BLOOD IN THE WATER

USS *Liberty*. (Photo courtesy of the National Security Agency.)

BLOOD
IN THE
WATER

HOW THE US AND ISRAEL CONSPIRED
TO AMBUSH THE USS LIBERTY

JOAN MELLEN

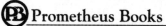
Prometheus Books

59 John Glenn Drive
Amherst, New York 14228

Inquiries should be addressed to
Prometheus Books
59 John Glenn Drive
Amherst, New York 14228
VOICE: 716–691–0133 • FAX: 716–691–0137
WWW.PROMETHEUSBOOKS.COM

22 21 20 19 18   5 4 3 2 1

Library of Congress Cataloging-in-Publication Data

Names: Mellen, Joan, author.
Title: Blood in the water : how the US and Israel conspired to ambush the USS Liberty /
    by Joan Mellen.
Description: Amherst, New York : Prometheus Books, 2018. | Includes bibliographical
    references and index.
Identifiers: LCCN 2018017164 (print) | LCCN 2018033098 (ebook) |
    ISBN 9781633884656 (ebook) | ISBN 9781633884649 (hardcover)
Subjects: LCSH: Israel-Arab War, 1967—Naval operations. | Liberty (Ship) | United States—
    Relations—Israel. | Israel—Relations—United States. | Israel. Mossad le Modiʻin ule
    Tafkidim Meyuḥadim.
Classification: LCC DS127.6.N3 (ebook) | LCC DS127.6.N3 M45 2018 (print) |
    DDC 956.04/645—dc23
LC record available at https://lccn.loc.gov/2018017164

Printed in the United States of America

This book is dedicated to Commander David Edwin Lewis, USN (Ret).

"*Historians must and ought to be exact, truthful, and absolutely free of passions, for neither interest, fear, rancor, nor affection should make them deviate from the path of the truth, whose mother is history, the rival of time, repository of great deeds, witness to the past, example and advisor to the present, and forewarning to the future.*"
—Miguel de Cervantes, *Don Quixote*

"*It is curious—curious that physical courage should be so common in the world, and moral courage so rare.*"
—Mark Twain

CONTENTS

FOREWORD

Joan Mellen, who has completed years of research into the deliberate Israeli attack on the USS *Liberty* on June 8, 1967, will provide answers that have heretofore eluded those seeking information as to why it was done and who was involved in an event that resulted in the murder of 34 Americans (31 sailors, 2 marines, and 1 NSA civilian), the wounding of 174, and the attempted murder of 294 Americans by the Israel Defense Forces. It is a continuation of her tireless and tenacious study of President Lyndon Baines Johnson and his administration, providing her readers with details that have not been made known to the American public.

Lyndon Baines Johnson. (Photo courtesy of the LBJ Library, Austin.)

Why is this accurate account so vital to the future of America? As an eyewitness, a survivor of the attack, and a witness to the US government's deception, I am very much aware of the events. My hometown, upbringing, and church and the US Navy provided me with the moral character and determination to complete our mission despite any adversities. It is my love of country that forces me to want the truth told. I have observed the whole scale of lies, deceit, and forgery by the US Navy, who were ordered to do so by our government officials, orchestrated by their commander in chief. The American public needs to know what was done to the USS *Liberty* crew and to our nation for the sole purpose of protecting our relationship with Israel and profiting for political gain on the backs of the *Liberty* crew.

Therefore, prepare to devour Ms. Mellen's account of this event and time period, *Blood in the Water: How the US and Israel Conspired to Ambush the USS* Liberty. She has uncovered details that have been deliberately hidden from your eyes to prevent you from forming a better understanding of the consequences of our silence. Please take this information to heart and share it with your family and friends. Joan Mellen's book is that important for future American generations to understand the abuses that took place during the Johnson years. I deeply appreciate Ms. Mellen's ability to document these events so that we can take steps to return to the form of governing our founding fathers gave us. If we do not learn from what her book provides us, our future is in jeopardy.

—Ernest A. Gallo, President, USS *Liberty* Veterans Association

PREFACE

There is a postage-stamp-sized image lodged permanently in my mind. It resides beside the flash of a golden-haired John F. Kennedy speaking at a podium on Fordham Road in the Bronx. Dating a few years into the future of that day is the image of a bulky man. He is dark haired and very tall as he surveys a roomful of people who have come to pay him homage. His skin is brown, his eyes are kindly, his expression is pleasant, and although he was a colonel in the army, there seems to be nothing military in his aspect.

Standing very quietly among the crowd, he does not invite intrusions. Yet in his short-sleeved, open-collared shirt, he is informal, not at all forbidding. He is a head of state come here to call on the president of the newly independent republic of Tanzania, until five years ago known as British Tanganyika. We are on the cusp of postcolonialism.

I had no idea that a US surveillance ship, the USNS *Valdez*, was at that very moment trolling the warmly sweet, turquoise-blue Indian Ocean just beyond our line of sight with its electronic surveillance trained on Dar es Salaam. The *Valdez* was helping CIA (whose officers never refer to it as "the CIA") track down Che Guevara, who had come to Congo to assist the beleaguered supporters of Prime Minister Patrice Lumumba, himself murdered with the assistance of CIA.[1]

Nor could I, a graduate student in English literature with a myopic education in history, have imagined that in fifty years I would be writing a book about a sister surveillance ship of the *Valdez*, the USS *Liberty*. History is the plaything of power, and so I certainly could not have imagined that *Liberty*, unarmed, would be brutally attacked as part of an operation designed to depose the man smiling at the crowd in this room at University College, Dar. That information was destined to remain secret well into the next millennium.

The year is 1966, and I am attending a reception for faculty and administrators where the guest of honor is Gamal Abdel Nasser. Nasser says a few words of pleasant, amiable fellowship with the president of the fledgling United Republic of Tanzania. I don't remember a word he said or the sound of his voice. He was mostly silent. But it was clear that he was a model to the leaders of the newly independent states of Africa in their effort to free themselves of the shackles of colonialism. Locals and foreigners alike, everyone is respectful.

The first president of Tanzania, Julius Nyerere, is present, but I retain no memory of him except that he wore a flowing white shirt and seemed always to be smiling. The countenance that has stayed with me, down all these years, is that of Gamal Abdel Nasser, whose presence will suffuse this history of the origins and cover-up of the bloody ambush of a technical research ship, the USS *Liberty*.

Soft-spoken, speaking all but perfect English, he seemed to be one of the "good guys." In my youthful abhorrence of imperialism, I knew nothing of the policy-making of intelligence agencies, and so it would have been impossible to penetrate why CIA counterintelligence chief James Angleton so despised this man that at this very moment he would be plotting his assassination. But I would not have been surprised that this man would ask the United States for an "evenhandedness" he would not be granted.[2]

At the dawn of the Six-Day War, only one year later, *Liberty* was rushed to the Eastern Mediterranean. On June 8, she was trolling in international waters at her normal cruise speed of five knots, the speed they traveled when they were on station and doing their intelligence collection, twelve and a half miles off the coast of Egypt. In a bloody, unprovoked, and systematic attack that continued for an hour and a half, Israeli jet fighter planes—their hulls blackened to conceal their country of origin, in defiance of international law—blasted the unarmed *Liberty*.[3] They were followed by torpedo boats brandishing machine guns.

The USS *Liberty* (IV). (Photo courtesy of the USS *Liberty* Veterans Association.)

For more than fifty years, the Survivors (the use of the uppercase is their designation) have sought an explanation for this attack, clearly designed to murder everyone on board and send their ship to the bottom of the sea. Intelligence gathering on the high seas is lawful, and it becomes illegal, naval historian Walter Jacobsen says, only when it infringes upon "protected features of the public order in the coastal state," which *Liberty* did not do.[4] It turns out that *Liberty* was not gathering intelligence on Israel at all.[5]

The United States professed that it was not a participant in any way in the Six-Day War, an event that Dr. Martin Luther King Jr. noted had "given Johnson the little respite he wanted from Vietnam." Yet the decimation of the Egyptian Air Force on the first day of the war would not have been possible without the participation of US F-4 planes doing aerial surveillance photography that Israel lacked the technological know-how itself to accomplish.

Where documents elucidating these events have emerged, they have been heavily redacted.

Blood in the Water is an effort to penetrate the motives for this attack. History may be defined as what is not yet known, hidden corners that illuminate events that seem otherwise inexplicable. Please be so kind as to consider this effort, this book, in the light of its unsatisfactory predecessors. Some components of one agency (CIA) will be revealed to have known the attack was coming, while others, appalled, were unable to stop it. CIA was not a monolith, and those who did not support this operation included Richard Helms, the director of Central Intelligence himself.[6]

Along the way, I have been guided by the words of members of the intelligence services with access to the truth of what happened and who refused to participate in the cover-up. Among them was a CIA asset named Wilbur Crane Eveland, who requested of Director of Central Intelligence Allen Dulles, his longtime friend, that he be removed from duty in the Middle East so that he would not be complicit in the injustices he was certain would come.

Allen Dulles acknowledged to his asset Eveland that "the CIA and Israel's Mossad had worked jointly to monitor developments within the Soviet Union and Russia's satellites, and even before the Egyptian-Czech arms agreement, the Israelis had warned that Russia had plans to arm the Arabs."[7] CIA had monitored Russian arms shipments to the Middle East.[8]

In 1959, Dulles had told Eveland that CIA's collaboration with Mossad, the Israeli intelligence service, left the United States exposed to blackmail and established Israel as the first nuclear power in the Middle East.[9] In 1972, General Matityahu Peled of the Israeli army stated in the Israeli daily, *Ha'aretz*, that "the thesis that the danger of genocide was hanging over us in June 1967 and that Israel was fighting for its physical existence is only bluff which was born and developed after the war."[10]

Government documents allow that Israel did not act alone in this operation and therefore cannot be blamed for the devastation by itself. The fifty-year cover-up has been tightly held and respected by every president from Lyndon Johnson, a principal in these events, through Barack Obama.

Available documents have been few and far between. Sometimes they arrive from the unlikeliest sources, like Mossad chief Meir Amit, who distributed the minutes of his pivotal May 1967 meeting with CIA station chief John Hadden to interested Israeli journalists.[11] Israel argued, falsely, that the USSR had "instigated" the Six-Day War and had targeted Dimona, Israel's secret nuclear arms facility.[12]

Israel continued for fifty years to argue that the attack on the ship was an "accident," passing along this disinformation to its assets like Avner Cohen, author of *Israel and the Bomb*, who attempted to pass it along to me. It was also Cohen, resident as a "scholar" in the United States, who reported to former Mossad chief Efraim Halevy that the memoir about Hadden written by Hadden's son, *Conversations with a Masked Man: My Father, the CIA, and Me*, had finally been published. Halevy replied, "I thought we had taken care of that."[13] It was a rare glimpse into Israel's shameless interference in US publishing.

Thomas Lowe Hughes, heading up State Department intelligence in the 1960s, told me there was no one in the government who saw any value in the truth about the USS *Liberty* emerging. That a cover-up had descended on these events was taken for granted. As Nicholas Katzenbach, then an undersecretary of state, remarked to Hughes, "What good would it do?"

Katzenbach was echoing the very view held in Israel after the collapse of its terrorist "Operation Susannah": "What good could come of an investigation?"[14] The truth was, at best, an inconvenience. Katzenbach had never been a proponent of speaking the truth to the public, as he revealed three days after the Kennedy assassination.

"The public must be satisfied that Oswald was the assassin," he wrote in a memorandum to Lyndon Johnson's aide, Bill Moyers, "that he did not have confederates who are still at large; and that evidence was such that he would have been convicted at a trial." Discussion was anathema. "Speculation about Oswald's motivation ought to be cut off," Katzenbach decreed. Katzenbach had been chosen by FBI chief J. Edgar Hoover "to head off public speculation or Congressional hearings of the wrong sort." Katzenbach began to write his memorandum on the Sunday after the assassination, the same general time when J. Edgar Hoover, writes historian Rex Bradford, was writing memos to the same effect.[15]

When Katzenbach was asked, "How are you going to pursue this with the Israelis, namely the *Liberty*?," he responded, "We're not going to. What good would it do?" He had gotten the message that *Liberty* was a nonissue, and that the sooner it was behind us, the better. "It will do nothing but damage our friends politically."

In conversation with me, Hughes speculated that Katzenbach "thought it would just produce an enormous maelstrom of political controversy."

I asked, "Wouldn't we have a better country if we had the truth?"

"Who knows?" Hughes said.[16]

History has revealed that some distinguished figures in American government were appalled by the attack and knew how it came about, but kept silent. They include the chief of naval operations, Admiral David Lamar McDonald, who published a series of autobiographical interviews with the Naval Institute Press, yet did not mention the USS *Liberty*.

To blame Israel alone for this attack on innocent Americans is like talking about the Holocaust, as Donald J. Trump did on International Holocaust Remembrance Day in January 2017, without mentioning the Jewish people. A Trump spokeswoman, Hope Hicks, told CNN the omission was intentional because the administration "took into account all of those who suffered"—echoing, the *New York Times* noted, "the position of neo-Nazis and Holocaust deniers who work to play down the genocide of Jews." Trump repeated this travesty of history in August 2017 when he wanted to blame "both sides" for the neo-Nazi rally in Charlottesville, Virginia.[17]

That his son-in-law's Holocaust-survivor grandmother was a founder of the United States Holocaust Memorial Museum fazed Trump not at all. So the fifty years of silence and obfuscation about the attack on the USS *Liberty* have a continuing legacy: it is acceptable to lie and distort, so long as you're not called out on it.

Over the years, one specious motive for the attack after another has been advanced. One has it that Israel feared that *Liberty* had discovered its plan to invade Syria the next day, June 9, and so had to pulverize the ship, to sink it with all hands, as it most obviously intended to do. In fact, Moshe Dayan, commanding the Israel Defense Forces, had not completed his plan for Syria before *Liberty* was bombarded, nor was the ship conducting surveillance on Israel. It was under instructions specifically *not* to process Israeli intercepts.

A variation submitted by Joseph Daichman in his history of Mossad was that the Soviets had been intercepting American radio signals.[18] Should *Liberty* not be removed, the Soviets would inform Egypt that Israel had moved troops to the Golan and left its border with Egypt undefended. None of this can be supported.

Wilbur Eveland came closest to the truth in his memoir, *Ropes of Sand:* "Unless the United States wished the Russians and Arabs to learn of joint CIA-Mossad covert operations in the Middle East and of Angleton's discussions before the 1967 fighting began, the questions of the lost American ship and how the war originated should be dropped."[19]

The CIA-Mossad joint covert operation was the attack on the USS *Liberty*, "the lost American ship." Nor can the attack on the ship be mentioned without the name "James Angleton" entering the discussion and his role being spelled out.

ACKNOWLEDGMENTS

C ommander Dave Lewis has been a mentor for me and a beacon of light from the time I began the research for this project in 2014. At the time of the attack on the surveillance ship USS *Liberty* on June 8, 1967, Lewis served as its chief intelligence officer. Modest to a fault, he has been committed to uncovering the motive behind Israel's unrelenting ambush of his ship and open to the question of whether Israel acted alone. That the attack was premeditated, despite Israel's denials, is a given. My heartfelt gratitude to Commander Lewis for reading this manuscript prior to publication and helping me, as he puts it, "to speak Navy."

Why Israel would murder thirty-four unarmed American sailors on a research vessel sailing in international waters and flying the Stars and Stripes has been a conundrum for those who survived and for authors who have attempted to unravel the motive for so vicious an attack. A fifty-plus-year cover-up has been maintained by both the state of Israel and the United States—its CIA, its executive branch, its Congress, the NSA, the Joint Chiefs of Staff—and the mainstream media. Agents of the Israeli Mossad have done their part in seeing that the truth remains inaccessible.

A lifelong Republican and a career naval officer, Commander Lewis surprised me by encouraging me to challenge the obvious lies, obfuscations, and contradictions that have been offered to the American public as credible history. Because I have enjoyed the confidence of Commander Lewis, many survivors of the attack have granted me personal interviews. I would like to thank Bryce Lockwood, Lloyd Painter, Jack Beattie, Ron Kukal, Ernie Gallo, Patricia Gallo, Dave Lucas, Joe Meadors, Jim Ennes, Joe Lentini, the late John Gidusko, Don Pageler, Moe Shafer, Phil Tourney, Jim Kavanagh, Ron Grantski, Bob Scarborough, Richard (Rocky) Sturman, Glenn Oliphant, Pat Blue, Gary Brummett, Kenneth

Schaley, Larry Weaver, Larry Broyles Sr. (of the USS *Davis*), Harold Six, and David McFeggan.

Were it not for the stalwart efforts of Jim Ennes, none of the subsequent books could have been written. We are all indebted to him for his courage in defying the highest military authorities. He wrote his book against specific orders that he remain silent. It is upon his valorous effort that other authors have based their efforts.

I am grateful to Tom Blaney and Carole Blaney for their generosity, particularly at Norfolk.

I would also like to thank for his support and wisdom Richard Russell, a former naval historian and the editorial director of the Naval Institute Press. Rick was always available to set my craft upright when I seemed in danger of capsizing and has been a loyal and treasured friend.

Others who contributed to my understanding include Thomas Lowe Hughes, who was director of State Department intelligence at the time of the attack on *Liberty*; Bill Knutson, one of the ace fighter pilots who was stationed at the time on the USS *America;* Ken Halliwell, a historian of the technical components of the *Liberty* story; Ron Gotcher, the lawyer who prepared the war crimes petition on behalf of the Survivors; John L. Hadden, whose father was CIA chief of station in Tel Aviv at the time; Dr. Peter Flynn, who saved Dave Lewis's eyesight; British journalist Peter Hounam, who of all authors has come closest to penetrating the operation that included the assault on *Liberty* as a key component; Tim Thompson, whose father, Richard Thompson, a CIA asset, organized and financed the film *USS* Liberty: *Dead in the Water*; Carol Moore and Rupert Christiansen, Thompson's friends; Captain Richard L. Block, an air force intelligence officer at the time; Adlai Stevenson III; Tom Schaaf; Admiral Bobby Inman, who perceived at once that the Israeli explanation that the attack was an "accident" was false; Dennis Helms, son of CIA officer Richard Helms; Ted Arens for his hospitality in Michigan; author Max Holland; Captain Robert Kamansky; Matthew Aid; Len Osanic; Mark Weber; and Dr. Molly Peeney, my former creative writing student, a PhD in Slavic languages and literatures, who generously contributed her Russian language skills. Thanks too to Susan Galpin-Tyree for sharing her NSA files.

I wish especially to thank my FOIA lawyer, Dan Alcorn, for his stalwart and untiring efforts to pry the records of the 303 Committee from the government and for refusing to cease and desist in his efforts. Dan's rectitude has earned him the Agency's respect. Still, in 2018 CIA wound up denying our request, claiming that they had no such records, although previously they had admitted that they did and asked for postponements.

Research librarians stand tall as heroes of any historical effort. I want to acknowledge in particular John F. Shortal, historian for the Joint Chiefs of Staff; Laura Waayers, reference archivist for the Naval History and Heritage Command; the staff of Syracuse University Libraries; Barbara Cline, Jennifer Cuddeback, and Lara Hall at the LBJ Library in Austin; Ted Jackson of Georgetown University's Special Collections; Andrew Diamond at Paley Library, Temple University; and Michael Lavergne, Information and Privacy Coordinator for the Central Intelligence Agency.

My gratitude goes to Audrey Szepinski, who has worked for several years as my research assistant and who created my USS *Liberty* archive. A more generous, intelligent, and enthusiastic collaborator could not possibly be found. I wish also to thank my webmaster at joanmellen.com, John C. Tripp, whose kindness has been unparalleled, and Jeff Higgins, a self-effacing IT expert.

Efforts to unlock history's secrets are inevitably collaborative. Among those who provided suggestions and wisdom were Burton Hersh; Malcolm Blunt, an old and trusted friend to whom I am once more indebted, this time for having first mentioned the name "John Hadden" to me; Rex Bradford; and Ralph Schoenman and Mya Shone, whose generosity and knowledge have always been sustaining.

Not least, I would like to express my gratitude to Karina Silva for her many kindnesses and her assistance with this project, and to Scott Allen;

ACKNOWLEDGMENTS

his help was a beacon of light. I would also like to send my gratitude to Jacqueline May Parkison at Prometheus Books for her help in shepherding this book through publication. For brilliant editing and insights at the penultimate moment, I am also grateful to Jade Zora Scibilia for her elegance, presence of mind, and moral stamina.

No literary agent in the times of Obama and Trump is likely to welcome a whistle-blowing author bringing truths no side finds comfortable. *Blood in the Water* deconstructs an event that even Richard Helms, the legendary director of Central Intelligence, with whom I occupy common ground on this subject, found appalling.

Thank you to my literary agent, Ellen Levine, who treated this project as no more challenging than any other even though I am advancing ideas that the institutions involved prefer remain absent from public scrutiny. Ellen represents an anachronistic triumph of professionalism in the literary sphere. Once more I am grateful.

CHAPTER 1

JOHN HADDEN CONFERS WITH MEIR AMIT

"Working for the CIA was not for anybody with a weak stomach—because you had to do things that were against all moral precepts and against the law."
—John Hadden, CIA chief of station,
Tel Aviv, June 1967

ohn Hadden was, officially, the "second political secretary." Perched on the top floor of the five-story US embassy, with views of the sparkling Mediterranean Sea below, he seemed so remote from the action, so out of the loop, that you might conclude, despite the presence of armed US Marines standing guard when you emerged from the elevator, that he was a functionary of no importance. You would be wrong.[1]

John Hadden was CIA's chief of station in Tel Aviv. He was a handsome, black-haired man, of middle size, with the intelligence operative's talent of making himself seem invisible. In his daughter Barbara's painting of him, he resembles that most engaging of police detectives of 1930s and 1940s comic strips, Dick Tracy.[2]

John Hadden was born on August 30, 1923. His father was a structural engineer, his mother the daughter of an Episcopal bishop. His education was privileged in keeping with the class background of his family, which had gotten rich in the China trade; during his childhood, his grandmother was driven around in a Pierce Arrow by a Russian chauffeur in uniform, cap, and black boots. The Depression seemed not to affect them.[3]

Hadden attended the prep school Groton, where everyone was against Roosevelt, a socialist who had "betrayed his class," and then

Harvard, where he was trained as an engineer.[4] His ambition had always been to attend West Point. A technicality delayed him, but he finally was accepted.

He was recruited in 1943 by OSS to be dropped into occupied France, as a support and liaison officer to a resistance group in the Pyrenees.[5] He was never dropped: the Germans got to the group before he did. His next stop was Algiers. He purchased currencies in Lisbon, Beirut, and other places.

He went on to the task of recruiting German prisoners of war, turning them into spies, and sending them back into Germany. He was able to foretell the Ardennes Offensive, "which Patton refused to believe. It acquainted me with one type of intelligence," he would tell his son, "which is still important and will always be so. We sent in a total of thirty-six missions and lost only three of them."[6]

After the war, he spent more than five years in Berlin. He was involved in organizing the digging of a tunnel into Soviet-occupied East Berlin, tapping into the main Soviet communications cable. Before long, he learned that the Russians knew about the tunnel from the start through a mole in MI-6 named George Blake.

When in 1951 his postwar posting in Germany came to a close, John Hadden joined CIA. In Germany, he married a fellow CIA officer, Kathryn Falck, known as "Betty," who had worked for counterintelligence chief James Angleton in Rome.[7] She saw that Angleton collected dirt on CIA directors, notably Richard Helms. Angleton invited her to work for him in Washington. She hadn't yet met John Hadden when she told Angleton she didn't want to leave Berlin. Her father had been the last mounted cavalry colonel in World War II, and he saved John Hadden's life.

The most important influence on Hadden was Peter Sichel, who was CIA chief of station in Berlin when Hadden met him, and who was replaced by William Harvey. When bellicose Bill Harvey with his lust for covert action was posted to Berlin, Hadden at once threw a wrench into his rogue border operations with Poland. Harvey blistered. Hadden successfully evaded Harvey, whom Hadden ultimately concluded was "a good administrator but also a nut-case."[8]

John Hadden was demoted to smaller and less significant posts. He moved on to Hamburg, then back to Washington. In 1961, he was present in the Bay of Pigs war room, where he foresaw that the operation wouldn't work, a view Hadden shared with Allen Dulles's protégé Edward Lansdale, who served CIA under US Air Force cover.[9]

After a stint as head of operations for Eastern Europe, John Hadden was in 1963 appointed to a dead-end job in Tel Aviv with a minuscule staff.

It was now spring of 1967, and Hadden was alarmed because he perceived a coming, catastrophic war. As long as we have an "imperial presidency," he thought, "we will engage in such activities, regardless of the political dangers involved."

John Hadden was a man of strong convictions. He shared the US embassy with Walworth Barbour, the American ambassador, a tall, fat man addicted to white suits worn with brown-and-white spectator shoes.[10] Unlike John Hadden, Barbour was a man with no convictions of his own and did not challenge anything the Israelis said or did.

Barbour was not troubled over reports of the proliferation of nuclear weapons at Dimona, site of the Israeli nuclear reactor operating undercover as "Dimona Textiles." Nor was he skeptical of Israeli denials that they were manufacturing nuclear bombs. John Hadden, with a very different moral compass, would become obsessed with the Israeli stockpiling of nuclear bombs. Yet Hadden told journalist Seymour Hersh that Barbour "was the finest man I've ever known in the government." A prerequisite of working for CIA was obfuscation, as Allen Dulles from the start had decreed.

Irony had long been Hadden's modus operandi. His dark, sardonic humor was for his own edification, and he rarely shared what he really believed with anyone. His son and namesake referred to this as his "misplaced sense of humor."[11]

Whenever John Hadden told the truth, it made him laugh.[12] If he seemed earnest, chances were that he was either shaping the truth or holding something back. He was a person of decency, erudition, and skepticism who found few like-minded people in his daily struggles. His limitation was, as he acknowledged, that his "experience with intelligence operations was entirely within the period of the Cold War." No one really knew him, this suave, black-haired man who smelled of Vitalis Hair Tonic.[13]

John Hadden was firmly opposed to the coming unprovoked war between Israel and Egypt, in which the Israeli side's strategies derived from the earliest programs of Zionism. The pretext for an Israeli invasion—that Gamal Abdel Nasser, Egypt's president, had removed the UN emergency forces and closed the Straits of Tiran to Israeli shipping—he found to be thin. Nasser had placed one hundred thousand troops in the Sinai in response to Soviet intelligence that Israel had eleven brigades on its northern border. All this might be summed up, to use Hadden's locution, as "the rattling of sabers."

Hadden knew that his superior at CIA counterintelligence, James Angleton, talked as if Nasser was the West's primary problem in the area. If Nasser could be eliminated, and the Egyptian army defeated without major power assistance, the Arabs would be left with no alternative but to make peace with Israel.[14]

From the time that President Dwight D. Eisenhower commented that he hoped "the Nasser problem could be eliminated,"[15] Dulles and Angleton launched a plan to assassinate Nasser. It was an obsession that would survive the administrations of both Eisenhower and John F. Kennedy. This plan was placed on hold with Kennedy's election and his more evenhanded approach to Israeli-Arab relations. John Hadden was a Kennedy supporter.

When Kennedy was elected, Angleton's efforts to privilege the state of Israel gave way to Kennedy's efforts to support a level playing field in the Middle East. Richard H. Curtiss, executive editor of the *Washington Report on Middle East Affairs*, said that Kennedy "was planning to take a whole new look at U.S. Mideast policy."[16] He would create new relationships with individual Arab leaders. He opposed the sale of Advanced Hawk missiles to Israel. "We have to concern ourselves with the whole Middle East," Kennedy told Israeli foreign minister Golda Meir. "We would like Israeli recognition that this partnership which we have with it produces strains for the United States in the Middle East." He was placing US interests, not Israel's interests alone, at the center of US Middle East policy.[17]

The Israelis bought Angleton's talk of an attack on Egypt with the objective of toppling Nasser, but were aware that it depended on Angleton's gaining the support of the White House. Under President Kennedy, this policy went nowhere. Kennedy was determined to be "evenhanded" in the conflict between Egypt and Israel.

Meanwhile American inspection teams of the Israeli nuclear facility were thwarted at every turn. Reports came back that "we lack sufficient proof, we cannot say to the best of our knowledge that the Israelis were developing a nuclear weapon." Kennedy was corresponding with Nasser and even wound up asking the Egyptians—who had overflights over the Negev, where Dimona was located—what was going on.

Nasser at one point explained to Kennedy that "continued Jewish immigration" created a pressure within Israel that had to explode and head for expansion."[18] Nasser contended that Israel "was constantly liable to be used by imperialism as a tool to divide the Arab nations geographically" and as a base from which to threaten the Arab Liberation Movement.

Kennedy met a stone wall in his peacemaking efforts; Israeli prime minister David Ben-Gurion categorically rejected Washington's suggestion that "Israel should begin the settlement process by taking back some of the Palestinian refugees." Kennedy, however, seems naïve in his "hope that both (the Arab nations and Israel) would be friends of the United States."[19]

Eisenhower had informed JFK of Israel's secret nuclear weapons program at Dimona. By the late 1950s, Angleton acknowledged what was happening in Dimona. "Yes, they've got it," he said.[20]

In March 1963, Sherman Kent, the chairman of the Board of

National Estimates at CIA, wrote a memo to the new director of Central Intelligence, John McCone, titled "Consequences of Israeli Acquisition of Nuclear Capability." Kent concluded that an Israeli bomb would cause "substantial damage" to the US position in the Arab world.

Israelis visited, like Rafi Eitan, Israeli diplomat and Mossad intimate, who played a major role in the capture of Nazi war criminal Adolf Eichmann and later directed US intelligence analyst Jonathan Pollard's espionage against the United States.

Under Lyndon Johnson, Angleton finally got his way.

John Hadden would later write that "Nasser had to create three casus belli in order to remain in power, so great were the popular pressures on him to face up to the Israelis."[21] Nasser threatened Dimona with preventive war and assumed the United States was playing along with Israel. (In an interview with *New York Times* reporter Clifton Daniel, Nasser was asked how he would feel if Israel got the atomic bomb. Nasser made no sign that he knew that Israel already had the bomb and was operating a facility where nuclear bombs were being manufactured.)

To appease Israel, the United States asked Israeli foreign minister Abba Eban, a former ambassador to the United States, to make the decision about whether the United States should sell jets to Jordan. He decided yes. It was cat and mouse every step of the way. Eban visited London, Paris, and Washington with a focus on Israel's fear of war, arguing that the Israelis would never attack Egypt unless Nasser attacked first, which was an outright lie, as history would demonstrate.

In the hothouse of 1967, Israel made much of Nasser's closing of the Gulf of Aqaba even though it was, in fact, of no strategic importance. Israel primarily utilized the port of Eilat, and only three Israeli ships a year went through the Gulf of Aqaba, no matter its symbolic resonance: it was Israel's only prize out of the 1956 war over the Suez Canal.

A quixotic man, John Hadden believed that he might be able to delay or postpone this war—he had to have known that he could not prevent it forever. His hope was that the Israelis might restrain themselves for at least three weeks to give the American president time to "'exhaust' all efforts to avoid war."[22]

Nothing had gone well for John Hadden in Tel Aviv. His family had to move often because he discovered that their house was bugged. The Shin Bet, the Israeli domestic intelligence service, attempted to seduce the US Marines who guarded the embassy with money and women. Hadden had concluded that the Israelis did not trust him. The Cold War was a high-stakes game, and he couldn't extricate himself from it. He came to believe that America was subordinating its own national interests to those of Israel. Mirage jets flew overhead every day. The scent of war pervaded the city.

Hadden helped his next-door neighbor construct a trench outside his home to "protect his wife and children," which was preposterous but was an indication of the success of the perpetual official propaganda that Israel faced imminent danger.[23] Hadden had told his neighbors there was no need for trenches, but they preferred to believe the war hysteria. Even Meir Amit, head of Mossad, was irritated that as a result of the war fever, many Israelis were leaving the country.[24] The Hadden family was evacuated back to the United States.

A civil man, John Hadden was accustomed to what he called the "card game" of tit-for-tat exchange between friendly intelligence services, like the British and the West German.[25] These meetings would conclude with everyone giving everyone else what they wanted. He understood the civilized intelligence world dramatized by novelist John le Carré. "Israeli intelligence is our main source of intelligence," Hadden noted, "unexamined, and that's another problem." Through the 1950s, "collaboration was particularly close between Israel's special services and the CIA."[26]

Meetings with the Israelis, Hadden soon discovered, were "crazed." More often than not, he would be subjected to a forty-five-minute diatribe and bombarded by a litany of threats attributed to all those ostensibly endangering Israeli security, challenges to Israel's existence that required immediate action. Next came a catalog of the military and intelligence matériel that Israel required from the United States, not only to ward off the threats but also for Israel's sanity and well-being.

"There you were in your chair," Hadden remembered later, "and they were shouting way over behind you! Absolutely outrageous. They were asking for the goddamn moon." At home, he sometimes fell into a bad temper and would shout *Ruhe!* ("Peace!") if any of his four children made noise when he was reading.

Hadden developed a strategy for dealing with the Israelis, whose brusque manners were so different from his own. He would sit and listen, quietly taking notes and expressing no emotion. Then he would speak for forty-five minutes, outlining the American position on a subject.

No interruptions were tolerated. In his remarks, he would "ignore everything that the Israelis said and do his best to be equally outrageous." One day he overheard Mossad chief Amit say, "Hadden sounds like he's really talking to you, telling you all sorts of interesting things, but he's not. On the contrary: you realize, as you walk off, that you're the one who's spilled all the beans." This pleased John Hadden.[27]

Learn Hebrew, he would advise his successor, and "just hold on to your hat and take the ride." Among his mantras was "Never trust anybody!"[28] His favorite pastimes were smoking his pipe, drinking Old-Fashioneds, and teaching his children how to play chess.

In 1963 in Tel Aviv, he had attended a dinner for diplomats. Already he was aware that the Israelis saw Americans as hard-drinking and likely then to be garrulous. Usually, Hadden kept his CIA-taught language skills to himself. He overheard the hostess say hopefully to an Israeli colonel that if Hadden kept imbibing, perhaps he would talk too much. This was a lapse John Hadden was unlikely to commit. He revealed little, even to his inquisitive children, a reticence that extended late into his life when his CIA years were long behind him.

John Hadden with his sons and as painted by his daughter, Barbara. Hadden was CIA chief of station in Tel Aviv at the time of the attack. Opposed to the Six-Day War, he is an unsung hero of this story. (Photos courtesy of John L. Hadden and Barbara Hadden.)

Hadden surprised his hosts then with his mastery of Hebrew: "*Nichnas yayin yotzeh sod!*" he said. This meant, "Wine goes in and a secret comes out."

CHAPTER 2

FIRE AT A SHIP!

"Get them to fire at something, a ship, for example."
—John Hadden

From his first days in Tel Aviv, John Hadden knew that Mossad did not consider him to be an ally. He in turn did not consider Israel to be "allied territory like Britain or enemy territory like East Germany." Israel occupied a category entirely of its own. In conversations with Mossad, familiarity with the jargon and pretexts of the Cold War was mandatory since the term "Soviet threat" was a blunt weapon, one more often than not wielded indiscriminately.

In their disregard for the rule of law, CIA and Mossad had much in common. Efraim Halevy, who was to serve Mossad for twenty-eight years and was Mossad director from 1998 to 2002, spoke frankly in a 2016 speech: "I studied law—which helped me to learn how to break the law when I needed to do so," Halevy said. "Did I break the law when I did what I did? Yes. I won't tell you how many times I broke [the law] because I don't want to spend the rest of my life in jail."[1] Asked by journalist Mehdir Hasan on November 22, 2016, whether Israel had nuclear weapons, Halevy replied, even now enlisting the ingrained Mossad culture of lying, "I don't know."[2] In fact, Israel had nuclear weapons at the time that John F. Kennedy was president in 1963.

Mossad chief Meir Amit summoned John Hadden to a meeting at his home on May 25, 1967. Amit not only headed Mossad and directed Mossad's European operations, but he was a veteran military intelligence (Aman) officer.[3] His personal mantra was very different from John Hadden's.

"If somebody is in your way you use the greatest firepower you can muster to blow him away," Amit believed. He had been a brigade commander in the War of Independence, coming to Moshe Dayan's attention when he attacked the Syrians on the Israeli side of the Jordan River. He had lived on kibbutzim all his life and was arrogant.[4]

Dayan appointed Amit chief of operations, the second-ranking officer in the army, and later recommended him to be the chief of military intelligence. Amit served as Dayan's second-in-command during the Suez campaign. It would be a seamless transition, Amit's working with Dayan on the attack on the USS *Liberty*. "The bomb is simply another weapon," Dayan argued, "and therefore there is no reason why Israel should not possess it or use it when necessary."[5]

The details of the conversation between John Hadden and Meir Amit at the end of May 1967 became available when years later Amit distributed a "Top Secret, For Your Eyes Only" memorandum to select journalists.[6] It reveals Hadden's desperation as he perceived how far Amit was prepared to go to precipitate a war with Israel's neighbors, and Amit's impatience that Israel had not already attacked Egypt.

In the memorandum, Amit wastes no time in concocting a pretext, that somehow Egypt will provoke Israel to attack—even as he doesn't believe he needs a pretext. Later, Amit would term his encounter with John Hadden "the most difficult meeting I have ever had with a representative of a foreign intelligence service."

Amit did not mince words in the meeting. "We are approaching a turning point that is more important for you than it is for us," he said. "After all, you people know everything." Flattery, along with lying, was, after all, a tool of the trade. "We are in a grave situation and I believe we have reached it, because we have not acted yet." It was as if the Six-Day War, in which Israel would double its territory, had not been inevitable since the time of Theodore Herzl and the early Zionists.

"Personally," Amit said, "I am sorry that we did not react immediately [to Nasser's closing of the Straits of Tiran]. It is possible that we may have broken some rules if we had, but the outcome would have been to your benefit. I was in favor of acting. We should have struck before the build-up." In fact, it was Israeli jets ranging into Syria as far as Damascus and shooting down six Syrian planes that provoked Nasser into closing the Straits of Tiran.[7]

Amit suggests that the interests of the United States and Israel were one and the same, which was far from the truth. Six Arab countries would break relations with the United States at the start of the Six-Day War.

Had Israel attacked Egypt, Hadden countered, "that would have brought Russia and the United States both against you." Hadden's suggestion that the Americans and the Soviets would act in concert seems absurd. Desperate to delay the start of what would be the Six-Day War, Hadden was grasping at straws.

Shrewd to a fault, Amit saw right through him.

"You are wrong," Amit said smoothly. "The other side has been operating as part of a grand design. We have now reached a new stage, after the expulsion of the UN inspectors. You should know that it's your problem, not ours."[8]

As Allen Dulles had founded CIA on the premise of a Soviet threat, and elements of the Agency were lifelong proponents of the view that the Soviet Union was dedicated to the demise of US power, so Amit invoked an undemonstrated Soviet threat to Israel, along with the even less credible view that the nationalist Nasser represented a threat to the United States.

Years later, Israeli prime minister Menachem Begin was to acknowledge that "the Egyptian army concentrations in the Sinai did not prove that Nasser was really about to attack us." But for a propagandist like Amit, a purported Soviet "grand design" could be converted into a pretext for Israel to attack its neighbors and seize their territory.

The "grand design" Amit charged was the Soviet ambition to gain control over the oil resources of the Middle East. At stake, Amit suggested, was the Israeli nuclear installation at Dimona, which Israel contended had become a Soviet target. All the while, Israel maintained the charade that Dimona was a secret. Into the millennium, Israel's stockpile of nuclear devices remained among taboo subjects for the mass media in the United States, rendering it a sham that a treaty with Iran would keep nuclear weapons from the Middle East.

Aware that Israel was churning out nuclear weapons at Dimona (John F. Kennedy's efforts at their containment had come to a close with his murder), John Hadden tried to postpone the coming aggression which it was clear to him would be initiated by Israel. According to Thomas Lowe Hughes, the Americans had been trying to divert the Israelis from their nuclear program for six years; everyone in the Kennedy administration had been united on this issue: Kennedy himself; Secretary of State Dean Rusk; diplomat George Ball; Secretary of Defense Robert McNamara; Richard Helms, who became Deputy Director for Plans, which meant head of the clandestine services, in 1961 and ascended to director of Central Intelligence in 1966; and even Assistant Secretary of Defense Cyrus Vance.[9]

Israel was working on nuclear power but not a bomb; David Ben-Gurion had lied to Kennedy at the White House in 1961. In 1937, Ben-Gurion had said, "We must expel Arabs and take their places," and this remained his position.[10] It would remain Israel's position too: "It is the duty of Israeli leaders to explain to public opinion, clearly and coura-geously, a certain number of facts that are forgotten with time," Prime Minister Ariel Sharon declared in 1998. "The first of these is that there is no Zionism, colonialization, or Jewish state without the eviction of the Arabs and the expropriation of their lands."[11] The term "Palestinian" never appears in this discourse.

In his pivotal conversation with Amit, Hadden rejected Amit's charges of Soviet belligerence and a Soviet threat to Dimona. Hadden argued that the Soviets were "exceedingly cautious and would never push 'brinksmanship' and threats too far. They would not risk war with the Americans and were reacting only defensively by 'rattling the nukes.'"

Lyndon Johnson had his eye on the election of 1968, the Jewish vote, and Jewish fund-raising. He appointed Nicholas Katzenbach as undersecretary of state because he thought, mistakenly, that Katzenbach was Jewish.[12] It was clear to Thomas Lowe Hughes that Johnson wanted to be thought of as pro-Israel in the service of garnering the Jewish vote in 1968, which Johnson believed was in jeopardy because many Jewish voters were opponents of his Vietnam War policy and so would not vote for him in the coming general election.

Close to Hadden's CIA superior James Angleton now, Johnson authorized Angleton to inform Eppy Evron, deputy ambassador from Israel to the United States, that the United States would prefer Israeli efforts to lessen the tension "but would not intervene to stop an attack on Egypt." He stipulated that there must be no Israeli military action against Jordan, Syria, or Lebanon."[13] If Angleton ever conveyed this stipulation to Evron, the Israelis would ignore it.

Johnson appointed Eugene Rostow as Assistant Secretary of State for Near Eastern Affairs and Asia precisely to support the coming Israeli war—and his own reelection. Out of the corner of his eye, Johnson saw Richard Nixon, his likely future opponent, saying, "I'm more pro-Israel than you are!" Indeed, Nixon and his future national security advisor, Henry Kissinger, had told the Israelis, "Don't worry about Dimona—we won't give you a problem on nuclear weapons!"[14]

This was the background to Meir Amit's revealing confrontation with John Hadden. Soon Amit arrived at a preposterous assertion: that the coming war was really "a confrontation between the United States and the Soviet Union."[15] The Soviets, Israel later would insist, instigated the Six-Day War in the hope of targeting the Dimona nuclear reactor.

As a CIA officer, Hadden had long pondered the "cultural differences between the two national types. If a disagreement arose, the Soviet reaction was to pull a gun and threaten the American opposite number. The American reaction was to never perceive a bluff and thus, if threatened with a weapon, to shoot first and ask questions later."

Hadden had supported John F. Kennedy. He remarked to author Michael Piper that "John F. Kennedy was the last American president to have really tried to stop the Israeli atomic bomb." Hadden was convinced that "Kennedy really wanted to stop it."[16] He offered the Israelis conventional weapons, like Hawk missiles, as an inducement.

"But the Israelis were way ahead of us," Hadden realized.[17] "They saw that if we were going to offer them arms to go easy on the bomb, once they had it we were going to send them a lot more, for fear that they would use it."[18]

Kennedy proposed that the Palestinians either be permitted to return to their homes in Israel or be compensated by Israel or resettled in the Arab countries or elsewhere. Meanwhile, Israel refused permission for inspections at Dimona to ensure that the program was peaceful in nature. The correspondence between Kennedy and Ben-Gurion grew sour over Dimona.

In one of his final communications with Kennedy, Ben-Gurion wrote: "Mr. President, my people have the right to exist . . . and this existence is in danger." Ben-Gurion demanded that Kennedy sign a security treaty with Israel. Kennedy refused. Ben-Gurion then confided his disgust with Kennedy to Angleton. On June 16, 1963, Ben-Gurion resigned as prime minister and defense minister, not for the last time.

On July 5, 1963, in a letter to Israel's new prime minister, Levi Eshkol, Kennedy wrote that he "welcomed" Ben-Gurion's "strong affirmation that Dimona will be devoted exclusively to peaceful purposes," along with Israel's "willingness to permit periodic visits to Dimona." He threatened that the United States' "commitment to and support of Israel could be seriously jeopardized" should it be discovered that weapons were being produced at Dimona. Kennedy demanded that the nuclear reactor at Dimona be subject to annual inspections to verify its "peaceful intent." Had John F. Kennedy remained as president, it seems apparent that there would have been no assault on the USS *Liberty*.

John Hadden had concluded that NUMEC (which stood for Nuclear Materials and Equipment Corporation) was "an Israeli [smuggling] operation from the beginning."[19] It was at this time that fund-raiser Abraham

Feinberg founded the American/Israel Public Affairs Committee (AIPAC) in time to oppose the policies of John F. Kennedy toward Israel.

Not only had James Angleton assisted Israel in obtaining nuclear weapons, he had helped to keep the program secret under the cover of "Dimona Textiles."

"Do you have nuclear weapons?" Kennedy demanded of Israeli deputy defense minister Shimon Peres on April 2, 1963, at the White House.

"Mr. President," Peres lied, "I can tell you most clearly that we will not introduce nuclear weapons to the region, and certainly will not be the first. Israel will not be the first to bring nuclear weapons into the Middle East."[20]

Israeli historian Tom Segev wrote in the *New York Times Sunday Review* of October 2, 2016: "Over the course of his political career, Mr. Peres participated in the oppression of the Palestinians who have been living for nearly half a century under Israeli occupation."[21]

By the end of 1967, the United States was wreathed in hypocrisy, with a public policy on arms balance in the region and a secret agreement to be Israel's major arms supplier.

John Hadden had established that nuclear weapons were being turned out at Dimona (under the "Dimona Textiles" cover) and that the uranium necessary had been smuggled into Israel by a company in Apollo, Pennsylvania.[22] Hadden looked hard at Nasser and saw that his administration was so fragile that a moment might arrive when he had to take steps to make war unavoidable, knowing he was going to lose.[23] Nasser, Hadden believed, feared he "would be toppled if he did not act against the Israelis as the Arab world was pressing him to do." In this spirit, Nasser had banished the UN emergency inspectors from the Sinai, granting Israel another pretext for war. He had narrowed, but not closed, the Gulf of Aqaba to Israeli shipping. Choosing to ignore their continuing access to the port of Eilat, the Israelis beat their familiar drum that Nasser was threatening their survival.[24]

Amit told John Hadden that Israel would penetrate only as far as Suez, but Hadden was dubious. He feared Israel planned to penetrate deep into Egypt and elsewhere. It was at this top secret meeting at Amit's home that the idea for the sinking of the USS *Liberty* and blaming Egypt, creating a false flag pretext for the bombing of Cairo, was born.

Desperate, Hadden spoke unwisely, if tongue-in-cheek. Inadvertently, he provided Meir Amit with a suggestion that would prove disastrous for the innocent sailors of the USS *Liberty*.

"Help us," Hadden cajoled, "by giving us a good reason to come in on your side. Get them to fire at something, a ship, for example."

Such an attack, Egypt attacking Israel, "would provide a US pretext for acting to defend the attacked state." The "attacked state" would be Israel, and the United States, defending an ally, would have every right to attack Egypt.

Not for a moment did John Hadden intend that Meir Amit take him up on the "suggestion" that Israel involve itself in firing on a ship, sinking *Liberty* as a pretext for a full-scale war against Egypt. He was goading Amit on, insisting that more than a pretext was required for Israeli aggression against Egypt.

On the ropes, having been bested by a wily adversary, Hadden had spoken words he could not possibly have meant. His son views that moment, his father suggesting to the head of Mossad that Israel perpetrate a crime on its own navy, as an example of his father's "misplaced sense of humor." Amit embraced the idea, only to twist it so that the attacked state would be the United States. Such an attack would surely provoke a US defense of the "attacked state," Hadden said. The United States could then have entered the coming Six-Day War legitimately.

In this Mossad-originating depiction of a pre–Six-Day War conversation between the Tel Aviv CIA station chief and the head of Mossad, we may discern the seeds of the attack on the USS *Liberty*.

"That is not the point," Amit said impatiently. He pretended to brush aside Hadden's suggestion that Israel provoke the Egyptians to fire on a ship as an absurdity. In two weeks, Israel would fire on the ship itself, while blaming Egypt. To provoke Egypt to fire on a ship was an obvious impossibility.

"If you attack," Hadden continued, "the United States will land forces on Egypt's side, in order to defend it."

"I can't believe what I'm hearing," Amit said, pretending to take Hadden literally, the idea that Israel could provoke the Egyptians to fire on a ship an absurdity.

Hadden, of course, was being facetious, knowing Israel could not goad Egypt into sinking a ship. It's inconceivable that John Hadden would advise Israel to attack an American ship. Cleverly, Amit reconfigured the idea so that Israel would do the firing, and then *blame* Egypt.

"Do not surprise us," Hadden said, presciently. He seemed aware that there was no way to predict what Meir Amit would do, although Hadden had to know with whom in the American intelligence services Amit was closest.

"Surprise is one of the secrets of success," Amit said.

"I don't know what the significance of American aid is for you," Hadden said, in those long-gone days before Israel had a blank check on American assistance. Amit had a ready reply. He was good at his job, which was to see into the future. "It isn't aid for us, it is for yourselves," he claimed.

Meir Amit, director of Mossad at the time of the attack on the USS *Liberty*: "Hadden sounds like he's really talking to you, telling you all sorts of interesting things, but he's not." (Photo courtesy of David Gurfinkel.)

So on this uncomfortable evening at the home of Meir Amit, the seeds were sown. In two weeks, they would blossom into a bloodthirsty reality. Attacking its own ships, however, had long been part of American intelligence and military history. The best-known example occurred at the turn of the twentieth century when the *Maine*, sitting in Havana Harbor, was fired on, with Spain blamed, justifying the US entrance into the Spanish-American War. The idea of a false flag operation, of firing on a ship and attributing the attack to another country, surfaced again in a 1962 document that Lyman Lemnitzer, chairman of the Joint Chiefs of Staff, had included in a list of covert actions. These were to be deployed to remove not Nasser but Cuba's Fidel Castro.

"We could blow up a US ship in Guantanamo Bay and blame Cuba," Lemnitzer had written in his proposed "Operation Northwoods."[25] He continued, "Casualty lists in US newspapers would cause a helpful wave of national indignation [against Castro]." Cuba would be destabilized, justifying a new invasion in a renewed effort to remove Castro. It was shades of "Remember the *Maine*" in Havana Harbor.

Firing on one's own ship was a casus belli, a pretext for a war of aggression. So Hadden had urged Israel to trap Egypt into supplying a pretext for Israel to go to war: Israel would be placing one of their own ships in harm's way, sinking one of their own ships as a casus belli, a pretext for waging war against Egypt and Syria.

"Operation Northwoods" had been delivered to President John F. Kennedy's secretary of defense, Robert McNamara. Kennedy rejected Lemnitzer's litany of macabre suggestions outright. But after Kennedy's death, the false flag operation of firing on a US ship surfaced in 1964 under the aegis of Lyndon Johnson. The United States fired on its own ship, the *Maddox*, in the Gulf of Tonkin, blaming the North Vietnamese and using this as a pretext for the bombing of Hanoi and Haiphong. Robert S. McNamara remained in place as Johnson's secretary of defense.

On May 26, unperturbed, Nasser declared that he did not fear losing a war. "We're going to send the whole crisis to The Hague," he said. He announced that he would not fire the first shot because the Soviets told him he was not to attack Israel. On that day, Israel sent a double agent to warn the Soviets that they planned to go to war and attack Nasser so Israel would hobble any possible Soviet retaliation.[26] A week before the start of the Six-Day War, the Israelis were confident that there would be no defense of Egypt by Egypt's ostensible Soviet allies.

That same month, still May, Lyndon Johnson invited Deputy Ambassador Eppy Evron to meet with him at the White House. Evron later said that Lyndon Johnson had told him, "You and I are going to pass another Tonkin resolution," referring to the false flag operation when the United States claimed, falsely, that the North Vietnamese fired on them, as a pretext for the US bombing of the north. So Johnson was enlisting the same strategy twice: once against North Vietnam, the other against Egypt.[27]

On Monday, May 29, Meir Amit met with Israeli prime minister Levi Eshkol three times. For the moment, the military was banned from an immediate attack against Egyptian troops in the Sinai. Eshkol's cabinet agreed that they must not go to war without one more endorsement and reassurance from the Americans.

McNamara had already indicated to Eshkol that the United States would not oppose the land grab to come. It was crucial, Eshkol and Amit agreed, that they be absolutely clear about the "American intentions" with respect to the war Israel hoped to initiate in less than a week's time.

The next day, Tuesday, May 30, the plan to fire on a ship percolating in his brain, Meir Amit flew to Washington, DC. The Israeli Security Cabinet had banned the military from an immediate attack against Egyptian troops in the Sinai, which was where the matter rested.

So urgent was this trip that Amit traveled by commercial airliner under an assumed name. He carried a letter he had drafted with foreign minister Abba Eban stressing the urgency of Israel's confronting Nasser. Signed by Levi Eshkol, it requested a military blank check from the Americans. This letter was part of a plan that included Abba Eban's address to the UN Security Council where he charged Egypt with the aggression Israel had itself committed.

Amit traveled in the company of John Hadden, as protocol decreed, and with Israeli ambassador to the United States Avraham Harman. His first meeting was with Hadden's superior at CIA counterintelligence, James Angleton, with whom he had developed an alliance that must be defined as transcending rapport. As time passed, Hadden and Angleton came to despise each other, and their visceral dislike would sour Hadden's remaining time in the Agency.

CHAPTER 3

JAMES JESUS ANGLETON: TREASON AT THE TOP

"I liked him as a person and I can understand why the Israelis trusted him so much, but I am convinced that he was mentally ill."
—CIA officer Arnold M. Silver, in an unpublished memoir[1]

"His treatment of those he felt less important than himself was disastrous. I came to think he needed mental help."
—John Hadden[2]

James Angleton, chief of CIA counterintelligence. Dulles and Angleton launched a plan to assassinate Nasser. (Photo from the US government.)

T he day after his arrival in Washington, Meir Amit began to send reports of his meetings back to Israel. His first report, received on Thursday, June 1, said that "there is a growing chance for American political backing if we act on our own." The United States would not endorse the Israeli military actions openly. But behind the scenes, the United States would support the Israeli aggression.

In the late afternoon of June 1, Israeli foreign minister Abba Eban received a report from "an American known for his close contact with government thinking." Israel learned that there were highly placed Americans who challenged its pretexts for war. Former ambassador to Morocco and Syria Charles W. Yost had traveled to Cairo as a presidential envoy. Yost wrote: "I cannot believe keeping the straits [of Aqaba] open was vital to Israel's existence, especially recalling that the straits were closed prior to 1957."

But Abba Eban decided that the report from Yost contained "no exhortation to us to stay our hand much longer." On that same day, Eshkol appointed Moshe Dayan to head the Ministry of Defense as a means of appeasing his military critics. Dayan had been close to Meir Amit for years, both being Sabras, born in Israel, with intertwined military careers.

Meir Amit's first meeting in Washington during those hurried few days in late May was with CIA's counterintelligence chief, James Jesus Angleton, who had managed to create a fiefdom within the Agency and was accountable to no one. Together with Meir Amit, Angleton would be the mastermind and engineer of the attack on the USS *Liberty*.

There is no documentary record of what was discussed at Angleton's meeting with Meir Amit, which took place on May 31, 1967. Most Israeli writers pretend that it never occurred, and write as if Amit met first with Richard Helms. But this was not so.

Like many of the first wave of CIA officers, Angleton had served with OSS (the Office of Strategic Services) in Europe during World War II, when he made the acquaintance of Jewish resistance groups based in London. He knew Allen Dulles and Richard Helms before CIA came into existence. Both went on, to their detriment, to tolerate his penchant for secrecy and for rogue covert operations for which he was answerable to no one.

The ink was scarcely dry on the CIA charter when Angleton began his involvement in terrorist operations. In Italy, Angleton was in the middle of Operation Gladio, in which CIA employed murder, sabotage, black ops, and assassination of political figures in a successful attempt to catapult the Christian Democrats into power and send an alliance between the socialists and Communists into oblivion.[3] It was Angleton, along with Frank Wisner, who would engineer in 1947 the fledgling CIA's relationship with the Mafia. Angleton imported a Mafia boss from Detroit to go to Italy to work with the Sicilian bandit Salvatore Giuliano in a terror campaign to subvert the election.[4] Director of Central Intelligence William Colby later wrote that the Communist and socialist coalition would have gained 60 percent of the vote without the Agency's sabotage.

George Kennan's "10/2" directive to the president's National Security Council in 1947 granted CIA these powers and more. (Kennan had served as deputy head of the US mission in Moscow until 1946. He returned home to serve at the State Department when he was enlisted to contribute to the effort to define the fledgling CIA's powers.) Angleton's involvement in Gladio was to remain part of the Agency's determination to cover up Angleton's participation in illegal and murderous activities, among them the attack on the USS *Liberty*. As for Colby, he refused to buy into the Angleton mystique. "I just could not figure out what they were doing at all," Colby said of Angleton and his counterintelligence staff.[5]

When at a 2012 Angleton conference outside Washington, DC, Carl Colby—the son of William Colby, the DCI who fired Angleton—requested that some light be shed on "Angleton's relationship to the Gladio" and the "Gladio group" in Italy with reference to the 1948 election, he was met by silence from the Agency assets and employees attending. William Colby himself wrote in his book, "I frankly didn't know what Angleton was doing."[6]

The Soviet Union had been the first state to recognize Israel, a detail that did not suit Angleton's vision of Israel as the eyes and ears of the United States in the Middle East, a reliable American military and economic outpost. In Italy, Angleton had developed networks of spies. He arranged, his biographer Tom Mangold writes, an operational intelligence exchange agreement with Mossad, upon which CIA relied for its intelligence about the Arab states.[7]

James Jesus Angleton affected a particular style. A cigarette dripped from his lips, and a cloud of smoke hovered over his head. His complexion was sallow, as if he rarely ventured out of doors, although among his hobbies was fly-fishing; his "piercing" eyes darted behind "horn-rimmed" tinted eyeglasses. A ghoulish figure, he was invariably clothed in a black morning coat and fedora and was excessively thin, cadaverous, and unappealing, so that his tall, bone-thin frame seemed like a walking question mark.

Angleton acolyte Tennent Bagley, who served with the Soviet Russia Division's counterintelligence, refers to "the air of mastery of recondite matters that hung about him [Angleton]."[8] Embarrassingly, given Angleton's role in the USS *Liberty* attack, Bagley refers to him as a "shining hero."[9] Counterintelligence, as author Joseph C. Goulden defines it, "is the means used to deny an enemy the capability to gather accurate information and to mislead him as to what is actually happening."[10] At this, Angleton was adept. Retired CIA officer Joseph Burkholder Smith told House Select Committee investigator Gaeton Fonzi that "Angleton's staff did 'strange things.'" Despite the fact that he only had counterintelligence jurisdiction, Angleton handled all Israeli operations. "This," said Smith, "had a strange effect on our activities in the Middle East," because unlike in other divisions, where station chiefs kept each other informed, Angleton wouldn't pass information to other stations in the Arab countries unless "he felt like it."

Smith added that he didn't know how Angleton "got all his power." He told Fonzi that "there could have been operations that Angleton staff was running that he wouldn't even tell the Director," although Angleton did have "a special relationship with Allen Dulles when he was running the Agency."[11] Apparently Angleton was accountable to no one, especially on matters relating to Israel.

Angleton's affect included encasing his frequent lies in double-talk because he didn't care if he was understood by most of his colleagues or not.[12] At Yale, editing a magazine called *furioso*, he had cultivated an interest in the poetry of Ezra Pound and T. S. Eliot, one openly a fascist, the other, Angleton's favorite, a bona fide anti-Semite.[13] In his Anglophile style, Angleton imitated Eliot. No one took him to task. He attended both Yale and Harvard, which does not say much for those temples of higher learning. Angleton's adventurism and reckless operations might have been inspired by his father, who had pursued the outlaw Pancho Villa, then married a seventeen-year-old. Angleton grew up in Italy because his father, Hugh Angleton, had founded the National Cash Register Company in Milan.

Chain-smoking Merit cigarettes, Angleton was a gourmet lunching at the best places in town. His voice was flat and without affect. He was a fraud, and to the ill fortune of the United States, he rose from OSS to a high place in CIA, his loyalties so profoundly with Israel that he could only be viewed as a traitor to his country.

Consistency was not among Angleton's qualities. Angleton was, CIA officer Arnold M. Silver was to note, "highly intelligent, uniquely articulate, and always wrong."[14]

In the Agency, Angleton cultivated higher-ups like Dulles and Helms, who were in a position to turn a blind eye to his policy-making operations, mostly irrational, for the United States. He knew how to manipulate Helms in particular, and when he insisted that Palestine Liberation Organization leader Yasser Arafat was a creature of the KGB, Helms believed him. All subjects would be incorporated into Angleton's Cold War mania and fevered anticommunism.

The discipline of "counterintelligence" depended on ferreting out spies who had burrowed into your ranks, collecting agents and double agents.[15] Angleton had met the Soviet spy Kim Philby in Britain. Philby came to the United States as the liaison for MI6. When Philby was revealed to be a Soviet spy, it was the burly former FBI agent Bill Harvey who penetrated his disguise. Later, it was said that "Philby was the greatest blow Angleton ever suffered."[16] At the same 2012 conference devoted to Angleton's work cited above, journalist Ronald Kessler remarked that "Angleton suspected everyone of being a Soviet spy except Philby."[17]

When Philby served as MI6 station chief in Washington, DC, Angleton had slipped him "the precise coordinates for every drop zone of the CIA in Albania." That Philby had been a Soviet spy, according to Tennent Bagley, tortured Angleton right up to his death.[18] Angleton wrote a four-page memo about the relationship between Philby and Guy Burgess, another Soviet spy, that was so tortured and opaque that William Harvey wrote at the bottom: "What is the rest of this story?"[19] (In 1960, Harvey returned from Berlin and was posted to CIA headquarters, where he was put in charge of the Agency's "Executive Actions" and "Operation Mongoose.")

John Whitten, Angleton's colleague at the counterintelligence division, told the House Select Committee on Assassinations in the late 1970s that Angleton's "understanding of human nature . . . his evaluation of people . . . was a very precarious thing." Herein lies a clue for the sailors of the USS *Liberty* with respect to who was to blame for their suffering.

A CIA historian noted that "the gears started to grind a little bit in Angleton's head." His ties to organized crime had emerged and so alarmed Richard Helms that he enlisted Whitten to investigate some of Angleton's activities, particularly in Latin America. David Robarge, an Agency historian, acknowledged that Angleton had created "a service within a service" and "that system became dysfunctional."[20]

In no sphere did Angleton's behavior better reflect his arrogance and subjective actions than in his dealings with Israel. His contacts predated his taking over the "Israeli desk" (Special Operations Group) in 1954.

His relationships with Israelis in high places dated back to 1950, when he met Teddy Kollek, an operative who later became mayor of Jerusalem, and Amos Manor of the Shin Bet, Israel's domestic intelligence service. It was Manor who suggested to Angleton that Israel's population of immigrants from the USSR and Eastern Europe made the country an indispensable source of information about what was going on in the USSR. "Even I was suspected by him, that I was a Soviet spy," Manor would say.[21]

In May 1951, David Ben-Gurion, the father of contemporary Israel, negotiated with Walter Bedell Smith and Allen Dulles that Mossad be enlisted in the service of CIA. The "special alliance"[22] between the United States and Mossad that would become the cornerstone of the attack on the USS *Liberty* had been proposed by Reuven Shiloah, Ben-Gurion's intelligence advisor.[23]

In June 1951, James Angleton met with Shiloah to work on a plan to use Jewish émigrés from Eastern Europe and the Soviet Union as spies. Among the services provided to CIA by Mossad were details of Soviet military capacities and intelligence capacities, including a map of a radar station that the Israelis had captured from the Arabs.[24]

April 1953 found Angleton in Tel Aviv meeting with the chief of Shin Bet. Through Angleton's efforts, "virtually every CIA man in the Middle East was working at second-hand for the Israelis." Meir Amit termed Angleton "the biggest Zionist of the lot" with a tone of admiration, as, indeed, Amit and Mossad could not have pulled off the operation against *Liberty* without him.[25] "As soon as you mention Mossad," Thomas Lowe Hughes told me, "Angleton is right in the middle of it. It's hard to imagine that the Six-Day War comes and goes without Angleton being involved in it."[26]

US interests, Angleton decided, "lay in propping up the Jewish state militarily and economically."[27] He enhanced his power base through his obsession with communism, a bête noire against which any method, any means of attack, was justified.

In October, Angleton visited Israel for the first time, reinforcing his friendship with Ben-Gurion, which played no small part in the operation against the USS *Liberty*. Regarding American-Israeli relations and the attack on the USS *Liberty*, it was at that moment that plans for the operation against the ship began. Angleton had been appointed officially head of CIA's newly created Israeli desk in 1954 and would be CIA's exclusive liaison with Israeli intelligence for the next twenty years. He treated the Israeli account "as a counterintelligence asset."[28]

At that moment in 1954, two Israeli intelligence officers were dispatched to Washington: Teddy Kollek, later mayor of Jerusalem, and Chaim Herzog. CIA was wary, concerned that Mossad might have been infiltrated by Soviet agents posing as Jewish refugees.[29] Israeli operative Kollek tried to warn Angleton that Kim Philby might be a Soviet agent— something wasn't right—but Angleton wouldn't listen.

Amos Manor, an Auschwitz survivor and refugee from Romania, arrived to convince Angleton that the presence of refugees from Russia and Eastern Europe could provide intelligence for CIA. Manor's contribution was, as he put it, to "persuade the anti-communist Angleton that we could be friends. Even I was suspected by him, that I was a Soviet spy." Manor managed to win over Angleton.

Tom Mangold uses this locution to describe Angleton's unique relationship with Israel: "I would like to place on the record . . . that Angleton's closest professional friends overseas, then and subsequently, came from the Mossad."[30] When an Arab American was nominated as a case officer for Israel, the Israeli government registered a protest.

Brushing aside the Agency's Near East Division as if it didn't exist, Angleton was now answerable only to the director of Central Intelligence. Years later, CIA officer Arnold M. Silver wrote that "one of Allen Dulles' gravest mistakes was appointing Angleton as chief of the new CI (Counter Intelligence) staff in 1954." Angleton mismanaged his staff, Silver concluded, and was "a neophyte" with respect to evaluating Soviet intelligence defectors." When Silver suggested to Angleton that his biggest source in the Vatican, a man on whom he had made his reputation, was a "fabricator,"

Angleton refused to listen. Angleton's "overriding interest was in his own activities, foremost of which was liaison with the Israelis."[31]

At Langley during these years, Angleton cultivated CIA officers who had access to classified information of possible use to Israel, as his loyalties bordered treason. One was Samuel Halpern, a Jew born in Brooklyn who had joined OSS in 1943 and CIA in 1947. Halpern went on to serve as executive assistant to Desmond Fitzgerald, chief of the Far East Division; later he joined CIA's task force on Cuba, working with William Harvey and Bobby Kennedy on Operation Mongoose.

Angleton set out to vet Halpern with respect to his loyalty to Israel. "Jim [Angleton] looked at me real hard," said "Sammy," as he was known affectionately to many of his CIA colleagues, later.[32] Aware of Angleton's relationships with Dulles and Helms, Halpern assured him that he would not interfere in matters involving Israel.

By 1954, Angleton was the only person authorized to talk to Israeli intelligence. By the late 1950s, Angleton would be helping Israel build an atomic bomb. John Hadden denied that Angleton had facilitated the transference to Israel of the nuclear materials they needed for a bomb, then had to admit that Angleton had no interest in stopping it either: "Why would someone whose whole life was dedicated to fighting communism have any interest in preventing a fiercely anti-Communist nation getting the means to defend itself?"[33]

That Nasser was not a Communist and that Moshe Sharett and Kollek and Amit's predecessor, Isser Harel, in 1956 were considering peace with Nasser (known as Operation Chameleon) did not influence Angleton. Kollek became one of John Hadden's favorite people from the moment Hadden arrived in Tel Aviv. Kollek called Angleton "an original thinker" who "often spoke in riddles that you had to interpret or feel, rather than analyze with cold logic."[34]

After the 1956 war, Eisenhower had to threaten to support UN sanctions and withdraw the tax-deductible status of private contributions to Israel. Israel retained rights to the Gulf of Aqaba. Israel's army had invaded Egypt and still occupied all of the Sinai Peninsula and the Gaza Strip. "Had it not been for Russia's threat to intervene on behalf of the Egyptians, the British, French and Israeli forces might now be sitting in Cairo, celebrating Nasser's ignominious fall from power," Eveland writes. "It was when some claimed that with the fall of Nasser, Soviet penetration into the Middle East and Africa would have collapsed." Out of his depth, with Angleton conspiring with his director of Central Intelligence and secretary of state, Eisenhower remarked "he hoped the Nasser problem could be eliminated."

Angleton brandished his fame from having been the first to obtain Khrushchev's 1956 Politburo speech denouncing Stalin, although in fact it was Amos Manor who brought the text to Ben-Gurion. Independently, the French had passed it to Frank Wisner—at the time, the DDP (Deputy Director for Plans), running CIA's clandestine services. When a staff member asked Angleton, "Will you at long last reveal how you happened to get a copy of that speech?" Angleton stared at him and in his flat voice, without affect, said, "No." "He was under the unfortunate impression," Arnold Silver noted, "that the cloak and dagger had been invented specifically for him and for nobody else."[35]

One day in 1956, Robert Amory, the deputy director for intelligence, confronted Allen Dulles during a meeting of CIA's Watch Committee.

"The taxpayer lays out $16,000 a year to me as your deputy director for me to give you the best intelligence available," Amory said. "Either you believe me or you believe this co-opted Israeli agent here."[36] He pointed at Angleton. Amory had overheard Angleton saying, "I can discount what Amory is saying. I spent last night with our friends and they have assured me they are carrying out protective measures against the Jordanians."[37] With respect to US relations with Israel, Angleton had been running a shadow government within CIA.

When he mentioned eliminating "the Nasser problem," Eisenhower meant that he hoped relations with the Egyptians could be improved. At that moment, however, Dulles and Angleton launched a plan to assassinate Nasser. The plan was placed on hold with John F. Kennedy's election and Kennedy's more evenhanded approach to Israeli-Arab relations. Ben-Gurion did not speak openly to Angleton regarding his plans to attack the Sinai, so that one day, Angleton visited Allen Dulles three times to assure him that an attack was not imminent, only for the attack on Sinai to be carried out. Isser Harel, then chief of Mossad, covered for Angleton, claiming that he had not told the Mossad station chief in Washington what was being planned.

Meir Amit became head of Mossad in 1963 and at once began to make frequent trips to Langley.[38] He promoted a military alliance of Israel, Jordan, and Saudi Arabia to be sponsored by the United States. Angleton was enlisted to make this happen with Arabist CIA officers.

Every CIA officer in the Middle East was now working "second hand" for the Israelis.[39]

Amit persuaded Angleton and CIA to provide millions of dollars to underwrite Israel's clandestine services which, say Dan Raviv and Yossi Melman in *Every Spy a Prince*, "were judged to be in the general interest of the West."[40] This enterprise was code-named "K Mountain."

At CIA, deep into the 1960s, Angleton handled the Israeli desk always within the Cold War anti-Soviet ideology that was his stock in trade. It was Angleton who would view Israel's instigation of the Six-Day War as necessary to protect Israel's nuclear reactor at Dimona from a "grand Soviet design" that included a nuclear attack on the United States.[41]

CIA agreed to provide extensive financial support for the Israeli service, and in turn, CIA used the intelligence it collected on Soviet military and intelligence capabilities.[42] Angleton's loyalty to Israel included infiltrating a Washington, DC, trash collector and having the trash from the Israeli embassy delivered to CIA.[43] Collecting everything by and about Israel was Angleton's characteristically irrational way of protecting them. During his tenure at the Agency, he visited Israel at least thirty times and insisted he could peer through the Iron Curtain only with the assistance of Israeli intelligence.[44]

Documentary support for Angleton's assertions was rare to nonexistent. At one point, Angleton admitted that he planted an Israeli agent in Cuba under the sway of an officer of the clandestine services, William Harvey, with whom the reader already has some acquaintance. Angleton acknowledged in this case that he had worked joint black operations with Mossad, a foreshadow of the joint operation in the attack on the USS *Liberty*. Did Harvey attempt to use this contact "to carry out the mission of eliminating the leader down there, or try to get any help out of him in that regard?" Angleton was asked. Angleton stirred from his torpor. "He knows that I would have cut his throat," Angleton said. The very fact that he was running an Israeli agent cast into doubt his loyalty to his country.

"That would have jeopardized your entire contact with the Israelis?" he was asked.

"Yes, sir," Angleton said.[45]

Angleton was a fraud never to be unmasked—for one thing, because you could never find him. Arnold Silver realized that "his overriding interest was in his own activities, foremost of which was liaison with the Israelis," and no one could stop him.[46] So Angleton sabotaged John F. Kennedy's policy to send international inspectors to Dimona, where false walls were erected, elevators hidden, and dummy installations built to conceal evidence of the nuclear weapons program.[47] Kennedy had hoped "to take a whole new look at U.S. Mideast policy."[48] According to Richard H. Curtiss, he planned to forge new relationships with individual Arab leaders and was dedicated to US, not Israeli, interests. This was not to be.

Angleton did have his apologists, like Thomas Powers, Richard Helms's biographer, who writes: "It is obvious that no one outside the CIA is ever going to know if Angleton overdid it."[49] On the same page, Powers writes: "Many other CIA people say that no one knew what was involved in some of Angleton's deeper operations." Powers also writes:

"When President Johnson planted himself directly in front of Angleton, and the cameras all focused in, Angleton's face expressed nothing whatever but pure horror."[50]

Angleton's loyalty was demonstrably not to the United States but to Israel. Seymour Hersh learned from a cache of Angleton's personal files connected to Operation Chaos[51] that he made a study of American Jews in the government, constructing "a matrix of the position and Jewishness of senior officials in the CIA and elsewhere who had access to classified information of use to Israel."[52]

Angleton looked for people who were active in Jewish affairs in their personal lives, or who had relatives who were Zionists.[53] These "scored high on what amounted to a Jewishness index." But Angleton's files were famously "disorganized," making it inevitable that no one find anything. This was a clear strategy to help him remain unaccountable to anyone.[54] Thomas Lowe Hughes remarked to me in our interview, with respect to Angleton's missing files: "I wonder what there is in Israel."[55] Then he added that to uncover the reality would release a "maelstrom," so they feel it best to leave things as they are." The "they" referred to those in high places.

Nor, as Arnold Silver noted, could Angleton "tolerate rebuttal." Meanwhile, he "had the confidence of Allen Dulles as Director, and that was what counted in keeping Angleton in his job as CI staff chief." At the Agency, Richard Helms was Angleton's "most important patron."[56] Helms and Angleton had danced warily around each other, each striving not to rock each other's boat. Their communication consisted of short telephone conversations on secure lines.

With Dulles and Helms—Helms reluctantly—turning a blind eye on his maneuvers and operations, Angleton was free to wreak whatever havoc suited him. When Helms left CIA, he ordered his secretary, Elizabeth Dunleavy, to destroy the bulk of his personal and office files. Angleton never shared his files with the Agency and said he destroyed those that were "embarrassing" to the Agency. He did not enter many of the official documents he horded in forty secret safes into the Agency's central filing system. He did file some records of the HT/LINGUAL mail-opening program, communications with the FBI (Angleton was Bureau Informant 100), and materials sent to and from the Warren Commission.

By the end, the consensus among his colleagues was that Angleton had "lost his judgment."[57] Partly that was a result of "the monster KGB conspiracy theories he sponsored in the 1960s"; these were fueled by historical ignorance, British author Christopher Andrew speculated. Fired up by Cold War hysteria, Angleton seems almost never to have bothered to have studied the actual political history of the Soviet Union.

It would be Angleton who would prevail in formulating, with Meir Amit, the configuration of the operation that would culminate in the attack on the USS *Liberty*.

And always Angleton's obsession with the Cold War lurked behind his relations with Israel. Deposing Nasser meant that oil resources would flow with less constraint. The accessibility of oil justified any subterfuge, any fabrication, such as that Yasser Arafat and the PLO were creatures of the KGB. They were not.

At his post, ruling over his own private shadow agency, Angleton viewed Nasser with alarm. He prohibited the CIA station in Tel Aviv from communicating with the Cairo station, or any other Middle Eastern capital.[58] All communications from Israel were routed not through the Deputy Director for Operations and the Near East Division but through Angleton's office in Washington, a policy he instituted in 1955.[59] CIA relied on Mossad for intelligence on both the Middle East and the Soviet Union.

From the fall of Egypt's monarchy and King Farouk, CIA had supported the Nasser-led coup of "Free Officers" and saw Nasser as the leader of the Muslim world and an American ally. In 1952, at the time of the coup, the United States (meaning CIA) supported him as the leader of the Muslim world. Nasser began as Saddam Hussein later would, with the support of the United States. First, the Agency would try to control him. Only when that proved impossible did CIA show their fangs. By 1967, Nasser had long been an Angleton enemy.

Meir Amit was Angleton's chief ally in Israel, but in the United States, he relied on another Mossad operative, Ephraim "Eppy" Evron, who in 1967, as a Mossad operative as well as deputy Israeli ambassador to Washington, enjoyed greater importance at the Israeli embassy than the ambassador, Avraham Harman.[60]

It was Evron who had arranged meetings between Angleton and Moshe Dayan, and Evron who encouraged Angleton in the view that Gamal Abdel Nasser was responsible for all of the West's problems in the area.[61] If Nasser could be eliminated and the Egyptian army defeated without overt assistance from a major power, the Arabs would be left with no alternative but to make peace with Israel. In this spirit, Evron arranged meetings between Angleton and Moshe Dayan and others to discuss the feasibility of an attack on Egypt with the objective of toppling Nasser.

Lyndon Johnson had authorized Angleton to inform Evron that the United States would not intervene to stop an attack on Egypt. Meanwhile, Eisenhower's plan to visit Egypt to improve Arab-American relations had been discouraged by Allen Dulles and his brother, John Foster Dulles, Eisenhower's secretary of state.[62]

On June 2, 1967, Eppy Evron was once again at the White House. The question was put to him: "Do we still have until June 11?" Evron hedged. There was nothing sacred about the two-week reprieve, he said. Then he had a question of his own: "What would you Americans think if there were a probe by an Israeli ship and the Egyptians opened fire and then we had to strike back. Would you recognize that we have exercised our legitimate right of self-defense under article 51 of the UN charter?" The next day, LBJ added a sentence to a letter to Prime Minister Eshkol: "We have completely and fully exchanged views with General Amit."[63]

In the matter of the attack on the USS *Liberty*, Helms learned of the heinous operation too late for him to stop it.

CHAPTER 4

TOPPLING NASSER

"If that Colonel of yours gives us too much trouble, we will break him in half."

—Allen Dulles

In 1952, Nasser was a "hawk-faced" colonel with a history of anti-British political activities who had come to power with a group of officers in a bloodless coup.[1] By the mid-1950s, Israel's goal had become to topple Nasser. The joint US-Israeli operation to sink the USS *Liberty*, to be followed by the bombing of Cairo and the toppling of Egyptian premier Gamal Abdel Nasser, was a continuation of a long-standing history.[2] The Israelis had wanted Nasser dead from the moment he and the other colonels overthrew King Farouk and the monarchy in an officers' rebellion.

Officers in the Egyptian army, trained by CIA, had formed links with Kermit Roosevelt and plotted to overthrow King Farouk. CIA had at first hesitated, having taken an active role in influencing the shape that the new government of Egypt would take following the fall of the monarchy. Kermit Roosevelt, senior officer in the Middle East Division, recommended that CIA approach Nasser, the leader of the Free Officers, to support a government amenable to US interests.

By 1956, the year Gamal Abdel Nasser became the second president of Egypt, the United States was committed to "inducing his downfall." So states a memorandum that was issued by the Office of the Secretary of Defense. Its title is "Emerging pattern—Arab-Israeli situation." It outlines the pattern for the 1967 Six-Day War with Nasser and Egypt as the central target, listing six points as "possible objectives of an Israeli attack on Egypt capable of being attained in the necessarily short blitzkrieg type of war." The first point of the six suggests the goal of the operation against the USS *Liberty*: "to induce the downfall of Nasser and his regime."[3]

From the moment in 1956 that Nasser became president of Egypt, Israel began to place in his mouth the words "We should destroy Israel." Then they would retract the statement as an "error," prescient words for Israel's explanation for its attack on the USS *Liberty*. Only after Nasser concluded, in the face of an Israeli army attack on Gaza, that there was "no chance for the [conciliatory] line adopted by Egypt until then, did he appeal for Soviet armaments." Prime Minister Moshe Sharett's diary "confirms beyond any doubt that Israel's security establishment strongly opposed all border security arrangements proposed by Egypt, Jordan or the UN," historian Livia Rokach writes.[4]

When President Eisenhower himself commented that he hoped "the Nasser problem could be eliminated," Allen Dulles and Angleton took that as a signal to begin to concoct plots to assassinate Nasser. The first of such schemes was aborted by Eisenhower's secretary of state, John Foster Dulles, but it remained on James Angleton's agenda.

Israel's own plans to provoke Egypt into war were on its own agenda at least as early as the autumn of 1953, almost a year before Gamal Abdel Nasser deposed President/Prime Minister Mohammed Naguib and consolidated his leadership by proclaiming himself the prime minister of the Republic by the ruling Revolutionary Command Council, the Nasser-led junta.[5] The Muslim Brotherhood, who supported Naguib, attempted to assassinate Nasser. The Israelis soon enough discovered that John Foster Dulles had promised aid to Nasser.

By 1954, the personal friendship between US Ambassador Henry A. Byroade and Nasser seemed to be producing a $50 million aid program for Egypt. At once this was viewed as a grave threat to the American dollars flowing into Israel, hopefully in perpetuity.[6] Also known as the Lavon affair, "Operation Susannah" was named for the girlfriend of one of the young Egyptian-Jewish terrorists, Victor Levy. The project itself was created by Israeli intelligence to reverse the direction of US aid away from Egypt to Israel.

On April 13, Byroade gave a speech in which he announced that US aid to Israel would be cut and aid to the Arabs increased.[7] Israeli military intelligence concluded that "what America really wants are bases to ring Russia completely."[8] Nasser wanted aid and nonalignment. Israel wanted to stop Britain's evacuation from the Suez Canal Zone. But Israel also was willing to provide military outposts for American interests.

The Israelis found their perfect solution thwarting US relations with Egypt in "sabotage actions" that everyone would believe were the work of the Muslim Brotherhood. Terrorist actions would break out all over Egypt. In so unreliable an environment, it would be wise not to invest American resources. With Nasser's Egypt destabilized, the Americans would do better to spend their money elsewhere and seek military services elsewhere too.

Handling Operation Susannah on the ground in Cairo was "Paul Frank," a.k.a. Avri el-Ad, or Avraham Seidenwerg. Avri el-Ad had long been an Israeli operative, and along the way had become a close acquaintance of James Angleton, linking Angleton with Susannah.[9] El-Ad had emigrated to Palestine from Europe in 1939 and joined the Zionist youth movement. After serving eight years in the terrorist *Haganah*, he was recruited into military intelligence (Aman) and became an expert in the field of demolitions. In Susannah, he operated undercover as a former Nazi who had become a German businessman. His alias was "Paul Frank," a non-Jew. To maintain his cover, he found a doctor to conceal his circumcision with a plastic foreskin.[10]

In Egypt in 1953, El-Ad, hitherto known as Paul Frank, set up a sleeper network. By 1954, Frank's handler in Israeli military intelligence, based in Paris, told him to prepare for political assassinations, with Nasser at the top of the list of targets.[11] The aim, as Andrew and Leslie Cockburn write, "was to destabilize Nasser's relations with the US and UK and maybe postpone the withdrawal of British bases on the Suez Canal."[12]

Moshe Sharett's diary reveals that the Israeli leadership—in particular Yitzhak Ben-Zvi, president of Israel from 1952–1963—had nurtured murderous intentions toward Nasser and Egypt and searched for means of drawing him into conflict for as long as Nasser had been a public figure.

"How wonderful it would be if the Egyptians started an offensive which we could defeat and follow with an invasion," Ben-Zvi said. Unfortunately, he lamented, the Egyptians have shown no tendency to "facilitate us in this task through a provocative challenge on their side."[13] The circumstances cried out for a false flag operation. What Egypt could not be lured into doing, the Israelis would accomplish in their name.

In Ben-Zvi's words are contained the seeds of the operation against the USS *Liberty*, a false flag operation blaming the Egyptians for an act of aggression that originated with Israel. Propaganda based on falsehoods would accompany this creation of pretexts for the bombing of Cairo. Clues for this pattern abound in the public statements of Israel leaders. In 1955, Moshe Dayan, Israel's chief of staff of the armed forces, said, "In order to have young men go to the Negev, we have to cry out that it is in danger." A pattern of false flag operations begun in the 1950s would persist into 1967 and the Six-Day War. "Arabs" would be demonized as Israel found pretexts for its own aggressions. Israel would persistently raise the false flag that its very existence was in jeopardy.

Employing ships with insidious intent became a frequently employed Israeli tactic. In September 1954, the Israelis decided to send the *Bat Gallim* through the Suez Canal with the understanding that Egypt was likely to seize the vessel as it had confiscated other Israeli ships when they had entered its territorial waters, as Israel itself had seized several Arab ships in Israeli waters. The *Bat Gallim* was the first Israeli ship to seek passage through the Suez Canal since 1949.[14] The Israeli government hoped that an incident in the canal would pressure Britain to force Egypt to end the blockade against Israeli shipping in the canal.

Bat Gallim was impounded, as expected, and the crew imprisoned, but Britain did not force an end to the blockade on the Egyptian government. Moshe Sharett, then the premier of Israel, received Nasser's peace initiative with interest, only for the more powerful Ben-Gurion to abort it and order a raid on Gaza. History reveals that Egypt was difficult to provoke, time after time robbing Israel of sought-after pretexts for invading.

The operation involving the sinking of the USS *Liberty* enjoyed its most overt antecedent in the Lavon affair, Operation Susannah, whose staged prelude was the retirement of David Ben-Gurion to a kibbutz on the Negev, out of sight and out of blame for the scheduled terrorism. For the moment, Ben-Gurion was succeeded by Moshe Sharett, who had been foreign minister since the founding of Israel, and whom Ben-Gurion believed he could manipulate. The new minister of defense while Ben-Gurion enjoyed his temporary exile in the desert was Pinhas Lavon, who, according to author Stewart Steven, "stood far above other members of the government. His sharp tongue was a feared weapon which he used to good effect. He was learned and a magnificent orator, but he lacked ministerial experience, and his ability to get on with people was always seriously in question."[15]

Historian Shabtai Teveth sums up the operation as designed "to undermine Western confidence in the existing [Egyptian] regime by generating public insecurity and actions, to bring about arrests, demonstrations, and acts of revenge while totally concealing the Israeli factor. . . . Suspicion [was to] fall on the Muslim Brotherhood, the [Egyptian] Communists, 'unspecified malcontents' or 'local nationalists.'"[16] The goal was to destabilize Egyptian society and alienate America from Egypt.

Before it was over, Pinhas Lavon, the Israeli minister responsible for intelligence in late 1954, would be (falsely) accused of giving the order for the bombings carried out in Cairo and Alexandria. In July 1954, angry at Nasser's friendly relations with the United States and Britain, and intending to disrupt these relationships, Lavon devised the plan to "break the West's confidence in Nasser" and to prevent aid from the West coming to Egypt.[17] The spy ring of young operatives, Jews resident in

Egypt, historian Livia Rokach writes, was "originally to serve as a fifth column." The role of the young recruits was to discredit the new Arab nationalist government.

Operation Susannah (1954–1955) became a Ben-Gurion operation, with his acolytes Moshe Dayan and Shimon Peres directly involved. It was a deplorable victimization of young Egyptian Zionists. The terrorist acts were carried out between July 2 and July 27, 1954. The perpetrators were young Egyptian Jews who hoped that their participation would lead to safe passage for emigration to Israel, a place they had never visited. They created the bombs and incendiaries themselves. For several years, the Israeli government denied its involvement in Susannah, only for it to a few years later assume responsibility and admit that the bombings were part of an Israeli government operation.

Meanwhile, Egyptians would be blamed for the deaths and destruction, and the Americans and British would increase their support to Israel. The Egyptians had hoped the United States would aid in the construction of the Aswan Dam; America hoped to induce Egyptian participation in the emerging Baghdad Pact. It would turn out that the necessary assistance for building the Aswan High Dam would come from the Soviet Union. While these issues were percolating, Israel created this ring of terrorism and mayhem to sabotage the prospect of Egypt's joining a US-sponsored Middle Eastern alliance organization. There was also a false flag incident with the *Bat Gallim*, foreshadowing the attack on the USS *Liberty*.

Operation Susannah began in the summer of 1954 when Colonel Binyamin Gibli, chief of Aman (Israeli military intelligence), organized the recruitment of the Egyptian Jews. These young Egyptians shared a belief in the state of Israel and in Zionism. They believed they were helping Israel; they had been given no briefing on what they were to do or say if they were captured by the Egyptian police. Nor were they provided with passports should they be forced to escape. Men and women of scant political sophistication, several of them graduate students, they were induced to plant bombs and incendiaries in post offices and libraries—United States Information Agency (USIA) libraries—in Cairo and Alexandria. Other targets were the Cairo railway station and two movie theaters. Another target was the automobiles of British envoys. The group of twelve terrorists made their own incendiary devices, many of which were small enough to fit into book covers.

Bags filled with acid were placed on top of nitroglycerine bombs, so that it took several hours for the acid to eat through the bag and ignite the bomb.[18] The bombs destined for the USIA libraries were placed on the shelves of the library just before closing time. Several hours later, a blast would occur, shattering glass and the shelves and setting fire to books and furniture. Similar bombs that also fit into book covers were placed in the Metro-Goldwyn-Mayer Theatre.

In the foyer of the Rio cinema in Cairo, ready to place his incendiary, Philip Natanson "sensed a wave of heat" searing his right thigh. The bomb in his trouser pocket had ignited! Flames leaped from his trousers; he squeezed his thigh with all his strength in a vain effort to stifle the flame. Following the explosion, he could see "the blackening skin on his thighs. His arms were scorched up to the elbows."[19]

It wasn't long before the Egyptian police discovered the notebook where Natanson had written down the formulas for manufacturing explosives that he copied from a microfilm that had been brought from Israel. The direct orders were given by Frank. "You wanted to burn the whole country, did you?" one Cairo policeman said to Natanson.

The government of Israel first reacted to the arrests by waving the flag of the Holocaust:

> The government of Israel strongly rejects the false accusations of the general Egyptian prosecution, which relegates to the Israeli authorities horrible deeds and diabolic conspiracies against the security and the international relations of Egypt. From this stand we have protested many times in the past persecution and false accusations of Jews in various countries. We see in the innocent Jews accused by the Egyp-

tian authorities of such severe crimes, victims of vicious hostility to the State of Israel and the Jewish people. If their crime is being Zionist and devoted to Israel, millions of Jews around the world share this crime. We do not think that the rulers of Egypt should be interested in being responsible for shedding Jewish blood. We call upon all those who believe in peace, stability and human relations among nations to prevent fatal injustice.[20]

It was an exercise in calumny and distortion. The accusations were not "false," the group not "innocent." The operation began with small packages of explosives thrust into the mail chute slot at the central post office in Alexandria and concluded with that incendiary that blew up in the pocket of Philip Natanson. The only frame-up was that invented against Egypt by the Ben-Gurion claque.

Operation Susannah sputtered out; eleven young terrorists, men and women, were sacrificed to world opinion, imprisoned, and served lengthy prison sentences. No match for the Egyptian services, they were pathetically and politically naïve. One, Shmuel Azar, was incapable of lying and admitted that he "was a full accomplice in everything his companions had done."[21]

"We are Jews and Zionists," Azar said proudly, "and we acted on behalf of the state of Israel," although how terrorist acts of arson and bombings contributed to the welfare of the state of Israel he could not say. Azar was one of two young Egyptian Jews who were executed in Cairo in 1955 in the wake of Susannah. Two were acquitted for lack of evidence, six given prison terms from seven years to life, and two condemned to death.

With no one to advise them, the group had considered calling themselves "Communists," only for Philip Natanson to note: "The Communists don't believe in terrorism."[22] The prosecutor at their trial depicted the attacks as a provocation aimed at "sowing dissension between Egypt and the West." A destabilized Egypt would not be a suitable recipient for American largesse.

The ruthlessness of the Israeli government, which would later be manifested in the attack on the unarmed sailors of the USS *Liberty*, was fully displayed in the sacrifice of these young idealists by David Ben-Gurion and the leaders of his Mapai party. Among the party could be found Moshe Dayan, who would give the order for the firing on *Liberty*, although the operation was not his idea. Prime minister though he might have been, Moshe Sharett knew nothing of the spy ring, and his party's newspaper, *Davar*, accused the Egyptian government of "a Nazi-inspired policy."[23] Moshe Sharett believed that those accused were entirely innocent and had been libeled, until army intelligence finally told him the truth.

They were young Zionists in the diaspora, their goal to migrate to Israel. Those who recruited them belonged to Israeli army intelligence, like Avraham Dar (a.k.a. John Darling). The Egyptians charged them not with terrorism but with espionage. The sole female, Marcelle Ninio, believed she was being recruited to organize Jewish emigration from Egypt. Willing to cooperate, to do whatever they could to help Israel, they were fervent believers in a Jewish homeland, only to be treated abominably by the Ben-Gurion faction behind Susannah. They had been in place to commit assassinations of government figures and military advisors, only for the operation to disintegrate. And they were obviously amateurs. Outside the Rio theater were found the remnants of an eyeglass case studded with explosive material.[24]

Another member of the group, Max Binnet, had been an Israeli agent in Iraq masquerading as a German priest, a major in military intelligence. He slashed his wrists with a rusty nail and committed suicide rather than stand trial.[25] Three of the Susannah conspirators were twenty-two years old, and went on to rot under unspeakable prison conditions: filth, degradation, torture, beatings, and starvation.[26]

The *Jerusalem Post* described them as having been instrumental "in helping to organize a group of young Jewish activists."[27] They had been cast adrift by military intelligence and tossed into horrific Egyptian prisons and had been given no instructions by their handler, Paul Frank, who was using Avraham Dar's Unit 131 of sleeper agents, as to what to do or say should they be apprehended.

The trial—at a military tribunal—began on December 11, 1954. The question of who was to blame occupied the press and the inner circles of the government. Based on a forged document by Shimon Peres and Moshe Dayan, the prosecution attempted to place the legal responsibility for the sabotage at Lavon's door.[28]

Because it seemed that the police were ready for them, and even had fire engines parked outside the cinema in Alexandria where Natanson was planting his bomb, the young conspirators came to believe that their handler, Paul Frank, had betrayed them. Frank himself served ten years in prison. He had lied to Pinhas Lavon, denying the July 2 post office sabotage. The young terrorists blamed Frank for threatening them into committing the sabotage. To blame Colonel Gibli would be to blame the army as "ridden with fascist tendencies" to the board of inquiry, so Frank lied, giving a false story Gibli had ordered him to present.[29] Accused of treason, Frank had in fact been recruited by army intelligence and Motke Ben-Nasur to lead the cell.

Both the young Zionists and Frank, who was arrested later, served more than a decade in horrific Egyptian prisons. One recruit named Meir Meyouhas, an Egyptian Jew and Mossad agent, received a lighter sentence and was released in 1960. The Egyptian police were assisted in their interrogations by German experts provided by CIA. Ultimately, the blame fell on Binyamin Gibli, Moshe Dayan, and Ben-Gurion himself.

With the September 1960 verdict in the Paul Frank case, the Lavon affair became public. Isser Harel, the Mossad chief, wanted to close in, but he could not risk condemning Peres and Dayan without incurring Ben-Gurion's wrath. Lavon was ushered out of government, and Ben-Gurion fired Isser Harel after discovering he had run his own programs behind Ben-Gurion's back. Harel's successor would be Meir Amit.

Along the way, Gibli's secretary admitted that she had been instructed to alter a vital letter of July 19, 1954, from Gibli to Dayan. The words "Following the conversation we had, the boys were activated" now read, "Upon Lavon's instructions, we have activated Susannah's boys." Gibli's secretary contended that the letter she had changed was not the one in question in which Lavon gave the order. Finally, a "Committee of Seven" concluded that Lavon did not give the direct order for the 1954 bombings. It was ruled that there was no need for further inquiry. Ben-Gurion insisted that "this country cannot live by whitewashing lies, misrepresenting facts and perverting justice," although this is exactly what happened in the fifty-year wake of the attack on the USS *Liberty*.

At a loss, in his diary for January 10, 1955, Sharett places the moral responsibility for the terrorist operation against Egypt on Pinhas Lavon, "who has constantly preached for acts of madness and taught the army leadership the diabolic lesson of how to set the Middle East on fire, how to cause friction, [and] cause bloody confrontations."[30]

Scholar Livia Rokach blames Sharett for "not denouncing those responsible and exposing his true convictions in regard to Israel's terrorist ideology." She accuses him of not proposing an alternative and not ordering "a radical housecleaning in the security establishment." The consequence would have been the downfall of Lavon and of the Ben-Gurionist gang headed by Dayan and Peres. "By not acting, Sharett was compelled to invite Ben-Gurion to reenter the cabinet as minister of defense in Lavon's place," Rokach writes.[31]

Before it was over, Paul Frank writes in his own memoir of these events, Lavon "was a nervous wreck. His face had paled at first, but now his hands were taut and trembling, his voice reduced to a whisper."[32]

While Egypt maintained that the whole thing was a "Zionist plot," Moshe Sharett denounced the trial of the conspirators as a "show trial" and charged that the young people had been victims of "false accusations, despicable slanders designed to harass the Jews in Egypt" and "heinous anti-Semitism." Duped by Ben-Gurion, Peres, Dayan, and Lavon, out of the loop, Sharett addressed the parliament, where he spoke of "the group of Jews who had fallen victim to false libels of espionage and from whom confessions to imaginary crimes appear to be extorted by threats and torture." He spoke of "the methods of medieval inquisitions" and of the Egyptian junta "spill[ing] Jewish blood."

"We see in the innocent Jews accused by the Egyptian authorities of such severe crimes, victims of vicious hostility to the State of Israel and the Jewish people," he said, and also lamented the "shedding of Jewish blood."[33] Others denounced the trials as a "pogrom." Sharett himself had been victimized by his political adversaries.

An international campaign was organized to rescue those sentenced to death. It was led by Labour MP Richard Crossman; French foreign minister Edgar Faure; and American lawyer Roger Baldwin, representing the US League of Human Rights, who all went to Cairo to plead with Nasser for the lives of the "innocent" defendants.[34] A month earlier, Nasser had refused to spare six members of the Muslim Brotherhood who were condemned to death by hanging for an attempt on his life. He felt he could not commute the two death sentences on Moshe Marzouk and Azar; they were hanged on January 28, 1955.[35] Moshe Sharett met with Roger Baldwin, who revealed that Nasser had "talked to him about Israel, saying that he is not among those who want to throw Israel into the Mediterranean. He believes in co-existence with Israel and knows that negotiations will open someday."[36] Allen Dulles tried to get Nasser to commute the death sentences, but he failed. CIA understood.

Three days later, on January 28, 1955, Abba Eban cabled Sharett, saying: "The U.S. is ready to sign an agreement with us whereby we shall make a commitment not to extend our borders by force; it will commit itself to come to our aid if we are attacked." Teddy Kollek, representing James Angleton and CIA counterintelligence, sent a message to Shin Bet: "The partners [CIA] renew their suggestion for a meeting with Nasser ... the initiative is now up to Israel." At the time, Kollek was director general of the prime minister's office. From 1965 to 1993, he would serve as mayor of Jerusalem, an office to which he was reelected five times.

The Israeli government was not a monolith, not then and not now. Ben-Gurion, having returned to the government as minister of defense, ordered an attack on a bus, resulting in the deaths of ten Bedouins. Ben-Gurion returned to Tel Aviv on February 21, 1955, accompanied by Golda Meir.

In the aftermath of the Lavon affair, the Mapai party broke up.[37] In 1955, Israeli paratroopers launched a raid on an Egyptian army post in Gaza and killed thirty-seven Egyptians, wounding more. This raid accomplished the rift between the United States and Nasser that Israel had hoped Operation Susannah would achieve. In October 1955, Ben-Gurion summoned his most stalwart officer, Moshe Dayan, back from a Paris vacation, to plan a war with Egypt in the Sinai Peninsula that would culminate in the Six-Day War. The climax of that effort, led in 1967 again by Moshe Dayan, would feature the ambush of the USS *Liberty*.

Israeli obfuscations notwithstanding, many in Egypt had perceived exactly what had taken place. The Egyptian newspaper *El Ahram* published an interview claiming that the acts of arson in the American libraries in Cairo and Alexandria and the attempted arson in foreign-owned cinemas "was directed by Israeli intelligence, and that its purpose was to disrupt Egypt's relations with the United States."[38]

When in 1955 this all came to light, Dayan was attempting to organize a coup d'état with Ben-Gurion's support. Lavon threatened to commit suicide.

Sharett experienced a failure of nerve and kept silent. "I walk around as a lunatic, horror-stricken and lost, completely helpless . . . what should I do?"[39] he confided to his diary. The plotters were in disarray. Gibli proposed, in Sharett's words, "a crazy plan to blow up the Egyptian embassy in Amman in case of death sentences in the Cairo trial."[40] Dayan, the most hotheaded of the group, "was ready to hijack planes and kidnap [Arab] officers from trains."[41]

Ben-Gurion now classified Operation Susannah as "Top Secret." His presence ensured that the words of Dayan and Shimon Peres would supersede anything Lavon had to say. Dayan had left for the United States five days after the attack on the General Post Office in Alexandria.[42] Later in 1955, Ben-Gurion was reelected prime minister, keeping the post of Minister of Defense. Lavon begged Ben-Gurion to exonerate him of having given the fatal order for Operation Susannah, of which he was innocent, but Ben-Gurion refused. Lavon also appealed to Sharett, arguing that "a criminal act has been committed." He pleaded: "An order which I had not given is attributed to me." Sharett was no fighter. Unable to stand up to Ben-Gurion, he receded from the fray.

Irish diplomat and historian Conor Cruise O'Brien wrote: "What seems surprising in retrospect is that the Operation [Susannah] did so little damage to relations between Israel and America." It had been an operation in which innocent Americans might well have been killed or wounded in the bombing of the USIA libraries. In retrospect, it seems to have been a dress rehearsal, Nasser in the crosshairs, for the attack on the USS *Liberty*. The United States was already granting Israel military carte blanche.

As for who ordered the attacks: some Israelis concluded that Avri el-Ad (Paul Frank) betrayed the ring. El-Ad believed Mossad betrayed the ring to discredit a rival operation (military intelligence). Some blamed Lavon, others Dayan. The operation failed in every respect. The British withdrew from the Canal Zone. Nasser's regime was not destabilized, and he continued to believe that a peaceful solution to his dispute with Israel was possible. CIA's Kermit Roosevelt came up with a scheme to use the affair to promote peace negotiations.

While public indignation remained fervent inside Israel, those in the inner circles of the government knew that Susannah had been an intelligence operation gone awry. But blaming Egypt for Israeli false flag militancy had become the norm. Moshe Dayan insisted that Israel did not need a security pact with the United States since "such a pact will only constitute an obstacle for us. We face no danger at all of an Arab advantage of force for the next 8-10 years."[43] Dayan believed that a security pact "would put handcuffs on our military freedom of action."

Ben-Gurion was now outspoken in his desire to instigate a war with Egypt. He said, "It would be worthwhile to pay an Arab a million pounds to start a war" and "Let us hope for a new war with the Arab countries, so that we may finally get rid of our troubles and acquire our space."[44] The distant thunder of the land grab of 1967 was already audible. An American Quaker named Elmer Jackson met in Cairo on August 14, 1955, with Egyptian foreign minister Mahmoud Fawzi and told Sharett that Nasser was still interested in normalizing relations with Israel. But Ben-Gurion was talking about Israel immediately occupying the Gaza Strip, this time for good. Isser Harel openly declared that the time had come for the occupation of Gaza now that oil had been discovered there.

In the aftermath of the Lavon affair, Ben-Gurion ordered a raid in Gaza on February 28, 1955. He used Susannah as the pretext, treating it as a false flag, as if the perpetrators of the terrorism were actually Egyptian terrorists.

A 1960 investigation in Israel called attention to the forgery of an important document, dubbed a "security mishap." It turned out that Lavon had not signed off on the operation. The blame ultimately fell on Benyamin Gibli, Moshe Dayan, and Ben-Gurion himself.

Paul Frank, a.k.a. Avri el-Ad, became involved briefly in the effort to blame Lavon. When he exposed the conspiracy, he was convicted of treason and sentenced to serve a decade in an Israeli prison, not unlike the later case of Mordechai Vanunu, who was punished for exposing to a British journalist that Israel had a cache of atomic bombs at Dimona and who served a jail term beginning in 1988. Ben-Gurion fought any reopening of the Susannah case, but a subsequent rehearing revealed that Lavon had been an innocent victim of the machinations of Peres, Dayan, and Gibli. All this led to the resignation of the Ben-Gurion government in 1961.

When the young Zionists who participated in Operation Susannah, four of whom spent fourteen years in prison, were released, outwardly they expressed no resentment. They did raise questions: "Why were we sent on a mission, without any prepared escape route?"[45] "Why were we forgotten after falling into captivity?" In prison, they had been denounced as "Israeli spies." The Muslim Brotherhood had been more sympathetic to them than the imprisoned Communists.

The last of the young recruits arrived in Israel in January 1968. Three of the Egyptian Jews recruited into the operation had died. A clerk at the Alexandria post office had been burned by an incendiary device, but no one had been killed. One recruit now noted that they had awaited a sign from Israel to guide them in their line of defense, only for "no such sign" to come. "The state of Israel dissociated itself from us," another said with bitterness. Israel had not told them what to do should the operation misfire—how to escape or what to say. They had been treated as expendable, an embarrassment to Ben-Gurion's Mapai party, and left to rot in prison. Israel did not provide them with passports, as had been promised, and the group had been starved out so that their health faltered as they scrounged for food amid grim prison conditions.

It had been feasible to procure the release of the Egyptian Jews rotting in their Cairo prisons in 1957. But Israel did not want them back or to reopen the topic of Operation Susannah. They were still in jail when Israel Defense Forces bombed the unarmed USS *Liberty*. In their testimony, published in 1978, there is no reference to any of them having knowledge of the attack on *Liberty*. They would have been skeptical of what Israel called an "accident" and a "mistake," having learned the hard way that in the name of their sacred cause, human lives were treated as expendable, whether they belonged to their ally, the United States, or to themselves as Egyptian Jews who were supporters of Israel.

When the group finally returned to Israel, they were compelled to live in isolation and prevented from speaking of their experiences in Cairo. When they did speak, they were instructed not to acknowledge their guilt, speak out against the Israeli government, or criticize Operation Susannah. In exchange, among his final acts in office, David Ben-Gurion personally offered them cursory thanks. As they were leaving their one brief meeting with Ben-Gurion, he told them, with breathtaking hypocrisy, that they had been "sold. And Lavon lied. You should write a book. Don't let what happened to you be forgotten."

This was after Ben-Gurion had covered up their travail for fifteen years. Knowingly, unthinkingly, they had committed acts of terrorism in the belief they were serving the cause of Israel. Even their Egyptian jailers had been astonished. "Israel didn't demand you, to our great surprise," one said at the time of Suez.[46] The instrument of their release in 1968 was General Meir Amit, now the head of Mossad and the architect of the attack on the USS *Liberty*, in a detail of exquisite irony.

Amit was now a veteran head of Israeli military intelligence as well. Amit sounds reasonable in his description of the Susannah activists. "They acted on instructions from Israel," he acknowledged, "and under the command of an emissary from Israel. Even though the instructions are a subject of disagreement and the emissary was a dubious person, Israel is responsible for their fate." At that moment, Amit said, Israel was holding five thousand Egyptian prisoners: "We can insist that our people be repatriated."

Most of the young terrorist-victims had never been to Israel. Amit called the prisoners "officers in the Israel army," something they had never been, except for Paul Frank. Israel undertook to keep their release secret, which was entirely in Israel's interest. At Frank's hearing, Moshe Dayan asked only one question: "Did you and your people carry out any actions prior to the twenty-second of July?" Serving Ben-Gurion, Dayan and Gibli set up Lavon. El-Ad concluded: "The black patch seemed to hide his [Dayan's] face from all commitment."[47]

Avri el-Ad had questions of his own: foremost, who was behind Operation Susannah? He was told it was "the Old Man," who had exiled himself from the government and gone to a kibbutz in the Negev, like Ivan the Terrible waiting to be summoned back to Moscow. "It was a golden opportunity for an Israeli agent," Avri had been told. His orders were to "cripple by sabotage, maim by death . . . poison the political atmosphere and spread sedition and unrest. . . . Sabotaging Anglo-American establishments would disrupt America's courtship of Nasser by making it appear as if Egypt's populace was actively subverting his promises."[48]

When it was finally over, Avri el-Ad migrated to California.

Sharett was finally informed by Pinhas Lavon that Susannah had been a security operation. Lavon had to admit that the accusations against the young Egyptian Jews were not false; the conspirators had been committing acts of sabotage in Egypt, and the highest authorities in Israel had organized Operation Susannah. Sharett retracted his wildly false accusations that the Egyptians had been motivated by "blood libel" and anti-Semitism.

Sharett, who was of a different temperament and values entirely from Ben-Gurion and his Mapai acolytes, had hesitated to expose this plot coming from the most powerful quarter of the Israeli government. He came away with some important insights. He saw that Lavon "inspired and cultivated the negative adventuristic trend in the army and preached the doctrine that not the Arab countries, but the Western powers are the enemy, and the only way to deter them from their plots is through direct actions that will terrorize them. Peres shares the same ideology: he wants to frighten the West into supporting Israel's aims."[49]

In a March 6, 1961, letter to Ben-Gurion, Sharett wrote: "Why did I refuse then the firing of Peres? Because his removal at that period would have been interpreted as an admission that the leadership of Israel's security establishment was responsible for the savage attacks in Cairo."[50] Sharett, a more ethical man than the Mapai leaders, made public that they attributed to Nasser falsely the phrase "we should destroy Israel," only to retract it as a "telex transmission error." Nasser had never threatened to "destroy Israel." Israel's attack on Gaza following the exposé of the Lavon affair unleashed huge demonstrations in the Gaza Strip and clashes between the local population and the Egyptian army. In May, the Egyptian government was forced to consent to the activities of Fedayeen guerrilla units for sabotage actions in Israel.

About to leave the government in 1956, Sharett had acknowledged that "reprisal actions," which Israel could not carry out if tied to a security pact, were necessary to "maintain a high level of tension among [Israel's] population and in the army. Without these actions they would have ceased to be a combative people."[51] Had they not cried out that the Negev was in danger, young men would not go there. The demonization of Egypt, attributing to Egypt his own expansionist agenda, had been articulated by Ben-Gurion at a six-hour cabinet meeting on March 29, 1955, fulfilling a function that the attack on the USS *Liberty* twelve years later would similarly serve:

> Egypt aspires to dominate Africa, westwards to Morocco and southwards to South Africa where one day the blacks will get up and massacre the two million white and then subject themselves to Egypt's moral authority. ... Nasser will probably not react to the occupation of the Gaza Strip because his regime is based solely on the army, and if he tries to fight back he will be defeated and his regime will collapse.[52]

Livia Rokach reasons that "Nasser had to be eliminated not because his regime constituted a danger for Israel, but because an alliance between the West and his [Nasser's] prestigious leadership in the third world, and in the Middle East, would inevitably lead to a peace agreement which in turn would cause the Zionist state to be relativized as just one of the region's national societies."[53]

Once Nasser made his arms deal with the USSR, the United States offered a "green light" for an Israeli invasion of Egypt. Teddy Kollek and Angleton were running this show. "When the Soviet arms arrive, you will hit Egypt, not one will protest," Kollek said, producing a CIA cable signed by Kermit Roosevelt, one of many green lights in these years in which the United States offered Israel carte blanche. Harel, the head of Mossad, concluded that "the US was hinting to us that as far as they are concerned, we have a free hand and God bless us if we act audaciously."

Nasser was now permanently in Israel's sights. On the matter of the Gaza Strip, Nasser was no match for them. A year later, Dayan's troops occupied the Gaza Strip, Sinai, and the Straits of Tiran. Ben-Gurion had succeeded in removing Sharett from the government and assumed the premiership himself, a month after the green light flashed.

In the next months, the United States authorized France to divert to Israel Mirage planes that had been earmarked for NATO. It was these planes that would bombard mercilessly the USS *Liberty*.

It was in the midst of the Lavon affair that James Angleton made the acquaintance of Eppy Evron, who would represent Mossad at the Israeli embassy in Washington, DC.[54] Angleton learned that Evron, together with Moshe Dayan, had plotted a covert operation in Cairo to blow up the US consulate and blame it on Nasser's nationalist supporters, and so destroy the possibility of US détente with Nasser. Evron, a Mossad liaison officer, lay low after the Lavon affair, while working for a reversal of US pro-Arab policy.[55]

Now, in 1965, secret meetings between CIA area representatives in the Middle East and members of the Mossad were held with an eye toward a military defeat for Egypt.[56] Attending were James Angleton; Ephraim Evron; Meir Amit, the new head of Mossad; and Brigadier General Aharon Yariv, director of military intelligence. W. W. Rostow was present, reflecting "almost totally the view of the CIA hierarchy."[57] Nasser had refused to call a meeting of the Defense Council of the Arab League on the grounds that Egypt was "not prepared to reveal her military secrets to governments in the pay of the CIA and the British Intelligence Services," isolating him further.

Nasser learned soon enough that the KGB had no intention of providing Egypt "with more than token materials and advisory help when the time came to fight." Moscow was not going to risk confrontation with the United States in the Middle East, and "Nasser was going to have to go it alone."[58] Stalin had long before imparted to the world communist movement that socialism in one country was what he wanted, and Russia was not about to aid others in their struggles in any efficacious way.

Journalist Anthony Pearson's most important source for his book *Conspiracy of Silence: The Attack on the U.S.S. Liberty* about the attack on the USS *Liberty* was a member of MI6's Middle East Division named Steven McKenna, operating as a "researcher" for the British Central Office of Information. MI6 discovered that when the KGB intercepted

CIA plans to depose Nasser, they saw this as an opportunity to supplement their own plans in Egypt without actually being responsible for the political upheaval. MI6 was aware that all CIA operations in the Middle East were the responsibility of Mossad.

Falsely accused, Pinhas Lavon resigned from the government. Ben-Gurion had returned from his voluntary exile to keep order within the Mapai ranks and take back the reins of power. In the background was Nasser's attempt to persuade John Foster Dulles and Eisenhower to finance the Aswan Dam, a task that by default fell to the Soviets. Egypt opposed the Baghdad Pact, and Dulles pressured Nasser by prohibiting the sale of arms to Egypt. Nasser had attended the Bandung Conference in April 1955, where he held talks with the heads of the Soviet delegation, paving the way for the Egyptian-Czechoslovakian arms deal. Chinese premier Chou En-Lai promised Nasser arms. In July, a delegation arrived in Cairo to offer what would be 200 Soviet bombers, 230 tanks, 200 troop carriers, and more.[59]

Dulles punished Egypt by withdrawing the aid promised for the construction of the Aswan Dam, and Nasser responded with the nationalization of the Suez Canal in 1956. The young Zionists, languishing in prisons in Egypt, asked: "Why was our imprisonment not even mentioned in 1956 when Israel held five thousand Egyptian prisoners of war captured in the Sinai campaign?" By the end of the Suez war, Nasser was ready to release the prisoners of Operation Susannah, only for the Israelis to fail to request their release, to Nasser's surprise.[60]

When John F. Kennedy was elected, Angleton's fevered efforts to favor the state of Israel gave way to Kennedy's efforts to maintain a level playing field in the Middle East. All the while, Angleton was aiding Israel in obtaining the uranium necessary to build atomic weapons, keeping the atomic program secret under the cover of "Dimona Textiles." On some occasions, Dimona was referred to by Israeli officials as a desalination plant.

After Kennedy's death, the operation to remove Nasser was resurrected. Author Alfred M. Lilienthal writes, "After President Nasser exposed an illegal American arms deal to Israel in 1965, James Angleton and several Mossad officers decided to oust Nasser for forcing Egypt to confront Israel."[61] According to Lilienthal, "Certain members of the Johnson administration along with Israelis had meetings in both Tel Aviv and Washington to 'promote a contained war between Israel and Egypt.'" According to author Richard Deacon, by the end of 1965, there was pressure within CIA to launch a coup within Egypt to get rid of Nasser.[62] A military defeat for Egypt would bring about Nasser's downfall.

The plan was organized in Tel Aviv by Meir Amit; Aharon Yariv, the head of army intelligence; Shimon Peres, the deputy minister of defense, who would later share a Nobel Peace Prize with Yitzhak Rabin and Yasser Arafat; and Moshe Dayan, among others. The interests of James Angleton coincided with those of the Israeli secret services long before the USS *Liberty* was dispatched by Lyndon Johnson's 303 Committee to the coast of Egypt and Israel, and indeed long before even the birth of the Israeli state. The Israelis assured the Americans that the ensuing war would follow an American "plan of containment."

"Do you have nuclear weapons?" President Kennedy had asked Peres, the mastermind behind the establishing of the nuclear facility at Dimona.

"Mr. President," Peres said, "Israel will not be the first to bring nuclear weapons into the Middle East." Later, Zionist writers would term the Six-Day War a "pre-emptive strike for the security of Dimona."[63] At heart, the Six-Day War "crowned the achievement of restoring the historical Jewish homeland," ensuring that Israel would not have to withdraw its borders to those of 1947. Soviet responses, eyed by the Israelis, were spun as responses to their intelligence (accurate) that the United States planned to attack Egypt, an event set in motion by the Israeli air attack on the USS *Liberty*.

The myth of an Arab threat was maintained for the next decade. John Hadden in his May 25, 1967, meeting with Meir Amit seemed to be engaging in sardonic irony in suggesting that the Israelis provoke the Egyptians into bombing a ship, but Dayan himself had proposed the same thing in 1954. Knowing that the Egyptians would not bomb a ship, Dayan suggested that the Israelis precipitate the incident, a suggestion spelled out in then-premier Moshe Sharett's diary entry of February 27, 1954.[64] Dayan suggested that direct action be taken to "force open the blockade in the straits of Eilat."

Moshe Dayan spelled out some of his Golan provocations for the newspaper *Yedioth Ahronoth*, and they have been confirmed by his daughter Yael, later a member of the Knesset.[65] A decade before the attack on *Liberty*, as early as January 1954 Moshe Dayan proposed several plans for "direct action" to force open a blockade of the Straits of Tiran and the port of Eilat. In Sharett's diary for February 27, 1954, he quotes Dayan: "A ship flying the Israeli flag should be sent and if the Egyptians will bomb it, we should bomb the Egyptian bases from the air, or conquer Ras-e-Naqueb or open our way from the South to the Gaza Strip up to the coast," Dayan said.

Sharett then asked Dayan, "Do you realize this would mean war with Egypt?"[66]

"Of course," Dayan said.

Sharett adds in his diary, "War with Egypt was to remain a major ambition of Israel's security establishment, but the time was not yet ripe."

Israel denied any part in Operation Susannah until 2005, when the surviving operatives were awarded "Certificates of Appreciation" by Moshe Katsav, the president of Israel. Finally the government admitted that Susannah had been a government operation.

So for fourteen years, up to the moment when the USS *Liberty* benightedly sailed through the Straits of Gibraltar in June 1967, Gamal Abdel Nasser had been targeted for removal from office by Israel. As Seymour Hersh puts it, in the ideology of the intelligence services of the United States and Israel, "Hitler and Nasser were interchangeable."[67]

Abba Eban addressed the UN Security Council, where he charged Egypt with aggressions Israel itself had committed. Sharett notes in his diary that five hundred officers had left the military services after Nasser came to power, and that his regime did not constitute any danger to Israel's existence, a fact well-known to the Israelis.[68] At the same time, at a cabinet meeting, Ben-Gurion declared that Nasser was "the most dangerous enemy of Israel and [was] plotting to destroy her." Constantly, Israeli officials lobbied against US aid to Nasser: they argued that his regime was unstable, and not worthy of Western aid and support. CIA reported to MI6 efforts to discredit Nasser and remove him from power.[69]

In 1964, wreathed in calumny, Lyndon Johnson wrote to Nasser: "We shall to the greatest extent possible, continue to avoid selling arms to the principal parties to the Arab-Israel dispute."[70] Johnson discovered on his desk a plan JFK had to invite Nasser to visit the United States in 1965. He chose to ignore it.

In February and March of 1967, British intelligence operative Steven McKenna charted meetings between "passing American civil servants" and Israeli figures Moshe Dayan, Shimon Peres, and Meir Amit. One such "passing American civil servant" was, of course, James Angleton. "Civil servant" was a euphemism for CIA.[71]

In the year leading up to the Six-Day War and the attack on the USS *Liberty*, James Angleton was in a state of moral and intellectual disarray. Angleton was devoting himself to what CIA writer Ted Gup called "the self-destructive hunt for Soviet moles inside the CIA." The consequence was that "the careers of honorable officers" were "ruined" and "vast resources being squandered chasing phantoms."[72]

By 1967, Angleton's psychological health had radically deteriorated. It was now that John Whitten, Angleton's colleague at the Counterintelligence Division, told the House Select Committee on Assassinations in the mid-seventies that "Angleton's understanding of human nature . . . his evaluation of people was a very precarious thing."

CIA historian David Robarge was to acknowledge after the millennium that Angleton had created "a service within a service" and "that system had become dysfunctional." And it must be said that only an intelligence officer who was deeply deranged and fiendishly loyal to murderous Cold War politics would participate in an operation involving the murder of unarmed American sailors.

Forty years after these events, John Hadden, well aware that Angleton was a fraud, told his son that he didn't know "what was wrong with Angleton."[73] Hadden could not talk to Richard Helms about Angleton "because of Helms' loyalty to Angleton. He could only talk to Helms if Helms asked him specifically about a matter."

All the while, Hadden was faced with a superior who "could not stand any questioning of his judgments." Nothing "could be permitted to disturb the Angleton aura of super-knowledge and super-ability." Making foreign policy for the United States in the Middle East was a highly disturbed individual accountable to no one and who would brook no opposition.

The April 4, 1967, edition of the Israeli newspaper *Ha'aretz* included speculation that Meir Amit had offered Nasser a deactivation of Dimona, an offer obviously rendered specious by Amit's conversations with John Hadden.[74]

And now, in late May of 1967, Meir Amit was at Angleton's door to request that he recover the favor. By now, Angleton was convinced that "if Nasser could be eliminated and the Egyptian army defeated without US assistance, the Arabs would be left with no alternative to making peace with Israel," an absurdity since Israel did not want peace.[75]

A National Security Agency official—whose name they never revealed—told authors Andrew and Leslie Cockburn that "Jim Angleton and the Israelis spent a year cooking up the '67 war. It was a CIA operation designed to get Nasser," exactly as the attack on the USS *Liberty* would be.[76] The attack on the ship was, in effect, 303 Committee approved, which meant that the president had been granted plausible deniability for the removal of Nasser. US involvement in an attack on Egypt would be the motive, the pretext for the Israeli attack on the USS *Liberty*.

303 was exercising its already established function as approving, authorizing, and designing covert operations that might otherwise be attributed to the president.[77] It turned out to be an arena allowing CIA to engage in policy-making. Under official cover, it was comprised of a high-level group of officials linked to plans for covert operations and granting them approval, in effect offering CIA a green light to move forward on policies it favored. (It was an example of President Kennedy's opposition to CIA's policy-making.)

The secretary of the 303 Committee was generally a CIA official appointed by the director of Central Intelligence, so that CIA controlled the agenda, kept the minutes, and wrote the directives.[78] Decisions reached by the committee were forwarded to the president for final approval, which he indicated by initialing either of two boxes: "approve" or "disapprove." So too "Operation Cyanide," the subject of an April 6, 1967, 303 Committee meeting, with its reference to "submarine in UAR waters," was authorized by Lyndon Johnson.[79] The president signed no documents so that he could "plausibly deny" he had been involved.

The structure of the 303 Committee is elucidated by Victor Marchetti and John Marks in their description of the "40 Committee," the predecessor for the name, in *The CIA and the Cult of Intelligence*.[80] The 40 Committee, they write, "functions in such a way that it rarely turns down CIA requests for covert action."[81] Its members included the undersecretary for political affairs, the deputy secretary of defense, the director of Central Intelligence, and the chairman of the Joint Chiefs of Staff. Minutes were "intentionally incomplete" and kept by a permanent staff member, always a CIA officer. All proposals for American intervention overseas "were drafted by the CIA's clandestine services."[82] To add to the confusion, given the absence of CIA transparency, is that "sometimes 303 matters were kicked upstairs to the president."[83]

An example of CIA's exercising power through the 303 Committee was that at one meeting, Allen Dulles expressed his displeasure that the State Department had failed to consult the Agency before announcing the reappointment of Philip Bonsal as US ambassador to Cuba. Dulles also saw to it that Douglas Dillon was not appointed head of CIA's Cuba task force. Not that the president was far from the proceedings: 303 met in the old Executive Office Building, around the corner from the White House.

The efforts to undermine and hopefully to topple Nasser progressed deep into the year 1967. In April 1967 the 303 Committee met to discuss the toppling of Nasser.

The single extant 303 document (as of 2018) regarding the USS *Liberty*, dated April 7, 1967, is a fragment of the minutes of one meeting.[84] Under discussion that day was a sensitive DOD [Department of Defense] project known as "FRONTLET 615." The operation is not defined other than by its name. It references a submarine "within UAR waters," although at that date the United Arab Republic consisted only of Egypt, Syria having dissolved its connection. The Polaris nuclear submarine *Andrew Jackson* was "stationed below *Liberty*" in a condition of "readiness state Red One."[85] Captain Lloyd Bucher of the *Pueblo* has said that every spy ship had a sub assigned to it, with orders to put the spy ship to the bottom of the sea if it got into trouble.[86]

Representing the Pentagon on that day was Lyndon Johnson's long-time confidant Cyrus Vance, now assistant secretary of defense. Also present was Johnson's national security advisor, W. W. Rostow, later to preside over the cover-up of the attack on the USS *Liberty*. Admiral Rufus Taylor, the deputy director of Central Intelligence, had been appointed by Lyndon Johnson eight months earlier and represented CIA.

Also present was Foy Kohler, a JFK appointee as ambassador to the USSR and now a newly appointed deputy undersecretary of state for political affairs. Kohler's career bore close CIA affiliations. He had been director of Voice of America and a member of the Council on Foreign Relations. (By the close of 1967, Foy Kohler had resigned from the State Department at the early age of fifty-nine. He had just taken the job and there was no reason why he would retire. Cyrus Vance too resigned shortly after the attack on the USS *Liberty*.)[87]

Vance had been in Lyndon Johnson's sights since the 1930s, and he worked for a New York law firm (Simpson, Thatcher) that also employed one of Johnson's fund-raisers. Vance was the stepson of John W. Davis, who had been a member of Congress, ambassador to the Court of St. James's, and the Democratic Party candidate for president in 1924. Vance bore resplendent Democratic Party credentials.

Under Johnson, Secretary of Defense Robert McNamara developed a close relationship with Cyrus Vance, even as McNamara was tormented by Johnson, who taunted him in 1964, "Wouldn't you like to be secretary of state?" McNamara also competed with Secretary of State Dean Rusk as to who would be briefed earlier in the morning.[88]

The 303 Committee document refers to a "US submarine in UAR waters." There is a reference to "615," which seems to suggest a date. Only later would the date of the operation be sped up and focus on the spy ship.

When the 303 Committee discussion concluded on April 7, it approved a proposal to "get Nasser." The attack on the USS *Liberty* would be part of an operation that the 303 Committee had approved two months earlier, with the president having been granted plausible deniability for the methods enlisted in the removal of Nasser. This one surviving 303 Committee document about the 1967 war was stored at the LBJ Library in a file marked "*Liberty*."

All that remained of the "submarine" was that a submarine, picked up at the submarine depot at Rota, Spain, would shadow the USS *Liberty*, only to be submerged, never to be seen again, except that its periscope would surface with sufficient time to photograph the attack. Sailor Rocky Sturman was smoking a cigarette on the bridge looking out over the moonlit waters of the Mediterranean on the night of June 7 when he saw a periscope on the conning tower of a submarine that would photograph the incident.[89]

A photograph of that effort later came into the possession of a *Liberty* survivor, Ernie Gallo, who had gone to work for CIA.[90] The term "Operation Cyanide" would have fallen into the abyss of hearsay, except that an air force intelligence officer named Richard L. Block, stationed in Iraklion, Crete, overheard conversations suggesting that Operation Cyanide was "a joint US-Israeli intelligence venture which involved the US Navy and its submarine arm."[91]

Midnight, June 7 into June 8: the last person to whom Lyndon Johnson spoke on the telephone was Mathilde Krim, a longtime Zionist and supporter of the terrorist organization *Irgun*.

CHAPTER 5

MEIR AMIT ON THE MOVE

"If a nation gets the intelligence service that it deserves, I suppose the performance of the CIA is a commentary on American character and naivety."
—Arnold M. Silver

"By the way of deception thou shalt do war."
—motto of Mossad[1]

I t is the last week of May 1967. Meir Amit and James Angleton remain behind closed doors, the content of their conversation never to be disclosed. James Angleton rarely submitted a narrative of his actions to paper—it was almost unthinkable—and was never to submit his records to the Agency that employed him. Only after his death did CIA gain access to some of his files. When they descended on his office, led by Richard Helms's successor, Thomas Karamessines, they carried away disorganized, abandoned paper that resided haphazardly there.[2]

Many concluded that by the 1960s Angleton had "lost his judgment," as he found KGB operatives around every door and nestled in every corner. Not least, he mistrusted those with whom he had worked at the Agency all his life. Among his plumpest targets was David Murphy, who directed the Soviet Russia division. British author Christopher Andrew observed that Angleton's "monster KGB conspiracy theories of the 1960s were fueled by historical ignorance," and this seems true.[3] Despite Angleton's outlandish pretensions about his admiration for the poetry of T. S. Eliot and Ezra Pound, his actions and speeches expose him to have been a profoundly ignorant man. Among the crudities of his thinking was his assumption that the Soviet Union was a monolith.

It is now June 1. Meir Amit eventually emerged from his meeting with James Angleton and moved on to the next encounter of this fateful trip. Second in importance among CIA leaders for Amit was Director of Central Intelligence Richard Helms.[4] But first, Angleton had a tidbit for Helms to present to President Johnson in his briefing, a task of the DCI. In the corridor, Angleton related to Helms that in the coming inevitable war with Egypt, the Israelis would "win and win big." It was this fragment of intelligence that, according to official CIA records, Helms numbered among his accomplishments as director of Central Intelligence. The estimate on the Six-Day War he termed "intelligence bingo because it was so apt, concentrated, you could see cause and effect," and it came to Helms, this piece of "intelligence work" from Meir Amit, courtesy of James Angleton.[5]

Not that Helms and Amit were strangers. According to Amit, Helms and his family had visited Amit at his home in Ramat Gan. Amit was confident now that he would "reap the seeds he had planted years ago" and receive reliable information. In particular, he hoped that Helms would convey that the United States would be sending a ship through the Straits of Tiran, upsetting Nasser. But this turned out to be more than Amit could expect or Helms could or would deliver. As the Six-Day War drew close, there seems always to have been a ship in the picture.

As he awaited the visit of Meir Amit, Helms was not alone. In the room, he confided in a memorandum for the president, were "some of my senior experts." In this memorandum about his meeting with Amit, Helms reported that based on his discussions with Amit, the Israelis were about "to strike." Amit estimated that the Israeli victory would take place in three to four weeks, with Israeli losses of about four thousand military personnel. Helms's source for the statement that the war would end quickly has been revealed to be James Angleton.[6] There would be "retaliatory damage to Israel from Egyptian air strikes." Israel "had some surprises of its own," Amit added.

Meanwhile, Israel wanted nothing from the United States, Amit declared, "except to continue to supply weapons already arranged for, to give diplomatic support and to keep the USSR out of the ring." Now, having arrived only two days earlier, Amit confided that he had been ordered to return to Israel.[7]

When the "experts" had departed, leaving him alone with Helms, Amit took the opportunity to expand upon his frequent theme: if Egyptian president Nasser were "left unimpeded," something Israel had determined not to do the day more than a decade earlier that Nasser had entered the Egyptian government, the result would be the loss of the whole area. Jordan, Saudi Arabia, and Lebanon would be forced into an accommodation with Egypt, with Turkey and Iran to follow. "Even Tunisia and Morocco will eventually topple to Nasser," Amit said, sounding like nothing so much as those mouthing the domino theory as they justified the repeated accelerated invasions of Vietnam.[8]

Now, behind the scenes, word was spread of an Israeli invasion of Syria, with the plum being Damascus. In response, the Soviets threatened to send Red Army paratroopers into Syria and place them in advance of the Israeli army in case they were needed—or so the Cold War Anglo-American war games, featuring one "toppling" or another, proposed.

In his conversation with Helms, Amit offered less ideological motives for war. Amit threatened that Nasser's moves, blocking the straits, "would ruin Israel's economy by forcing Israel to keep its reserves mobilized," a version of blaming the victim. The Israeli people were starving, the economy suffering, and the harvest still standing, Amit argued, but with eighty-two thousand Egyptian troops remaining in the Sinai, Israel could not demobilize its reserves and send them back to their homes and fields.

Preparing Helms for Israel's imminent war of aggression, Amit said that "if Israel continues to do nothing, a surprise Egyptian air strike against Dimona or airfields is very possible," a statement for which there is no available corroborative evidence.

"It is better to die fighting than from starving," Amit said melodramatically. He was jealous of the US involvement in South Vietnam. "The Middle East offers the United States a chance to demonstrate its commitment at a much lower price than in Vietnam," he declared. "In Israel, the United States has people on whom it can rely." Not surprisingly, there is a racist taint to that statement.

Nasser was trying to provoke Israel "so that he could point to Israel as the aggressor," Amit said. He did not need to add that Israel embraced being provoked. Rather, he said petulantly, "Israel is being forced to act because of the inaction of others, and it cannot wait longer than a few days or a week." In fact, four days would be all it took.

Amit knew what the United States wanted: it was that Israel play along with the myth that the Americans would take no part in the coming war. He was not looking for "'collusion' with the United States in any action Israel might undertake against Egypt," he said, nor did Israel want the Americans to fight for Israel. "The assurance of a rapid supply of arms, preventing the Soviets from intervening, and understanding and political support," would be enough.

There is an intriguing unsigned memo titled "DRAFT MEMO: SUZANNA" among Richard Thompson's papers with respect to Meir Amit and his part in the Six-Day War:

> Meir Amit was both head of Mossad and Military Intelligence. Known for his theory: If somebody is in your way you use the great firepower you can muster to blow him away. Integrated military special operations into Mossad, replaced at military intelligence by his deputy Aharon Yariv who brought management skills that distributed collected data to field commands. The two made use of both military intelligence, operational skills of special operations and eliminated the competition between the service. . . .
>
> Fact: Liberty on station had intercepted and routed to US Israeli radio traffic.

Fact: Israeli ambassador to US called to State dept and advised that the US would support Egypt's call for a cease fire. ALSO: The US knew that the Jordanians had been lured into the fight by false signals manufactured by Israel.

Fact: Israel knew of Liberty's presence and resources and believed that the interception of their radio field traffic poses a threat because they believed that the US signals transmitted to the US were being intercepted by the Soviets.

Fact: Israel had made detained battle plans for the capture of the Golan and when the ambassador was threatened with US support of Egypt's call for a cease fire Amit pressed for the removal of the threat.

Fact: On direct order from Dayan the Liberty on 7 June was alerted to the Israeli knowledge of their mission and successes and was alerted that they expected the ship to move.

Fact: First of June Amit visited Washington DC, Angleton/ Helms, CIA and sec. defense Bob Mc. Advised that operation Cyanide had been compromised and the US was delaying action until after discussions with Soviets.

Fact: Israel moved up its battle plans and struck the first blow 7:30 AM, 5 June, Egypt air force destroyed on the ground.

Fact: Israeli interception and rerouting of Egypt signal traffic created a distorted response on the ground. For example an Israeli actually commanded an Egyptian tank force by changing the radio frequencies used and directed all movement away from the battle and to a POW site.

Fact: Israel advised US of displeasure about the USS Liberty and its mission.

Fact: Liberty alerted by being provided a copy of the transmittal.

Fact: Amit pressed Dayan to sink the ship with hands and US would blame Egypt because of the rerouted traffic.

Fact: Israeli air & Naval units ordered to sink the ship, command knew it was US but following Amit's direction of "Mighty force to blow it away" attacked 8 June.

Fact: Johnson, dod, state all informed on the 7th of pending attack.

Fact: Attacked ship, pressed on to Golan's capture and took the position that the US knowingly sent the ship into hostile waters to collect sensitive field commands that would have alerted their enemies to Israel's troop movements/timing/etc. and was a major threat that had to be removed because they felt the US persons not sensitive to Israeli interest might knowing share the date with Soviets who in turn would share with their friends or Soviets intercept and reroute traffic to alert conflicting forces.

Fact: Retaliation was discussed and ruled out because of political considerations.

Fact: Navy ordered to cover up the court of inquiry proceedings and finding alerted to meet the political requirements not the truth.

Fact: Cover up continues but cracks appearing, Capt Ward Boston, Admirals Starring, Moorer, and others speaking out.

Fact: Intelligence operations that were to have been used with Operation Cyanide are now beginning to surface.

John Hadden's name does not seem to have surfaced, but he was very much a presence in Amit's discourse. "The lives that will be lost in any action by Israel will be placed against the account of those who urged Israel not to react earlier," Amit said. This was what Hadden had done. "It was a mistake on the part of the United States to hold Israel back," Amit said.

Richard Helms submitted the memo of his encounter with Meir Amit to the Agency. It contains no mention of the sinking of a ship, although Helms, as we shall see, was soon made aware of the US plan to bomb Cairo. In his "Secret" report of his private conversation with Amit, Helms offers no assessment of the Israeli plans for war. Coolly, he depicts Amit's arguments. Only his later reactions to the events that followed reveal how appalled Helms was by Amit's self-serving statements.

Helms arranged a meeting for Amit with Secretary of Defense Robert McNamara. McNamara's stance was satisfactory to Israel; he had said, "I can understand why Israel wanted a nuclear bomb. . . . The existence of Israel has been a question mark in history, and that's the essential issue."

Before meeting with McNamara, Amit had already concluded that Israel would meet with no opposition to its coming war from the secretary of defense. Amit concluded that "the only ones opposed at this point are the people in the State Department."[9]

McNamara informed Amit that Lyndon Johnson was aware that he was there and had promised, "I read you loud and clear." Certainly Amit came away with the view that Johnson did not object to an invasion of Egypt.[10]

From Amit, McNamara wanted to know how long the conflict would last, a question entirely in character for this icy logician of war. How many casualties? Amit was happy to engage: fewer than six thousand, lower than in the War of Independence. Amit talked about a multinational fleet, but McNamara evaded any promise of open US involvement in the coming war. McNamara did volunteer that he "admire[d] Moshe Dayan."

Twice, McNamara was interrupted to speak with Johnson on the telephone while Meir Amit waited in the room, a telltale sign of the collaboration that was being reinforced.[11] All the while, Amit claimed that the Israelis could do the job on their own without the open involvement of the United States. Yet, in reality, the United States was about to collaborate with Mossad in the attack on the USS *Liberty*, even as Allen Dulles had confided to Wilbur Crane Eveland in 1959 that "the CIA's collaboration with Mossad left us exposed to blackmail and established Israel as the first nuclear power in the Middle East." Angleton prevailed, so that when the chairman of the Joint Chiefs of Staff stated publicly that US military assistance to Israel had jeopardized America's defense capabilities, he was accused in the press of being anti-Semitic, that familiar cudgel enlisted against anyone who criticized the policies of the State of Israel.[12]

Later, Amit mythologized with a cover story of his own. He claimed that he had asked McNamara if he should remain in Washington for another week or go home right away.

"Young man, go home," McNamara supposedly said. "That is where you are needed now." In fact, Amit and US ambassador Avraham Harman had already been called back to Israel. Later, Amit oversimplified his talk with McNamara. "I drew the conclusion it was a 'flickering green light,'" Amit said.[13]

In fact, in the Six-Day War, Israel was following an agenda involving attacks on Egypt and its other neighbors formulated by Zionist leader Theodore Herzl in 1904 and outlined in Moshe Sharett's diary a decade earlier. Israel hardly required permission to annex territory that had been outlined in the Zionist project since the turn of the century and so did not require a green light, flickering or otherwise.

Later, caught red-handed in his most perfidious act—the calling back of rescue planes sent to assist the sailors whose lives were in jeopardy on the foundering, listing *Liberty*, about at any moment to sink to the bottom of the sea—McNamara denied that he had given a green light to anything. "Absolutely not," he insisted. According to McNamara, he, Johnson, and Secretary of State Dean Rusk had agreed that "should Israel call on the United States, we had to be in a position to get the support of the American people, which we would not have had had Israel attacked Egypt." This of course is gibberish, since Israel did openly attack Egypt. McNamara claimed to have told Amit not to initiate the attack.

According to Israeli historian Tom Segev, Lyndon Johnson set up a special task force to handle what became known as the Six-Day War and the US role in it.[14] It was headed by McGeorge Bundy, Johnson's former national security advisor, and endorsed by James Angleton. Angleton requested absolute secrecy regarding what this task force did, Segev relates, a request that was to be honored for more than fifty years. Amit had succeeded in lulling the Arabs by not attacking the previous week. The attack would be a surprise, even as Amit had told John Hadden that essential to his operation was the element of "surprise."

There were in fact few surprises. Documents reveal that at the time of the Six-Day War, the United States ran a senior Israeli cabinet minister as a spy.[15] By conservative estimates, James Angleton and Israel had been planning the Six-Day War from at least 1966 on.[16]

On his whirlwind trip to Washington, DC, Amit managed to find time to meet with Secretary of State Dean Rusk on the Friday before his departure.[17] Rusk also met that day with Thomas Lowe Hughes, the director of State Department Intelligence and Research, but he did not mention to Hughes he had met with Meir Amit. Rusk asked Hughes whether the intelligence community believed the Israelis would strike that weekend. He thought they had another week to go, Hughes said cautiously. Hughes was Rusk's closest colleague, but Rusk was not forthcoming regarding what Amit confided to him.[18]

Later, Amit admitted that he had allowed himself a theatrical outburst in Rusk's presence. Those who bore the responsibility for Israel's fate would not accept another Munich, Amit declaimed, invoking the tired cliché of Chamberlain appeasing Hitler at Munich in 1938: "Must Israel have to accept ten thousand casualties . . . before the US will agree that aggression has occurred?"[19]

The Israelis did not trust Rusk, who had been opposed to Israel being the sole state in the Middle East enjoying the benefits of atomic weapons. When he had been Kennedy's secretary of state, Dean Rusk told the Israeli ambassador, Abba Eban, that the dissembling regarding Israel's stockpiling of nuclear weapons was becoming a handicap to US-Israeli relations. The Israelis at once accused Rusk of being "unfriendly." Hadn't he opposed President Truman's recognition of Israel in the first place?

One meeting between Lyndon Johnson and Abba Eban, now serving as foreign minister, was arranged by Eppy Evron. Eban was accompanied by Avraham Harman, the Israeli ambassador. They discussed the breaking of the blockade of the Straits of Tiran. Eban lied and told LBJ that Egypt was about to attack Israel, whereas in fact CIA had been involved in a covert plan with Israel to promote a war against Egypt with the purpose of overthrowing Nasser.

Meir Amit returned to Tel Aviv with the one assurance he had sought, that the United States would not act against Israel should Israel invade Egypt (or anyone else). Later, he revised his story and told the Israeli cabinet that if the Americans were given one more week to exhaust their diplomatic efforts, "they [would] hesitate to act against us."[20] (The next day, the Israeli cabinet decided to begin the Six-Day War immediately.)

Unencumbered by the duplicitous presence of Meir Amit, John Hadden returned to Lod Airport nine miles outside Tel Aviv via Rome on Saturday morning, June 3. "The first class El Al compartment was filled with cases of morphine ampoules," he told his son and namesake. "It was clear that the Israelis were prepared for major losses and that we had only a few hours to go."

Hadden went straight to his office at the American embassy. As soon as he arrived, his code clerk rushed into his office with what Hadden later termed a "hot cable."[21] It was a direct order to him from Desmond Fitzgerald, the CIA chief of operations, as Hadden later remembered. "Go at once to the chief of Israeli intelligence and advise him that we think it's OK to go ahead and bomb Cairo," the cable read, in Hadden's later partial paraphrase.

It was a direct order, Hadden said years later, "to promote an action that would have been catastrophic." He never revealed whether the target in that cable was the USS *Liberty* or Cairo, with the understanding that the operation involved bombing *Liberty* as the prelude to bombing Cairo, the exact scenario that almost did occur.

"Some gung ho idiot," as Hadden described Fitzgerald without including his name, had authorized Israel to do something unthinkable. "It was the days of the proconsuls," Hadden said. It is clear that the cable went beyond authorizing a predictable military operation, such as the bombing of Cairo, which would not have been issued by CIA. It may well have been that Hadden received CIA's order that the Sixth Fleet bomb Cairo, an event that is incomprehensible unless one adds the component of Israel sinking the USS *Liberty* and blaming Egypt for an act of war against the United

States that was the pretext for US retaliation. In 2013, Hadden described the incident as follows: "My respect for Des Fitzgerald disappeared when he told me to pass a message to the Israeli PM via Mossad to bomb Cairo. Helms or Millet canceled the cable after the weekend."[22]

Without consulting anyone at Langley, and wary, always, of his superior James Angleton, Hadden, outraged and appalled, dropped the cable in what was called the "burn bag"; these were papers destined for the shredder. He assessed the crisis as too urgent for him to wait for any further cable traffic or discussion with his Agency superiors. He was not going to follow the orders outlined in that cable. He was not going to be responsible for the deaths of civilians in Cairo. Hadden, an honorable man, considered himself "lucky . . . I could say I'd never seen the damn thing," he said. "It was how you thought if you belonged to a bureaucracy like CIA. You attempted to do as little harm as possible, and wrestled with how that was to be defined."

John Hadden never recounted what was written in that cable, to the knowledge of this author, including to his son, who interviewed him for twenty hours shortly before his death. Without awaiting further word from the Agency, Hadden tossed the cable into the burn bag.

This we know: James Angleton had instructed that all communications with Tel Aviv be sent through his office. Richard Helms, the director of Central Intelligence, knew nothing about this cable, which had been hastily dispatched by Desmond Fitzgerald on the Saturday before the beginning of the Six-Day War on Monday. Since Meir Amit, obsessed with the plan to bomb Egypt and the USS *Liberty* both, had visited with Angleton first in his visit to Washington, DC, that week, circumstantial evidence, if nothing else, places Angleton at the heart of the operation to bomb the USS *Liberty*. Later, Hadden would speak of the attack as an "incredible blunder because of rivalry between the [Israeli] Air Force and Israeli intelligence, by which one group knew and the other didn't, and the other blew up the ship," which is vague enough. We are here being offered a rare opening into "Agencyspeak."

What Hadden surmised about who had been in on the creation of this cable, we do not know. We do know the order definitely had not been sanctioned by Richard Helms and did not originate with Helms but with Desmond Fitzgerald. It required that Hadden communicate with someone at Israeli intelligence, necessitating that the Israelis take immediate action. Hadden had been ordered to sanction that action.

On Monday morning, Hadden's immediate superior at CIA saw the cable and rushed to Helms as soon as he came into the office. "My God, what do we do now?" he said.

"Christ, someone get hold of Hadden and tell him to ignore it!" Helms said. Helms added, as Hadden learned, "Tell Hadden if he hasn't handed it over not to hand it over."

Then Hadden's superior, Fitzgerald, sent him a cable signed by Richard Helms. It read, as Hadden would later describe it, "Disregard Cable XYZ, 1-2-3-4-5!" It was too outrageous an action to be spelled out, even decades later.

"Have you taken action?" Helms asked Hadden. Helms ordered Hadden to destroy the cable. Helms needn't have worried.

"I have so far been unable to carry out the order," Hadden replied. This was as cryptic as he needed to be. At that moment, Hadden apparently thought he had dodged a bullet, thwarted CIA's endorsement of an Israeli bombing of Cairo with US endorsement. He seems to have had no inkling that the bombing of Cairo was already part of Meir Amit and Levi Eshkol's agenda and had been endorsed by the United States through CIA's chief of counterintelligence.

Neither John Hadden nor Richard Helms would have authorized so monstrous an action as the sinking of an American ship, murdering several hundred unarmed American sailors for the purpose of creating a pretext for removing Nasser from power. "No excuse can be found," Helms, still angry, said later, referring to the attack on the USS *Liberty*, "that this was a mistake." In a rare public statement, Helms challenged Israel's excuse that it had been an "accident" in attacking the USS *Liberty*:

"There could be no doubt that the Israeli's knew exactly what they were doing in attacking the *Liberty*," Helms said. It was "no mistake."

Fifty years of a cover-up have left that cable impenetrable, although we do know that it was the US Navy and the Sixth Fleet that were to be sent off to bomb Cairo, not the Israeli air force, because Admiral William Inman Martin, in a moment of panic, admitted that he had sent planes off the USS *America* with instructions to bomb Cairo. When former USS *Liberty* sailor Ernie Gallo, employed by CIA, requested records pertaining to *Liberty*, Fitzgerald's cable, which we know reached John Hadden, was not included.[23] Years later, John Hadden would write that "I really liked Helms—both as Chief and human being."

Flying home on a jumbo jet loaded with military equipment, Meir Amit arrived back in Tel Aviv at midnight on that same Saturday evening, June 3.[24] This flight had traveled via London and Frankfurt, where it was loaded up with gas masks. There were only two passengers, Amit and Ambassador Avraham Harman, and they headed directly for a meeting at Levi Eshkol's apartment.[25] Awaiting them were Eshkol; Moshe Dayan, who two days earlier had been named chief of the Israel Defense Forces; Shimon Peres; Yitzhak Rabin; Abba Eban; and Israel Lior.

Amit reassured the group of Ben-Gurion acolytes. There were no significant differences between US and Israel intelligence, he said, an indication to the group that he had discussed everything with Angleton. "I am given to understand," Amit told this upper echelon of Israeli power, "that the Americans would bless us if we were to break Nasser in pieces."

Lior was stunned.[26] The group had believed the United States would oppose their going to war, and now they were informed that this was not the case. They didn't even require a cabinet endorsement or a declaration of war. The task at hand was the destruction of Nasser as a political force, a reprise of the 1956 campaign.

At this early stage of events, a debate raged between Dayan, Ben-Gurion's attack dog, who wanted to begin the war at once, and Ambassador Harman. At the center of the debate was the use of an Israeli ship, which would be sent through the Straits of Aqaba, provoking the Egyptians to fire on it. This would provide the Israelis with a pretext for beginning the war. Amit talked specifically of sending a ship into the Gulf of Aqaba, then goading the Egyptians into firing on it.

"The United States won't go into mourning if Israel attacks Egypt," Amit said. "The Americans will hesitate to act against us and there is reason to hope that they will even support us." On May 22, Nasser had closed the Gulf of Aqaba, blockading the Straits of Tiran. Israel at once had claimed that its oil lifeline had been cut off when it was denied access to the port of Eilat, at the head of the Gulf of Aqaba. This was an overstatement, since Haifa remained available and Israel sent only a handful of ships through the Gulf of Aqaba each year. But Israel was shopping for pretexts, and demonizing Nasser in its customary manner.

On that Saturday night, Eshkol embraced the idea of provoking Egypt to fire on an Israeli ship, directing himself to Dayan, the new head of the Israel Defense Forces: "We'll send a ship. They'll open fire. Then there'll be a cause for action." Impatient to begin, the chief of the army general staff, Yitzhak Rabin, supported Dayan. With every passing day, Rabin insisted, it was harder for the IDF. The allies Dayan and Rabin—within a year to be named ambassador to the United States; within a decade, prime minister of Israel; and a future assassination victim—doubted that Israel's existence was in danger. They doubted that Egypt would attack first, and agreed that "a war would improve Israel's situation."[27] They also shared the opinion that Israel needed a pretext, a justification for going as far as they planned to go.

Israel did not wait to provoke Egypt to fire on a ship and to begin this war. Israel never sent a stooge ship through the Gulf of Aqaba to provoke Egypt. Without the fig leaf of a pretext, they sent guns blazing. The ploy of firing on a ship would not be left to the Egyptians to fire on an Israeli ship, but would be the work of the Israelis themselves four days into the war as they fired on an American ship. But from the moment when John Hadden facetiously advised Meir Amit to fire on a ship in a false flag operation, a ship had been part of the Israeli war plans.

Monday, June 5, dawned. In sixteen hours, the Arabs lost more than four hundred planes. The Israelis lost nineteen. Eleven thousand, five hundred Egyptians were killed in action, with 5,600 prisoners captured. Israel was to double its territory, bringing one million more Arabs under Israeli control. Despite the US claims to neutrality in this conflict, six Arab states broke relations with Washington.

W. W. Rostow, Lyndon Johnson's national security advisor, called the Israeli air attacks on Egypt on the first day of the Six-Day War, Monday, June 5, a "turkey shoot." In short order, the Israelis took Jerusalem and the West Bank, using "liberal doses of napalm on refugee columns fleeing to the east." The opening of the Northern Front (Syria) can be viewed as an afterthought by Dayan, after Yitzhak Rabin, the army chief of staff, had warned against it, so the attack on *Liberty* had nothing to do with Syria: "I do not believe that Nasser wanted war," Rabin said. "The two divisions he sent into Sinai on May 14 would not have been enough to unleash an offensive against Israel. He knew it and we knew it."[28]

The Cockburns write: "There is a body of opinion within the American intelligence community that [James] Angleton played a leading part in orchestrating the events leading up to the June 1967 war. One long-serving official at CIA's ancient rival, the code-breaking National Security Agency, states flatly that 'Jim Angleton and the Israelis spent a year cooking up the '67 war.'"

Amit was to admit: "Angleton was an extraordinary asset for us. We could not have found ourselves a better advocate."[29]

CHAPTER 6

"HEROES IN THE SEAWEED"

"Have you casualties?"

—US naval attaché Ernest Castle

Later, the Chief of Naval Operations, Admiral David Lamar McDonald, who would never have acquiesced in such an operation, would wonder with profound irritation who placed the USS *Liberty* thirteen miles off the coast of Egypt in the middle of the Six-Day War. Admiral McDonald reserved his indignation for internal communications. He said nothing about the USS *Liberty* in the autobiographical interviews published with him by the Naval Institute Press. From the start, he surmised that there was little of intelligence value to be gained by perching the USS *Liberty* blatantly in harm's way.

The physical order to dispatch *Liberty* from its assignment on the west coast of Africa to Rota, Spain, and then onward east of Suez came to *Liberty* before the first shots of the Six-Day War had been fired. It was sent to Lieutenant Commander David Edwin Lewis, who served on *Liberty* as chief intelligence officer, by the Joint Chiefs of Staff. A night-time message came to Commander Lewis to move the ship at "full flank speed" by the dark of the moon, to Rota and ultimately to that position thirteen and a half miles off the coast of Egypt that so infuriated Admiral McDonald.[1]

Only decades later, with the release of the transcript of the Joint Chiefs fact-finding team, would some of the truth emerge. The order to place *Liberty* in a war zone had originated with the 303 Committee and one particular individual sitting on the committee: Cyrus Vance, representing the Pentagon and, directly, Lyndon Johnson. The Joint Chiefs of Staff had neglected to redact this one sentence on page 6 of the report of its fact-finding team: "It was the Deputy Secretary of Defense (Cyrus Vance) and the 303 Committee which 'initiated movement of the USS *Liberty* to the Eastern Mediterranean by way of Rota, Spain.'" *Liberty* sailed "subsequent to approval by the JCS/JRC, the Deputy Secretary of Defense and the 303 Committee."[2] Cyrus Vance was the strongest presence on the 303 Committee on the matter of covert actions involving Egypt (UAR).[3]

Admiral William Inman Martin, commander of the Sixth Fleet, was to tell the Joint Chiefs' investigators that "he would trade one ship for effective communications," emphasizing his "dissatisfaction with current capabilities of equipment and facilities."[4]

As for the remnants of Operation Susannah, "Paul Frank," an Israeli, remained in prison, as did several of the younger Egyptian-Jewish terrorists.

Robert Wilson, a CIA officer under cover with the National Security Agency, joined the *Liberty* ship's company at Rota, where he retrieved "two or three classified working aids in a little black satchel with a lock affixed. One was a dictionary." There was no voice communication they could pick up, except from the Israelis. Wilson (he asks to be called "Bob") told the sailors that he worked for the NSA. He would serve with CIA until 2002. Fifty years after the attack, his shipmates would either never have heard of him or believe he was with NSA. "I never talk about my intelligence work on the ship," Wilson told the author at the fiftieth reunion that he attended with his shipmates in 2017.[5] He didn't recall the name of John Hadden, although he did know the naval attaché, Ernest Castle, who, late on the afternoon of the attack, following the hasty departure of two Israeli helicopters loaded with commandos with machine guns at the ready, flew over the ship in an Israeli helicopter.[6]

Looking down from his helicopter, Castle threw onto the deck of *Liberty* a bag weighted with oranges. Inside was his calling card, on which he had scribbled, "Have you casualties?" The bag landed next to a bloody severed leg lonely on a deck washed with blood. The men stared in disbelief. Captain William McGonagle denied Castle, who had been misidentified as "the American Ambassador," permission to board the ship. Castle's helicopter flew away at 7:05 in the evening. But all that came later.

Robert Wilson was not part of James Angleton's counterintelligence component. If he said anything later, it was to complain about the failure of communication between the intelligence services and the ship. It has never emerged why CIA needed to be a presence on a ship reporting to NSA and the Joint Chiefs, unless it was one agency watching another on the precipice of a false flag operation. That Wilson might have sacrificed his life in this service seems to have escaped everyone's attention.

Robert Wilson was nonplussed by the author's remark that CIA was not a monolith. That was always the case, observed this sophisticated, worldly man.

On the way from Rota, learning of the Israeli-Egyptian conflict brewing, the sailors, among them Terry McFarland, were concerned that they would be out there on their own without protection during a war. According to Clyde Way, there was a brawl between the regular crew and the SIGINT (signals intelligence) because they wouldn't say what the ship's mission was. It seems more likely that they did not know. Sunbathing, playing cards, listening to boom boxes, enjoying cookouts notwithstanding, the sailors worried.

On Sunday, June 4, Jim Ennes writes in the first book-length account of these events, that officers and enlisted men alike continued to worry openly about the safety of the ship and the wisdom of their mission. They expected that with the onset of war, the following day, their assignment would be reexamined. Dave Lewis drafted an appeal through "General Services Communications" (which meant Captain McGonagle), to Vice Admiral William Inman Martin, commander of the Sixth Fleet, requesting that a destroyer be sent to remain within five miles of *Liberty* and serve as an armed escort.[7]

The USS *Liberty* had set sail from Norfolk on May 2, 1967, bound for Abidjan, the capital of the Ivory Coast. The intelligence officer in charge, Lieutenant Commander David Edwin Lewis, and the captain, William E. McGonagle, were piped aboard by the boatswain using a small whistle-like instrument. He used one pitched sound for the commanding officer coming aboard and another for a department head like Dave Lewis. It was a challenge to become proficient on a boatswain's pipe.

They had not gotten off to an auspicious start. Lewis had just arrived at his new office and locked himself inside to read the myriad of instructions awaiting him. He heard a knock on the door out in the hall. Lewis ignored it. The knocking became louder and more insistent until someone opened the door and the captain came storming into the office.

William McGonagle, son of a Wichita sharecropper who was later a janitor, had joined the navy to escape the vegetable fields of California, where his family had relocated out of the Dust Bowl. A petty man, concerned about his prerogatives, McGonagle told Lewis, in no uncertain terms, that he "would never again be kept out of *his* spaces on the ship." Apparently he lacked a security clearance to enter the research spaces; at that time, the Naval Security Group did not automatically clear commanding officers. Lewis, mild mannered and NOT petty, immediately got on the phone to Washington.

McGonagle was an insecure man, and a control freak. He wasn't satisfied with his own messages that came in from "COMSIXTH FLEET COMUSNAVEURCOM" or "COMMANDER USNAVAL FORCES EUROPE." He wanted to see Lewis's (clip)board as well.

Captain William McGonagle, at left: a stickler for the rules and a fan of Doris Day films. (Photo courtesy of Tom and Carole Blaney.)

McGonagle did not socialize with the men, but remained in his stateroom. A man of few intellectual interests, Doris Day movies were his obsession. For these he would emerge from his isolation. Lewis, affable, without any sense of class superiority, insisted that he be called "Mr. Lewis" and did not use the title "Lieutenant Commander." He was admired by the men who served under his command. Ernie Gallo calls him "salt of the earth" and adds, "This country was lucky to have him."

Among their assignments in Africa was to find out what government was being overthrown and whether the Russians or Cubans were involved in the former French territories and in Portuguese Angola.[8] *Liberty* had French and Portuguese linguists on board and was soon to add Russian and Arabic speakers. The Middle East was not part of their assignment, which focused primarily on Russian influence in West Africa. *Liberty's* mission up to the time of the Six-Day War was to troll "like a ferret" to determine which governments were in upheaval and determine whether the Russians were involved.[9] They collected voice transmissions even from nondescript Russian fishing trawlers and recorded everything except what could positively be Israeli or from the British Commonwealth.[10] Israeli transmissions were encrypted, and *Liberty* cryptologists were unable to identify them.

Shortly after he reported aboard *Liberty*, Dave Lewis, who was the only French linguist on board, was briefed by Lieutenant James Pierce, the communications officer. Pierce described certain sealed orders in his safe that concerned "emergency communications via U.S. submarines in the event of hostilities and that were part of a project called 'Cyanide.'"[11] Pierce was the only one in possession of these sealed orders, which were to be opened up only in the event of a detonation, a nuclear blast. According to Dave Lewis, CIA was not involved in the cable tapping that was part of these instructions, and Operation Cyanide was "not part of the attack on the USS *Liberty*" per se.[12] (Years later, Dick Thompson, a CIA asset who committed the latter part of his life to research into what happened to *Liberty*, admitted to Lewis, regarding his efforts on behalf of Peter Hounam's book, "the title sounded good," adding no bona fides to the term "Operation Cyanide.")

What Lewis came to understand of Operation Cyanide was that it involved communications in a postnuclear environment. In a radiation-contaminated atmosphere where high-frequency communication would be impossible, signals could proceed through water at the extremely low frequency available to submarines. Information could be transferred up to ten words a minute. So a submarine waited on the scene at Rota and followed *Liberty* to the East Med to be present for the nuclear war that almost came to pass. "If there was a nuclear war and an electromagnetic pulse from the airborne blast wiped out all HF [high-frequency] communications, we could contact a US submarine and send our communications via the submarine so that they communicated through water," Lewis says.

Those sealed orders, which Dave Lewis was destined never to read, had to have been written at least two months before the Six-Day War. That there was a submarine shadowing *Liberty* has been established, not only by eyewitnesses but in that 303 Committee document of April that referred to a submarine "in UAR waters." The two best candidates were the *Amberjack* and the *Andrew Jackson*.

Amberjack had been positioned in the Eastern Mediterranean from May 15 on and had been on duty with the Sixth Fleet since 1961. To the day of his death, the captain of the USS *Amberjack*, Augustine Hubal, refused to discuss what his submarine was doing out there so close to *Liberty*. Even when questioned by his former classmate at the Naval Academy, Tom Schaaf, Hubal maintained his silence. Jack Hyatt questioned him as well, only for Hyatt, Dave Lewis's roommate at the Naval Academy, to assure Lewis that Hubal knew nothing about the *Liberty* incident. Hubal maintained that his submarine was submerged at the time at least one hundred miles from *Liberty*.

When we first encounter *Liberty*, she has just pulled into Abidjan, known as "the Paris of Africa." There were fleshpots and establishments purveying alcohol. Several sailors, including the executive officer, were alcoholic, and at such ports they replenished their supply. A beer cost two cents. There were exploits with women, and a sailor named Petoom, deep in his cups, peed off a balcony, landing on the president of the Republic. Petoom found himself court-martialed. No one thought these people had anything to do with being serious or took themselves seriously, not least the XO, Phillip Armstrong.

Executive Officer Phillip Armstrong, shortly to perish on the USS *Liberty*. (Photo courtesy of Tom and Carole Blaney.)

In Abidjan, Captain McGonagle made a pass at a comely French blonde, Yvonne de Villeneuves, wife of the local chief of naval operations. Corruption was in full flower, and during Dave Lewis's first deployment to Abidjan in 1966, Madame de Villeneuves had sent her husband's private plane to Paris for fresh oysters to impress the Americans. On this trip, Madame, adorned by a bikini that scarcely formed a thread, taught Lewis to water-ski in the Grand-Bassam lagoon east of Abidjan, which was full of crocodiles.

A measure of McGonagle's relationship to the men and his awkwardness was that at a reception at the American embassy he ordered them to wear dress blues. It was steamy, and the ambassador, in possession of greater common sense, sent them back to change into shorts.

They were in Abidjan making their port call when the message came in from the Joint Chiefs of Staff: "Proceed at best speed to the Eastern Med."[13] At 1 a.m., Captain McGonagle stood waiting for Dave Lewis on the quarterdeck with the news that they had emergency orders to leave, a "sudden change of mission." Best speed was top speed. "The Klaxon went 'Bang! Bang! Bang! Bang!' It was a lot louder than a drum, let alone a siren or bell."

The date was May 24. LBJ had canceled their sailing to Cape Town lest any involvement with South Africa mar his civil rights record, but they were slated to go to Lagos, then Angola. McGonagle sent Dave Lewis to tender his apologies, making use of his French. The order carried such urgency that Lewis grabbed a lower-ranking seaman to drive the ship's pickup truck. Then they hit all the houses of ill repute, picking up *Liberty* sailors and ferrying them back to the ship. At full flank speed, they took off for Rota, Spain, which housed an American submarine base. The sailors were not told anything about their mission. Only after they left Rota did they learn that the Israeli-Egypt conflict had erupted.

At Rota, where they were allowed only one day, they tried to have the hydraulics of the moon dish refitted, while six new people clambered on board: three Russian translators, including US Marine Bryce

Lockwood, and three translators of Arabic. Lockwood's message from the Joint Chiefs of Staff ordered him to remain on twenty-four-hour duty.[14] He was assigned to work for Dave Lewis in the Naval Security Group detachment and told his primary mission was to go after the Russians. The government was also definitely interested in the United Arab Republic, Lockwood says.

When he sat down with "Mr. Lewis," Lockwood was told specifically that they were not targeting Israel. "As linguists we were told that if we identified an Israel target, a Hebrew target, we were to identify it and drop it. If intercepted, links should be identified as Israeli, or British Commonwealth, then we dropped it and no further action was taken on them." Lewis says they tapped underwater cables and discarded everything except what came from the Soviets. They were now looking for any reactions to the Six-Day War from the Soviets, such as if they were moving nukes into the area.[15] No one on the ship was fluent in Hebrew. NSA translator Allen Blue was Jewish, but he knew only a smattering of Hebrew.

They departed from Rota on June 2, with the captain having been "ordered to use 'best speed.'" Later, the captain would remark that this was "the first instance in which he had ever been ordered to use best speed," the fastest the ship could move. There was an urgency about getting the ship in place that would never be explained.

Realizing they were in a perfect location to be attacked, several sailors expressed their concern. Both McFarland and Way were told by McGonagle that if any situation developed, "we had five-minute air support, that's how quick they'd be with us. Help would be on the way." They trusted the Sixth Fleet and "believed in them." Later, some were told that their mission was to pick up civilians who wanted to be evacuated—this would be the cover story. Dusty (Paddy) Rhodes, an R brancher, was "told to tell everybody we were to aid in the evacuation of US embassy personnel, which is a little ridiculous. Those boats out there with antennae draping in the water. Any fool can know what they are for." There was no antenna in the water, of course; Rhodes was enlisting a certain literary license. Rhodes, like others, concluded: "I don't think there was that much ever accomplished."

"I think they wasted a whole hell of a lot of money, because I don't recall much of any intercept, intelligence, anything being gathered. ... If they did gather anything it was the run of the mill intercept that you pick up all the time," Rhodes added. Asked if they produced anything worthwhile in the way of intelligence to warrant the ship being sent out to the East Med in harm's way, Rhodes echoed several of his shipmates: "I doubt it," he told his NSA interviewers. "I doubt if they produced anything worthwhile."[16]

Both Dave Lewis and Commander "Bud" C. Fossett confirm that the tasking was exclusively against Arab targets, specifically UAR.[17] There was no tasking against Israeli elements. Later, interviewing some of the officers, NSA would be amazed that they did not pick up Hebrew linguists, nor did anyone have any real command of Hebrew; Allen Blue knew no more than a few words.

Sailor James O'Connor later reiterated: "We were targeted mainly against Egyptian targets, low level comms. We could hear a lot of the troops on the battlefield talking back and forth." In his 1980 interview, the NSA kept trying to prompt him, only for O'Connor to repeat, "We wouldn't have the need to be targeting against Israel. Israel was an ally, and in that case you would not be going against your ally."[18] Were they to intercept messages from friendly nations, like the United Kingdom or Israel, the communications technicians were instructed that these not be translated. They listened to the Soviets but couldn't tell what they were saying. They just copied it and forwarded it to what Dave Lewis sometimes calls, pejorative intended, "NO SUCH AGENCY" (National Security Agency). They listened for plain language because they couldn't read anything that had been encrypted, and they had no capability of listening to the Soviets, who might have been listening to the Israelis.[19] Usually, they set up a circuit in English or Russian. Once a message was encrypted, there was nothing they could do about it.

A lightheartedness persisted. Lieutenant Lloyd Painter bet someone who could lose the most weight on the ship; Painter ate "like a pig," Lewis says, then one day out, he got Dr. Richard Kiepfer to give him diuretics and so won.[20] Painter had been drafted by the army to serve in Vietnam. Quickly he joined the navy, as several of the sailors did to avoid that cruel, bloody, senseless war.

"I have always believed that the Israelis would never have conducted such a cowardly, murderous act without a 'green light' or at least a blinking 'yellow light' from the Johnson administration." (Photo courtesy of Lloyd Painter.)

McGonagle asked Dave Lewis if the mission would be affected if he moved fifty miles from Gaza. "It would hurt us, Captain," Lewis said. "We want to work in the UHF [ultra high frequency] range, line of sight. If we're over the horizon, we might as well be back in Abidjan. It would degrade our mission by about twenty percent." McGonagle then decided to "go all the way in," to remain "on station."[21] It is to be noted that Dave Lewis took the mission very seriously, even as the NSA does not seem to have done.

LIEUTENANT COMMANDER DAVID EDWIN LEWIS

David Edwin Lewis was born on April 28, 1931, in rural New Hampshire. He came from an old American family, his ninth great-grandfather, Edmund Lewis, having embarked at Ipswich, England, on the *Elizabeth*, a wooden ship, on April 10, 1634.[22] They disembarked in New Amsterdam, which in 1664 became New York. Lewis died the day they arrived; one of his sons, John Lewis, came to own three-quarters of Westerly, Rhode Island. Dave Lewis grew up to be a man who lived in history.

Dave, a member of the Congregational Church from the time he was one year old, grew up poor and humble, religious, hardworking, and upright. Helping his mother with the washing, he put his right hand through the wringer and so became left-handed. No one noticed that he had any special talents. He was one of seven children, five boys and two girls, and all of the men became officers in the US military. He worked all his life; at the age of seven or eight, he was pitching hay. For five years, he was a teenage gravedigger. As a mason, he hauled bricks up to chimneys; he also clerked in a grocery store and caddied at the local golf course.

When Dave was eight or nine, one day his father asked him to go for a ride in his old truck. They stopped at the drugstore, where Dave picked up a pack of gum and stuck it in his pocket. They then drove forty-five miles north into the old Indian Stream Republic, an entity claimed by both Canada and the United States until the Webster-Ashburton Treaty was signed, establishing the boundary between the two nations. It lasted for about six or eight years, then became the town of Pittsburg, the largest town in acreage east of the Mississippi. Dave's father had a camp up there.

Dave pulled out the packet of gum and offered his father a stick.

"Where did you get that?" his father said. Dave knew better than to lie. His father turned the truck around and drove the forty-five miles back. He handed Dave a nickel and pointed. Never a word. It meant a lot more than yelling, which his mother did. The children didn't pay attention to their mother, but if Dad said something, they jumped.

When he was ten years old, his father told him, "You will probably live long enough to see a president other than Franklin Delano Roosevelt." This was a fate devoutly to be embraced. So the political ethos of the family was instilled. Dave Lewis was to be a Republican all his life.

As Dave Lewis was completing an indifferent high school education, he spotted a notice on the bulletin board of the local post office announcing that university entrance examinations would be held there on the coming Saturday. Had Lewis read the fine print, he would have realized that these exams were for entrance into the service academies. His acceptance into the US Naval Academy at Annapolis came as a surprise.

When he was sworn in, he was handed a bill for $3,800 or $3,900. Payment came out of his $78 monthly pay, and he was given $3 a month in cash for personal expenses, but Dave Lewis was already no stranger to austerity. The rest went to pay down the bill, which was not satisfied until two months before his graduation. He did not enjoy the Naval Academy and early on begged his mother to permit him to return home. You required a parent's permission to be set free. Mrs. Lewis refused.

Dutiful, obedient, he remained and graduated in June 1954 as a cryptologist. To obtain his security clearance, they interrogated everyone in his hometown of Colebrook. There were all kinds of clearances that went beyond TOP SECRET. His was TOP SECRET CODE WORD SPECIAL COMPARTMENT.

He married a hometown girl, a Roman Catholic, and took instruction, as was required. The teacher asked if he believed in divorce.

"Father, I am opposed to divorce myself, but I have to acknowledge the existence of it. I can't deny that," Dave Lewis said. This newly ordained priest forbade the marriage. The local priest then labeled this man a "damn fool," went to the bishop in Manchester, and got the order rescinded. Dave remained a member of the Congregational Church, underlining his identification with his Puritan ancestry and reflecting the church's reformation of the Church of England. Dave and Dolores Lewis had two sons. Like their father and four uncles, both sons embraced the

US military. One served in the air force. The other had asked his father if he should apply for appointment to the Naval Academy.

"Hell no," Dave said. "With the chip you have on your shoulder, you wouldn't get past first base."[23] Four months or so later, his son Michael threw a paper at him, his appointment to the Naval Academy.

Dave Lewis, Memorial Day, 2014. (Photo courtesy of Commander David Edwin Lewis, US Navy [Ret.].)

Three Lewis brothers, from left, Lieutenant Colonel Palmer Lewis, US Air Force (Ret.); master sgt. Charles Jarvis Lewis, Jr., US Army (Ret.); Commander David Edwin Lewis, US Navy (Ret.). (Photo courtesy of Dave Lewis.)

Dave Lewis having survived the attack, and Left, Dr. Peter Flynn with Dave Lewis aboard the USS *America*. "Don't move your eyeballs." (Photos courtesy of the USS *Liberty* Veterans Association.)

Dave Lewis and his four brothers, members of the military services, and his sister. Dave Lewis is at the center rear. (Photo courtesy of Dave Lewis.)

Dave Lewis, Memorial Day, 2014. (Photo courtesy of Commander David Edwin Lewis, USN [Ret.].)

THE SIX-DAY WAR

By the close of the first day of what would become known as the Six-Day War, June 5, 1967, Israel had destroyed Egypt's air force, appropriated the Sinai and the West Bank, subdued Jordan, and annexed East Jerusalem with its holy sites, including the Temple renamed the "Wailing Wall." All that remained waiting to be conquered was Syria, the plum of the fertile Golan Heights and, with luck, Damascus. All the while, Israel would claim that this was not a "land grab."

The Johnson government was to claim that there had been no US secret participation in the Six-Day War, but this was not so. Before a shot was fired, US reconnaissance F-4 aircraft had taken off from the American base at Torrejon de Ardoz, Spain, for the Egyptian airfields. Torrejon housed the largest bombers in the Strategic Air Command. The purpose of this mission was to provide aerial surveillance in the form of high-tech photographs; they utilized cameras that were not available to Israel at the time, although Israel claimed responsibility falsely for the pictures that appeared in *Time* and *Life* magazines.[24]

According to Stephen Green in *Taking Sides*, the planes flew from Ramstein, West Germany. The pilots were told they were enlisted in a NATO fair-weather training exercise. The photo equipment was highly sophisticated. The cover for those involved was that they were civilian employees, Americans, contracted to the Aero-Tec Corporation in Dallas-Fort Worth. It was an "ultra-secret exercise," operational assistance for the Six-Day War. The RF-4C planes were painted over so as to obscure their US identity.[25]

The pilots were stripped of their US military uniforms.[26] It is direct evidence of US involvement in the Six-Day War prior to the operation involving the USS *Liberty*. Later, Nasser would charge that US aircraft had participated in the Israeli air strikes against the United Arab Republic on the first day of the war. An air force participant named Greg Reight told author Peter Hounam, "I think we were *the* photographic intelligence. The only thing the Israelis had were gun-cameras."[27] These American aircraft had operated beneath a "hurry-up paint job" to make them seem as if they were Israeli in origin.

Another aspect of US participation in the Six-Day War was that the United States had leaked to Israel "each and every gap in the Egyptian radar," which was used by Israel in its preemptive first strikes on June 5, several days after the Egyptians had ordered their Sharm el-Sheikh garrison to stand down, downgrading and ending the crisis. These penetrable gaps in their strung-out radar were known only to the United States.

There is further evidence of US involvement in the Six-Day War, indicating that the United States was far from neutral. On May 23, Lyndon Johnson "authorized a total shipment of armored personnel carriers, tank spare parts, spare parts for the Hawk missile air defense system, bomb fuses, artillery ammunition, gas masks and other items."[28] In 1966, the United States had provided Israel with $92 million worth of military assistance.[29]

SOVIETS AT THE READY

While the United States was supplying Israel with the photography necessary to bomb the Egyptian airfields on June 4, as Soviet fleet admiral Ivan Kapitanets later recounted, Soviet ships stationed in the Mediterranean were informed that they would be placed in a state of complete war alert within the next twelve hours. The number of Soviet submarines in the East Med was doubled and reached ten. A nuclear torpedo had been added. Five large diesel submarines were added on June 6. Submarine K-131, Project 675, on the night of June 5–6 was ordered to reach the coast of Israel and to be ready to attack coastal targets. The Soviet naval forces in the East Med had been "considerably strengthened."

Later, Captain Nikolai Shashkov, commander of submarine K-172, said that "in a critical situation, the Soviet Union would support them [the Arabs] by any means, including nuclear." According to Shashkov, their targets were Israeli cities. The Russian orders were that should the Americans intervene, should the United States bomb Cairo, the Soviet submarines would retaliate by attacking the Israeli mainland at the Dome of the Rock, with its golden cupola glittering in the sunlight on the Temple Mount in the Old City of Jerusalem.[30]

The Soviets concluded there was "at least one" nuclear submarine of the US Navy as part of the Sixth Fleet. This was the *Amberjack*, performing a "reconnaissance mission within the territorial waters of the United Arab Republic." The Soviets later said that the *Amberjack* "witnessed an attack on the intelligence ship the *Liberty*."[31] Soviet journalist Nikolai Cherkashin concluded that "the Six-Day war was the third crisis (after Berlin in 1953 and Cuba in 1962) that could have provoked a Third World War in a thermonuclear way." To communicate with Moscow for orders, Captain Shashkov brought submarine K-172 up to the surface every two hours.

His orders, to be complied with at his own discretion, were to launch nuclear warheads as soon as the first US bomb was dropped on Cairo. So the Russians waited to see whether the Israeli jets, torpedo boats, and helicopters would succeed in sinking the USS *Liberty*, creating the pretext for a US bombing of Cairo. (The Soviets were well aware of the details of the operation.) Meanwhile, the Soviet Union launched paratroopers into Syria, awaiting a siege upon Damascus by Israel. As journalist Joseph C. Harsh wrote in the *Christian Science Monitor*: "Israel can only do what Washington allows it to do. It dare not conduct a single military operation without the tacit consent of Washington."[32]

Nikolai Shashkov's Echo II missile submarine, K-172, patrolled the Israeli coast throughout the Six-Day War. It had eight nuclear missiles at the ready. Back in February or March, Shashkov had received orders "to be ready for firing nuclear missiles at the Israeli shore" in response to a "joint Israeli and American landing on the Syrian coast."[33] If the Israelis continued to Damascus, the Red Army would execute a massive airborne drop into Syria and confront the Israeli army.

It was Lyndon Johnson who ordered that the Israelis not move toward Damascus. On June 10, Soviet premier Alexei Kosygin sent a message to Johnson that mentioned the possible use of military force if the Israelis didn't halt their advance into Syria, something they had already done. All this was part of what John Hadden had called "rattl[ing] the sabers" on the part of the Soviets.

Later, Shashkov explained to journalist Nikolai Cherkashin in *Rodina* magazine that he was under the water with two nuclear reactors, twenty-odd torpedoes, and eight rockets. He was aware of American nuclear-powered vessels that held Moscow and the industrial areas of the Urals in their sights. They could also have had the honor—or, rather, misfortune—to start the Third World War. Shashkov added, "The USSR was just as capable of making a nuclear strike as American strategists defending their [own] geo-political interests. Personally, I have not and do not feel any hostility towards Israel itself."

Asked what his crew knew, he replied, "They must have known we hadn't come to Haifa for a friendly visit. Only I knew about the order to be ready to strike." Shashkov's father had been in the Secret Service, the head of a special department of the 2nd Strike Army, fighting the Nazis. Shashkov's father shot himself when his commander, Vlasov, surrendered. Nikolai Shashkov retired from the military on March 8, 1968. (Among those on the American side disgusted by the sacrifice of the USS *Liberty* who retired shortly after the attack were Cyrus Vance and Admiral David Lamar McDonald, the chief of naval operations.)

THE USS LIBERTY

The USS *Liberty*, whose name was intended to recall the Liberty Bell, was gray and old, a refurbished "Henry Kaiser special." She was a hastily constructed freighter put together near the close of World War II and not built to last. We won the war, Commander Lewis remarked sardonically to the author, "because Kaiser could build them faster than Japan could sink them." Temporary bulkheads (walls) separated the holds. *Liberty*, under other appellations, had served in both World War II and Korea, then was brought out of retirement by the navy and in 1963 classified as a "technical research ship."

Liberty, originally named *Simmons Victory*, had since been studded with forty-five deck antennas and a giant moon dish sitting on a platform forty feet wide and thirty-five feet high, the only one in existence. (The construction of a second had been begun, but it was never finished.) This configuration was so unique that it might have served as an alternate American flag. There was no doubt as to whom this ship belonged. After the attack, all AGTRs (Auxiliary, General, Technical Research) and GERs (a much smaller version, such as the *Pueblo*) were scrapped.

Once you turned the moon dish on, it had every flashing light and gadget known to man on it, the flashing lights impossible to ignore. It was sixteen feet in diameter, and any pilot overflying the ship could identify it easily. In communication with the moon, this satellite dish turned inquisitively and was the forerunner of the communications satellite. It was mounted pompously on a special stand. Unfortunately, it suffered from hydraulic structural flaws—the moon dish had been installed in the shipyard with 1,500-psi fittings when they should have installed 3,000-psi fittings. That explains why when they first fired it off in the shipyard, an elbow broke loose, penetrated two bulkheads, and fell in front of Lewis's stateroom door. It was usually either leaking hydraulic fluid or blowing fittings. When *Liberty* called at Rota, Dave Lewis had contacted the sub base commander and asked him if he could seal the leaky joints on the moon dish or repair them. The commander had only time sufficient to weld the joints. The moon dish otherwise was operative all thirty-one days of the month. Moe Shafer and Jim Kavanagh were assigned to transfer direct intelligence to the National Security Agency through the TRSSCOM basket's microwave antenna that looked like a basket. The antenna was eighteen feet in diameter, set on the platform.

As for spying on Israel, this was not their assignment. The only way they could have communicated was in the clear, and if they were spying on Israel, it wouldn't make much sense to transmit the material where Israel and Russia both could pick it up. In retrospect, the whole project was farcical. That didn't matter because there had, so far, been no assignment, no calls to urgency, no threat, and no particular information sought.

The satellite dish worked until the entire dish was blown off the ship. A message included in the fact-finding report later issued by the Joint Chiefs seems to have been ignored. It was dated May 30 and read: "Request you take action to hold the USS *Liberty* at Rota, Spain until directed otherwise."[34] From the start, the men and their ship were treated as if they were expendable.

So the ship creaked eastward on behalf of the superannuated CIA-inspired Cold War. She was, Admiral Thomas Moorer, later a passionate advocate of the sailors, would remark, "the ugliest, strangest looking ship in the U.S. Navy" and "looked like a lobster with all those projections moving every which way."[35]

The sailors were segregated: there were the cryptologists with their security clearances, and there were those who followed the sea. "There was a big door with a cipher lock on it and nobody but us can get in," Clyde Way said.[36] The signals intelligence people were called "spies," and they were doing something classified, possibly connected to the NSA, CIA, or FBI. The only thing was they "didn't wear a trench coat." They were CTs (communications technicians) of six distinct branches. The CTs monitored radio signals issuing from the Soviets or from Egypt. The political subtext of their operation, Dave Lewis says, was "Don't blame Israel." *Liberty* was structured according to class parameters, with hostility between the intelligence types, who alone had access to the "research spaces" on the second deck, and everyone else.

Dave Lewis's boss was Rear Admiral Ralph E. Cook, commander of the Naval Security Group. Admiral Cook maintained the independence of the Naval Security Group. Lewis's ultimate boss was the chief of Naval Operations, Admiral David Lamar McDonald, and above him, the chairman of the Joint Chiefs of Staff. To task *Liberty*, the NSA had to go through the Joint Chiefs. Orders came down to the ship from SERVRON (Service Squadron) 8. If NSA set up the whole thing, "they would have had to go through the chairman of the Joint Chiefs and the Naval Security Group."

Liberty carried no cannon, only four machine guns mounted on deck, which would be of no use in self-defense. Meanwhile, false flag information swirled: that the justification for the secret atom bomb factory at Dimona was incomplete German denazification; that the Soviets instigated the Six-Day War and the Israelis invaded Egypt to "save Dimona, and Israeli security."[37] Israeli security being in jeopardy meant anything was acceptable, and there had even been speculation in the *Ha'aretz* newspaper on April 4, 1967, that Meir Amit had offered Nasser a deactivation of Dimona. Later, the Israelis put forth the explanation that their invasion of Egypt had been to "save Dimona." It had all been a preemptive strike for the security of Dimona.

Meanwhile, Dave Lewis on *Liberty* was given orders so vague as to amount to gibberish: "Find out who is doing what to whom," Dave Lewis told the author, was all he had been told with respect to *Liberty*'s sudden reassignment to the Eastern Mediterranean. There was no specific intelligence assignment, a fact reinforced by survivors decades later. The Soviets were entrenched in the area and had been authorized to use "nuclear tipped" weapons, as were the American pilots on the USS *America*, who were briefed on the topography of Cairo and sent on their way to target (Cairo) simultaneously with the attack on the USS *Liberty*. Nuclear-armed aircraft were launched "hot" on their way to Cairo from the aircraft carrier *America*.[38]

Liberty departed from Rota on June 2. That afternoon, the ship passed through the Straits of Gibraltar. All the while, the Soviet Navy was watching. By now, the Soviet Union had moved at least thirty warships and ten submarines into the area, foremost the nuclear sub K-172. At the same time, *Liberty* was technically (automatically) chopped (assigned) to Vice Admiral William Inman Martin, commander of the Sixth Fleet. Chopping to a new location meant you were transferring from one command to another.[39] So *Liberty* transferred command from Service Squadron 8 Norfolk to the Sixth Fleet. Martin, who had foreknowledge of the attack, would later distort this history by claiming this wasn't done until June 6, and documentation materialized to confirm this date.

Admiral William Inman Martin. "I emphatically deny that she was a spy ship."

As it departed from Rota, *Liberty* was trailed by three Soviet AGIs (surveillance ships) that could do thirty knots, as opposed to *Liberty*'s eighteen at its flank speed. So *Liberty* was humping along at eighteen knots, with the Soviet intelligence collectors sailing circles around it. By the next morning, June 3, the Soviet spy ships had disappeared.

For the record, Admiral John S. McCain, commander of Naval Operations for Europe, out of London, informed commander, Sixth Fleet, Vice Admiral William I. Martin on June 3 that "the *Liberty*'s mission" was to conduct an "extended independent surveillance operation in the eastern Mediterranean" and that "Sixth Fleet might be called upon to provide logistic and other support."[40] That June 3 date belies the later assertion that *Liberty* was not chopped to the Sixth Fleet until June 6.

When on June 5 Israel attacked the Egyptian airfields, McCain and Martin both noted the movement of some twenty Soviet warships with supporting vessels and an estimated eight or nine Soviet submarines into the Eastern Mediterranean. Although Admiral Martin was ordered to keep his ships and aircraft one hundred miles from the coasts of Lebanon, Syria, and Israel and twenty-five miles from Cyprus, nothing was said about the positioning of the USS *Liberty* until after the fact.

It wasn't until Memorial Day 2017 that the Naval History and Heritage Command released a history of *Liberty* III (AGTR-5) stating that it wasn't until June 6 that CINCUSNAVEUR (commander in chief, US Naval Forces, Europe) informed Admiral Martin that *Liberty* "would come under his control at the start of the mid watch on 7 June to facilitate area command and control and any possible requirement for protection during the Middle East hostilities."[41] This is history written too far after the fact to pass without skepticism.

It was as if *Liberty* were a ghost ship venturing alone into a war zone. So the Joint Chiefs' confidential message states that *Liberty*, the name redacted in the report, may be "required to provide logistic support or other assistance during these operations. It is expected that *Liberty* will make short port visits in the Eastern Med at 3 to 4 week intervals although her endurance extends well beyond this time." This makes no sense given the events to come.

In his interview with NSA, sailor Clyde Way said: "We put the word out to the crew that we were being sent to Israel because the Americans might be evacuated. . . . We were the closest AGTR there." This was the cover story.

Way remembered that it was Lieutenant Maurice Bennett and Commander Lewis who told him to tell the crew that "we were going to help the Americans in case of evacuation from Israel. The Israelis were on our side and they were going to allow us to go in and get our Americans in case they got in danger." Cold War propaganda was enlisted to justify actions that might later be challenged and found questionable. On some of the orders, the USS *Liberty* was not even an "addee," the Joint Chiefs' investigators discovered.

The mission was hardly all sunbathing, taking photographs, and shooting at tin cans floating in the blue sea. On June 6, *Liberty* received these orders: "In view present Arab/Israeli situation and unpredictability of UAR actions, maintain a high state of vigilance against attack or threat of attack, report by FLASH precedent any threatening or suspicious actions directed against you or suspicious actions directed against you or any diversion from schedule necessitated by external threat." This seems ominous indeed. They were ordered to "submit reports of ships, aircraft and submarines which are unidentified, hostile . . . or engaged in harassment."

Admiral Martin did not act to include USS *Liberty* in his order previously issued to all other Sixth Fleet surface and air "to stand off at least 100 miles from the coasts of belligerent nations." The Joint Chiefs supposedly sent a series of five messages, they claim.[42] This was on June 7. All were misrouted, lost, or delayed.[43] They call it "one of the most incredible failures of communications in the history of the Department of Defense." One message ordered the ship to be moved twenty nautical miles from the UAR and fifteen from Israel; the next gave the one-hundred-mile figure. In retrospect, these messages appear to have been inserted into the record after the fact. Better that messages be misrouted than that a ship, wittingly on the part of those in command, have been placed in harm's way.

There is ample reason to doubt the story that if only the lost messages ordering *Liberty* to move one hundred miles away from the coast—or alternately, twenty miles—had been delivered, the attack could have been avoided. Dave Lewis finds the entire story of the lost messages, which would have placed *Liberty* out of harm's way, dubious. Communications

Technician (E-6) Joe Lentini believes the messages were sent after the fact because there was no way to send them and have them not arrive but go elsewhere.[44] They would have been put in the circuit for broadcasts destined for the Sixth Fleet and, as such, would have been repeated on many frequencies. The message would have been decrypted; everyone read everyone else's mail, with other ships' messages being placed in burn bags.

Joe Lentini contends that the messages to move the ship were configured after the fact. "Why would anyone send a ship of the Sixth Fleet a message and route it to a shore station?"
(Photo courtesy of Joe Lentini.)

Should such a message have been sent to the USS *Liberty*, it would have been recognized as a Sixth Fleet message. Such a message within the Naval Security Group could not go astray. Lentini's group sent and received all traffic to and from the ship; they dealt with Fleet broadcasts and with encryption and decryption of all material coming to or going from the ships they were assigned to. According to Lentini, orders to *Liberty* would come via the Med Fleet Broadcast, where the message would be broadcast over multiple frequencies, multiple times, and copied by all Med Fleet ships. There was no way the message would have gone to any shore station.

Drawing of the USS *Liberty* by Colleen Lentini.

Any legitimate navy order to move the ship would also be sent from NSA via Naval Security Group special broadcast frequencies. No such message regarding moving the ship was ever sent or received. The format of this supposed message to move one hundred miles was also all wrong. "The ship's routing indicator should have shown to whom *Liberty* was attached (the Sixth Fleet) and the proper circuits to get a message to us. There was no way for a message to travel to the places our message was purported to have gone," Lentini says.

But even as writers persist in perpetuating this component of the cover-up, Joseph Lentini demonstrates persuasively that no such message to move *Liberty* one hundred miles had been sent prior to the attack via the only channel through which *Liberty* customarily received messages. The Joint Chiefs had concocted a false story to cover their having placed the ship in harm's way. Dave Lewis notes that Israel "has attacked vessels over a hundred miles offshore, so moving the ship would have done no good in any case." Lentini, who had been a communications technician and O branch supervisor, and who became a US Navy CT instructor, says the message idea to move to a new position one hundred miles off land was an after-the-fact effort.

Lentini is certain that had NSA decided to move *Liberty* prior to the attack, they knew how to do it. The only people the story of the misdirected messages made sense to were those with no clue as to how navy and NSA communications worked. There would have been two messages, two copies. *Liberty* was a member of the Sixth Fleet, so one copy would have come via Sixth Fleet Broadcast. There is no way a message concerning ship movement would go to any shore station other than the broadcast comm center.

The second copy would come through NSA circuits over entirely different frequencies and using different equipment and routing indicators. There has never been a report confirming the existence of this message. Any message directing *Liberty* offshore would have had to be sent by fleet broadcast. Lentini is adamant: "There is no way any order intended for the *Liberty* would be sent the way official histories have recounted how it was misrouted. Such an order to a ship known to be attached to the Sixth Fleet would never go anywhere other than the Comm Center for that Fleet!" Lentini concludes that such a message "did not exist!"

In another interpretation of these events, the trajectory of this narrative suggests that Admiral William Inman Martin had advance notice of the order that the ship be moved. Receiving these orders from Admiral John S. McCain, he delayed sending the order to the USS *Liberty*. What has been made to appear to be an innocent error in fact reveals that Admiral Martin intentionally delayed sending the message to the ship. Instead, he allowed it to float from the USS *Little Rock* to the Navy Communications Station in Greece, to the Army DCS station at Asmara, so that by the time of the attack, it still had not arrived. The attack depended on the compliance of Admirals McCain and Martin, without whose cooperation the Israelis could not have bombed the USS *Liberty*.

It was on June 7 too that the Chief of Naval Operations, Admiral McDonald, registered in print his dismay that the USS *Liberty* had been placed 12.5 miles off the coast of Egypt and 6.5 miles from Israel. "I don't know why we do something like this now," he wrote in red pencil.[45] To those who were not in on the operation, placing *Liberty* at such a location made no sense. But even the highest officials of the navy did not rank high in US government transparency.

Admiral David Lamar McDonald, Chief of Naval Operations at the time of the attack. He resigned shortly after. "I don't know why we do something like this now." (Photo courtesy of US Navy.)

There were others of like mind, like Frank Raven, a group head at NSA specializing in the Soviet Union and monitoring its unencrypted traffic. Raven argued that *Liberty* would be "defenseless" alone in the Mediterranean. He was overruled, just as Admiral McDonald discovered that *Liberty* had been posted to the Eastern Mediterranean too late to prevent it. (Only reading between the lines of his internal communications do we discover how appalled Admiral McDonald was about the hijacking of the USS *Liberty*.) The sinking of the *Liberty* came after information regarding Egypt's signal to downgrade and thus end the crisis had been sent to the United States, probably via *Liberty*.[46]

In an essay written in 1946 on the question of whether we need a CIA, OSS wartime London chief and future ambassador David K. E. Bruce notes that at the table of power, the navy was "seated somewhere below the salt." The metaphor dates from medieval times, when salt was scarce and available only at the high table, where the aristocracy sat. Commoners were at lower trestle tables. Salt was placed at the center of the high table, so those of the lower classes, at the lower table, were "below the salt."[47] Admiral McDonald, in the waning days of his service as Chief of Naval Operations, was no match for ruthless figures like James Angleton and Lyndon Johnson.

The reply to Admiral McDonald was received at 2:37 p.m. It acknowledged that increased distances to CPAs—UAR twenty miles, Israel fifteen miles—had been recommended to the Joint Chiefs of Staff. But McDonald was not satisfied with this minor adjustment. He added to his memo, "I wouldn't even let her go down that way now!" The Chief of Naval Operations was not in the loop that included the 303 Committee and Cyrus Vance, who had placed *Liberty* in this position, or John S. McCain and Vice Admiral William Inman Martin, who saw to it that *Liberty* remained there.

On the morning of June 8, before the attack, the Israel Defense Forces killed 850 Egyptian prisoners of war, whom they had captured on June 6 and 7 near the town of El Arish, after first ordering them to dig their own graves. The story was broken by two Israeli journalists, one television, the other print. Later, the Israelis offered as one of their bag of pretexts for their attack on *Liberty* that they thought the United States had detected their mass murder of the prisoners of war. But if NSA knew about this particular war crime, they didn't tell anyone on the ship. The story made the front page of the *New York Times* on September 21, 1995.[48]

His assignment, as we know, was to "find out who is doing what to whom," Dave Lewis had been told, and not much more than that. Only after all these events were concluded did some of these *Liberty* "spies" concede that they had not discovered much intelligence about the Soviets or anything else. "I wore two hats on the *Liberty*," Dave Lewis says.[49] He was Officer in Charge of USN-855, the cryptologic unit, and he was the Naval Security Group department head in the ship's organization. USN-855 reported through the captain to the Naval Security Group Headquarters in Washington, DC. The ship reported to Service Squadron 8 in Norfolk.

A cable was sent to the US embassy in Cairo informing them that an air attack was coming.

"One thing we were told. If anything were to happen we were within ten minutes of air strike and help. None of us were very worried," Dusty Rhodes told his NSA interrogators later. The sailors were lied to: the aircraft carriers of the Sixth Fleet were between 350 and 400 miles away, hardly within ten minutes of an air strike.[50] Rhodes remained livid: "They send a boat out there and something happens, they leave you out there to die. They don't give a damn about you. They should have been there immediately with aid. Even if it meant going in and wiping the whole Israeli outfit out, they should have done it."

Along the way, the NSA asked their representative at the Joint Reconnaissance Center, John Connell, whether there would be any changes in the ship's schedule because of the outbreak of the war between Israel and Egypt. They learned that the Joint Chiefs "didn't plan any change at the time."[51] This was on June 5.

Richard Harvey, an NSA scheduler, said that the mission "was primarily against Middle East targets," which was vague enough. On the issue of Hebrew linguists, he said, "There would not have been any need for it. We had no tasking." The majority of his reply remains redacted.[52]

Evidence that *Liberty* was chopped to the Sixth Fleet closer to June 2 than the official date of June 6 is reflected in the fact that Dave Lewis requested of Admiral Martin that an escort be assigned to accompany the ship to its assignment off the coast of Egypt immediately after they crossed the Straits of Gibraltar on June 2. What followed was a series of communiqués and responses. Lewis made the request only after consulting with Captain McGonagle. The destroyer would remain five miles off *Liberty* and serve as both an armed escort and an auxiliary communications center.[53] This fact does not appear in the recent official history of *Liberty* or in other pro-Israeli accounts of the attack.

The request for an escort was denied the same day or the following day—the exact date remains ambiguous. Admiral Martin would claim, falsely, that he did not know that *Liberty* was under his command until June 7, but that is unlikely and can only be accounted for by Admiral Martin's being part of the operation against the USS *Liberty*.[54] Martin sent one message saying he had never heard of an AGTR, implying that he did not know they were in his chain of command.

There were several exchanges between Lewis and Admiral Martin or his staff. Upon receiving the request, Vice Admiral Martin, three stars, nickname "Fast Charger," said he had never seen an intelligence collector and wanted to pay the USS *Liberty* a visit. He claimed he didn't know "who we were or what we were," Dave Lewis says.[55] He professed not to know that *Liberty* was in his command, which surprised Lewis, since by navy protocol, the ship would be chopped to the Sixth Fleet automatically upon its passing through the Straits of Gibraltar.

Admiral Martin ultimately offered a terse reply to the request for an escort. Jet-fighter protection was ten minutes away, he claimed. (This was false.) They were sailing in international waters, the ship's hull well marked, the ship flying the American flag. No escort was necessary, Admiral Martin insisted. To the Joint Chiefs of Staff fact-finding team, after the fact, and contradicting Israeli spokesman Aharon Jay Cristol, who insists in his apologia for Israel that an escort was never requested, Martin said that he had wanted to visit *Liberty* "to see what he could do for her and what she could do for him in other than ... [*redacted*]." So Admiral Martin made liars of both Lewis and McGonagle.

He had rejected the request for an escort because, he said, "previous instruction had been issued stating that association of the SIXTHFLT with the USS *Intrepid* should be avoided: 'based on this precedent, the visit to the USS *Liberty* was not accomplished.'" Admiral Martin asserted that the ship "was not a reasonable subject for attack by any nation, not a participant in the conflict, [and was a] clearly marked United States ship in international waters."

Dave Lewis concluded that Admiral Martin's refusal of an escort—and his change of mind about visiting the ship—had something to do with trepidations about having to go aboard on a bosun's chair, being high-lined.[56] When he learned that *Liberty* could not accommodate a helicopter, Martin suddenly claimed that he had too much to do and canceled out. Former MI6 agent Anthony Wells's supposition that Martin refused the escort because it would expose *Liberty*'s presence in the East Med is fatuous.[57] Their presence had been common knowledge in Rota, Dave Lewis says, and they were followed by the Russians most of the way to the Med. Prior to the attack on *Liberty*, both the United States and Russia had built unarmed intelligence collectors. None had ever bothered the other.[58]

Back home, there remained those who were concerned about the ship. Gene Sheck, at NSA's K Group section, which was responsible for managing the various mobile collection platforms, intervened. He reminded John Connell at the Joint Reconnaissance Center that during the Cuban missile crisis, the *Oxford* had been pulled back from the Havana area. Was consideration being given to doing the same for *Liberty*? Connell spoke to the ship movement officer at the Joint Reconnaissance Center, but the operation was tight enough that no action was taken and his concerns were brushed aside.[59]

The National Security Agency did not participate in the operation. On June 7, Frank Raven at NSA was asked by an analyst, "For God's sake do you know where the *Liberty* is?" Raven believed she was sitting off Crete, only for the analyst to add, "They've got her heading straight for the beach!" As author James Bamford discovered, Raven ordered *Liberty* out of the area and told Bamford that "there was nothing to be gained by having her in there that close … whatever they could ascertain from their position, nothing nobody in the world gave a damn about."[60] The later "Keystone Kops foul-up," as Bamford calls it, about a message that supposedly was misrouted was disinformation and part of the cover-up.

Without chastising Admiral Martin by name, in their report, the Joint Chiefs concluded that an operational commander could not protect a ship like *Liberty* "without providing escort and combat air patrol; he can only react to attack once initiated or threatened which in this case was too late."[61]

Later, Admiral Martin would tell the Joint Chiefs' fact-finding team that he had expected on June 5, the day the war broke out, that "higher authority" would have modified *Liberty*'s orders "in the interest of her safety" and that he would therefore be off the hook. He added that *Liberty* was not under his "complete operations control." He urged *Liberty* to "vigilance against attack or threat of attack and to report any threatening or suspicious actions directed against her or any diversion from schedule necessitated by external threat. Advise if local situation dictates change in area of operation assigned by reference JCS schedule."

This message included the instruction that *Liberty* utilize TF-60 tactical circuits, and it never reached Captain McGonagle. Admiral Martin initiated "tracer action through the ship-shore terminal to ascertain if it had been delivered, an action which was not completed before the attack. The message had not arrived prior to the attack."[62]

A communications technician on *Liberty* named David McFeggan, who reported to both the Office of Naval Intelligence (ONI) and CIA, would remark of Admiral Martin fifty years later, regarding Admiral Martin's foreknowledge of the attack, "Of course he knew."[63] ONI was "working with" CIA on this operation, he said. McFeggan had TOP SECRET CRYPTO clearance and worked out of his own research space. He didn't know that Dave Lewis had TOP SECRET clearance. He was not authorized to tell Lewis anything about his own mission and never did.

McFeggan had two years of junior college when he joined the navy and then went to intelligence school for six months, only to find himself in the ONI. This was in 1964. His cover was that on the USS *Liberty* he worked for Jim Pierce in the communications center. He had access to Dave Lewis's spaces, but Dave didn't have access to his.

McFeggan held CT2 rank, petty officer second class intermediate, but was not an officer. "Within our spaces," Lewis says, "people could wander around wherever they wanted. You had to go through a locked combination door to get in, but once in you could go anywhere." McFeggan reported to no one on board. He was a pale, nondescript navy volunteer, and years later Dave Lewis did not remember his name, nor could he conjure up an image of McFeggan's face. There had long been a rumor that CIA had assigned someone to the ship.

Dave McFeggan.
"Of course he knew."
(Photo courtesy of Ted Arens.)

Through ONI, McFeggan says, he was "patched" to CIA. He says he functioned on the ship as a lay chaplain and was proud that he "ordered a kid," as he put it, to close an open hatch as water poured in from the torpedo attack, which had blasted a forty-foot hole in the ship. He passed out rosaries, although he was a Protestant, and Bibles. He gave away his personal Bible.

McFeggan added that the original target for attack, the ship chosen for the mission, was not the USS *Liberty* but the USNS *Valdez*, a technical research ship manned by National Security Agency civilians and monitoring the east coast of Africa as CIA hunted down Che Guevara and intercepted messages from Fidel Castro.[64] Che had traveled to Congo to offer assistance to the vulnerable supporters of the murdered Patrice Lumumba, premier of Congo. *Valdez*'s history included eavesdropping on Soviet missile tests. On board were French, Portuguese, Spanish, and Russian linguists. McFeggan remembered it as the "USS *Alvarez*," but he had to have been referring to the *Valdez*.

Should *Liberty* not have been summoned to the coast of Egypt, its next assignment was to relieve the *Valdez*, proceeding south to the Cape of Good Hope and up the east coast of Africa, through the Suez Canal, and then home. Dave Lewis approved this assignment. Told that the *Valdez* had to return home, he thought it was a good idea to assume its assignments, since *Liberty* was so close.

Valdez moved at only eight to ten knots (as opposed to *Liberty*'s eighteen knots). Having suffered damage from its travails on the Congo River, the *Valdez* began its journey home even as the USS *Liberty* assumed its new assignment in the East Med. The officers in charge saw no point in keeping the *Valdez* in the Middle East, so it made its way through the Suez Canal. In the night, on the way to the Eastern Mediterranean, *Liberty* passed the *Valdez*.[65]

Liberty proceeded on its lonely journey to the coast of Egypt, all other ships having been called away. In the predawn hours of June 5, the Monday, Israeli jets attacked twenty-five Arab airbases from Damascus in Syria to Luxor in Egypt. On June 6, Admiral Martin sent a message to the USS *Liberty*, a schizophrenic warning given his foreknowledge of the attack: "In view of present Arab/Israeli situation and unpredictability of UAR actions, maintain a high state of vigilance against attack or threat of attack, report by flash precedence any threatening or suspicious actions directed against you or any diversion from schedule necessitated by external threat. Advise if local situation dictates change in area of Ops assigned . . . keep COMSIXTHFLT [himself] and CTF63 informed of logistic needs sufficiently in advance to enable orderly logs . . . include COMSIXTHFLT as info addee on reports required . . . submit reports of contact with ships, aircraft and submarines which are unident, hostile, of intel interest or engaged in harassment."

This warning came in a two-page telegram from COMSIXTHFLT—Admiral Martin—and was copied to more than seventeen places, five of those redacted. They include the Joint Chiefs. The "unpredictability" of UAR actions amounts to disinformation. As the UN peacekeepers were brutally attacked by Israeli tank columns, so Israel Defense Forces at El Arish, just opposite where *Liberty* had been positioned, murdered their Egyptian prisoners with machine guns and tossed their bodies into mass graves.[66] When *Liberty* arrived at the East Med, there was a lot of static on the frequencies, and they had a difficult time copying.

Apparently it didn't matter what they copied. They had been placed to be attacked and had no discernible intelligence mission. On June 6, *Liberty* was directed by NSA to "maintain a high state of readiness" because of the "unpredictability of the UAR" and to report by FLASH any "threatening or suspicious actions." (A FLASH message took precedence over ordinary traffic.) By June 6, Egypt, its air force in shambles, was in no position to bother anyone.

Among the more forthright witnesses has been sailor James O'Connor: "We were pretty much out there on a limb, by ourselves, if anything happened," he told the NSA later. "It didn't look like there was anybody around to get to us." Yet "we really didn't think anything was going to happen to us."

When they arrived at their assigned position, Captain McGonagle called Dave Lewis to his stateroom.

"Lewis, do we have to be this close in?" McGonagle said.

"Well, Captain, if you want to get all the VHF [very high frequency] communications, yes."

Center, chief engineer George Golden. Both a Mason and a Jew, he saved the ship. Golden concluded that "this was a well-planned attack against us, and they knew we were an American ship." (Photo courtesy of Tom and Carole Blaney.)

"OK. We'll stay here then," McGonagle said. Lewis later reflected: "I did what was right from my point of view, but if I hadn't told him that, he would have moved offshore. If we had been one hundred miles away, then line of sight would start to apply, and we would receive no tactical communications."

On their way to their assigned position, *Liberty* passed three Soviet ships "streaming in column."[67] Officer Jim Ennes, in charge of the ship's division of electronic maintenance technicians, and author of the first account of the attack, published in 1980, reports they also saw a huge Texaco tanker. The captain, on the bridge, peered at *Liberty* through binoculars. Planted on the bridge, McGonagle assumed the burden and the prestige of command, and there he would remain through most of the events to follow, just as the ship's chief engineer, George Golden, would remain at the helm of his boiler, thwarting the encroachment of the cold water that threatened to send them all down to the bottom of the sea.

Some time prior to the attack, according to Dave McFeggan, a message involving "Frontlet 615" or "Operation Cyanide" was delivered to McGonagle marked "FOR CAPTAIN'S EYES ONLY."[68] The name "Operation Cyanide" also survives in the recollections of Captain Richard Block. It was recognized by Israeli intelligence operative Rafi Eitan, who was notorious for having been instrumental in the kidnapping and extradition of SS Obersturmbannführer Adolf Eichmann. In an interview with the BBC, Eitan acknowledged the existence of an "Operation Cyanide." Asked to define what this meant, Eitan cut the interview short. "Out of signature and loyalty to my country . . . I know what I'm allowed and where I stop," he said nervously.

What "Frontlet 615" meant derives from one particular source. It was Richard Thompson, who had been recruited by CIA and who became a fervent student of the history of the USS *Liberty*. Thompson's father had served with the OSS during World War II; he himself had worked for a subsidiary of a CIA proprietary, ARAMCO, for years, and had been a diver for a group that later became the Navy Seals. He attained the rank of full commander in the navy, but he never owned a uniform. He had gone on to serve in navy intelligence (ONI) only to be recruited for

CIA by John Shinneman, a maritime lawyer who practiced in New York. Shinneman became an undersecretary of state under John F. Kennedy. Kennedy himself had recruited him.

"How would you like to be recruited?" Shinneman said one day to Dick Thompson. Later, Thompson remarked to his son, "I wouldn't let him down."

CIA asset Dick Thompson, center, with John Shinneman, the maritime lawyer who recruited him to the Agency. "How would you like to be recruited?" (Photo courtesy of Tim Thompson.)

One day he was house sitting for his son, Tim, taking care of Tim's dog. When Tim opened the door, he discovered his father chatting with two men whom Dick introduced as CIA employees. Nothing more was said.

There was other evidence of Dick Thompson's James Bondish activities. He was a big man, six foot two, with big blue eyes, and was athletic, outgoing, charming, gregarious, and without apparent ego.[69] He liked to help people and was free of self-promotion. He preferred to remain in the background. He threw himself into anything he undertook, and he gave it his all.

Thompson's friend Carol Moore told the author: "He grabbed the *Liberty* story like a dog with a bone and ran with it. It was a grave injustice and someone should bring it to light and make them own up to the flag. . . . He was a loyal American and thought the *Liberty* crew should be in the forefront, they should get the spotlight. He was a facilitator. Everything he did, he was always the person in the background . . . he didn't want to take the credit."[70] He was a mentor to Moore in her business and was "selfless," Moore said: "He introduced you to his friends, he gave of himself, helped out wherever he could. A stellar person. He also loved art and was a patron to young people and bought their paintings and introduced them to people who could help them." Carol Moore also told the author that it was unmistakable to most people close to Dick Thompson that he was with CIA.[71]

After years of CIA activity, his passport had an accordion-pleated insert that would tumble to the floor if you opened it, chock-full of visas, many in Arabic or Cyrillic, and he spent a lot of time in Russia researching the *Liberty* story, as well as in Jordan, Syria, Abu Dhabi, Lebanon. He traveled the Middle East regularly, and once, arriving in Cairo, he remarked sardonically, "We slit a lot of throats here." Dick had been lunching with CIA officer William Buckley, later kidnapped and assassinated, who made him aware of the story of the USS *Liberty*. Thompson was too smart and too politically savvy to place all the blame on Israel; he knew that it was inconceivable that Israel would murder unarmed American sailors and cast them and their ship to the bottom of the sea without a prior handshake from the US government, endorsing the project.

Clever and savvy, Thompson developed a close relationship with Richard Helms, and one can infer that regarding the truth behind the attack on the USS *Liberty*, Helms and Thompson were of the same persuasion: they agreed that the truth should come out. Yet for all his contacts, Dick Thompson was unable to "crack Hollywood" with distribution of the *Liberty* story, as Carol Moore put it. He went through two or three potential movie distributors before he tried overseas. He needed an American, but everyone was afraid of the story except Thompson, Dave Lewis remembers. Thompson's efforts included research into "Cyanide" and "Frontlet 615." As a CIA asset, Thompson was able to penetrate the reality behind these mysterious entities. Thompson believed that because Operation Cyanide was called off by the United States, Israel refused to accept the fact and began Operation Frontlet 615 early.

In a scenario found among Dick Thompson's papers is a partial memoir by "An Unknown Israeli writer," who admits to having been a "covert operator." This man predicts that "the massing of American ships in the area would be accepted, and Russia could be clobbered without time for retaliation. China would present no threat, and the USA—or the 303 Committee could rule the world."[72] That he knows of the existence of the highly secret 303 Committee suggests that the author is highly placed in the intelligence community.

In this document, the anonymous operative explains that this "secret US committee which decides military policy, ensured that the President is not called to account for any actions that may go wrong," which is a textbook definition of the 303 Committee. He notes that the United States had moved the Sixth Fleet into the area to make sure a nuclear submarine was stationed off the Gaza Strip, with orders to sink *Liberty* if the Israelis had any problems. The orders were to "leave no witnesses." Dave Lewis says that "it makes sense for the 303 Committee to be blamed for ordering the hit [on the USS *Liberty*]."[73]

"What was 'Operation Cyanide,'" this operative ponders. "A scheme cooked up whereby the USA could legitimately back Israel in attacking the Arabs without incurring the wrath of Europe-Russia-China. The plan was for the USA to do a pre-emptive strike on Russia immediately afterwards." The actual response of the Russian leaders, readying their nuclear submarine in the Eastern Mediterranean, certainly reflects awareness of Operation Cyanide.

Dick Thompson. According to Dick Thompson, "It was '303' who ordered the dispatch of three 'air ready' planes directly to Cairo." (Photo courtesy of Tim Thompson.)

The key, this operative writes, was to "sacrifice the *Liberty*. The intent was for Israeli aircraft to attack the unarmed ship with unmarked aircraft, destroy its communication first strike, and then sink it with all hands." With no evidence other than the fact that it had been sunk in view of the shore, it would be assumed that Egyptian planes (what few remained after the Israeli attacks of Monday, June 5) had sunk it.

Blaming Egypt, the United States was to land the ready battalion of Marines in Lebanon, securing Israel's flank. Thompson believed the Soviets confronted the Johnson administration with the facts of Operation Cyanide, thanks to Philby's relationship with Angleton, among the consequences of Kim Philby's defection. In an email of July 23, 2003, Thompson speculates that the planned visit of Meir Amit to CIA/DOD on June 1 involved the confirmation of the planned Operation Frontlet 615 (referred to in that extant 303 Committee memo of April). The Soviet Union sent the Soviet ambassador to the White House on June 2, revealing that the Frontlet 615 Operation had been blown and resulting in moving up the date of Israel's June 5 attack on Egypt.

Thompson reveals that Amit pressed Dayan to sink the USS *Liberty* with all hands, and the United States would blame Egypt because of the rerouted traffic. According to Thompson, "Israeli air & naval units were ordered to sink the ship. Command knew it was US but [were] following Amit's direction." Thompson's words come from the above email and interview with people with whom he shared this information, like Ernie Gallo. Thompson replies to a question long pondered by those studying the attack: who gave the order to sink the USS *Liberty*?

The Israeli operative whose memoir was buried among Dick Thompson's papers believes that "those [Israeli] pilots were not to blame. They carried out orders only after questioning repeatedly over the air to confirm it was a US ship they were attacking. . . . From memory," he writes, "six sailors lost their lives on that first sortie to cripple the communications. When the next sorties arrived—again it was only after heated debate between pilots and headquarters that they did attack."

The writer had to have been close to the attack. "If memory serves me," he writes, four separate torpedoes were launched, only the final one hit the target. The crew death toll rose to thirty-four men (true). "The amount of radio traffic was almost impossible to keep up with. We heard *Liberty* get off a jerry-rigged low-power SOS signal requesting assistance. We heard the response from the Sixth Fleet in the Mediterranean some five hundred and twelve miles west of *Liberty*."

This Israeli operative notes that despite urgent requests, the fleet did not send the stricken ship help. "Orders not to interfere came directly from Washington. We picked up a signal from the fleet commander stating three strike aircraft were standing 'air ready' which meant they were carrying nuclear not conventional weapons."

The author of this document near the end reveals that his name is "Frank." He was close enough to fear a dose of radiation poisoning. "Room 47," not defined in this document, was "informed pronto, top priority." Frank reveals that he was in contact with "USA HQ" and "picked up a series of airborne exchanges." He realized that "303 had ordered the dispatch of the three 'air ready' planes directly to Cairo. That meant there was less than an hour to the use of nuclear weapons on Egypt." (We know the time was in fact seven minutes.) These details also reveal that Admiral William Inman Martin was getting his orders from 303.

"In this inside view," Frank writes,

> we learn it took eighteen clammy minutes to get the urgency of the situation to the Top Brass of the Kremlin, and convince them the shit would hit the fan in Cairo in just as a few minutes—and RUSSIA would be next with MOSCOW the prime target.
>
> All Russian nuclear missiles were primed and pointed, and that the first mushroom in Egypt would be the signal for a Russian mass launch.
>
> We listened in and picked up the instructions direct from the US Navy Commander in Washington to abort the attack mission and return to base. The heated discussion between the Sixth Fleet commander and his boss was suddenly cut short as the President's voice, and L.B.J. personally ordered the immediate abort. THE PLANES WERE ONLY SEVEN MINUTES FROM TARGET—AND THE STARTING OF WORLD WAR 3.

Frank knows that the "un-named US submarine commander defied orders to sink it [*Liberty*], refusing to kill the innocent American crew." He was never disciplined for disobeying the order." Certainly it has been speculated that a submarine was given this order. This Israeli operative knows that the life rafts were damaged by Israeli gunboats following instructions to make sure there were no survivors. He reasons that they feared the life rafts might contain survivors. He speculates, or knows, that US planes from Spain had "hurriedly received a new paint-job to give them Israeli markings and were dispatched to assess damage."

Frank is a tough customer. He casts a wary eye on the men who accepted Purple Hearts and swore "never ever" to speak about the event. "Those guys accepted honour and payment in return for silence, and were a disgrace to themselves, to their dead comrades, the United States Navy and the US they served."

The spelling of "honour" reveals that whatever nationality the speaker commanded, he was not an American. "Shame on them all—and the bosses they served," he cries out. "303 decided it best to drop 'Operation Acid Drop,'" he writes, "the attack on Russia, mighty quick and attempted to cover up 'Operation Cyanide,' as far as possible." This the United States and Israel, working in concert, succeeded in doing.

According to this unsigned document from Dick Thompson's archives, the remembrances of an "unknown Israeli writer," a "covert operator," and a double agent" who calls himself "Frank," it was 303 that ordered the dispatch of three "air ready" planes directly to Cairo. There was less than an hour to the use of nuclear weapons on Egypt. The implication was that Russia would be next, with Moscow the prime target (the plan was named "Operation Acid Drop"). Then Lyndon Johnson personally ordered an immediate abort.

The planes were only seven minutes from target, as Admiral William Inman Martin would at an unguarded moment later corroborate. In his description of these events, Frank comes close to blowing the whistle on the *Liberty* operation: "The Sam gave bell to almond-eyes" refers to Uncle Sam sacrificing an American naval surveillance ship ("bell" as in the Liberty Bell), and its crew. According to Frank's descriptions, *Liberty* was "a ship bristling with equipment to spy on friend and foe alike. It had been dispatched to sit off-shore of the Gaza Strip to do the same monitoring we were—or so the Captain thought!"

"Frank" had been "doubling as a Mossad operator" and had been up in the Himalayas doing covert checking on Chinese military action in the area. He was called back to Alexandria to coordinate assessment of the Middle East crisis because he had extensive knowledge of Egypt, Jordan, Iraq, and Syria and had worked as a double agent for the Israelis.

"'Almond eyes' refers to 'Operation Cyanide'—Almonds—cyanide!" That was the plot hatched by "Mk14" (Mk 14—a .303 caliber rifle). 303, of course, was the secret US committee deciding military policy—particularly in ensuring that the president not be called to account for any actions that may go wrong.

Finding Mk14 meant we had "locked on to their communications channels." The author sounds like an Israeli who knows about how Israel had fire locked on to the USS *Liberty*. At other moments, he sounds as if he is a Russian, as he refers to *Liberty* as doing "the same monitoring we were."

"What was 'Operation Cyanide'?" the author asks. "A scheme cooked up whereby the USA could legitimately back Israel in attacking the Arabs without incurring the wrath of Europe-Russia-China. The plan was for the USA to do a pre-emptive strike on Russia immediately afterwards."

"How did '303' intend to achieve this?" Frank asks. The key was "Operation Cyanide—sacrifice *Liberty*. The intent was for Israeli aircraft to attack the unarmed ship with unmarked aircraft, destroy its communication first strike, and then sink it with all hands." With no evidence other than the fact that it had been sunk in view of the shore, it would be assumed that Egyptian warplanes had done the deed. (Obviously the friendly Israelis would not attack a ship flying the American flag.)

Frank suggests that the United States had stationed a nuclear submarine off the ship with orders to sink *Liberty* if the Israelis had any problems. The orders were to "Leave no witnesses." The fly in the ointment was Terence Halbardier's resurrection of an antenna that would allow *Liberty* to communicate with the outside. "We," the author admits, heard *Liberty* get off a jury-rigged low power SOS signal requesting assistance.

With no evidence other than that it had been sunk in view of the shore, it would be assumed that Egyptian warplanes had perpetuated the attack. This unprovoked attack on an American unarmed ship would legitimize the US entering the war. Arab oil would become the property of Israel and the USA. The presence of American ships in the area would be accepted and Russia would be clobbered without time for retaliation. China would present no threat, and the USA (or the 303 Committee) would rule the world.

One has only to consult the papers of George Rufus Brown, of defense contractor Brown & Root, at Rice University in Houston to find this exact sentiment: Arab oil belonged to the United States for the taking, and if Gamal Abdel Nasser got in the way, we had imaginative plans for him.[74] At the time, in 1953, of the CIA coup in Iran against the democratically elected prime minister, Mohammad Mosaddegh, George Brown and his brother Herman breathed a sigh of relief. As USS *Liberty* Survivor Ernie Gallo put it, "Israel was a giant aircraft carrier. ... We needed an ally for our oil."[75]

Both Herman and George Brown were already assets of CIA's clandestine services, as a CIA document reveals.[76] After the overthrow of Mosaddegh, George noted the "different approach the U.S. government was now taking."

"Now I think we have at least half of the reserves of the Middle East oil," George exulted. Brown & Root had surveyed the "hot and disease-infested poor countries within the equatorial belt, and discovered, 'that's where all of the oil is too!'" James Angleton's views were far from unique among the powerful. They were shared by defense contractors like Lyndon Johnson's supporters, Herman and George Rufus Brown of Brown & Root.

Center, Herman Brown; at the right, George Rufus Brown at a Brown & Root meeting. "Arab oil belonged to the US for the taking." (Photo from Brown & Root / George R. Brown Executive Files, MS 488, courtesy of the Woodson Research Center, Fondren Library, Rice University.)

George Rufus Brown and Herman Brown. (Photo from Brown & Root / George R. Brown Executive Files, MS 488, courtesy of the Woodson Research Center, Fondren Library, Rice University.)

"Seventy percent of the known oil reserves of the world today are in the Middle East," George Brown wrote to Senator Lyndon Johnson on February 25, 1957, "and we cannot afford any foreign policy that would run a chance of our losing control of these reserves because we would be at the mercy of our enemy if this should happen."

The role of Brown & Root was plain: it was to create "a partnership arrangement between our companies who are working abroad and our government . . . to keep us supplied with raw materials or natural resources to keep our economy from sinking." As Israel's enthusiastic supporter and unquestioning ally, Cold War fanatic Angleton cast that country in the role of US outpost in the Middle East.

"Might not the land grab of 1967, planned for years," Israeli premier Moshe Sharett had speculated, "be attributed to the discovery of oil near the Gaza Strip?" Referring to the USS *Liberty*, Sharett refers to "the use of terror and aggression" by Israel and talks about "the long chain of false incidents and hostilities we have invented and on the many clashes we have provoked which cost so much blood, and on the violations of law by our men—all of which have brought grave disaster and determined the whole course of events."[77] The attack on the American sailors was hardly the first of the malfeasances committed by Israel, acts of terrorism originating in imperial hunger and complicity with the United States.

In an alternative intelligence-inspired scenario, Anthony Wells writes, fancifully and less than accurately, "The *Liberty* was a key source in the NSA network. She read the traffic." In fact, Dave Lewis reveals that *Liberty*, where he commanded the intelligence collection, was specifically ordered *not* to collect intelligence from Israel or the United Kingdom, but to focus solely and exclusively on Egypt and the Soviet Union.

Wells offers no corroborative evidence because none exists. "The information sent shudders down the spines of President Lyndon B.

Johnson, Secretary of State Rusk, and key advisor [Benjamin] Sonnen-feldt," he writes, naming as a "key advisor" an operative whose name appears only infrequently in the literature about the USS *Liberty*. Wells did interview Dean Rusk—an interview he has chosen to classify and not share with history.

His perspective driven by the Cold War, Wells writes that "Moscow made it clear: if the Israelis did not desist, the Red Army would execute a massive airborne drop into Syria and confront the Israeli Army." According to Wells, Rusk confided to him that "had the Israelis not halted when they did"—that is, short of Damascus—"the Sixth Fleet would have landed aircraft in Israel to deter the Soviets from invading that country." That the Sixth Fleet would have landed aircraft in Israel seems, with the hindsight of history, to be preposterous.

Did *Liberty*'s sensitive antennas pick up Israeli orders for the June 9 attack on Syria and relay them to Washington? No. *Liberty* was far over the horizon from Tel Aviv, as well as from Israel's Northern Command, which was responsible for the Syrian front. Strategic communications are normally not line of sight. If somehow *Liberty* had a direct link with NSA, why didn't she receive her standoff orders from that same link?

The answer, according to Dave Lewis, is that *Liberty* didn't have real-time communications; their high-frequency communications were not always reliable; the moon dish was frequently inoperative. Only on the occasions that it worked were they able to obtain eighteen hours a day of coverage by bouncing off the moon.

Wells's goal is to place exclusive blame for the attack on *Liberty* on Moshe Dayan. So he writes that Dayan had "taken the law into his own hands and ordered the attack on Syria. . . . The Prime Minister and the other key Israeli leaders had no role at all in the decision to attack Syria and the USS *Liberty*." Ignoring the roles of Meir Amit and James Angleton, as well as Lyndon Johnson and Cyrus Vance, in these events, Wells presents in this document the indefensible view that "Moshe Dayan was taking the West to the brink with the Soviet Union by attacking Syria." Making the goal clear, Wells repeats that it was "a personal decision and order to attack the US spy ship." This could "have taken the Soviet Union over the edge if the United States had mistaken the perpetrator and taken action against, for example, Egypt."

Wells acknowledges that the Sixth Fleet launched aircraft against Egypt. But he fantasizes that this was retaliation against the Soviets' plan to take the Golan Heights, something that nowhere occurs in Soviet history. Israel did not advance on Damascus, precipitating a supposed Sixth Fleet aircraft encounter with the Soviets that did not take place. It was all a war games fantasy.

So in the literature about the attack on the USS *Liberty*, from several quarters, history is ignored in favor of disinformation. The goal is to remove both the United States and Israel from responsibility for the attack. According to Anthony Wells, all the trouble issued from one demon, Moshe Dayan: "No asset was better placed than the USS *Liberty*. Moshe Dayan knew this and wanted zero collection of Israel communications."[78]

Dave Lewis puts the lie to all of this: "*Liberty* was not collecting Israeli communications," he told me. He has not spoken widely about this issue, and Wells must have believed he was safe from challenge. Uneasy for some reason, Wells adds that Dayan "was a great Israeli patriot and leader . . . personally courageous and gave of his all for his country."

Wells has not been alone in isolating Dayan as the mastermind of the attack. Joining him was Cyrus Vance, the person who sent *Liberty* up to the East Med on behalf of the 303 Committee. In his memoir, *Hard Choices*, Vance praises Dayan: "I had come to admire Dayan, whom I found to be a brilliant, imaginative and honest man," paying reparations to the scapegoat.[79] Vance does not mention the USS *Liberty*, in whose fate he played no small role. Of another participant in *Liberty*'s destruction, Vance refers to the "mutual trust and confidence that I had enjoyed with Bob McNamara."[80]

In this scenario, the efforts of Johnson (and Rusk) to prevent Israel from heading for Damascus are what prevented World War III, turning LBJ into a hero, a prince of peace—rather than someone who brought his country to the brink of World War III by authorizing the bombing of Cairo, someone who lays claim to the title of "the scourge of Vietnam" (with Richard Nixon coming in second). Wells does do history a service by acknowledging that the United States indeed had plans to attack Cairo. According to Wells, the Israeli advance into Syria brought a confrontation between the superpowers deadly close to reality. In Wells's scenario, the Sixth Fleet's immediate response to the attack on *Liberty* was to launch aircraft against Egypt, only to be "recalled just in time, as they were heading toward Egypt." (There are those who still doubt that the United States launched aircraft on their way to bomb Cairo.)

For the remaining three years of President Gamal Abdel Nasser's lifetime, and beyond, Egypt receded as a dominant power in the region. No American or Israeli has discussed what really happened in the attack on the USS *Liberty*, either how the idea for the attack originated or with whom. No Israeli leader has discussed the attack, fifty years later. Among the national security considerations that required silence were James Angleton's discussions with Eppy Evron before the fighting began. They included Israel's interception of communications among Arab leaders and transmission of doctored texts to encourage Jordan and Syria to commit their armies in the erroneous belief that Nasser's army had repelled the Israelis.

According to Wilbur Eveland, "President Johnson's annoyance with Nasser was well-known to James Angleton, who was a man searching for vindication after the defection of Kim Philby. Angleton was eager to show that CIA's liaison with Israeli intelligence could assist the US in achieving its objectives in the Middle East. Angleton concluded that 'Gamal Abdel Nasser was responsible for the West's only problem.... If Nasser could be eliminated and the Egyptian army defeated without overt major power assistance, the Arabs would be left with no alternative to making peace with Israel.'"

Minister Ephraim Evron was Angleton's steady contact. Evron arranged for Angleton to meet with Moshe Dayan. It wasn't that Dayan made crucial decisions about the Israeli aggression, but the long-planned war with Egypt necessitated the appointment of Dayan. It has been part of the cover-up that the literature of the USS *Liberty* ignores overwhelmingly the figures of James Angleton and Meir Amit as principals of these events.

Thanks to Philby's relationship with Angleton, Israel had a detailed battle plan prepared and rehearsed for the Golan Heights. The press of the right wing of Israel's government moved the attack date from June 15 ("Frontlet 615") to June 5. Another provocative note by Dick Thompson is that the Israeli plan for the Golan had been in play for many months prior to June 1967. US communications, both defensive and blocking, were in place, and *Liberty*'s signals were actually blocked at first by US systems provided, resulting in knowledge of all channels used.[81]

Thompson suggests that "the reason that opening the facts today is very difficult [is] that it would show the grip that Israel has on the US government." Lurking behind these events as well was Israel's suspicion that the United States would support Egypt's call for a cease-fire and the equal suspicion that USS *Liberty* signals transmitted to the United States were being intercepted by the Soviets.

Never satisfied with what he knew from his intelligence sources, in the late 1990s Thompson confronted Robert S. McNamara at a fancy country club and demanded the truth. All he could elicit was McNamara's double-fault response: "I don't remember anything about the USS *Liberty*."[82]

Dave McFeggan told the author he reported to ONI and CIA right up to the time of the attack. One of his functions for CIA was to save one antenna, McFeggan had learned, which is how it happened to be available to be rescued by Terence Halbardier, who was in charge of communications equipment; apparently CIA's role was to help the sailors to sabotage the operation.[83] This coincides with Richard Helms's effort to sabotage the US bombing of Cairo, as reflected in his attempt to thwart the CIA cable to John Hadden, and his several later statements that the attack on *Liberty* was no accident, no mistake, contrary to official Israeli assertions.

According to author Peter Hounam, later a CIA witness told Congress that the US embassy in Tel Aviv (John Hadden) informed Washington on the evening of June 7 that the Israelis would attack *Liberty* if it continued on its course. This, according to Hounam, was confirmed "by one of the *Liberty* crew [Dave McFeggan], a petty officer working . . . below decks in a high security area of the ship and picked up a message transmitted by the Israelis in English that the ship would be in danger if it remained. This message was FLASHed to Washington in the early hours of 8 June." Later, McFeggan told Hounam that a strike on the ship could be blamed on Cairo, just as the Gulf of Tonkin affair had been the pretext for the bombing of Hanoi and Haiphong. There were rumors circulating among the enlisted men that there was a spy aboard the ship, Dave Lewis heard. Most believed it was an officer.[84]

CHAPTER 7

CONSPICUOUS GALLANTRY[1]

"I don't need the Mossad and the Shin Bet knocking on my door."

—Seth Mintz

At first light on the morning of June 8, a minute after sunrise, the operation against the USS *Liberty* commenced. A French-made 2501 Noratlas, lumbered over the ship. An ensign saw it through his binoculars but could not discover any markings. It had a double fuselage and looked like "an old P-38 or a small flying boxcar."

On that morning, a message came to Captain McGonagle. It was titled "operation cyanide" and read "Captain's Eyes Only." It announced the presence of the *Andrew Jackson*, a Polaris nuclear submarine, close below *Liberty*.

Throughout the morning, there were thirteen such overflights over *Liberty*. Lieutenant Lloyd Painter heard a buzz and went topside to check it out. When he reached the bridge area, he saw a slow-moving aircraft with the Star of David visible on the side. He saw the same slow-moving Israeli plane again between noon and 1 p.m. when he was assigned to bridge duty as officer of the deck.

Robert Wilson saw a Noratlas overflying them and concluded it was Israeli. "What else is flying out there at this point in the war, coming from the direction of Israel and going back to Israel?" he later remarked. This plane circled about three or four times off the port beam and then took off in a "true direction" toward Tel Aviv.[2]

And so it went all morning. At 8:50, a single jet crossed astern of the ship, circling from starboard to port and returning to the mainland in the direction of the UAR. At 10:30, two unidentified jet aircraft orbited the ship three times at about ten thousand feet and at a distance of approximately two miles. At about 10:56, another aircraft crossed astern of the ship at a distance of three to five miles, circled around the starboard side, then headed back to the Sinai Peninsula. Overflights occurred at 11:45, 12:20, and 12:45.

It was a quiet morning. Sailors sometimes waved to the reconnaissance planes, and Larry Weaver, who would suffer a lifetime for the many wounds he endured in the attack now four hours off, observed, "I could see the brightness of their teeth." Jack Beattie, age nineteen, waved to a pilot who did not wave back. A separate "situation report" (SITREP) was sent to the Pentagon for each overflight. This record of the surveillance flights alone demonstrates that the attack, which commenced at 1:58, was preplanned and no accident.

That trouble was afoot is reflected in *Liberty*'s message to the Naval Security Station Command at 11:00 that she had destroyed all superseded May publications (CRYPTO documents) and intended to destroy all irregularly superseded material daily because of the "current situation and shallow water in the operating area."

At 11:45, there was an explosion at El Arish, the closest town on the coast. Smoke filled the air and would be enlisted as a pretext that *Liberty* had been firing weapons, an Israeli pretext that had to be rejected when Israel discovered that *Liberty* lacked the capability to fire on land. It carried no such weapons.

The overflights had particular goals. The "flying boxcars" were calculating *Liberty*'s coordinates, including what speed the ship was moving— which was five knots, giving the lie to Israel's later contention that they thought the ship was moving at twenty-eight knots and thus was a warship vulnerable to attack. Bob Scarborough explains that the Israelis obtained "fire control lock" so that the attackers had the ship's coordinates, including how fast it was going.[3] All they had to do was push a button, and "fire control" was locked on *Liberty*. They discovered Israel had done this from morning intercepts of Morse code that were sent via "SECRET CRYPTO CRITIC to Washington."

The intercepts revealed that the Israelis were going to attack "an American base," according to Ron Grantski.[4] This message was forwarded as top secret to the White House. (Both Dave Lewis and Bob Scarborough are dubious that there could have been an intercept of an Israeli message: for one thing, they were instructed not to intercept Israeli messages, for another they had no means of decrypting them. Further, when their equipment registered the fire lock, the Israelis were already firing at the *Liberty*.)

Grantski's information may be incomplete, but he is certain that there was such an intercept.[5] As Grantski explained to the author, "The American base was us!" Grantski, age nineteen at the time, says, "They jammed our radio frequencies and so knew everything about us."[6] In fact, the navy had provided Israel with the frequencies because the United States had joint ops with them. The radios were jammed on both the US Navy tactical and international maritime distress frequencies. Chief radioman Wayne Smith told author Stephen Green that five of *Liberty*'s six shore circuits were jammed, and whoever was doing it "went searching for the last circuit."[7]

Grantski was in T branch (techno branch) with TOP SECRET CRYPTO clearance and knew "through its [*Liberty*'s] radar they had fire control locked on us all morning long, which meant the plane could release its weapons within a few seconds." He kept calling the bridge, domain of the captain. "Someone is getting ready to shoot at us," he reported. The captain did not seem to take the warning seriously. Grantski says, "The Israelis didn't know we had this 'gear.'"[8]

Moe Shafer and Jim Kavanagh, doing the cleanup on the TRSSCOM basket, watched a twin engine prop plane circle the ship five times with its big doors open and "guys hanging out taking photographs." They waved. The pilot waved back.[9] The Star of David was visible on the hull. The last of the thirteen overflights on the morning of June 8 arrived at close to 1 p.m. Eight were low-level reconnaissance planes, passing as low as two hundred feet above the main mast.

Midmorning at the Israel Defense Forces war room, *Liberty* was designated with a green mark on the plot board as a "neutral American Vessel" as early as the first reconnaissance sortie. One surveillance pilot reported to Israeli naval headquarters that

AGTR-5

was written on the ship in ten-foot-high white letters on both sides of the bow and in three-foot letters on both sides of the stern, identifying it as an American ship.

Present in the Israel Defense Forces war room that morning was Major Seth Mintz.[10] Mintz had been born in the United States and had gone to Israel at the age of fifteen and a half, in 1962, to join a kibbutz. He was assigned to Kibbutz Nirum in the Negev at the edge of the Gaza Strip. His "kibbutz father" was Mordecai Gur (beni Moti), who, coincidentally, was one of the implementers of Operation Susannah. Mintz hoped to be a dual citizen, although the United States did not at the time recognize dual citizenship. He enlisted in the IDF reserves in 1965. When his enlistment time of one and a half years was up, he stayed on in Israel and attained the rank of major.

So on June 8, 1967, Seth Mintz was in the war room at Ramat Gan. Later, he said he could hear the pilots reporting during the attack that the ship flew an American flag. When Mintz entered the room, a conversation was going on about a US ship that had been under reconnaissance for several hours. The consensus in the room was that it was the USS *Liberty*.

A query to the US embassy yielded the reply that there was no US ship in that area. Aerial photographs were taken and ordered delivered to the US embassy in Tel Aviv. Mintz was present when word came back from the embassy by courier. The courier said, in Hebrew, "They still say it isn't a US ship."

There was talk of the ship being an Egyptian freighter, but Mintz believed "there was no question in anyone's mind but that it was a US ship." The attitude, however, was "Either it's our ally or it's our enemy."

Mintz was in the war room between three and a half and four hours. He concluded that attitude overruled conviction (laced with doubt), and the attack order was given. Later, he revealed June 7 embassy radio intercepts that showed that Israel attacked "with the knowledge that it was a US ship." They had consulted the standard compendium, *Jane's Fighting Ships*, and had identified the American flag. As reported in the *Washington Post* by Rowland Evans and Robert Novak ("Twenty-Five Years of Cover-Up"), Mintz said: "They knew . . . even when it was happening. Pilots in the Mirage attack were saying that it was an American ship. You could read the numbers on the side of the ship."[11] Mintz told Evans and Novak that "the order to sink the spy ship came not from the war room, but from superior officers. Immediately thereafter . . . many Israeli officers 'had doubts whether they had done the right thing.'"[12]

On November 7, 1991, Mintz in *Ha'aretz* expressed "grave anxiety over the media interested in him" with regard to the *Liberty* affair. "Everyone is after me now, and that is what I'm afraid of. I don't need the Mossad and Shin Bet knocking on my door."[13] Coolly, Israel claimed that *Liberty's* marker was removed from the "plotting board" because "the data was old" and identifications were supposedly erased after each watch and restored with each oncoming watch.[14]

Mintz later explained that each oncoming watch had to learn of *Liberty's* existence from scratch. Then updates of *Liberty's* whereabouts ceased altogether. Mintz stated that everyone in the Israeli war room and the attacking pilots knew they were attacking an American ship.

Mintz returned to the United States, where he encountered difficulties. In Washington at the invitation of Thames Television, he was told that he had been discredited and accused of having lied. No further interviews were conducted. He remembered the name of the person who attacked his credibility as a "Mr. Pennink." In June 1991, Mintz gave an interview where he offered the view that the United States, not Israel, was ultimately to blame for the attack, which "was ordered by a top military commander of Mossad"; the Prime Minister would not have been informed or asked before the order to "shut it down" was given from a war room near Tel Aviv.

Later, living in Houlton, Maine, where he owned a car dealership, Mintz attended a talk on the attack by *Liberty* Survivor Rich Carlson.[15] Mintz confirmed: the item representing *Liberty* on the board to show where they were was removed when the watch changed. Mintz was questioned by the FBI, but when agents returned a second time, Major Mintz had left the country. Having received threatening telephone calls from Israel, Mintz disappeared beneath the radar of historical accountability, and from then on remained unavailable for clarifications.[16]

By midmorning of June 8, Commander Pinchas Pinchasy, the naval liaison officer at Israeli air force headquarters, knew about the presence of an American ship. "I reported this detection to Naval Headquarters," he said, "and I imagine that Naval Headquarters received this report from Air Force ground control." Pinchasy had pulled out a copy of *Jane's Fighting Ships*, then sent a report to Israeli navy headquarters in Haifa, identifying an "electromagnetic audio surveillance ship of the U.S. Navy named *Liberty* whose marking was GTR-5."[17] So Israel's own records give the lie to Israel's later "apology" and assertion that the attack was an unpremeditated "accident" and they did not know that they were killing American sailors and attacking an American ship.

On *Liberty*, responding to the alarming fire control lock-in, Captain McGonagle ordered a General Quarters Drill, an exercise he had been calling regularly as *Liberty* moved toward its assigned position. This was at 1:02 p.m., less than an hour before the ship would be attacked. With the hindsight of McGonagle's having initiated the cover-up, the question is inevitable: what did he know? Meanwhile, in the sailors' quarters, some displayed little Star of David flags in support of the Six-Day War.

Sailors sunbathing on the morning of June 8, 1967. Left image: Lieutenant George Golden (background) and Lieutenant Commander Phillip Armstrong (foreground); right image: Captain William McGonagle. Officers sunbathed on the foredeck, and enlisted men had to remain aft. The captain had a special place reserved exclusively for himself. (Photos courtesy of Don Pageler and the USS *Liberty* Veterans Association.)

"General Quarters, General Quarters, all hands man your battle station!" was the order, followed by the sounding of the Klaxon. Each man had three minutes to reach his particular General Quarters duty station. Then all hatches were sealed, and the watertight integrity of the ship was established. The captain timed how long it would take for everyone to be prepared and in a state of readiness. It was, Phil Tourney writes in *Erasing the Liberty*, "almost as if Captain McGonagle knew we were to be attacked."[18]

By 1:45, the cryptologists had returned to work, reporting data. Arabic linguist Robert Wilson, in the analysis and reporting area, thought he might go up on deck for some sunbathing.[19] The sailors were mostly idle. McFarland was copying "low level material" from the Egyp-

tian army and air force, some Moroccan, some Algerian. Their surveillance was all about nothing. They had uncovered no smoking guns. They
tested weapons by firing at tin cans set afloat in the Mediterranean Sea—
with limited success.

Sailors of the USS *Liberty*. Left to right: Moe Shafer, unknown
name behind Moe, Ron Grantski, Paddy Rhodes, Jim Kavanagh,
Donald Lundin, Harold Six in front with glasses: "They shot our
life rafts out of the water." (Photo courtesy of Ron Grantski.)

Lieutenant James G. O'Connor had just been serving as officer of the
deck and, at the conclusion of the drill, had gone up to 04 level above
the bridge to see if he could locate approaching airplanes that had been
picked up on radar by the lookouts.

At 1:58, Captain McGonagle from the starboard wing of the bridge
observed a single jet aircraft. It was five to six miles from the ship, trav-

eling parallel to and in the same direction as *Liberty*. He had his binoculars out and trained on this plane and so didn't spot a second plane swooping in from the port side to launch a rocket, which exploded two levels below the bridge.

White hats, four sailors. Ranking below chief petty officer, they were enlisted men, grades E1–E6. Left to right: Don Pageler, Ron Grantski, Ken Ecker, and Ron Buck. (Photo courtesy of Ron Grantski.)

Rocket attack. (Photo courtesy of the National Security Agency.)

The single aircraft sighted approaching the ship at 1:58 had similar, if not identical, features to the jet aircraft that had orbited the ship at 10:30. The markings had been blackened over, and there was no doubt of its intent. The captain directed the officer of the deck to alert the forward gun mounts (two .50 machine guns). They could not raise the forward mounts. They were entirely helpless, between four and five hundred miles from the Sixth Fleet.

Without warning, *Liberty* was attacked by three Dassault Mirage III fighter planes, firing rockets, two thirty-millimeter cannon, and machine guns. Rockets hung under each wing. They were each armed with three thirty-millimeter cannon, one air-to-air missile, and two one-thousand-pound bombs, as well as four rocket pods with eighteen rockets apiece.[20]

Sailors saw flickers of light coming through the bulkhead, armor-piercing tracer bullets slicing through *Liberty*'s thin skin.[21] The metallic sound was if somebody was moving a chain back and forth—as if bullets were hitting the hull at an angle, not penetrating but being diverted down. Rockets blew out the portholes, sending broken glass everywhere. The flag, in tatters, was quickly replaced with *Liberty*'s holiday flag, seven feet by thirteen feet, a flag normally raised on holidays like the Fourth of July or Memorial Day when the ship was in port, never at sea. They raised the holiday colors on the number 4 port halyard. Later, Israeli denials that a flag had been visible were part of the cover-up. The flag was replaced twice, first by Russell David, who was the leading signalman. When that flag too was shot down by the Israelis, it was replaced by a flag hoisted by Frank Brown and Joe Meadors.[22] There was never a time when the American flag was not extended in the breeze.[23]

The later contention that the Israelis mistook *Liberty* for an Egyptian horse carrier half its size was preposterous, among the more transparent facets of the cover-up. They could not have been shooting at *El Quseir*, which was in port in Alexandria at the time because its boilers were inoperable. There was such a difference between the keel and waterline in the two ships that had they been shooting at the Quseir, they would have missed. *El Quseir* was an out-of-service Egyptian horse carrier designed to carry forty horses and their riders for the Egyptian cavalry in the 1920s.[24]

USS *Liberty* with American flag in the breeze.

The moon bounce system (AN/SRC33 XN-1) worked until it was blown off the ship by Israeli aircraft.

Those manning the four Browning machine guns on deck were among the first to die. The noise was so loud that sailors on the nearby submarine *Amberjack* thought they were being fired on by depth charges. As far as anyone knew, that submarine was there to tap into underwater cables in search of Soviet message traffic. Dave Lewis's brother, Captain Harold Stephen Lewis, administrative officer in charge of all submarines in the Mediterranean, told him that the *Amberjack* was not involved in an operation with *Liberty*. But those subs involved in black ops did not come under Harold's jurisdiction: he wouldn't have known.

Tom Schaaf confided to Dave Lewis that *Amberjack* was on a black mission at the time of the attack on *Liberty*. Captain Augustine Hubal insisted that *Amberjack* was fifty miles away; sometimes he said one hundred miles. Even Admiral Thomas Moorer, who became Chief of Naval Operations later in 1967, could not get answers from the submarine people in the Pentagon, apparently because *Amberjack* was involved in a black program using top secret photo equipment. On the matter of the relationship between *Liberty* and a submarine, the truth remains submerged.[25]

Later, Harold Lewis confirmed that Hubal was on a black op, perhaps tapping into underwater submarine cables. Dave says the strong suspicion was that they were engaged in "Operation Cyanide," a tapping of submarine cables "which had nothing to do with us."[26]

Nor was there any doubt as to the intent of the Mirage jets. The ship's photographer, Charles L. Rowley, climbed one deck to the signal bridge, the ship's highest platform, to take pictures. "Look out," someone yelled, "he's shooting!" Rowley tried to take a photograph of the planes, only for the Israelis to shoot the camera out of his hands. Russell David switched on a twelve-inch signal lamp and flashed *USS LIBERTY, U.S. NAVY SHIP* until he was hit by gunfire.

The attacking airplanes aimed heat-seeking missiles at the tuning section of every HF antenna. There was another message sent to LBJ on June 8, before the attack, information conveyed by Ron Grantski. It was that the Israelis were going to attack an "American base" disguised as Arabs. If they could pin the aggression on Egypt, the United States could legitimately send help for Israel to bomb Cairo. They said they had all the coordinates that would wipe "them" out, the "them" being the USS *Liberty*.

Fire control was indeed locked on the ship, and the Israelis had spent all those hours of surveillance getting the fire control locked on. Clyde Way said in his NSA interview they had "an Israeli voice communications link." It proved that the attack was not an accident. Ron Grantski concluded from his discovery of the fire control, "After the attack I knew about our country. We were expendable."[27]

That the Israelis had mentioned an "American base" is evidence coming from Ron Grantski, who conveyed to the author that he had overheard one of the T branchers reporting the fire control to the bridge. On the morning of the attack, a T brancher discovered through Morse code that Israel planned to attack "an American base," information that he kept to himself.

The tape was on a seven-and-a-half-inch reel. It was removed when they lost power, put in an envelope, and held. It was a possible Israeli intercept that they sent back to NSA, so *Liberty* had a voice intercept going at the time of the attack, before and during, until they lost all the antennas. Way told NSA he didn't know what happened to that tape.

Every antenna was hit twice. Dusty Rhodes said, "They snapped our antennas with the first pass, most all of them. Then they beat the hell out of the bridge because if you want to destroy a chain of command, that's where you're going to go for."

The machine on *Liberty* that registered the fire control was nicknamed SPOOFO, standing for AN/WLRI. "We could tell if somebody was locking on, was trying to get our speed and distance. If they came to attack, all they would have to do was push a button. It meant that they were getting ready to launch weapons at us," Grantski says. The signal was coming from the general direction of Tel Aviv. Grantski didn't know that the captain never informed Dave Lewis, who was in charge of station USN-855 and was to be informed; it was a court-martial offense for a T branch sailor not to inform him of such information. According to the chain of command, a T brancher should inform Dave Lewis before he told "the old man" (McGonagle).

Ron Grantski is the witness who heard the noise from the equipment (SPOOFO (An/WLRI) that registered that the ship had "fire control" locked on to them, coordinates, speed, and distance. SPOOFO was a receiver that picked up multiband receivers that covered all the frequencies. Grantski described it this way: "There's a loud noise, BLAT! that copied that lock-in. It gave off a signal. You had to be tuned to the frequency of the fire control radar to hear it." This machine told you that someone had locked into your coordinates and details.

So when the Israelis pushed the button that locked in *Liberty*'s coordinates, the ship's own surveillance equipment automatically copied that lock-in by giving off a signal. Technicians also translated the Israeli Morse code, which revealed that they planned to attack "an American base." According to the information on TRSSCOM, the Israel message was in numbers, each of which represented a letter of the alphabet, in blocks of five. The captain had been informed, but he said that the only planes in the area were Israeli—i.e., "friendlies"—so they had nothing to worry about. (A special antenna was required for ultra and very high frequencies.)

Unalarmed, the captain replied to Grantski that the only planes in the area were Israeli jets, and the only boats were Israeli boats. It was beyond William McGonagle's limited imagination and flimsy political education that they could conceivably be unfriendly. So chatter centered on the fact that the Egyptians wouldn't dare attack us since the Israelis were right there. And wasn't the Sixth Fleet fifteen minutes away by air?

Paddy Rhodes was on the damage control team. A receive antenna (blue), a whip, remained intact, which Dave McFeggan suggests reflects one of his own secret CIA functions, to save one antenna. The red light was off on the TRSSCOM parabolic satellite dish, which meant that it was not transmitting.

It wouldn't have made any difference. Three Mirage jets had come roaring over the ship, firing rockets, cannon, and machine guns. Rockets hung under each wing. They were as black as U-2s, empty of identity as the planes that had flown to do aerial photography for Israel from Torrejon. The sound of the Israeli machine guns firing was like ball bearings hitting glass.

The captain was on the bridge with Lloyd Painter, watching the jets bear down. Everyone assumed the attacker had to be either Egypt or the Soviet Union; Egypt believed that US military assistance in the form of carrier aircraft had been "involved in the Israeli attack," a charge the Joint Chiefs denied—on behalf of the Sixth Fleet. Two fifty-five-gallon gasoline drums stowed below the bridge on the port side were set on fire by an exploding rocket on *Liberty*'s portside 01 level.

A bomb hit the whaleboat on the starboard side aft of the bridge, throwing the executive officer, Lieutenant Commander Phillip M. Armstrong, back into the bridge. He tried to jettison the burning gasoline drums, which had been hit with napalm and were burning. Armstrong was trying to get the drums off the ship before they exploded. In the attempt, he was hit by a rocket that shattered his legs. There were no visible wounds, but his heart was leaking.[28]

Armstrong was talking to Dave Lewis, and the next minute he was dead. He was killed by a small piece of shrapnel that severed an artery in his chest. His autopsy would reveal that his chest had filled with blood, putting pressure on his heart, which stopped it.

James O'Connor remembered that he had been standing up there "trying to be John Wayne," ready to dive down on the bridge, and as he fell, he looked up and saw the American flag flying, not obscured by smoke, as the Israelis later mythologized. It was "standing straight up." During the attack, O'Connor fell down a ladder and lost all feeling from the waist down. He dragged himself into the Combat Information Center behind the bridge, where the floor was soon awash with blood. It was his. He had two great big holes in his back, and blood was pouring out. He told a young ensign to take off his T-shirt and stuff it into the holes in his back. The bleeding stopped. O'Connor survived.

XO Lieutenant Commander Armstrong with Chiefs Carlyle F. Lamkin, Joseph Allen Benkert, and Melvin Douglas Smith. Armstrong and Smith died in the attack. (Photo courtesy of the USS *Liberty* Veterans Association.)

The motor whaleboat on the starboard side on the 02 level aft of the bridge was set ablaze. The first pass set the captain's "gig," which could carry thirty men to shore, on fire and blew it off the side of the ship. The ship would sustain 821 rocket and machine gun holes. The bridge started burning, and the captain yelled to come and help fight the fires.

The captain's gig. (Photo courtesy of Commander David Edwin Lewis, US Navy [Ret.].)

The jet fighters began delivering heat-seeking missiles to the coil of each of the forty-five deck antennas, a single-minded effort to eliminate any possibility that *Liberty* could call successfully for help. They knew exactly where to strike the coil that generated heat at the base of the antenna. They had to pick out a small tuning section of the HF antennas. Every antenna and its transmitter was at once rendered inoperative, cutting off contact between *Liberty* and the rest of the world. One inactive antenna did not generate heat and so was not susceptible to the heat-seeking missiles utilized by the Israelis. It was not destroyed because it wasn't hot. If it had been operative, Dave Lewis speculated, no SOS would have gone out, and all the sailors would have found themselves at the bottom of the sea, as was obviously intended.[29]

View from forecastle looking aft toward superstructure(83)

Bridge area seen from helicopter(76)

Rocket holes, port side(96)

Rocket holes. There were 821. (Photo courtesy of Don Pageler.)

Systematically, as they struck the coil of each antenna, they aimed at every moving target on deck, slicing the men with shrapnel, like hunters in a forest. Stephen Toth tried to take pictures of the planes and was killed by a rocket.[30]

Those manning the four Browning .50 caliber machine guns on deck were eliminated. Scrambling, bleeding, their bodies ripped open by shrapnel, the sailors rushed for cover. Soon the deck was awash with blood and body parts. Twenty-one-year-old Larry Weaver, caught out on deck, could find no shelter but behind a bollard, an object around which you wrap a rope or the chain used to hold the anchor. His eyes met those of an encroaching pilot. Weaver gave him the finger, at which point the pilot zeroed in on him mercilessly, firing his machine gun, round after round, until Weaver lay helpless and bleeding on the deck. He says he stanched the phosphorus fire on his stomach with his blood.[31] Multiple pieces of shrapnel had penetrated his body, some to remain for a lifetime. The blood of helpless, trapped sailors flowed as the wounded joined the dead in a horrific scene reminiscent of Pieter Bruegel's painting *The Triumph of Death*. Working on the bleeding and wounded sailors, Dr. Kiepfer was hit by more shrapnel.

The dead of the USS *Liberty*.

During a second wave of strafings and firings, Super Mystère jets sent canisters of napalm that burned hot and clean onto the deck. When sailors arrived topside with hoses to put out the fires, the planes, swooping low, targeted the hoses and the firefighters, and riddled the hoses with holes and the men with shrapnel. It was the war in Vietnam, turned against American innocents. When sailors carried stretchers onto the deck to rescue the wounded, the planes took aim at the stretcher bearers. There were to be no survivors.

Ron Grantski was among those who tried to fight the fire, which was like jelly, burning his hands.

With all this firepower, there was virtually no margin for error. Sinking the ship and drowning everyone on it had been, it seemed, a no-brainer. Yet these navy professionals—some in their forties, having served in World War II, like chief engineer George Golden; some in their thirties; some still in their teens—kept the USS *Liberty* afloat. During World War II, no victory hull that took a torpedo hit didn't go down. Golden had joined the navy at the age of seventeen after the attack on Pearl Harbor. He had survived two torpedo attacks in World War II, had served in Korea and Vietnam, and earned before it was over thirty-four medals including two Purple Hearts. He became executive officer after Phillip Armstrong died, and acting commanding officer for a short period.[32]

The air force contributed to identifying the assailants, who had arrogantly believed they could conceal their identities. Based in Iraklion, the capital of Crete, where the United States maintained a base at Souda Bay, Captain Richard Block, who was duty watch captain with the USAF 6931 Security Squadron and an expert in signals intelligence, served on a C-130 reconnaissance aircraft. Reporting to the National Security

Agency, at the time of the attack Block was on duty listening to Israeli ground-to-air communications.

Block had been the first intelligence officer at the onset of the Six-Day War to send a CRITIC message to the White House, with the statement "Israel Attacks Egypt," leaving no doubt as to who was the aggressor. Block's reports went to the Air Force All Source Reconnaissance Center in San Antonio. Block then produced intercepts of an Israeli pilot, who radioed his controller at the Israel Defense Forces headquarters.

Unlike the USS *Liberty*, Block had a Hebrew translator in his unit as well as an Arab linguist permanently on duty. And so they translated a deeply distressed pilot questioning his handler at ground control. "It's an American ship! It's an American ship! It's an American flag!" he cried, assuming there must have been some mistake.

Air force intelligence also intercepted the ground control's reply: "Never mind, hit it!" "You have your orders!" "Attack it! Follow orders!"[33] When the pilot continued to object, the controller became more vehement. "DO attack this ship!" he said. Block sent a transcript of this conversation to President Lyndon Johnson as a CRITIC, a message that went directly to the White House.

Captain Block concluded that the attack on the USS *Liberty* was not only premeditated but was a pretext, like the 1964 incident at the Gulf of Tonkin when an American ship falsely accused the North Vietnamese of firing on it, like "Remember the Maine." Of the three pilots attacking the USS *Liberty*, each asked that their orders be confirmed. They had been ordered to aim for the antennas and radar-tracking gear. One was a native-born Israeli, another a Vietnam vet who had served with the US Navy Air Corps.[34]

"It was a setup," Block told me, which was the identical conclusion drawn by *Liberty*'s chief engineer, George Golden. In addition to the C-130s, the air force had an eavesdropping CD-121, with Hebrew linguists aboard. When the pilot said, "I'm not doing it," Block's NSA friends "went nuts." He said, "It's an American ship. He definitely identified it as an American ship."

All around the area, the Israelis had been identified as the attackers, and the victim as an "American ship." Block's superiors reacted fiercely to his saying Israel was the aggressor: "If you're wrong, you're dead meat." Before it was over, they gave him an Air Force Commendation Medal for his actions during the Six-Day War. But it was kept top secret.

I asked Block: "There's no way they would do this without a handshake from the United States?"

"Absolutely," Block said. "Johnson and McNamara were involved up to their smelly armpits. . . . The whole thing fell apart because the captain, McGonagle, and his men saved the ship. They did everything in their power to do the ship."[35]

There was also a navy plane with Hebrew linguists aboard hovering overhead. Charles B. Tiffany was flying in a navy EC-121 electronic surveillance aircraft twenty miles off the Egyptian coast when he was warned of "something crazy on UHF." The code they were given meant "You are about to be shot down." Tiffany thought the source was Egyptian or Soviet fighters. "Little did I know that a fleet of Mirages were heading to kill us because we had just stumbled on the *Liberty* slaughters," he wrote in a memo titled "The *Liberty* Cover Up and Me."[36]

Tiffany was a flight commander on Crete. His knowledge was limited to "Airborne intelligence gathering, UAR radar plotting and a few other messages." He knew of Operation Cyanide from conversations. "At that moment, we all knew, including full Colonel Rosenow, the Pentagon Special Security Officer (NSA) that the Israelis had conducted their June 1967 dawn raid on the Egyptian Air Force by filtering through Egyptian radar gaps previously sensed by the US that no one else should have known about, not even the Israelis." The plan included a preemptive strike on the Soviet Union immediately afterward.

Aboard an EC-121M aircraft taking off originally from Rota for the Naval Security Group and tasked to the East Med was an American Zionist named Marvin E. Nowicki, who was the "chief Hebrew-language analyst aboard." He was trained in Russian as well and reported to a laundry list of "consumers," including COMSIXTHFLT, CINCUS-NAVEUR, CIA, and the Joint Chiefs.

In search of Russian voice activity in VHF, dubbing himself a "spook linguist," Nowicki on June 5 was tasked to fly into the combat zone in the dead of night to the coasts of Egypt and Israel.[37] On Crete, he "reported to the area off the coasts of Egypt and Israel, equipped with a special piece of intercept equipment called the 'Big Look' to intercept, identify and reverse-locate the source of radar signals."

Nowicki asked himself: It was pitch-black, in the middle of a war zone. "What in the devil were we doing out here?"[38] They also monitored the Israelis using UHF on June 6, watching as the Egyptians "were shot out of the sky by IAF Mirage aircraft." On June 8, they were "wheels in the well" at midday when Nowicki received a call on the secure intercom from a Hebrew linguist to the effect that he had "odd activity" on UHF.

Nowicki flew over only to observe "Israeli aircraft completing an attack on some object," having "heard a couple of references to the flag during an apparent attack." What could the "object" flying an American flag diagonally to El Arish be? Nowicki requested the frequency, rolled up to it, and "sure as the devil Israeli aircraft were completing an attack on some object." The ship, identified as flying an American flag, and being attacked by what would soon be air and surface units, was of course the USS *Liberty*.[39]

Nowicki's reports would reach as far as Dwight Porter, the American ambassador to Lebanon. Porter learned that the air attack had been led by a pilot who informed his controlling officer that it was an American ship, flying an American flag, and who expressed great reluctance to attack, but did. Porter insisted that there was no case of mistaken identity. He confided in William Chandler, president and CEO of the Trans-Arabian Pipeline Company at the time. He spoke in 1986: "Bill, you probably wondered why our Beirut embassy was so large, with so many people. We were the communications center for the USG in the Middle East, and we had a highly sophisticated communications system, capable of listening in on everything going on in the area, including Hebrew. . . . On the day of the attack on the *Liberty* we heard the pilot of an Israeli aircraft say to his ground control: 'But Sir, it's an American ship: I can see the flag.' And we heard the ground control respond: 'Never mind! Hit it!'"[40]

Oliver Kirby, a former NSA Ops boss who was called back to NSA in 1967, said, "I can tell you for an absolute certainty that they knew they were attacking an American ship."[41]

Through navy monitoring, another of the attacking pilots was heard to complain that he wished he had "iron bombs," heavier weapons, the more efficiently to send *Liberty* to the bottom of the sea. James Ronald Gotcher, a US Air Force intelligence analyst with the 6924 Security Squadron at Da Nang Air Force Base in Vietnam, heard the same intercepts. Horrified by the attack, people in air force intelligence, Gotcher later said, were taking bets on which Israeli city would be obliterated by morning. It did not occur to anyone that so purposeful an attack could be an "accident," let alone that the United States would not immediately retaliate.

A few months later, Army colonel Patrick Lang saw these intercepts during a course taught by NSA people from Fort Meade at Fort Holabird, Maryland. The flight leader spoke to his base to report that he had the ship in view.[42]

The one medical doctor aboard, thirty-year-old Richard Kiepfer, created a "hospital" on the mess deck, where he placed men with their insides lying on their chests as he struggled to save their lives. Aided only by corpsmen (nurses) and sailors he pressed into service, Dr. Kiepfer was alone to tend to the wounded. Everyone became a doctor, and Clyde Way said that he "learned how to do a tracheotomy. We dressed wounds, we did stitches, anything we needed to do to help that doctor."[43]

While he was operating on a sailor, Kiepfer was hit with eleven pieces of shrapnel in his abdomen. He received a gunshot to his leg, a variety of burns, and a broken kneecap.[44] His memories were vivid: "While I was on the deck, I got hit by a fifty caliber machine gun bullet to my leg that came from the torpedo boats. I was bleeding into my shoes and not until the next day when I was able to lie down did the bleeding slow down."

"All I could think about was keeping limbs attached to sailors," he said later.[45] He self-injected morphine and carried on. The pain was intense. The fragments that penetrated him were so hot they cauterized his wounds. He applied surgical dressings. He grabbed a life jacket and strapped it on as tightly as he could to control the bleeding. Then he gave himself a shot of morphine. Dr. Kiepfer remained on his feet for the next twenty-eight hours. Two corpsmen worked by his side.

"It was important that the doctor not look as if he was injured," he said. Captain McGonagle ordered him, "Take it [the life vest] off or people will think the ship is sinking."[46] Richard Kiepfer ignored him and walked away, eager to tend to what would be the 195 wounded.

Dr. Kiepfer, a true hero of this story, performed surgeries and blood transfusions through the night of June 8 into June 9. One among many untrained volunteers to assist Dr. Kiepfer was a college dropout named Don Pageler. The sailor receiving the transfusion had both kidneys shot out. "I have to sew him up," Dr. Kiepfer said. "I can't save him." Pageler, like others, drew the obvious conclusion as Dr. Kiepfer's efforts lasted through the night: "The White House left us for dead."[47]

Don Pageler in Rota, Spain, a subtender and submarine in the background. (Photo courtesy of Don Pageler.)

"In LBJ's mind we were just an average day's losses in Vietnam. I doubt Israel would have attacked without the knowledge or complicity of our State Department's willingness to sacrifice a few hundred sailors to have a 'stabilized' Middle East and all that oil," Dr. Kiepfer concluded.[48]

In *Liberty*'s research spaces, CTs began to destroy the key cards. When a signal is put in, the key card sends a "baud" to its intended location. A crypto machine scrambles the bauds, and the receiving crypto machine descrambles them and sends them to the teletypewriter. There were 7.42 bauds to every letter. The radioman topside sets up the circuit and knows from the key card where to send it. The recipient, which was the NSA back at Fort Meade, had to have the same key card to add the baud, and then they would get plain language in English.

En route to their destination, the sailors on the USS *Liberty* learned that there had been a break in diplomatic communications between the United States and the North African countries, such as Morocco and Tunisia. Everybody was breaking diplomatic relations with the United States because they thought the Americans were helping Israel with planes that took photographs of the Egyptian airfields, which was true.

As the planes struck the ship, fore and aft, panic registered on everyone's faces. Then emergency destruction was ordered. Protection of the cryptographic equipment was of the first importance. They used an ax. The key cards went into burn bags, destined for the deck incinerator, only they couldn't get to it because the Israeli jets were shooting everyone who came on deck.

The sailors set fires in the passageway to burn the bags, creating dark clouds of smoke. They took full bags on deck to jettison them, but no more than six bags made it. There was a lead weight in the bottom of ten to fifteen pounds. A bag weighed two hundred pounds, maybe more. After they managed to get some into the sea, they decided not to jeopardize lives to throw those bags over.[49] They were unable to destroy all the machines.

Part of the air attack involved the jamming of the US Navy frequencies. Dave Lewis says we had told the Israelis what they were, and they were jamming them. More specifically, Richard Sturman said that it had to have taken time for the attackers to find the frequencies on which a source could broadcast.[50] The search must have been made by shore-based Israeli radio installations before the attack, further evidence that the attack had been premeditated.

A buzzing sound was all you heard on the receivers. When the sailors tried to get the SOS out, all they heard was a buzz saw. But the planes couldn't both fire and cut off the jammers at the same time, and that allowed the ship to send out the distress signal. There was a space of a few seconds.

The sailor in charge of the electronics equipment was Terence Halbardier. Halbardier had repaired a transmitter, and he discovered that one antenna was cold because it had never been hooked up, so heat-seeking missiles didn't find it. They had one transmitter and one antenna. Halbardier connected a coaxial cable from the transmitter to the antenna. He was hit three times by shrapnel from things exploding near him. Under heavy Israeli rocket fire, Halbardier walked across the deck dragging a cable to connect the surviving antenna with a transmitter in the after deckhouse. Halbardier ran some "spare co-ax from the base of the antenna tuner directly to a transmitter in the after deckhouse."[51] He managed to get off a high-frequency SOS during a lull when the jets were trying to reload.

Otherwise, the Israelis jammed all the ship's transmitting frequencies. The navy had provided Israel, as an ally, with these frequencies. One of the pilots was a US citizen (Amnon Tavni), and when the ship was identified, he refused to comply and so was court-martialed and imprisoned. The United States made no attempt to secure his freedom.

In 2011, Halbardier, a petty officer third class who was an electronics technician, received a Silver Star, recommended by Jim Ennes and Dave Lewis, for repairing the damaged antenna in an open deck area during heavy aerial attacks. He risked his life, being hit three times by rocket fire. Halbardier had shut down one antenna because there were problems in the tuner. Offline, it had not been hit by the Israeli rockets because it wasn't generating any heat. Because it was inactive, and not generating any heat, the Israelis missed it.

In summary, Halbardier had grabbed a roll of cable and run out onto the open deck to attach new connecting coaxial cable to this antenna and "jury rig" the spare coax from the base of the antenna tuner directly to a transmitter in the After Deckhouse in the main transmitter room so that a radioman could get out the SOS. Spotting this moving target, the gunner on one of the attacking planes attempted to take him down.

Radioman second class Richard Sturman says they were jammed on all their tactical frequencies. When the Israelis fired cannon and rockets, there was no jamming. When they stopped, they jammed. They didn't want the radio jamming to interfere with the guidance of the missiles.

It wasn't easy. Wayne Smith figured out that the frequency dial was one kilocycle off. He adjusted it, and the radio operators tried again to send out the SOS. The message was not encrypted but in "plain language": "*Liberty* is under attack by unknown enemy air and surface units. Request assistance." The reply to the SOS was "Help Is On The Way." With a humility characteristic of these sailors, Halbardier claimed he was "just a guy from Texas who could do a lot with simple stuff like baling wire."[52]

Further obfuscation derived from Lewis's assistant, Maurice Bennett, who claimed that the attackers were Soviet MIGs. According to Jim Ennes, Bennett kept himself off the watch bell and didn't stand bridge watches as everyone else did. He told Dave Lewis that "he was scared. He couldn't take that responsibility."

During the attack, Lloyd Painter also observed Bennett hiding in a storage locker or closet. Ennes says he hid there until the attack was over.[53]

Bennett, George Golden told A. J. Cristol, was a spook rather than a ship's officer, a fitting source for Cristol, whose work was sponsored and controlled by the state of Israel. Dave Lewis says that Bennett ingratiated himself with XO Armstrong and his drinking group rather than with Lewis, his immediate superior.

After the attack, Bennett approached George Golden, complaining, "How come everyone got a medal for heroism and I didn't?" "What did you do?" Golden said. "Write it up and I'll see if it flies." Bennett produced so glowing a report that he was recommended for a Silver Star, only for the Chief of Naval Operations, Admiral McDonald, to downgrade it to a Bronze Star. Still, Bennett came away with a Silver Star, courtesy of Admiral William Inman Martin, who was part of the cover-up.

"Any station, this is 'Rockstar' [the ship's code name], we are under attack by unknown sources," the caller cried. The signal went out rapidly because a decade earlier President Eisenhower had put the CRITICOM system in place, which meant any Naval Security Group message went out as a CRITIC to both the USS *Saratoga* and the USS *America*, and straight to the Joint Chiefs and the president as information addees. This was how Robert McNamara knew that the men had survived. A CRITIC message went automatically because an act of war, which includes the launching of planes, requires that a CRITIC message go to Washington. That CRITIC shuts down all other communications en route. The message was a teletype with "CRITIC" typed at the top, which meant it went directly to the White House within ten minutes, the established goal. McNamara's reply came by the AUTOVON system in the form of a telephone call.

In plain language—not encrypted; there was no time for that—the SOS went out to the Sixth Fleet: "*Liberty* is under attack by unknown enemy air and surface units. Request assistance." The USS *Saratoga* demanded an identifying code: "Give us your authentication." Someone managed to look it up. Still, Rockstar could not identify by whom she was being attacked, although the Sixth Fleet heard the sound of exploding rockets on the transmission. Reportedly, Captain Donald D. Engen of the USS *America* hesitated, asking Admiral Lawrence Geis, "Should we not clear this with our political masters in Washington?," to which, according to this source, Geis replied in the affirmative.[54]

The Mayday went out nine minutes into the attack.

The pilots who were ordered to attack the USS *Liberty* met with unhappy consequences. One pilot, Amnon Tavni (a.k.a. Even Tov), the aforementioned American citizen, told California representative Paul "Pete" N. McCloskey and a lawyer that when he came upon the ship, he saw immediately that it was an American ship.[55] Tavni was the executive officer of a six- or eight-plane attack wing. He was twenty-two years old, born in a town near Tel Aviv but grew up on a kibbutz.[56] By age forty-one, he believed Israel, to be secure, had two choices: "either expand to include all of Palestine and force the Arabs out of the country, or accept a Palestinian state on the West Bank and Gaza, but either way Jerusalem always belonging to us." He had seen the American flag and refused to join in the attack, but been ordered to do so by his base commander. He saw both black and white sailors on the deck, he claimed, so it had to have been an American ship. There was a small American flag at first, but they ran up a much bigger American flag (the holiday flag).

He refused to attack when he was ordered to attack anyway. When he went home, he was taken into custody. Tavni's subsequent court-martial in Israel was for "refusing orders" and "making a flight without permission" (presumably returning home).

In view of his outstanding record, Tavni was given no prison sentence. His second-in-command had refused to participate in the attack, as he had. He was handsome, suave, and, as his lawyer, Joseph Adragna, thought, "For real." He moved to the United States after that, entering the country on a false passport. He obtained a green card but surrendered it upon his last entry to the United States, when he traveled on an Israel Defense Forces colonel's visa. From the time he refused to fire on the USS *Liberty*, his life took irregular turns as he straddled the boundaries of the law and moved between the United States and Israel.

Tavni was arrested in New York on a bank fraud scheme. He had become acquainted with people doing business with Chemical Bank and discovered a way to engage in transactions that allowed him to extract large sums from its banking system. He enlisted other people in this purpose, apparently including several women, and it was one of these contacts that led to his arrest and conviction. He received a ten-year sentence, and since he was an Israeli citizen, he would be reviewed for possible deportation. Tavni complained of anti-Semitism at Springfield federal prison and was told if he wrote any more letters to the editor, he would spend the rest of his sentence in solitary confinement ("the hole").

He was interviewed by Rep. Pete McCloskey, who had taken an interest in the *Liberty* events, at Springfield prison, where Tavni, now known by his real name, Even Tov, told McCloskey he feared for his life from Mossad.[57] McCloskey had a friend contact Tov and so learned: "Tov wishes to remain anonymous because he feels he could be assassinated by the Mossad if his whereabouts were known to them and the fact that he is a potential revealer of the fact that the attack on the *Liberty* was intentional." He requested being placed in a witness protection program and to testify before a congressional committee, requests that were denied. The lawyers with whom Tov was in contact told McCloskey: "We are fearful that if the Israelis should ever learn that Tov has made contact with the crew of the U.S.S. *Liberty*, his life might indeed be in danger."[58] McCloskey facilitated his release and was in constant touch with Stan Aderman of the Anti-Defamation League of B'nai B'rith.

Just as Tov was about to be released, a representative of Thames Television in London named Adrian Pennick called him at Springfield, at McCloskey's suggestion. It was July 23, 1986. When Tov called Pennick back, it was only to deny that he had ever been an Israeli pilot or participated in the *Liberty* attack. "That may have been Mr. McCloskey's interpretation," Tov said. In a subsequent letter to McCloskey, dated August 4, 1986, and signed "Amnon Even-Tov (Tavni)," he said he would not participate in the Thames Television documentary until he was "given the opportunity to prove (undoubtedly) my true identity and what my court martial, while serving in the Israeli air force, was all about. . . . With all respect and understanding, Mr. Ennas [*sic*] fails to tell the truth in his book. As any other Israeli citizen, I am fully convinced that the attack on the liberty was nothing but a terrible mistake of identification. There could not be any other reason."[59]

After he completed his sentence, Even Tov, a.k.a. Amnon Tavni, was escorted to New York by a federal agent. He had served five years and was deported to Israel in 1986. In a later letter, dated October 16, 1991, an obviously terrified Tov repeated the cover story: "the attack on the *Liberty* was nothing but a terrible mistake of identification."

Confirming Tov's story was Seth Mintz, who had been in the

Israeli war room on the morning of the attack (and who claimed a "Mr. Pennink" had attacked his credibility, perhaps misremembering the name of Adrian Pennick). Asked about Even Tov, Mintz said, "He may very well not be alive." He felt that Tov's "fears were justified." In Washington, Mintz said that two Israeli pilots received sentences of eighteen years at hard labor for refusing to take part in the attack. Former Mossad officer Victor Ostrovsky echoed Mintz and told Representative McCloskey that "Tavni's story was credible" and that there were secret courts-martial, as Tov had alleged. Ostrovsky had been born in Canada in 1949, migrated to Israel as a fervent Zionist, served in both the Israeli army and navy, and was then recruited into Mossad, which he served for seven years. Disaffected, and with considerable trepidation, he returned to Canada.[60]

Let us return to the attack itself. During this terrifying hour and a half, one communicator rolled into a ball, having defecated in his pants, and crawled into a corner. Lieutenant Commander Lewis gave him a boot and told him to get on the circuit and send out an SOS. "I can't. I don't have keying material," he pleaded, which meant cryptographic keying material to keep the message secret. "I don't care," Lewis told him angrily. "Send it in plain language. We break the law now!"

The sailor died complying with that order. Eventually everyone in the communications shack was killed. The next message from *Liberty* reported: "Hit by torpedo starboard side. Listing badly. Need assistance immediately."

At 10:13 a.m. eastern standard time on June 8, the day of the attack, Admiral Martin reported to the Pentagon that Sixth Fleet planes were at the scene—a falsehood, and directly following LBJ's lie to Alexei Kosygin that US planes were flying to *Liberty*.[61] These discrepancies reflect nothing so much as that the survival of the ship was unanticipated by those in highest authority. Robert McNamara learned of the attack by 8:30 EST, while the Pentagon was not officially notified until 9 a.m. McNamara's chief public relations officer, Phil Goulding, in his 1970 book called *Confirm or Deny*, poses questions that were logical only for someone who was out of the loop: "How in the name of heaven was the Pentagon to learn whether the attackers knew that the *Liberty* was an American ship? How was it to know why the attack had been made and who ordered it?"[62]

Goulding had been placed in an embarrassing position by his boss, McNamara. He admits that when he left the government nineteen months after the attack, "we still did not have from Israel the answers to why it happened or who ordered it or who was to blame."[63] In his naïveté, Goulding is honest. "By 1970, he was fully immersed in the cover-up," Goulding acknowledges.

Before his departure from the Pentagon at about at 8 p.m. on June 8, Admiral McDonald discussed the matter with "Op-002." Op-001 is Chief of Naval Operations, and 002 is Vice Chief of Naval Operations. (Dave Lewis was Op-94GR, his official CNO title.) McDonald said that in effect he saw no justification for *Liberty* to operate along the coast of Syria, Israel, or Egypt; that the hazards were too great; and that the political cost was by no means worth the intelligence that might be gained. His assistant wrote in his memo that Admiral McDonald "notes especially that the presence of *Liberty* close-in to the coast in these waters runs counter to the great effort that the United States is presently making to refute Arab allegations that U.S. Naval Forces have participated in the hostilities [of the Six-Day War] and our efforts to prove that no U.S. ships or aircraft had been in these waters for several days."[64]

McDonald's assistant had left the building, as had General Steakley, director of the Joint Reconnaissance Center. But his deputies, Captain Vineyard and Captain Rorex, came to Op-002's office at about 6:40 p.m. Op-002 outlined McDonald's position and requested Vineyard to clear with the NMCC Deputy Director of Operations to release a directive to the Commander in Chief, European Command (CINCEUR) to order

Liberty to stay at least one hundred miles from Egypt, Syria, and Israel, and at least twenty-five miles from Cyprus.

Vineyard balked, saying he did not see the need to send a message. He did agree to phone CINCEUR immediately for passing to *Liberty*, something John S. McCain would not do. The Joint Chiefs' report records some of McDonald's concerns: "Chief Naval Operations again required his staff to press for modification of USS *Liberty*'s movements, at least to conform to SIXTHFLT."[65]

On that evening, Chuck Rowley received a message marked "For Command Officer's Eyes Only" for delivery to Captain McGonagle. The message was sealed in an envelope. Rowley had been cleared for a submarine project under the code name "Cyanide," as had O'Connor, Carpenter, and Dodd. Shortly before the attack, he intercepted some very low frequency signals, which he reported by FLASH message. He said he learned later that the president was awakened because of his message.

The forensic evidence that this was a premeditated attack is overwhelming. In Omaha, Nebraska, at Offutt Air Force Base, Stephen Forslund, an intelligence analyst for the 544th Air Reconnaissance Technical Wing of the Strategic Air Command, viewed an NSA transcript of raw translations of intercepts of communications between the attacking jet aircraft and their ground controllers.

There was a "detectable level of frustration evident in the transmissions over the fact that the aircraft were unable to accomplish the mission quickly and totally." Forslund was serving as an all source intelligence analyst for the US Air Force during the Six-Day War: "I and many others like me," he would say, "read transcripts of the air-to-air and air-to-ground communications of the fighters who attacked the USS *Liberty*. We read these in real time during the day the attack occurred."

Forslund remembered that on the day of the attack on *Liberty*, he read yellow teletype sheets that spewed from the machines in front of me all day. . . . The teletypes were raw translations of intercepts of Israeli air-to-air and air-to-ground communications between jet aircraft and their ground controller. . . . The transcripts made specific reference to the efforts to direct the jets to the target, which was identified as American numerous times by the ground controller. Upon arrival, the aircraft specifically identified the target and mentioned the American flag was flying. . . . There were frequent operational transmissions from the pilots to the ground base describing the strafing runs.

The ground control began asking about the status of the target and whether it was sinking. They stressed that the target must be sunk and leave no trace.

Forslund also learned of a US State Department message to Israel stating that the United States had full knowledge of what had occurred on the attack on the *Liberty* and strongly warning Israel "to cease activities immediately."

That night, Forslund saw a segment on the evening news referring, vaguely, to a mistaken attack by Israel upon an American ship off Sinai. The next day, a small newspaper article referred to an "accidental attack" on the USS *Liberty*. For thirty-six years after that, he heard nothing. Inadvertently, he had exposed the cover-up and happened upon evidence of a deliberate attack. "We all lost our virginity that day," Forslund said.[66]

Further evidence of US government foreknowledge of the attack is that in the early morning hours of June 8, the US nuclear force was at the ready, on call. A unit of the US Air Force, the 601 Direct Air Support Squadron, based in Germany, was placed on standby alert. The 744th Bomb Squadron 4556 Strategic Air Wing at Beale Air Force Base, north of Sacramento, was also placed on alert. Air force pilot Jim Nanjo came forward to author Peter Hounam and recounted that he was sent to take off in his nuclear-armed plane between 2 and 4 a.m., Pacific Time. Nanjo had two and a half minutes to dash to his plane, start the engines, and listen for an incoming message. Nanjo took his H-bomb–configured B-52 to the end of the runway and waited four hours for the coded message from Offutt Air Force Base. He would then proceed toward target, where he would "deliver nuclear weapons."[67]

The "go-code," which could be given only upon direct orders of the president of the United States, never arrived. Then Nanjo was ordered to stand down. Neither in Germany nor in Sacramento were the pilots ever briefed as to why they had been placed on alert. Bryce Lockwood subsequently learned that the entire nuclear force of the United States was on alert starting the morning of June 8.[68]

The US embassy in Cairo was informed that an attack on Cairo was imminent. The two best sources for the planes on their way to Cairo being nuclear armed are the captain of the USS *America*, Donald D. Engen, and officer Charles B. Tiffany, who reported that "aircraft were launched 'hot' and headed toward Cairo with nukes, only to be called back."[69]

Later, NSA releases posted on the NSA website would participate in the cover-up and the operation itself. An Israeli pilot says, choking on disinformation, "People jumped into the water from the warship" and "the ship has now been identified as an Egyptian ship." Neither of these statements bears any relation to the truth. An air controller orders, "You will try to pull the people out of the water." In reality, no one jumped into the water.

Liberty was described as "smoking a lot," the better to support Israeli disinformation that they couldn't read the hull number, or spot the American flag, and so struck the ship by mistake, not knowing it was an American ship. One pilot tells another, "When you pick up the first man, find out what his nationality is." So a tale was spun. "If they speak Arabic,

Egyptians, you're taking them to El Arish. If they speak English and are non-Egyptians, you're taking them to LOD," the airport 9.3 miles southeast of Tel Aviv.

Finally, the interceptions reveal Israeli ground control to be particularly brutal, with ugly sexual innuendos. Shmuel Kislev, chief air controller at general headquarters in Tel Aviv, is particularly heartless, as his conversations with his cohort "Menachem" reveal. Menachem replies, "She's not shooting back." Kislev says only, "Great, wonderful. She's burning! She's burning!" Kislev tells Menachem that if "ROYAL [the Mystère jets] has napalm, it would be more efficient. You can sink her," he adds.[70]

Kislev wants to know: "Is he screwing her?," to which Menachem adds, "He's going down on her with napalm all the time." At another point, Kislev picks up an internal phone to speak with his superior at Air Control Central. "What do you say?" he asks. But no one wants responsibility. "I don't say. I don't want to know," the superior says. The disinformation was in place from the start. Kursa, the Israeli in charge of the first jets, the Mirages, insists on the tape, courtesy of a transcript provided by the *Jerusalem Post*, saying, "It's a military ship," for which there was no evidence. The *Jerusalem Post* implies that the pilots were searching for an identifying flag. One pilot declares, "There's no flag on her!"

ROYAL, the Mystère group, says, "She looks like a minesweeper with that marking CTR" (actually GTR). Then comes the false statement, "People are jumping into the water!" Finally, Menachem asks Kislev, "What country?" And Kislev says, "Apparently American." In the fraudulent transcript released by Israeli apologist A. J. Cristol, Kislev tells "Robert," "It's an Egyptian supply boat." Menachem is chief air controller at Air Control South. Robert is chief air controller at Air Control Central, twenty-five miles south of Tel Aviv. "Shimon," the deputy chief air controller at Air Control Central, orders, "Have them rescue the people with the torpedo boats to help." All this is contrived falsification.

Other fraudulent moments have ROYAL, the Super Mystère jets, saying, "Careful of her antennas," when in fact the antennas had already been blasted out of commission by the Mirage jets led by Brigadier General Iftach Spector, the lead pilot in the attack by the Mirage jets. Among Spector's lies were that he made two or three sorties, full circles of the vessel. In fact, there were thirty or more.[71]

At 4:04 p.m., Shimon tells Kislev, "The ship hasn't sunk yet," and when Ernest Castle is misidentified as the "American Ambassador" and is being brought to the ship, Shimon says, "Is he afraid they'll open fire on him?," even as Castle looks down from his Israeli military helicopter at the deck splashed with blood and strewn with severed body parts.

Once the attackers were identified as Israeli, Dave Lewis's four watch supervisors—crew men, all inferior to him in rank, chief petty officers and petty officers, and of whom Stan White was in charge, gave orders to find out what they were saying from the planes to Tel Aviv in plain language. It was breaking the law, Dave knew, but the old rules no longer applied.[72] "We don't worry about security," Dave said.[73]

CHAPTER 8

WITH THE SIXTH FLEET

"I sent jet aircraft with nuclear-tipped weapons to Cairo."
—Captain Donald D. Engen, USS *America*,
to a shipmate (as told to Captain Richard L. Block)

At 12:05, nearly an hour before the Israeli planes attacked the ship, three Israeli motor torpedo boats left Ashdod, the largest port in Israel, twenty miles south of Tel Aviv, at high speed and headed toward *Liberty*. A message went off to the Sixth Fleet, for all the good it would do: "Unidentified gunboats approaching vessel now."

The Israeli assumption was that the torpedo boats would complete the sinking of the ship. So at 2:24 p.m. local time, three French-built sixty-two-ton Israeli motor torpedo boats approached in attack formation. The bombers were still on the scene as the three torpedo boats steamed into position alongside *Liberty*, although later the Israelis added another lie and insisted that their pilots departed the area before the torpedo boats arrived. As Joe Meadors observed, "Their crew looked us over very closely and motioned to the bridge area." *Liberty*'s forward machine gun mounts had been destroyed in the first air assault, and two sailors who had been manning the machine guns were killed. At general headquarters in Tel Aviv, the chief air controller, Lieutenant Colonel Shmuel Kislev, who had ordered two Super Mystère jets to join the attack armed with napalm, was informed by a pilot of *Liberty*'s hull number. "At that point in time," Kislev admitted later in a BBC documentary, "I was sure it was an American ship."[1]

The torpedo boats launched five German-made nineteen-inch torpedoes at the ship. One struck the target, hitting the starboard side, penetrating directly into the research spaces. A hole thirty-nine feet wide at the bottom and twenty-four feet wide near the waterline was opened. Seawater rushed in. Twenty-five men immediately floated to their deaths. Had the torpedo hit the boiler, as it was intended to do, the ship would have gone down with no survivors.

The bulkheads exploded, and water filled the research spaces. Drowning men scrambled for something to hold on to in the blackened room as they attempted to reach the hatch, which had been closed as per the prerogatives of the General Quarters drill. Bob Scarborough hung from an overhead pipe and heard the water splashing around him. For the moment, he treaded water.

Captain McGonagle called for the men to "prepare to abandon ship!" Lieutenant Lloyd Painter was to supervise the evacuation of the wounded crew members, who were to proceed to the muster area, topside near the rafts. Painter opened the hatch and "observed with my own eyes the Israeli motor torpedo crew members methodically machine-gunning the USS *Liberty* rafts as they floated away. The rubber rafts had been set on fire by the napalm canister and had to be cut from our ship," Painter remembered later. At once, the rafts were riddled with holes. For another forty minutes, the torpedo boats machine-gunned the ship with armor-piercing projectiles. "It was clear they didn't want anyone to live," Petty Officer Chuck Rowley said.

"You see, it really wasn't until that torpedo boat pulled up alongside the ship, and then I saw the Israeli flag and I was in shock," Glenn Oliphant would recount later. "Everybody thought Israel was our ally, you know, or at least we were friendly with them, and here we were in international waters being attacked by Israel. Nobody could believe it. We were numb."[2]

"Sending aircraft to cover you"—the Sixth Fleet sent a message that *Liberty* could not receive because it lacked a receiver.

Dave Lewis, two levels below deck when the attack began, felt the paint on the bulkheads burn onto his body. His skin turned charcoal, then so ashen that Dr. Kiepfer thought he was dead. His eyes were sealed shut. His skin was wildly tattooed. One eardrum was nonexistent; the other was 85 percent burned out. Lewis, close to where the torpedo hit, waist-deep in swirling water, was clinging to the remains of the ladder going up to the next deck. With Lewis were Robert "Buddha" Schnell and John Horne. Later, Maurice Bennett claimed to have rescued Lewis, but Lewis denies that, awarding the credit to Schnell.

"NSA" civilian Robert L. Wilson (Bob), whose role was "to observe," and suggesting that at least one component of CIA was not part of the operation (many people are unaware that most CIA people work under cover identities such as Wilson's), noted that "there was no panic. For the most part, solidarity governed the ship and the men." When a man was ordered to do something, he did it. Helping the wounded became everyone's job. Men learned to dress the wounded and to sew surgical stitches. "With the lengthening hours of darkness," Wilson told the NSA later, "deepening depression and shock caused some men to break down and succumb to the fears they had been able to restrain during the attack."[3]

There were "heroes in the seaweed" (the phrase comes from Canadian artist Leonard Cohen's sublime song "Suzanne"), like Bryce Lockwood, the US Marine sergeant ("Old Sarge") and Russian translator who pulled three men out of the water and carried them, one by one, up a ladder. Shot in the head (he obviously was expendable to both ONI and CIA), Dave McFeggan found himself in the water, about to drown, when Lockwood found him. As Lockwood attempted to hoist McFeggan up the ladder, he dropped him, a moment neither man would ever forget. Lockwood carried McFeggan to safety, McFeggan's head bumping up the ladder as they made their way in the darkness.

Later, recovering on the USS *America*, McFeggan did not endear himself to his shipmates who had also been wounded. He "behaved badly in the hospital," Harold Six recounted to the author fifty years after that fateful day. Six could not know why McFeggan believed he deserved better treatment. He had no idea that McFeggan had been working for CIA and communicating with them and that he did not expect to be anywhere near the line of fire, to be a sacrificial victim. McFeggan was a CT under cover, which was why Dave Lewis, who was supervisor of all the communications technicians, did not remember his name or anything at all about him. Nor could Lewis recall anything about Robert Wilson, who was a National Security Agency translator and also a CT under cover for CIA.

Splashed with old paint during the attack, Bryce Lockwood pulled three sailors to safety, the sole US Marine Survivor of the attack. (Photo courtesy of Bryce Lockwood.)

Harold Six, a CT, was ten feet from the torpedo when it exploded. Two decades later, he didn't know who had saved him. Only in 1995, at his first reunion, did Six learn the identity of his savior. He recognized Bryce Lockwood immediately: he was the marine called "Sarge" with whom Six had picked a fight at Rota out of hotheaded anti-marine antipathy.[4] Years later, Six apologized on the grounds that he had been alcoholic: "I just didn't feel right about being alive." He subsequently went to Vietnam to "get myself killed."

Chief engineer George Golden described the bulkhead aft of the torpedo as "breathing" and illustrated it by pulsing his hand.[5] He could feel the beating of the ship's heart. Sheet steel doesn't retain its integrity very long when being flexed, and that was a critical point in keeping the sea out and the ship afloat.

Golden acted swiftly and without undue speculation. He had given the order to "flood the voids" (the empty tanks along the bottom of the port and starboard sides). This was known as "counterflooding." The tanks would be filled with seawater. He flooded the port side with seawater; he opened the ballast vents to take on seawater and create stability. They didn't have much "free board" left. With a full load, the ship sits lower in the water. *Liberty* did settle, went down more, giving them less footage above the surface of the sea. They sank a little lower, but they didn't have as much list and did not capsize. They survived.

Golden took a calculated risk that they wouldn't sink, and he put up four-by-eight-foot sheets of plywood to plug the holes in the walls; they had very little watertight integrity. Golden had tried this method unsuccessfully during World War II when his ships were hit by German torpedoes. Both times, the ship went down. By all reason, *Liberty* should not have remained afloat.

Golden concluded that "this was a well-planned attack against us, and they knew we were an American ship." He was not a man who lost his nerve.

The order to "abandon ship" came from the captain, and the remaining life rafts were lowered into the water. Lloyd Painter was topside in time to witness a torpedo boat shoot a life raft to ribbons, in violation of international law. One torpedo boat snatched up a life raft as a souvenir and sped away, heading back to base with its treasure. The life raft was taken to reside at an Israeli naval museum.

For forty minutes, the torpedo boats continued to fire on the ship with machine guns. When they departed at last, by CIA calculations, two Israeli SA 321 Super Frelon ("Super Hornet") helicopters arrived to finish the job and sink *Liberty*. Stars of David were painted on their sides. Their doors were open, and inside you could see soldiers in camouflage brandishing machine guns in the open doorways. One Israeli soldier fixed his eyes on sailor Glenn Oliphant, who stood on deck watching. The soldier aimed his gun directly at Oliphant. Their eyes met.

Captain McGonagle, bleeding on the bridge. (Photo by and courtesy of Lloyd Painter.)

Captain McGonagle remained immobile in his chair on the bridge, dazed and wounded, his leg oozing blood. He didn't say much. Then he issued an order: "Prepare to repel boarders!" All they had with which to defend themselves were World War II–issue M1 rifles and .45 caliber automatic pistols—and their bare hands. Phil Tourney and Rick Aimetti rushed to the small-arms locker, only to find it secured with a huge steel lock. No one could locate the key. They did not succeed in ripping the locker open with an ax.

Tourney rushed on deck, only to observe a helicopter no more than ten feet off the starboard gun mount. One of the commandos sat on the side of the helicopter with his foot on the skid. Neither said a word. Then, abruptly, without warning, the helicopters whirled away and turned into the wind. Their mission had been aborted. Apparently Israeli listening posts had picked up the launching of US jet fighters from *Saratoga* and *America*.

There are some missing pieces to this narrative. Let us return in time to the moment when *Liberty* succeeded with the aid of Terence Halbardier in restoring its communications with the Sixth Fleet. As soon as *Liberty*'s SOS reached the Joint Chiefs, they authorized a retaliatory air attack on the Israeli naval base at Haifa.[6] Two wings of Sixth Fleet Skyhawks were to be sent from *Saratoga* and *America*. "An incident which could have sucked the United States into that war had the Joint Chiefs of Staff's impulsive advice, which I witnessed, been followed," CIA officer Patrick McGarvey said later.[7] "They proposed a quick, retaliatory air strike on the Israeli naval base which had launched the attack."

Richard Deacon, who had been with British intelligence, was one of the few writers to acknowledge that the Joint Chiefs of Staff were ready immediately to take retaliatory action. After the attack: "At first the US chief of state [he means Joint Chiefs of Staff] were goaded [by whom, he doesn't say] into proposing a quick retaliatory air strike on the Israeli naval base which launched this attack." Deacon adds that such a move "would have dire consequences all around."[8] Deacon does not suggest that there was justice in the self-defense of the United States striking back.

The retaliatory attack proposed by the Joint Chiefs was quickly canceled by Lyndon Johnson.

WITH THE SIXTH FLEET

There is no documentary record of the time that on the USS *America*, Sixth Fleet commander Admiral William Inman Martin, having conducted briefing sessions for pilots on the topography and landmarks of Cairo, dispatched three "air ready" jets with nuclear capability to bomb the city of Cairo. We do know that briefing sessions exploring the topography of Cairo had been held aboard the USS *America*. Given that Admiral Martin had foreknowledge of the attack, it should come as no surprise that the antiseptic deck logs of the USS *America* make no mention of planes having been launched with the target destination of Cairo.

Years later, a navy aviator named Brad Knickerbocker recounted that he had been about to take off from the USS *Saratoga* and had been briefed by officers using large maps of Egypt. They highlighted surface-to-air missile sites, antiaircraft emplacements, port facilities, and other military targets. Knickerbocker's account is garbled; the planes bound for Cairo were launched not from *Saratoga*, as he writes, but from *America*. Knickerbocker's plane, according to his account, did not launch at all: "The first flight of aircraft from the *Saratoga* was recalled without engaging in combat, and my flight did not launch."

What is significant about Knickerbocker's account is not the cancellation of his flight but the preparation that he underwent, the study of the topography of Cairo—evidence that the United States had indeed prepared to bomb Cairo and had been thwarted only at the last minute when *Liberty* had miraculously, successfully sent its SOS to the Sixth Fleet.[9]

"My combat initiation would have to wait for Vietnam," Knickerbocker writes in an article published in the *Christian Science Monitor*.

Wittingly or unwittingly, Knickerbocker misidentifies his ship as *Saratoga;* it was in fact the USS *America.*

There were two carriers with fighter planes on board. The planes equipped with nuclear warheads and bound for Cairo were launched from the USS *America*, the only one of the ships in the Sixth Fleet with nuclear capabilities.

The officer who received the SOS from *Liberty* and responded immediately to its call for help was Captain Joseph Tully of the USS *Saratoga.*

There was a covey of embedded journalists on *America*. Among them was Harry Stathos, who later said he personally saw nuclear-armed aircraft launched from *America*. Then, Jim Ennes later said, a chief performance officer with the Naval Security Group unit told him the same story, as did a catapult operator who recorded nuclear weapons launched.[10] Captain Engen of *America* chased Harry Stathos, who had come upon the launch to Cairo, from the scene. Engen covered up with the pretext of a nuclear drill, accounting for the nuclear-armed planes being brought up from their subterranean resting place, but it had been a close call. In fact, Stathos, and the other reporters, including Bob Goralski, witnessed the launch of nuclear weapons in the direction of Cairo.

Once the SOS from the USS *Liberty* reached the USS *Saratoga*, Captain Joseph Tully wasted no time. Ready to launch planes to come to the aid of *Liberty*, consulting only his own righteous heart—at 2:09 p.m., Captain Tully acknowledged *Liberty*'s call for help and dispatched four F-4 Phantom jets to *Liberty*'s location. A pilot on one of the planes launched by Captain Tully from *Saratoga* was heard to say, "Who is the enemy?" By now, it was no later than 2:25 p.m.

"Defense of USS *Liberty* means exactly that," the message to the pilots reads. "Destroy or drive off any attackers who are clearly making attacks on *Liberty*."

The pilots were to remain over international waters and defend themselves if attacked. Their orders were very specific: "You are authorized to use force including destruction as necessary to control the situation. Do not use more force than required. Do not pursue any unit toward land. Do not fly between *Liberty* and shoreline except as required." It never came to that. The Sixth Fleet was located 512 miles west of *Liberty*. Captain Tully's message was immediately intercepted by the Israeli intelligence services, who now knew that an SOS had been gotten out.

A good man, a navy captain of the old school resembling the stalwart adventurers of the sea in the novels of Joseph Conrad, Joe Tully couldn't imagine that Admiral William Inman Martin, commander of the Sixth Fleet, would be participating in a conspiracy that involved the United States firing on its own ship. He couldn't imagine his country involved in a false flag attack on Egypt.

Noticing that the USS *America* had not launched any planes in response to the SOS, Captain Tully signaled to Captain Donald D. Engen: "WTH?" (What the hell?) Engen did not reply. Eighty or ninety minutes later, Tully was authorized to launch again. He did not remember ever seeing any aircraft launched from the USS *America*, only that his own second launch of rescue aircraft was also recalled.

In the chain of command, Engen and Tully worked for Rear Admiral Lawrence Geis, two stars, the carrier division officer, while all of the Sixth Fleet worked for Martin. Admiral Geis, operating as part of the Sixth Fleet Carrier Striking Force, was commander of Carrier Division 4 (Mediterranean). Violations of hierarchy were antithetical to the culture of the Navy.

With *Saratoga*'s planes still in sight, Captain Tully noticed that *America* had not launched. Captain Tully was "perplexed," his word. Why didn't Captain Engen simultaneously launch rescue planes? Tully himself was able to launch at once because although he had been authorized to relax from the high alert posture that the fleet had maintained, he had kept his pilots, airplanes, and catapults prepared for immediate reaction.[11]

Captain Tully learned that Admiral Martin was on the flag bridge, ostensibly conducting a maneuvering exercise. Using Admiral Martin's personal call sign, using the primary tactical radio circuit, he signaled that "UNODIR"—unless otherwise directed—he was turning into the wind and launching airplanes to defend *Liberty*. He checked with his navigation officer, Max K. Morris, and was told that they were fifteen to twenty minutes' flight time from the USS *Liberty* and could be of immediate assistance. It was only then that he personally called Vice Admiral Martin via the primary tactical radio circuit and said he planned to launch his "Red Strike Group."

But Admiral Martin was busy recalling the four nuclear-armed planes he and Captain Engen had secretly dispatched to Cairo, and so it was only the USS *Saratoga* and not the USS *America* that answered the first SOS by sending jet planes to defend *Liberty*.

Captain Tully launched twelve fighter-bombers and four tanker planes.[12] He launched immediately and without authorization.[13] Moments later, Tully was ordered to recall his planes.

Captain Tully's launch had been discovered by the Israeli intelligence services, and presumably it was the combination of the launch and the recall of those planes bound for Cairo that precipitated the Israelis calling off their attack on *Liberty*. Dave Lewis is persuaded that had the first group of rescue planes arrived, they would have preceded the torpedo boats, and twenty-eight people would have remained alive.[14]

Admiral William Inman Martin had assumed that the two waves of Israeli jets had succeeded in sinking the USS *Liberty*—the ship was defenseless. "Fast Charger" had been authorized to move to the next phase of the operation—which was that the United States bomb Egypt in retaliation for Nasser's having (ostensibly) attacked the USS *Liberty*. This time the task would fall not to Israel but to the United States itself, so reckless had Lyndon Johnson become.

Once the SOS reached the USS *Saratoga*, Admiral Martin, commander of the Sixth Fleet, had no choice but to recall the nuclear-armed planes that had been dispatched to bomb Cairo. They had been raised to the deck, with reporters on board, and so there were those who observed the nuclear-armed planes. To cover up the use of the nuclear-armed planes, Admiral Martin had offered up the pretext that there was a nuclear drill in place.

The commanding officer of a destroyer alongside and the catapult operator confirm that aircraft carrying nuclear bombs were launched from *America*.[15] The nuclear loading "exercise" was ostensibly to ensure that the wiring in the weapons and the wiring in the aircraft were compatible.[16] They were at anchor north of Crete, the island between the USS *America*, the Mediterranean, and Egypt.

The "Israeli author" whose diary is included in Richard Thompson's papers states that "303" had ordered the dispatch of three "air ready" planes directly to Cairo. (Actually there were four planes.) That meant there was less than an hour to the use of nuclear weapons on Egypt—and then the target would be Russia. Meanwhile, the author shared what he knew with his Kenyan controller and another senior officer under cover with Spetsnaz (Russian special forces), who was a British double agent. "'The first mushroom in Egypt would be the signal for a Russian mass launch."

This double agent notes that "the un-named submarine commander defied orders to sink it [*Liberty*] refusing to kill the innocent American crew. He was never disciplined for disobeying the order."

The facts support the account of the anonymous Israeli agent whose memoir resides in Dick Thompson's archive. On June 8, Admiral Martin was conducting a SIOP (Single Integrated Operational Plan) drill, a special intelligence nuclear weapons drill. "Integrated" meant that it included the air force and navy. SIOP, however, in the cryptonyms of that day, did not refer to a "drill" at all. It meant that the nukes were being activated, readied for launch. You did not do a SIOP if you were not readying your weapons for action, for actual battle, Dave Lewis says.[17]

George E. Sokol, a third class aircraft structural mechanic in hydraulics, noticed that the hangar bay fire doors were almost completely closed, because the six nuclear bombers resided there, protected by US Marines. Along with the announcement "*Liberty* under fire," he heard the words "SET CONDITION ZULU." "Condition Zulu" meant airtight security pending a nuclear attack. It meant "Stand by for attack," and on an aircraft carrier with nuclear capacity, it meant something more than that.[18]

The saltwater washdown system, which, in case of nuclear attack, would go all over the ship to wash the fallout over the side, was pressurized and ready to go. Sokol thus assumed that we were at war with Russia, the consequence of *Liberty* having gone to the bottom of the sea.

The nuclear weapons brought up from the hold to the main deck were witnessed by some of the journalists embedded on *America*. It didn't seem to them as if anything was untoward. It's apparent that there was no "drill." The idea of a drill was cover for the attack on Cairo. There was no "exercise." Four planes took off, bound for Cairo. Two were nuclear loaded.

There is further evidence that the planes heading for Cairo were loaded with nuclear weapons. It comes from Rich Young, a member of the USS *America* aircraft crash crew: "All hands had to clear the flight deck except essential crew, and I watched nuclear bombs being loaded on planes—we knew they were nukes because they each had two marines guarding them, each one locked and loaded."[19]

The attempted attack on Cairo was witnessed by yet another sailor: Chuck Rowley told Jim Ennes when he was writing his book that he had talked with a pilot on the USS *America* who said he flew one of the planes and they "definitely carried nuclear weapons and were headed toward Cairo."[20]

Ted Phil, chief of staff to Admiral Geis, says there's confirmation that the nuclear weapons were on deck being loaded. Captain Engen launched "ready" aircraft toward Cairo, two planes that carried "nuclear-tipped weapons."

"I sent jet aircraft with nuclear-tipped weapons to Cairo," Captain Engen told fellow officers on *America*, who recounted his words to their friend, US Air Force Captain Richard L. Block.[21] But Captain Block added a disclaimer in his interview with the author at his home in Florida:

The part I had to play in the *Liberty* affair is limited to intercept from our airborne intelligence gathering, UAR, and a few other messages which our unit received from other sources. All this information, due to the sensitivity of the incident, was quickly compartmentalized and sucked into the "black hole" of "need to know eyes only" category. . . . From what I know from conversations, it was a joint US-Israeli intelligence venture which involved the US Navy and its submarine arm.

. . . The nuclear armed aircraft launched hot from the aircraft carrier *America* was brought to light by naval personnel on the carrier.[22]

US Air Force Captain Richard L. Block (right). Stationed in Iraklion, Crete, at the time of the attack. "It was a joint US-Israeli intelligence venture which involved the US Navy and its submarine arm." (Photo courtesy of Richard L. Block.)

Captain Engen made no public statements as to why he did not launch planes toward *Liberty* at the same time that Captain Tully did. (Engen would rise to the rank of admiral before he retired from the navy.)

The planned bombing of Cairo was predicated on there being no survivors from the USS *Liberty* to bear witness to the fact that they had not been attacked by Egypt or the Soviet Union. The US attack on Cairo would be represented as retaliation for Egypt's bombing of *Liberty*.

The planes dispatched from the USS *America* were seven minutes from target in Cairo when Admiral William Inman Martin recalled them.[23]

The combination of the launch and the recall of planes bound for Cairo precipitated the Israelis calling off their attack on *Liberty*. Unbeknownst to Captain Tully, when he informed Admiral Martin that he had launched, Martin now knew that the jig was up.

Where Lyndon Johnson was when he ordered the planes to be recalled is not known. According to White House records, Johnson did not make his way from his bedroom to the Situation Room until late morning. Neither Johnson nor McNamara were ever to admit they had recalled the rescue planes bound for the USS *Liberty*.

It was when, years later, Joseph Tully spoke about these events that he pronounced himself "puzzled" at the failure of the USS *America* to launch immediately following the arrival of *Liberty*'s SOS, as he had done.[24] Whether or not the rescue planes would have arrived in time to stop even a portion of the Israeli attack has been much debated.

"It would have taken us over an hour to reach *Liberty*," says Bill Knutson, who flew an F-4B, which could "fast cruise" at 450–500 knots.[25] A-4 attack aircraft could not maintain even that fast a pace. The A-1s, prop aircraft, "would have taken . . . over two hours to reach *Liberty*." But Knutson took off at least an hour and a half after Captain Tully's first launch.

Lyndon Baines Johnson.
Photograph inscribed to
Billie Sol Estes.
(Photo courtesy of the late
Billie Sol Estes.)

In the lead plane dispatched by the USS *America*, when it finally launched toward *Liberty*, was W. D. (Bill) Knutson, who was among the pilots participating in the launch against Cairo and now the pilot of the lead plane launched to the side of *Liberty* by *America*.[26] Having set forth at full throttle, knowing he had five hundred miles to cover to reach the USS *Liberty*, Knutson was startled to be recalled fifteen or twenty minutes into the flight.

"We were vectored toward Rockstar," Knutson remembered for me, "and told she was under attack by unknown aircraft. . . . I kept asking distance to Rockstar/*Liberty* and when we were told it was over four hundred miles, we came out of afterburner and maximum speed so we could have enough fuel to get there and defend the ship. We had not gone more than one hundred miles when 'Courage,' the USS *America*, told us to abort the mission and return for landing." "Courage" gave no reason and said only that the recall had been ordered by Sixth Fleet "Fast Charger," who was Admiral Martin.[27]

At the left is navy aviator Bill Knutson, lieutenant commander and operations officer of VF-84 on his way to a combat cruise in Vietnam in 1965. The plane is a Phantom F-4B on the flight deck of the USS *Independence* and is the same type of plane Knutson flew from the USS *America* in 1967 on his way to respond to the attack on *Liberty*. With Knutson, to his right, is Lieutenant Rodney A. Knutson (no relation). The big boys "called us Big K and Little K," Knutson says. (Photo courtesy of William Knutson.)

No explanation would ever be forthcoming.

Being recalled and not given any reason except that the Sixth Fleet made the recall, Knutson says, was "indeed aggravating." A pilot of an A-3 "was so pissed about the recall that he took out his anger by making a barrel roll over the carrier," a maneuver not only not authorized but "usually not performed by such a large aircraft as the A-3!" Some pilots had heard the voices from *Liberty* requesting help while they were being recalled.[28] One wrote a magazine article about it in *Counterattack* magazine that appeared in July 1967. Author John Borne recounts that he searched all New York City public libraries for that issue of the magazine, only to find it missing everywhere.[29]

In later years, Captain Engen covered for himself as well as for William Inman Martin. Engen contended that *America* was caught up in an SIOP drill and was occupied with the loading and moving of weapons, and so when he learned that *Liberty* needed help, he found "one gloriosky spotting mess on our hands." Therefore "we were late launching and responding to *Liberty*'s need because of this. I stopped the [drill]," Engen writes, "as *Liberty* reported being attacked." He does not refer to the fact that the planes that had gone to Cairo had to come back first.

He justified his having failed to launch upon the arrival of the SOS from *Liberty*, as Captain Tully had done: "I could not launch aircraft because of the weapons mess that I had on my hands," which is vague enough. In a letter to Captain Tully, Captain Engen writes, disingenuously, "I do not know why your aircraft was recalled from the first launch that you made."[30] He pretends to have been bedeviled by "a lot of confusion on the flag bridge as they tried to figure out who was doing what to whom."

Engen evades the actual chronology. He estimates that he launched A-4s and F-4s, "as you [Captain Tully] did," about one hour and ten minutes after the reported attack. In fact, Captain Tully launched about a half hour after the attack. Engen insists he still does not know the identity of the "enemy." Both captains launched together ninety minutes after Captain Tully's first launch.

USS *Liberty* on June 9, no longer alone.

USS *Liberty* on June 9. (Photos courtesy of the USS *Liberty* Veterans Association.)

Engen does acknowledge his "understanding that the President talked directly to RADM Geis and said, 'Bring back your striking airplanes.' That decision was White House driven and above the pay grade of the Sixth Fleet Commander, Bill Martin."

Having regained his bearings following his order to recall the planes he had dispatched to Cairo, Admiral Martin sent a message to both carriers that a rescue flight should be sent to the USS *Liberty* in ninety minutes, a time having been set by McNamara. Tully replied that his planes would be ready. At 3:50, a second convoy of rescue planes was launched, this time from both carriers. Admiral Geis informed McNamara that he was dispatching planes without any nuclear capability. Now came McNamara's second message.

As per protocol, Captain Tully used the Critical Intelligence Communications network, or "CRITICOM," an instantaneous communications signal. Admiral Geis also contacted the White House and the Pentagon so that both the president and the Joint Chiefs were alerted that Captain Tully had sent "ready" aircraft to the rescue.

Engen and Martin stuck together. They insisted they responded immediately to the SOS from *Liberty*, although only Captain Tully did. They did not admit there were two launches. Captain Engen told Congressman Paul Findley, "President Johnson had very strict control. Even though we knew the *Liberty* was under attack, I couldn't just go and order a rescue."[31] Yet that is exactly what Captain Tully did.

At Port Lyautey, the naval station in Morocco, routing the AUTOVON (Automatic Voice Network), an unclassified worldwide telephone service of the US military serving the Mediterranean area, NSA communications technician and petty officer Julian ("Tony") Hart was listening in.[32] Hart heard the voice of Secretary of Defense Robert Strange McNamara speaking on an unsecured open line to Admiral Geis. McNamara was calling back the planes that had been dispatched to the USS *Liberty* by Captain Tully. Hart specifically heard McNamara identify himself.

When Admiral Geis recalled the aircraft from *Saratoga*, it was with instructions not to jettison their five-hundred-pound bombs. There was a NATO ammunitions depot in Crete, and so four of *Saratoga's* aircraft were directed to the NATO Ammo Depot and Airfield. That was Captain Tully's first launch.

At a loss, Admiral Geis speculated that Washington had concluded that the aircraft dispatched by Captain Tully carried nuclear weapons, and Tully concluded that he should launch again with reassurances that there not be nuclear weapons aboard.

After the first group of planes dispatched by Captain Tully had returned, Admiral Martin sent a message to both carriers that a rescue flight should be sent in ninety minutes. The time was set by McNamara. Tully replied that his planes were ready to depart—he believed he had only to clear up McNamara's misunderstanding regarding the planes he had sent and their nuclear capability. In sending out a second sortie at three in the afternoon, Captain Tully made a point that he was now dispatching planes with no nuclear capability.

At 3:50, a second convoy of rescue planes was launched, this time from both carriers. Admiral Geis now sent a CRITIC straight to the White House, informing McNamara that he was dispatching planes without any nuclear capability. Fifteen minutes later, McNamara was back on the line. "I told you to get those damned aircraft back!" he snarled. "Call them back!"

After McNamara's second call, in clear violation of the code of no man being left behind on a field of battle, Admiral Geis requested confirmation of the order. He required higher authority than a mere secretary of defense to abandon American sailors to certain deaths in violation of the code of military justice. (Dave Lewis calls McNamara "Johnson's flunky. He didn't have to think, just obey.")[33]

Admiral Geis demurred. "These people are under attack!" he said. These were men for whose lives he was responsible. He refused to obey McNamara. It was now that Lyndon Johnson grabbed the telephone and made his wishes known. "I don't give a damn if the ship sinks," Johnson said. "I will not embarrass my allies." So he revealed an hour before Israel admitted that it had been the aggressor that he knew precisely who was responsible for the attack on *Liberty*.[34] The military code of "No Man Left Behind" had been rendered a mockery by this man who had garnered a Silver Star fraudulently in another war, courtesy of General Douglas MacArthur, as part of a political arrangement.

Receiving such orders, Admiral Geis had no choice but to obey.

II

At the time of the attack, Johnson had been meeting with a secretary discussing his 1968 presidential campaign. He instructed the secretary to compile a list of the states he had visited since he became president. "Eliminate 1964," Johnson ordered. "Compile only 1965, 1966, and 1967."

History would have remained ignorant of Lyndon Johnson's perfidious role in the events of the Six-Day War had Admiral Geis, appalled, not felt a need to convey the reality of Johnson's call to one of the survivors of the attack. He chose Dave Lewis, the highest-ranking surviving officer on *Liberty*, whom he trusted would not speak out until Admiral Geis's death. Lewis promised to wait.

After he had spent a week recuperating on the USS *America*, Lewis had received a message that as soon as he was able, he was to visit Admiral Geis in his stateroom. "I want someone to know what happened," Admiral Geis said, adding, "I have to swear you to secrecy in my lifetime."[35]

Admiral Geis would die twenty-three years later, in 1980. He had chosen Lewis, Dave Lewis believes, because he was the senior officer available on *America* who had survived the attack and was likely to keep the confidence. It was no small matter because in recounting Lyndon Johnson's intervention to Dave Lewis, Admiral Geis was violating Naval Security regulations.

They shared a cup of coffee. Admiral Geis explained how he had configured a launch using aircraft incapable of carrying nukes and relaunched. So there had been two distinct rescue launches, one ordered by Captain Tully and a second by Captains Tully and Engen. Admiral Geis wanted somebody to know that the sailors had not been forgotten; attempts had been made to come to their assistance.

Admiral Geis told him that as soon as he learned of the distress signals, Lewis says, he—through Captain Tully—dispatched aircraft to defend the *Liberty*. He then called the White House, sending McNamara a CRITIC, and it was then that McNamara ordered him to recall the aircraft. Julian Hart heard McNamara reply, "We're not going to war over a bunch of dead sailors." Hanging up, Admiral Geis had been incredulous. He couldn't believe McNamara thought he had launched nuclear weapons in the direction of *Liberty*.

Admiral Geis found McNamara's order incomprehensible. No reason for aborting the rescue flights was given. Yet American sailors under attack and unable to defend themselves were being abandoned at sea. Perhaps— Geis, out of the loop, thought—McNamara was under the misapprehension that he had dispatched planes with nuclear capabilities.

Richard Sturman, a radioman, wondered: "How did LBJ know it was Israel? The Israeli apology came at 4:14 p.m. two hours and forty-five minutes after the attack."[36]

Israel had doubled its territory and increased the number of people under its sway by one million. The denial that the war was about the acquisition of land (a "land grab") was rendered preposterous, as the settlements in what had been Palestinian territory began at once.

LBJ had revealed that he knew not only the identity of the attackers but that the attack itself had been a collaboration. The purpose was to remove Nasser.

During all this time, the embedded reporters on *America*—among them Harry Stathos, Bob Goralski, and Neil Sheehan—were kept in the dark about the attack.

In retrospect, it seems that neither Admiral Geis nor Captain Tully knew that Captain Engen of *America* and Admiral Martin had sent jet aircraft with nuclear-tipped weapons to Cairo. Later, Captain Engen blamed others for his not having a clear understanding of what was going on. He blamed "the spooks keeping so quiet about what they were doing," he wrote many years later to Captain Tully, obfuscating and attempting to absolve himself from responsibility for the unconscionable act of failing to send rescue planes when the SOS first arrived from *Liberty*.[37] In noting that "the spooks" were involved, Captain Engen inadvertently lets us know that CIA had entered the action.

In fact, Engen was late because the planes on their way to Cairo had to be redirected. "I stopped the LSP [the nuclear drill] as *Liberty* reported being attacked," he said. The key word in that sentence is "as." Events proceeded in logical sequence. First, the planes on their way to Cairo had to be turned around. Only then could planes be launched to assist *Liberty*.

Engen estimates that he launched A-4s and F-4s "as you [Captain Tully] did about one hour and ten or twenty minutes after the reported attack." He is referring, of course, to Tully's second launch. He says his aircraft left the ship "fully loaded with conventional ordnance," as was true of all three launches. Conventional ordnance meant not nuclear.

It was the first launch, toward Cairo, from *America*, that carried nuclear warheads. Captain Engen insists he still did not know who the enemy was but knew that *America*'s A-4s "binged to Souda Bay to download the Bullpups," air-to-ground missiles. These were the planes that could not return to the aircraft carrier because they carried nuclear weapons.

Engen supports Admiral Martin. "It is my understanding that the President talked directly to RADM Geis and said, 'Bring back your striking airplanes.'" Later, Engen and Martin claimed that they responded immediately to the SOS. They did not admit there were three launches toward *Liberty*, the first from Captain Tully, the second and third from Captain Tully and Captain Engen. When it was all over, Donald Engen received three stars, Captain Tully none.[38]

Hidden in the chaos were the aborted planes that had almost reached Cairo. These were directed to Crete, since nuclear-armed planes were forbidden to land back on an aircraft carrier. During the afternoon of June 8, the carriers *America* and *Saratoga* were drenched in chaos and misdirection, with Admiral Martin contradicting himself at every turn. A "Memorandum for the Record" was issued by CIA almost immediately, the "spooks" Captain Engen had treated with disdain. It referred to the Israelis "erroneously" attacking a vessel "which was thought to be a US Navy ship."[39] CIA writes that "Israeli helicopters were conducting rescue operations," a fantasy. Most of the government documents, particularly the summary authored by CIA, discussed at length in chapter 11, were designed to exonerate Israel of any responsibility for the attack they had conducted.

To his lasting credit, Admiral Geis became one of the happy few, joining, among others, Admiral David Lamar McDonald, in not signing on to this nefarious operation. These were men for whose lives he was responsible. Calling back the rescue planes, whether they would have been too late to save the ship or not, whether they could have prevented the torpedo attack or not, violated every principle for which he and the navy stood.

When Admiral Geis requested confirmation of the second order to recall rescue aircraft, Lyndon Baines Johnson came on the line, the commander in chief himself. He was on the open line, AUTOVON. His voice, with its Texas Hill Country accent, was unmistakable. He would not have his allies embarrassed, Johnson said. He didn't care who was killed or what happened to the ship. Had Captain Tully's first launch proceeded unimpeded, the lives of twenty-eight men might have been spared.

"I don't care if the ship sinks," Johnson said, as Admiral Geis later recalled to Dave Lewis aboard the USS *America*. "I don't give a damn if the ship sinks. I will not embarrass my allies." Sailors all the way to Morocco heard his Texas twang with its unmistakable curl of menace. It was recognizable to every American. Or he may have said, "I will not embarrass an ally." So in his panic that the operation be exposed, Johnson revealed to a high-ranking officer of the US Navy that he knew the identity of the attackers and hence that the attack had been a collaboration between Israel and the United States. Among Johnson's lies was a message to Soviet premier Alexei Kosygin on the morning of June 8 apologizing for US planes crossing Egyptian territory. His explanation was that "they were going to help the *Liberty*."

Cliff Carter, at the left, his man on the ground in Texas, with Lyndon Baines Johnson. "I will not embarrass an ally." (Photo courtesy of the LBJ Library, Austin.)

By 7:30 a.m. on June 8, LBJ should have been called by Rostow, Bundy, or McNamara, who would have received the FLASH message saying the ship was being attacked. No phone call to Johnson was recorded by anybody at the White House. At 8:08, LBJ called Senator Mike Mansfield, and at 8:13, he called Mansfield again. At 9:48, Kosygin called LBJ. At 9:49, there is another call recorded from Kosygin to LBJ. All of this suggests Johnson's foreknowledge of the attack and that he was not taken by surprise.

By 4:40 p.m., all rescue aircraft had been recalled. But in the mess of contradictions, evasions, and outright lies, five minutes later, at 16:45, via high-frequency voice, a message came to *Liberty* from COMSIX-THFLT: "Assistance is on the way." This was taken from the *Liberty* deck log. At 4:14, the Israelis reported they had "mistakenly" attacked a US ship at 1400: "Rescue efforts are under way."

The first launch of planes by Captain Tully would have arrived, according to Terence Halbardier, prior to the arrival of the motor torpedo boats, saving at once twenty-five lives. Admiral Moorer concurred: had the rescue aircraft not been recalled, "they would have arrived at the *Liberty* before the torpedo attack, reducing the death toll by twenty-five."[40] After the SOS arrived, Israel either intercepted it or was informed. The pretext that Egypt had sunk the ship could no longer be maintained. Abruptly, the two helicopters that had been assigned to complete the operation— sink the ship and be sure there were no survivors—were recalled without having fired a shot.

At 4:13 p.m. *Liberty*'s time, Admiral Martin, COMSIXTHFLT, notified his superiors that aircraft were dispatched from the two carriers and those aircraft "were on the scene at approximately 3:45 *Liberty* time." Martin knew that both flights had been recalled. He lied. In 1984, Admiral Martin wrote to Jim Ennes: "Comment on the USS *Liberty* INCIDENT: I was not informed that *Liberty* would enter the Mediterranean or that she had entered. I received no requests from *Liberty*—no communication until she was under attack." All of this was also contrary to fact.[41]

On June 9, Admiral Martin made a personal inspection of the ship.[42] The wounded were rescued and medevacked to the USS *America*, where there was a full hospital and where Dr. Peter Flynn would lance open Dave Lewis's eyelids. "Don't move your eyeballs or I can't guarantee where the scalpel will go," Dr. Flynn, a hard-boiled type, said.[43] His hand was steady as he gently shaved the paint off the surface of the eye.

And when there was no longer any space to tend to the wounded aboard *America*, the remaining wounded were brought to Admiral Martin's flagship, the USS *Little Rock*, a guided missile light cruiser. There were minimal facilities and no doctor on board. Five wounded sailors were placed in a small room, where bunks were set up.

To console these very young men, Admiral Martin, the highest-ranking officer in the Sixth Fleet, came into the room.[44] He was there to console them, still somewhat in shock. Admiral Martin sat down on the edge of Moe Shafer's bunk and asked him, as he did each of the others, if they were OK. "I just want you all to know we wanted to protect you. We launched four airplanes off the *Saratoga* with conventional weapons to come and help your ship. We [also] launched four planes with nuclear warheads off the USS *America* and they were targeted to go to Cairo. Lyndon Johnson, the White House, contacted us and said to call the planes back."[45]

Admiral Martin added that he had been "helpless. I couldn't help you."[46]

Moe Shafer was twenty years old. He was bewildered. Apparently Israel's radar had picked up the planes. Moe concluded that when the president says call back the planes, they call *all* the planes back. The planes with nuclear warheads couldn't land back on an aircraft carrier, they were told. They went to Crete. Admiral William Inman Martin went to each sailor's bed, touched him, asked if he was all right. In his effort to console, Admiral Martin made the most startling revelation, one that has not yet entered the history of the Six-Day War, as it should have.

Looking into the eyes of each of the sailors, speaking a few words to each man personally, he wanted to tell them that he had not abandoned them, that he had been active on their behalf. He knew what they had been through and he was trying to convey to them: this is what I tried to do to come to your aid. The second you called, I sent planes to help you. He wanted to tell them how close he had brought them to World War III.

Moe Shafer had been in the research spaces at his General Quarters station and so took the full brunt of the torpedo. He was blown into the ceiling, at once suffering a concussion. Admiral Martin, a tall, trim man, sat down at the edge of Moe's bunk. The gist of what Admiral Martin had to say was astonishing.

"I'm Admiral Martin," he said, "and I want you to know that we launched four planes with nuclear warheads off the USS *America* and four planes armed with conventional weapons off the *Saratoga*, only for the White House, Lyndon Johnson, to call the planes back." They were seven minutes from target in Cairo when he was ordered to call them back." Wide-eyed, these twenty-year-olds stared at him.[47]

Later, Moe Shafer gave interviews to both CNN and to *Nightline* in which he told this story. This was in 1982 or 1983. He was interviewed for twenty-five minutes by CNN. "I made twenty-five seconds on the air, during which I was made to seem anti-Semitic," Shafer told the author. Friends called him and were indignant. Moe's interview with Ted Koppel for *Nightline* did not make the air. Not a word of Koppel's interview, in which Shafer participated only reluctantly, was broadcast.

Of the five men on *Little Rock* who had been visited by Admiral Martin, Gene Kirk grew despondent and refused to revisit the subject, even with his shipmates. Kirk chose to disappear, a hermit in the American hinterland. He retired into the Midwestern wilds, an area of Minnesota, as Moe described it, of which no one had ever heard. By 2017, another of the men, Porky Eakins, had died, and Moe did not remember the names of the other two.[48] So the men who were witnesses to Admiral Martin's confession that he had sent nuclear-enhanced planes on a mission to Cairo, only for them to be called back when they were only seven minutes from target, had died or fallen silent. In his landmark book, Jim Ennes does not include Admiral Martin's having admitted that he had sent planes to Cairo on June 8, 1967, but Ennes did not interview his shipmate Moe Shafer.[49]

During the afternoon of June 8, periodically the Soviet submarine K-172, situated in the East Med and awaiting orders, would surface for instructions on whether to fire. Soviet captain Shashkov tells his story in Hebrew in a 1992 edition of the newspaper *Yedioth Ahronoth*. "We were to order the launch of a nuclear missile on Israel," he says. The article quotes a Jewish crewman on the same submarine who later emigrated to Israel. The third officer in charge of firing the Soviet missiles was named Fellsman, and he also was Jewish. A GRU (foreign intelligence) colonel, ex-KGB, says that Moscow regarded the *Liberty* attack as a deliberate "provocation," a pretext to precipitate open US involvement in the Six-Day War.

A Soviet submarine in the Eastern Mediterranean. "We were to order the launch of a nuclear missile on Israel." (Photo from the archive of Dick Thompson, courtesy of Tim Thompson.)

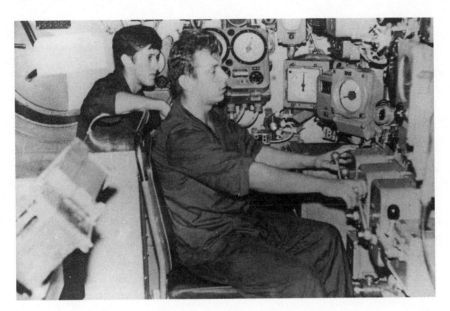

Scenes on the K-172 Soviet submarine: "A joint action by two special services, the USA and Israel, which had one goal, combining forces for a war with Egypt." (Photo from the archive of Dick Thompson, courtesy of Tim Thompson.)

The primary Soviet target in retaliation for the bombing of Cairo was to be the golden Dome of the Rock in Jerusalem—the sub lacked the range to go farther.[50] That week, the Israeli flag had been hoisted over the Dome of the Rock, only to be immediately lowered on the orders of Moshe Dayan. It was a politically sensitive place, and as the Israelis took possession of the areas they had conquered—the Old City of Jerusalem being one—they were wary. The rock was a sacred place, the last location of Mohammad before he ascended to heaven.

On the USS *America* on June 9, guards were stationed at the door of *Liberty*'s men's ward; if a man had to leave the ward, a guard went along.[51] Jim

Kavanagh went on to experience three surgeries in Frankfurt, Germany. The day after one, two ONI officers entered his room. "Do you think it was on purpose?" one asked. Kavanagh said that he did think so.

"Let me tell you how this works," an ONI officer said. "If you ever repeat what you told us, you will spend a few years in Leavenworth." Kavanagh was nineteen years old. He never spoke a word about what he thought about the attack on his ship. He became a math teacher.

After *Liberty*'s SOS went out, Admiral Martin followed the plan by sending a message to the Pentagon through the Morocco station: "*Liberty* under attack by Egyptian forces."[52] There wasn't a shred of evidence confirming this "fact." It remains as a vestige of the false flag operation of sinking *Liberty* and blaming Egypt.

There is other evidence of US determination to bomb Cairo—a plot thwarted by the determination of the sailors, and George Golden in particular, that they not sink. David G. Nes, acting ambassador at the US embassy in Cairo, and the *charge d'affaires*, since Nasser had not accepted the new ambassador, was warned to expect an imminent bombing attack on Cairo by US planes.

At once, Nes ordered the destruction of sensitive documents. There were five or six hundred Americans resident in Cairo, and Nes had to find a way to send their possessions home. Their cars were parked all over Cairo. Nes assigned this task to the CIA station chief.

Then Nes went on the emergency radio. The embassy received an immediate message that *Liberty* was being attacked by the Egyptians and that planes were being launched in a retaliatory raid on Cairo from *Saratoga*, he said. (This version of events coincides with Brad Knickerbocker's account of how he was about to launch from *Saratoga* to Cairo until his flight was canceled.)

Nes explained that they expected American planes over Cairo at any minute. Then, within the hour, a second message came in "saying that the attackers had been identified as the Israelis." That they were planning an evacuation from North Africa and the Middle East that would have comprised thirty thousand Americans was confirmed by George G. Bogardus, who was American consul at Stuttgart, Germany, at the time of the attack.[53]

Nes was too worldly not to be skeptical that the attack was some kind of accident. A few months later, back in Washington, he gave a talk at the National War College. Nes said that at lunch one afternoon, "I sat next to one of the commanders of the Destroyers [the *Massey* or the *Davis*] escorting the *Saratoga*, and he confirmed the launching of aircraft, the original mission being targets in Egypt. So it was a pretty close thing."[54]

Another indication that the United States had embarked on an attack on Cairo was the hotline message from LBJ to Kosygin apologizing for US planes crossing Egyptian territory. Johnson's explanation, "They were going to help the *Liberty*," makes no sense. The route to *Liberty* made no detour over Egypt.

After his week on the USS *America*, Dave Lewis was flown to a hospital in Naples. There he asked the morgue officer how many of "my sailors" had drowned in the flooded compartment. None, Lewis was told.

Johnson lied to Soviet premier Kosygin on the newly activated hotline. He claimed he had instructed the carrier *Saratoga* "to dispatch aircraft on the scene to investigate the attack on the USS *Liberty*." The truth was the reverse: Johnson and McNamara twice canceled aircraft on their way to the scene of the attack.

CHAPTER 9

COVER-UP

"I emphatically deny that she was a spy ship."
—Admiral William Inman Martin

I srael made its public admission that it had conducted the attack on the USS *Liberty* on June 8 at 5:45 p.m. local time, three hours and forty-five minutes after the bombing of the ship. A declassified cable on file in the LBJ Library reveals that "hours after the incident he [Ambassador Barbour] reported that Israel did not intend to admit to the incident."[1] Nothing was straightforward or unambiguous. The guilty scrambled, none more egregiously than in Admiral Martin's emphatic denial "that she was a spy ship."[2] A desultory ambassador, Barbour was a Kennedy appointee. In *The Samson Option*, Seymour Hersh quotes Barbour as having told his new deputy chief of mission, William N. Dale, that he was on assignment personally from Lyndon Johnson himself: "I'm here under orders from Johnson, who told me, 'I don't care a thing about what happens to Israel, but your job is to keep the Jews off my back.'" A man wanting in subtlety, Barbour added, "Everything I do is designed to keep the Jews off the President's back, to keep them happy." The well-being of the US military stationed in the Middle East occupied a very low priority.[3] Hersh quotes John Hadden as calling Barbour "the finest man I've ever known in the government." It seems obvious that irony kept Hadden sane in that climate, and that his tongue was planted deeply in his cheek when he made that remark.

Barbour was strictly a pragmatist, as he told Dale: "Arab oil is not as important as Israel is to us. Therefore I'm going to side with Israel in all my reporting." Barbour could add no moral compass or historical depth to the situation. Seymour Hersh acknowledges that there was a long history of Israeli-US joint intelligence operations both before and after the attack on the USS *Liberty*. William J. Casey, CIA director under Ronald Reagan, ordered that Israeli liaison officers be provided with a private office near CIA headquarters.[4] But that came later, when overt collusion was the order of the day.

Hersh writes that "Barbour urged that Washington downplay the Israeli Air Force's rocket and strafing attack on the USS *Liberty*." Only at the end of the day did Barbour cable the secretary of state that "Israelis [were] obviously shocked by error and tender sincere apologies. Investigation now under way to obtain more info about vessel. Israelis do not intend to give any publicity to incident. Urge strongly that we too avoid publicity. If it is US flag vessel its proximity to scene conflict could feed Arab suspicions of US-Israel collusion."[5]

Falsifying the records meant presenting a united, corrupted version of the truth. The lying began with the attack itself. At 2:11 p.m., IAF audio-tapes declare that the air attack was over. At 2:17, Motor Torpedo Boat Division 914 was ordered that they "might need to give help." The Israeli helicopters that came next were ordered to assume there were Egyptian survivors—following the original plan that the ship was an Egyptian freighter, in keeping with the scenario of bombing Cairo in retaliation for Egyptian aggression.

There is chat on one Israeli air force tape about the lack of armed personnel to guard any Egyptians picked up by the helicopters. Israeli records have the motor torpedo boat division "closely approach in order to identify the vessel" and state that two helicopters were on their way. Unaware that *Liberty*'s SOS call had been received by *Saratoga*, the Israelis ordered the two dispatched helicopters held until the attack by the motor torpedo boats had been completed.

By the end of the day June 8, the politicians knew that a watertight cover-up was urgently required. The appointed US ambassador to Egypt,

Richard Nolte, not yet having been granted an opportunity to present his credentials to Nasser, and observing the lay of the land, sent a telegram on June 8 back home to his superiors: "We better get story on torpedoing of USS *Liberty* out fast and it had better be good."[6]

LBJ was livid. He wanted to know where this unknown ambassador of his came from. In fact, Nolte had been a classmate of the ubiquitous Nicholas Katzenbach and Thomas Lowe Hughes at Oxford. The truth was not an option. Nasser expelled Nolte on June 10, and Johnson, perceiving shrewdly that Nolte knew too much, chose not to post him elsewhere.

Scarcely had the firing ceased when Captain McGonagle initiated his own cover-up. Some observed that the captain's "demeanor had undergone a transformation. He was cold, distant and bitter, curt, off-balance, irritated and anxious."[7] Were it not for the captain's participation in the cover-up, it could not have been engineered as successfully and with the longevity that it has. The captain had been semiconscious and had lost a lot of blood, and the doctor, Richard Kiepfer, had considered relieving him of his command. Then it was decided that George Golden would actually control the ship, making all essential decisions. Jim Ennes has described how Lieutenant Maurice Bennett told him he had sent "the battle report on this thing to the Chief of Naval Operations."[8]

It was after the attack was over, too, that McGonagle berated Dr. Kiepfer for keeping his life jacket on because he was frightening the men with fear that the ship was in danger of sinking.[9] Kiepfer had not informed the captain that he had been wounded so as not to make the saving of lives about him personally. He was the most deserving of recipients of the Silver Star and, as Dave Lewis suggests, the Congressional Medal of Honor that went, instead, to the captain.

Liberty steamed on. At seven in the evening of June 8, Captain McGonagle, lying in bed, dictated a report enumerating ten dead, fifteen severely wounded, and seventy-five total wounded, with an undetermined number missing. Three musters were taken to identify the dead, the seriously injured, and the missing. Taking down McGonagle's testimony, the same obfuscating testimony he would give to Admiral Isaac Kidd for his naval court inquiry, was Maurice Bennett.

By 5:15 on June 8, McGonagle had radioed his falsified account of the attack to the Sixth Fleet commander, Admiral William Inman Martin. He referred to six strafing runs beginning at 2:00 p.m., although there had to have been many more than that. He mentioned the torpedo attack at 2:35 but neglected to mention that the torpedo boats had continued a machine gun attack on the ship for another forty minutes. There is no reference to the torpedo boats having machine-gunned the life rafts to ribbons.

Maurice Bennett himself added: "From reading the report, you'd think almost nothing happened at all. The report says there were just one or two airplanes that made a total of maybe five or six strafing runs over a period of maybe five or six minutes. Then, bam, the torpedo, and it was all over."

His faith in the honesty and integrity of McGonagle intact still, Ennes was incredulous. He blamed Bennett for accepting McGonagle's distorted report. Ennes writes: "When I mentioned the report to Lloyd Painter and others during the night, they reacted with bewilderment. No one could understand why McGonagle's report so minimized the incident and so ignored crucial details."[10]

This message was the first detailed report to leave the ship. It came a few hours after the attack and was riddled with lies, and it was repeated by McGonagle when he later testified before the Naval Court of Inquiry. It was erroneous, minimized the incident, and, in retrospect, seems to have been part of a preconceived plan. In substance, it was how the Pentagon would thereafter describe the incident, essentially verbatim, to the press.

Into that night of June 8, living through seventeen hours without help from the Sixth Fleet, the men were nervous and fearful. People gathered on the bridge, looking out for the rescue planes that would never come, or for the return of their tormentors. "We were just kind of waiting for whoever it was that had come and gotten us," sailor James O'Connor said, "to come back and finish us off."[11] All the sailors felt the stress of adversity, which would endure among many of them for a lifetime. Most had responded with unselfishness and valor, no one more than George Golden, to whom many believe they owed their lives. It was engineer Golden to whom Joseph Conrad's insight best applied: "For surely it is a great thing to have commanded a handful of men worthy of one's undying regard."[12] It was George Golden who best deserved the gratitude of his shipmates.

USS *Liberty* after the attack.

"By nightfall of June 8, everyone on board," Lloyd Painter says, "had a deep feeling of betrayal, bewilderment and abandonment. And, yes, a deep-seated anger at those who had murdered our ship mates. Because it was, in fact, cold-blooded murder."[13] George Golden said they had been "scape-goats," set up by their own government. They had been flying the US flag and had been a plainly marked US Navy noncombatant ship in near perfect weather, in international waters, and our "ally," Israel, had attacked us.

"This left us all in a conflicted state and very angry," Painter said. He added: "It wasn't until the Court of Inquiry began that we realized what a massive cover-up had been put in place. Then a real sense of abandonment, anger and frustration emerged. It is still inside of me today."

In Washington, on the morning of June 9, the cover-up was already well in place. At the National Security Agency by 9 a.m., Deputy Director Louis Tordella was discussing the torpedo attack with Captain Merriwell Vineyard of the Joint Reconnaissance Center. Tordella and General Marshall Carter wondered about "classified materials" on board and electronic equipment that would reveal US capability to "demultiplex the VHF and UHF multichannel interceptions." Vineyard confided that "consideration was then being given by some unnamed Washington authorities to sink *Liberty* 'to shield Israel' in order that newspaper men would be unable to photograph her and thus inflame public opinion against the Israelis." Official US action was discussed as if the United States and Israel were one entity.

Not in the loop, Tordella "made an impolite comment about that idea," wrote a memo of his conversation with Vineyard, and stored it away.[14] That Johnson, McNamara, and W. W. Rostow were already determined to stand by the falsehood that the attack had been an "accident" or a "mistake" is clear.

Far from being indifferent to the fate of *Liberty* on the morning of June 8, Robert McNamara had called General Carter, the NSA director, "wanting precise information" as to the ship's complement, the number of civilians on board, the exact meaning of the designation AGTR, and other facts. There were three civilians on board; other facts would be provided by Captain Thomas of the Naval Security Group.

The government did not function as a monolith. Johnson, McNamara, and Admiral William Inman Martin, and, in the shadows, CIA counterintelligence director James Angleton, operated on one side, with foreknowledge of the attack. Other officers, Richard Helms, Louis Tordella, Admiral David Lamar McDonald (Chief of Naval Operations), and John Hadden (CIA) represented quite another perspective. That McNamara, the technocrat and scourge of Vietnam (with Johnson equally deserving of that title), would not have hesitated to sacrifice the *Liberty* sailors should surprise no one.

Now McNamara lobbied unsuccessfully for scuttling the ship. William Inman Martin had gone from a heroic career of 440 night landings during World War II to an ignominious moment. He had been appointed commander of the Sixth Fleet just two months before the attack, only to refuse the destroyer escort that had been requested by *Liberty*'s captain and chief intelligence officer. A year later, in a letter to a friend, he referred to the "unbelievable carnage!"[15] In the aftermath of the attack, he lied obviously and outrageously.

On Saturday, June 10, 1967, Admiral Martin held a press conference. Regurgitating the official Pentagon line, he denied that the USS *Liberty* was a spy ship. The Norfolk *Virginian Pilot* of June 11 quotes the commander of the Sixth Fleet as stating: "I emphatically deny that she was a spy ship."

Martin revealed simultaneously that the United States was not prepared with a credible cover-up. "I emphatically tell you that she was there to be a communications guard in case we had to mass evacuate," he told the reporters, offering a view that seems to be an obvious product of CIA's Office of Cover and Deception.[16] "I have tried to be just as open and frank with you as I know how to be."[17]

As for motive, one turns to the US antipathy to the anticolonial struggles, and to capitalism's greed in obtaining control over the natural resources and markets of the newly independent states of the Middle East and of

Africa. Nasser symbolized independent nations that defined themselves as "neutral," neither pro-American nor pro-Soviet. Sinking the (unarmed) US surveillance ship and blaming Nasser was essential to ridding the region of economic interlopers who might compete against American interests.

Nasser's 1956 occupation of the Suez Canal was not far from anyone's mind. How great an impediment the Soviets would ultimately be to US interests was not yet clear. The view of a retired Soviet colonel, Oleg Korneevitch Sergeev, was that the Soviets knew what was coming, as Sergeev put it in describing the attack on the USS *Liberty*: "a joint action by two special services, the USA and Israel, which had one goal, combining forces for a war with Egypt."[18]

The Americans, the Soviets speculated, were not prepared to enter the conflict because of the Soviet forces in the Mediterranean Sea and the threat to Israel. It would have required a major military commitment and brought a full-blown conflict with the Soviets. As one of Sergeev's colleagues put it, "It is common for the secret services of countries to use their own forces for provocations to justify military actions."

During that night of June 8, after midnight, a 626/4 Soviet missile destroyer had signaled to *Liberty* in English, offering help.[19] "No thanks" was *Liberty*'s reply. Fifty years later, some of the sailors would still be thinking in Cold War terms. Their offer of assistance having been declined, the Soviets then added that they would remain at the horizon, and if the ship was going to go down, they would help out. For the next six hours, the Soviet ship followed a parallel course to *Liberty* at a distance of several miles. At 4 a.m., *Liberty* sighted a Russian merchant ship, *Proletarsk*.

In the early morning hours of June 9, Israel stormed into the Golan Heights. The pretext for a US entrance into the war—Egypt's sinking of a US intelligence ship—had vanished, and Israel's march to Damascus was canceled. Israel acquiesced in halting the land grab that would have carried it into Damascus, and by three in the afternoon, Radio Damascus had accepted a cease-fire.

June 9, 1967. Helicopters transported the wounded to the hospital on the USS *America*.

On the morning of June 9, at 6:25 the destroyers USS *Davis* and USS *Massey* drew up. "It was the prettiest sight I had ever seen," *Liberty* sailor Ron Kukal said. *America* was 138 miles behind, along with *Saratoga* and *Little Rock*. Finally, helicopters arrived, and nine dead and fifteen seriously wounded were transferred to the USS *America*, which had full hospital facilities.

The USS *Liberty*, photographed from the USS *America* on June 9, 1967. (Photo courtesy of Ernie Gallo.)

The flooded spaces remained 90 percent full of water and heavy oil fumes. There were no signals or noise to indicate that any sailors trapped below remained alive. Sailors from the USS *Davis* boarded *Liberty* and went below to remove the dead, repair the ship's navigational gyro system, restore fire main pressure, repair boilers, repair electrical and electronics

systems, and, above all, save the ship from sinking by shoring up the ballooned bulkheads below decks. They went in under battle conditions,
"locked and loaded."

Sailors of the USS *Liberty*, June 10, 1967: Left to right: Richard
Carlson, Lowell T. Bingham, Ron Kukal, Jeff Carpenter.

Larry Broyles entered the spaces where there was the greatest possibility for further flooding and which could have caused the ship to
sink. Descending below, Broyles, who was "an electrician's mate striker"
(working toward a rating as an electrician's mate, who is responsible for
the ship's electrical equipment), says, they risked their lives. The hatch
was locked behind them. Should the ship start to sink, they would be
trapped. There was no power, no water pressure. Once they went below
deck, the scuttle hatch was "dogged down" and locked so there would be

no way for them to escape. If the steel bulkheads were to give way, Broyles said, "we were dead." On the first night, they slept outside in life jackets.[20]

Larry Broyles (above left) of the USS *Davis* serving on the USS *Liberty*. "If the steel bulkheads were to give way, we were dead." (Photo courtesy of Larry Broyles.)

They were a contingent of twenty-one. Their task was enormous: they were to prevent any further attack, give medical assistance, prevent the ship from sinking, and restore all systems. The water pump had to be started so they could have enough pressure to clean up the blood and the napalm. They required electricity to get the boilers going, the turbine turning.

They had to shore up the steel bulkhead that had ballooned and warped from the torpedo blast. The walls were stretched, and there was seepage, so they could hear the salty seawater splashing up against the walls where the torpedo hit. Opening up some cargo hatches, they could see bodies floating around. One was caught high up in the wiring. There were only bones because the flesh had been blown off. Broyles remained aboard *Liberty* as, the next morning, having leveled the ship as much as possible, they moved off at four knots to Valletta, Malta. All the while, they expected to go under. (They arrived in Malta on June 15.)

On his way back to the United States, Larry Broyles passed through Rota. His camera and exposed film were at the bottom of his seabag, which was stowed in a locker as he waited in Rota for the plane that would take him back to Brooklyn. The next time he looked, the film and camera were gone. Two weeks later, he saw his photographs in *LIFE Magazine*.

Later, the sailors of the USS *Davis* were denied the commendations awarded to sailors on *Liberty* because they had not done their work in the heat of battle. The policy remained that the less *Liberty* was noticed, the better.

On June 9, James O'Connor shipped a canister of sixteen-millimeter film of *Liberty* to the Naval Photographic Center. Under the cover of night, his film was sent by special plane to Washington, DC. He himself was urinating pure blood and was sent to the *America* by himself. The doctor said he'd lost more than half his blood. "I don't know why you're alive," he said. O'Connor lost consciousness on his wire stretcher twice. He had nerve damage in his back. He lost a kidney. One of his legs never regained total feeling. At Landstuhl hospital in Germany, he was assigned an assumed name, "Private Loveland."

Later, NSA asked O'Connor whether *Liberty* produced any useful intelligence. O'Connor evaded the question. "I would hope it did," he said, but he "could not recall any." Bud Fossett at NSA was asked the same question during an investigative postmortem about *Liberty*. Did he believe *Liberty* produced some useful intelligence? "Any outstanding examples that you might cite?"

"I'm not aware of anything that was produced," Fossett said. "Certainly none against Middle East or North African targets of use by the *Liberty*."[21] CIA's Robert L. Wilson replied to the same question: "I sure wish I could say that we produced a couple of really neat things that were probably unique. Unfortunately, one of the things I thought was really nice was a message that had already been reported by another field station. . . . I don't think we really got anything significant out of it at all. . . . It [the operation] was a failure. . . . I thought it was a waste of a lot of lives and just a needless waste, and it had quite a shocking effect on me. I also felt almost guilty because I was alive and some were dead."[22]

"It was an attack on the United States!" Dave Lewis would say indignantly, his passion intact fifty years later. "And no one did anything about it."

On the afternoon of June 9, *Liberty* was finally visited by Admiral Martin. After meeting with the captain and crew, he gave the order that the ship proceed to Malta, rather than to Souda Bay in Crete, which had an adequate dry dock and was 16 hours away—three days of travel, versus 125 hours and seven days to reach Malta.

First class petty officer Ron Kukal says that "the excuse was given that at Souda Bay they didn't have facilities to repair our severe damage."[23] "The long voyage to Malta meant," Lloyd Painter says, "that the US government wanted us to sink." Malta had other advantages for higher authority. In Malta, they were less likely to be accosted by the press, who might have questions.

The primary necessity, according to Admiral Martin, having secured the approval of Admiral McCain in London, was to protect the crypto-material and equipment, even as most had been destroyed anyway. Lieutenant Bennett arranged that a team from the Naval Security Group, Europe, meet *Liberty* at Malta.

USS *Liberty* on June 9, 1967. Rescued at last.

On June 10, Vice Admiral John S. McCain, four stars, father of the future bellicose Arizona senator, ordered Rear Admiral Isaac Kidd, two stars, to convene a Naval Court of Inquiry, an official investigation of the incident.

On the way to Malta, McGonagle showed his statement for the court of inquiry to Dr. Kiepfer and George Golden. Kiepfer and Golden both objected, arguing that the planes had attacked for at least twenty-five minutes and that the offer of help came two hours after the torpedo attack, not before.[24]

But McGonagle apparently had asked for their views only to pull rank and to ensure the credibility of his part in the cover-up. He told them he "trusted that their story would not conflict with his." McGonagle told

Kiepfer, "Our best course of action is don't volunteer a thing. Answer their questions, but don't tell them anything you don't have to tell them." Dr. Kiepfer noted, nonetheless, that "the Russians arrived to help before our own ships did."[25]

On the Sunday of that week, as *Liberty* limped toward Malta, Kidd and his counsel, Ward Boston, set out on the destroyer USS *Fred T. Berry*. From a small boat, Kidd clambered aboard *Liberty* to begin what sailor Jack Beattie called "the most dishonest investigation in naval history." Bryce Lockwood would remark, "Everything McGonagle did until the morning after the attack was marvelous. Then Kidd came aboard, and suddenly McGonagle was a yes-man. He went to his grave with a guilty conscience."[26]

Admiral Isaac C. Kidd Jr.: "Ward, they aren't interested in the facts of what happened. It's a political issue. They want to cover it up." (Photo from the US Navy.)

Beattie had spent the night of June 8 in a small boat with his life jacket on. Suddenly, there was Kidd, with his belt buckle decorated with stars, in his face. He was a short, fat man. Don Pageler would remember that Kidd had brought with him a small bottle of brandy to give everybody. He was intimidating as he told the sailors, "Keep your mouth shut or you'll end up in Leavenworth prison."

On June 12, the order was broadcast, "Everyone on the ship muster on the forecastle on the aft deck." George Golden conducted a head count and was so rattled by the threatening and unpleasant atmosphere that he forgot to count himself. Glenn Oliphant remembered Isaac Kidd's threat as "If you guys talk about this, I'll make sure you're in prison."[27] They were to grant no interviews. They were to go ashore only in civilian clothes. They were not to mention the name of the ship. "Just forget it ever happened," they were ordered. The CTs were told that everything was classified.

"You have a CRYPTO clearance; you cannot divulge what you saw or what you think, or you can be court-martialed and will be court-martialed. You still have time in the navy. You would spend the rest of your time in jail. The officers have the right to shoot you."[28] The tone was frantic, verging on hysterical—as well it might have been. What was at stake was that the US role in collaborating with Israel to murder its own sailors be kept secret, a devil's bargain mandating that both the United States and Israel stay silent. And so through 2018 they have done, despite pressure from the surviving sailors.

In the late 1980s, Pageler found himself in group therapy for post-traumatic stress disorder. One night in group, a marine who had served in Vietnam looked into his eyes and said, "You guys got screwed as bad if not worse than anyone I knew in Viet Nam. You have every right to be as angry as you can be."[29]

It was treated by higher authority as a matter of life and death that what had happened to these sailors be kept secret. Lloyd Painter and Bob Scarborough received their Purple Hearts in Germany, where Painter was ordered, "Never say where you got it!" They would never be told why they were to maintain silence for the rest of their lives. (Two hundred and eight Purple Hearts were awarded to the sailors, along with 294

Combat Action citations, 9 Navy Commendations, 2 Navy Crosses, 20 Bronze Stars, and 12 Silver Stars. *Liberty* would be the most highly decorated ship in naval history for a single engagement, even as this one-sided ambush could hardly be termed "combat."[30])

Resigning his naval commission after the attack, Lloyd Painter went on to serve twenty-eight years with the United States Secret Service as a special agent. He would be assigned to protect, among others, Mamie Eisenhower, Pat Nixon, Pope John Paul, and Henry Kissinger. He was never assigned to any member of LBJ's family. "I consider myself lucky in that respect," he says.[31]

On the day *Liberty* arrived in Malta, McNamara ordered a news blackout.

As soon as they docked in Malta, the crew members of the USS *Davis* were ordered to be ready to depart. They assembled with their seabags and were escorted down the gangplank by armed navy personnel in white short-sleeved shirts and white pants, .45 caliber pistols strapped to their waists. Then they were marched single file down the pier until they came to the USS *Davis* captain's motorboat.

Sailor Don Pageler in dry dock at Malta after two days bringing the dead up from the flooded research spaces. (Photos courtesy of Don Pageler.)

Malta: caskets and body bags. (Photos courtesy of Don Pageler.)

Liberty in dry dock in Malta. (Photo courtesy of the National Security Agency.)

No one spoke to them, and they didn't talk to anyone as they were hustled aboard the USS *Davis*. It was as if there was something shameful about the whole incident. They were not awarded "hostile pay" because "there was too much paperwork involved."[32] Like the *Liberty* sailors, the sailors who had come aboard from the destroyer *Davis* to help save the ship were warned never to speak of what they had seen or what they had done.

In Malta, the navy hierarchy closed ranks around the sailors. Local newspapers were forbidden from photographing the battered ship, and the sailors were ordered not to talk to reporters. George Golden told Colin Frost of Reuters that a massive cover-up was under way. Soon Golden was warned by a navy captain and two government agents, "If you don't shut up, your career in the navy is over and you won't be able to get a job flipping burgers." Golden was flown back home that night.

Malta: men retrieving the corpses of their fallen comrades. (Photo courtesy of the National Security Agency.)

Malta: sailors entering the ruined research spaces of *Liberty* in dry dock. (Photos courtesy of Don Pageler.)

Only people who had TOP SECRET clearance were permitted to go down into the flooded spaces to collect the broken, decaying bodies. Invariably, they vomited. There were pieces of bodies that couldn't be identified. Catching Ron Kukal, the highest-ranking enlisted man, whom he found slipping and sliding on blood in the passageway, Lieutenant O'Connor told him, "You're the man for the body recovery."[33]

Pieces of bodies were pulled out of steam pipes. Kukal tried to put them together like a jigsaw puzzle, laying out torsos, arms, and legs. A head had been severed in the gun mount. There was unburned napalm everywhere. Kukal had been in the navy for eight years. After the attack, he resigned.

Meanwhile, Admiral McCain was directing the Sixth Fleet to do "whatever is feasible to keep any Soviet ships out of *Liberty*'s wake," as if *Liberty* had generated useful intelligence and something terrible would happen should it fall into the hands of the Russians.[34] The nonsense of the Cold War, so vital to James Angleton, persisted, embedded in the consciousness of the military, officers and enlisted men alike.

At a congressional hearing a day or two later, initiated by Senator Sykes of Florida to look into the attack, NSA director Marshall Carter was asked whether or not he thought the attack was deliberate. "It couldn't be anything else but deliberate. There's just no way you could have a series of circumstances that would justify it being an accident," Carter said firmly.[35]

Cyrus Vance, who had sent *Liberty* to the East Med on behalf of the 303 Committee, was present to shut Marshall Carter down. "I think it's premature to make a judgment like that," he said. Vance took charge of the cover-up within the United States.[36] When Marshall Carter returned to NSA, he told his chief of staff, Gerard Burke, "Cy Vance told me to keep my mouth shut. These were his exact words."[37]

Vance sent his own cable to the naval forces in Europe that all information on *Liberty* must come from or must be approved by the Department of Defense, mainly himself. The president of the United States leaned on Admiral Kidd to ensure that the one inquiry into the attack would not expose the truth—not least that he personally had intervened to prevent rescue planes from flying to the side of *Liberty*. 303 had ensured Lyndon Johnson's plausible deniability.

In the documentary *USS* Liberty: *Dead in the Water*, George Golden says that Captain McGonagle had told him that if the ship sank, blame would go to Egypt and the Soviet Union, and then the United States would step in and engage in the war openly. Golden also confides that Kidd kept him out of the hearing room so that his testimony wouldn't be recorded.

George Golden was born Jewish, but this attack at the hands of the Israelis, with the collaboration of his own government, embittered him. He renounced his Judaism and converted to the Baptist faith.[38] He told Bryce Lockwood at the 1997 reunion of the surviving sailors that he was a "Pentecostal Baptist," which for Lockwood was an oxymoron.[39] George Koromah, one of the few people of color among the crew, called Golden the "best officer on the ship."[40]

In Malta, members of the officer class showed little regard for the sailors. Don Pageler, a compulsive amateur photographer, was up on the dock taking pictures when he overheard three officers who had arrived from Washington for the court of inquiry. "I don't know what every-body's making such a big deal about that for," one said. "That hole doesn't look that big to me." The hole in the ship made by the torpedo was forty feet wide. A third classman, one rank above Pageler, turned around and said, "Fuck you, sir!"

Near the end of his stay in Malta, Pageler was in a bar when he met a Royal Air Force officer who said, "Ah, you guys deserved to get shot up. You shouldn't have been over there anyway." At every turn, the sailors were blamed for having been attacked, blamed for having been where they had been ordered to be.

Bob Wilson was given "the rush treatment to get out of there, and don't talk to anybody." When the ship had begun its move to Malta, he had been looking over the side and saw some "Top Secret Codeword stuff floating out of the torpedo hole. Then some men with little hooks picked it up, people with no clearance." There was something farcical about the efforts to suggest that *Liberty* had been on a credible, urgent surveil-lance mission, that any of the intelligence they collected had any value or relevance.

Wilson was offered to stay a day and recuperate, an offer he declined. When he heard the official story that they were in the Eastern Med because there were "some U.S. civilians in the area at the time . . . and in case any of these civilians were attempting to get in contact with the United States in order to get out of this area, we were there to intercept any communica-tions." He had trouble saying these words "with a straight face."[41]

He landed at JFK, and he and his escort boarded a little helicopter so as not to have to go through the airport. A customs official asked him, "So you were on the *Liberty*, how was it?"

"Not so nice," Wilson said, and walked off. A marine lieutenant colonel accompanied Wilson all the way back to Friendship Airport in Balti-more. He didn't run into any journalists, but the officer was "extremely nervous the entire time, afraid I was going to say something wrong or some reporter was going to come up to me. I think he was going to have a heart attack." Despite his CIA affiliation, Wilson was never debriefed. He was afforded only a two- or three-minute visit with Deputy Director Louis Tordella at NSA. Among dishonorable people, he retained his code of honor, which meant never violating his oaths of secrecy.

Kidd's "inquiry" was completed in a scant week, rendering it a travesty that this should be the only official US government investigation into the attack on the USS *Liberty* for fifty years and counting. Kidd interviewed no one in Israel. Years later, in 1983, Admiral Kidd wrote to Jim Ennes that "any dealings with any other nation or any like sources beyond our own people were precluded."

During the entire process of interviewing, Kidd's mantra remained: "You will never, repeat, never, discuss this with anyone, not even your wives. If you do, you will be court-martialed and will end your lives in prison or worse." So he intimidated into silence even shrewd officers like Lloyd Painter, someone not easily browbeaten.

On the tugboat *Papago*, assigned to accompany *Liberty* to Malta, crew member James M. Makris watched as bloated corpses floated out of the torpedo hole while officers drilled orders into the men: put the cameras away, don't take pictures, don't ask questions. If anybody had pictures, they were to turn them in to superior officers.[42]

Papago used boat hooks and crab nets to pick up floating material. Enhancing the farce, lights were rigged on *Papago*'s bridge wing. It ran over some material with her propeller, then backed down over it, shredding the paper into small pieces. When paper did not disintegrate in nine hours after being placed in the water, it balled up and sank.

Torpedo hole, seen at waterline[31]

Shots of the torpedo hole. (Photo courtesy of Don Pageler.)

Malta: torpedo hole in dry dock (Malta) with scuba divers.
(Photos courtesy of Don Pageler.)

Dave Lucas, the first sailor witness at Kidd's court of inquiry, contradicted McGonagle's June 8 testimony dictated to Maurice Bennett. You will not find his descriptions of the injuries to the men in the final report because part of the purpose of the inquiry was to minimize the ferocity of the attack. Nor is there mention of the napalm that was tossed on deck, although Lucas had brought a sample of the jellied napalm in a container to the hearing.

Dave Lucas testified that the torpedo boats signaled *after* the torpedo attack, not before, as McGonagle claimed. McGonagle said that a sailor fired on the Israeli boats and claimed that the Israelis were accurate in claiming the ship had fired on them. Lucas said he had investigated and found that the machine gun had gone off by itself in the heat of battle. The sailor manning that machine gun had already been killed.

Malta: Torpedoed compartment and torpedo hole seen in dry dock. Most of the hole is below the waterline. (Photo courtesy of Don Pageler.)

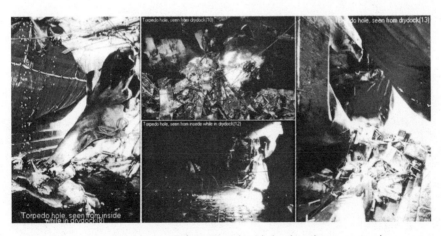

Malta: torpedo hole seen from inside while the ship was in dry dock. (Photos courtesy of Don Pageler.)

Captain McGonagle on bridge with large rocket hole (34)

Battle damage (59)

Ensign David Lucas with battle damage (37)

Ensign David Lucas with battle damage to the ship. (Photos courtesy of Don Pageler.)

After Lucas was sent off to a hospital, Captain McGonagle took the stand. McGonagle repeated the obfuscations and untruths that he had dictated in the report he made on the day of the attack. He claimed that the attack lasted "five to six minutes"—at the most, eight—when in fact, the bombardment took closer to an hour and a half.

McGonagle said nothing about the torpedo boats' machine-gunning of the life rafts. Lloyd Painter testified to that Israeli war crime; Captain McGonagle did not mention it, and it does not appear in the final report. McGonagle ignored entirely that the torpedo boats had machine-gunned *Liberty* for an additional forty minutes after they had fired their torpedoes.

McGonagle claimed, preposterously, that machine gun fire issuing from *Liberty* was effective, adding, "I am sure that they felt they were under fire," as if the Israeli torpedo boats had been provoked into defensive retaliation, as if they were the victims rather than the aggressors. After the torpedo attack, he claimed that he did not order any preparations be made to abandon ship. In fact, his order to abandon ship is what led to the men to lowering the life rafts into the water in the first place.

James Scott writes in his book that there is a handwritten copy of *Liberty*'s Combat Information Center log showing that at 2:33 p.m., the demolition bill was set, an order to destroy classified materials, set explosive charges, and open valves to scuttle a ship. McGonagle lied about the number of reconnaissance flights on the morning of the attack; he lied about the time the first flight arrived, claiming it came at 10:30 a.m. rather than at 5:15 a.m. He lied when he said that after the torpedo attack at 2:25, the boats made no further attacks. He lied about the ship's log, which stated that at 2:38, he had issued the order to abandon ship.

McGonagle's testimony is ragged and replete with non sequiturs. He revealed inadvertently that both he and Admiral William Inman Martin were part of the operation and enjoyed foreknowledge of the attack. He echoed Inman Martin's statement that operational control of *Liberty* chopped from CINCUSNAVEUR to COMSIXTHFLT only on June 7, when in reality that had occurred when the ship passed through the Straits of Gibraltar on June 2, as an automatic protocol.

He offered into evidence an altered ship's log, in which for the time between 1:55 and 2:46 p.m. of June 8, there are no entries at all.

There are other obfuscations in McGonagle's testimony. McGonagle insisted that he did not "order any preparations to be made to abandon ship," although sailors had heard him do that. Some on the bridge with the captain heard the order, but then George Golden intercepted it, and indeed they did not abandon ship. Captain McGonagle insisted that the two helicopters "did not approach the ship in a hostile manner, but kept pointed parallel to the ship." Glenn Oliphant witnessed otherwise. He saw a soldier manning a machine gun in a helicopter's open door: "He was aiming the gun at me. I don't think we would have had a chance against those commandos," Oliphant says.[43]

In retrospect, it would seem clear that McGonagle's logic was to claim that he had maintained his position on the bridge, issuing orders throughout the ordeal. Unfortunately for the captain, there was a witness to this untruth. Lloyd Painter had been summoned to find McGonagle lying on a stretcher; Dr. Kiepfer corroborated his testimony. McGonagle did not maintain his position on the bridge, fully conscious and issuing orders. There is a photograph taken by Lloyd Painter of Captain McGonagle lying semiconscious on the bridge, blood oozing from his leg. Blood sloshed in his shoes, and his trousers were soaked with blood. He was supine and unconscious. Medal of Honor or no, he was no hero.

At one point, Lloyd Painter had encountered Isaac Kidd alone on the ship. He had removed his stars and told Painter to treat him like any other sailor. "Tell me what really happened," Kidd said.

Painter testified for about two hours.[44] He talked about how the captain lapsed in and out of consciousness during the attack. He testified as to the low-flying reconnaissance aircraft before the attack, with the Star of David plainly visible; he witnessed the machine-gunning of the life rafts. Only about 35 percent of Painter's testimony made it into the record. All the while, Painter says, he was made to feel as if the sailors of Liberty were the "bad guys." Painter added: "Notice I do not address him [Kidd] as Admiral—he does not deserve the title."[45] (This reminds the author of Robert J. Kleberg Jr. refusing to call his old acquaintance Lyndon Johnson "Mr. President.")

Painter concluded: "Unlike the Gulf of Tonkin incident, Operation Cyanide went dreadfully wrong. Liberty did not sink. We all did not die. We were able to ID our attackers. Then we were ordered to sail across the Med on a fatally damaged ship, in the hopes that we would sink. If the Liberty had sunk, at least there would be no evidence of what had transpired."[46]

"Daddy lied," McGonagle's daughter Sandy confided to sailor Gary Brummett, who asked whether her father ever told her he lied. "He told us years ago he lied about it," she said.[47]

Kidd's final report focuses almost exclusively on McGonagle's testimony, giving great weight to how the captain relied on the North Star on the night of June 8 to guide the ship to safety. Years later, in his cups, McGonagle told George Golden that he had been bribed to distort the facts.[48]

Indeed, he was at once promoted to the rank of captain and given a new ship to command. In 2007, Admiral Kidd's counsel, Ward Boston, would state, speaking of both himself and Kidd: "We both believed with certainty that this attack was a deliberate effort to sink an American ship and murder its entire crew. . . . The Israelis intended that there be no survivors."[49]

At the time, however, the inquiry concluded falsely that the attack was "in fact a case of mistaken identity," the American flag "difficult to identify." In fact, the flag was replaced twice, first by Russell David, the leading signalman. When that one was shot down, Frank Brown and Joe Meadors raised the holiday colors, the oversized flag, on the number 4 port halyard.

Yet Kidd's report states that there were "no available indications that the attack was intended against a U.S. ship." The report repeats that "the Israeli Defense Forces conducted air and surface searches for survivors . . . responding to a U.S. attack." There is nothing about the machine-gunning of the life rafts; nothing about those helicopters with commandos, their weapons at the ready; nothing about how the rescue planes were called back.

At the inquiry, a radioman who kept talking about the Israelis' jamming of the circuits was removed from the room and ordered to be silent.[50] When Dr. Kiepfer remarked, "The only help we had was from the Russians," he was ordered, "You will drop that line of reasoning, doctor!"[51]

If anyone criticized Israel, they were told, "We don't want to hear about that." An officer brought the "Ship Weather Observation Sheet," which showed that there was a breeze sufficient to make the flag stand out on June 8. There was a sprightly breeze, no clouds, no rain—only sun. The blue sea of June put up no resistance.

When the court showed no interest, he removed the weather report from the courtroom, wisely anticipating that it would disappear.

Nine years later, he gave it to Jim Ennes, who would write the first book describing the attack, in defiance of Admiral Kidd's orders that the sailors remain silent in perpetuity. The court of inquiry ruled that it was a windless day and there was no flag.[52] Yet for fifty years, the government would contend that this was a legitimate investigation, rendering any further investigation unnecessary.

Kidd carried the report to London, where the protocol was to show it for the endorsement of Captain Merlin Staring "in a legal review capacity." For several days, Staring was "heavily engaged" in a review of the testimony and evidence gathered and reported by Admiral Kidd. The logistics were accomplished at the London headquarters of CINCUSNAVEUR (John S. McCain, commander in chief, US Naval Forces Europe. Staring was "Force Legal Officer."[53])

The report was several hundred pages long. Staring's early study of the transcript "produced many pages of personal notes and questions which I would have to resolve and/or comment upon in the proposed endorsement which I contemplated preparing for consideration by the Commander-in Chief." Staring had spent two long days and nights when an inquiry came to him from Admiral McCain.

According to a letter from Staring to writer David Walsh, McCain had demanded an endorsement by "that evening." When Staring "stated that I could not hope to complete my work and conscientiously fulfill my professional responsibilities as Force Legal Officer within that time frame," he was told that the endorsement "would be prepared elsewhere within the staff."[54]

According to other sources, the report was removed from Staring's office overnight without his knowledge. He was the senior navy lawyer on CINCUSNAVEUR's staff and knew that he would be held responsible for the endorsement. Immediately, he put himself on the record as having "neither prepared the endorsement . . . nor been given an opportunity to conduct a complete review of the record and to advise before that endorsement was sent forward."

In a slightly different version of these events, Staring said: "I had the

650-page record for a total of 18 hours, during 15 of which I concentrated on it."[55] He had "been having problems finding evidence in the record to support some of the court's findings, and was only about a third of the way through it when the Admiral had the record withdrawn from me." Staring never saw the manuscript again.

Staring was a timid man, supine before authority, and he did not tell anyone what had happened with the draft of the naval inquiry.[56] A few years later, when Staring was promoted to admiral and became the navy's chief legal officer (Judge Advocate General), he saw the alterations made by John S. McCain, and he revealed the truth of what had happened.

By 2005, now Admiral Staring called "the Navy Court of Inquiry of 1967 a near-total farce. . . . It could neither then nor now be considered an honest or a thorough, or a reliable investigation of the major tragedy that was the attack upon the USS *Liberty*."[57]

Ron Kukal, left in the white T-shirt; on his right, Admiral Merlin Staring. (Photo courtesy of Ron Kukal.)

Armed with a gun to "protect the evidence," in itself farcical, Kidd traveled from London to Washington. Civilians from the White House then sat down with Kidd and edited the transcript. In Washington, Isaac Kidd met with the Chief of Naval Operations, Admiral David Lamar McDonald.

Kidd's further-edited summary had arrived in the fourth-floor office of Admiral McDonald for review on June 22.[58] An accompanying memo warned that "strong Navy non-concurrence in the draft is anticipated" and that the Pentagon's press officers had "their marching orders from Secretary Vance."[59] Once again, the shadow of Cyrus Vance looms over these events.

"Ike, was it intentional?" Admiral McDonald asked Kidd. The Chief of Naval Operations clearly had not been in the loop.

McDonald, now sixty years old, despised Robert McNamara's leadership of the Pentagon, as McNamara ignored the chain of command and discounted the views of senior military leaders, whose experience he dismissed. McDonald openly praised McNamara as "probably the best defense secretary ever," while his own view was the opposite.[60]

McDonald attacked the draft summary of the court of inquiry report with his customary red pencil. Beside one statement, McDonald wrote, "I don't believe it." Utilizing every means open to him, he dissociated himself from Admiral Kidd's history of the attack on the USS *Liberty*.[61]

David Lamar McDonald was a no-nonsense, simple man. He was born September 12, 1906, in a small town in northeast Georgia, his father a country preacher. He was a longtime foe of cover-ups. He had served in his long career aboard the USS *Saratoga*. John Sidney McCain, who was a traitor to these sailors, and would be rewarded with a battleship being christened in his name, had been one of his students. McDonald had been commander of the Sixth Fleet, like Admiral Martin. McDonald was appointed Chief of Naval Operations by President John F. Kennedy in August 1963, having just been awarded his fourth star.[62]

"It isn't Watergate," McDonald remarked. "It's the unwillingness to come clean."

So he set himself on a collision course with Isaac Kidd, Robert McNamara, and, behind them all, Cyrus Vance.

What McDonald liked about serving on a carrier was the camaraderie: "The way you have to rely on each other, the teamwork, is just unbelievable. And these men do this night and day."[63] When he was appointed CNO, he thought the "Navy did itself proud in World War II. Here I was, the son of a country preacher in Georgia and the existing system made it possible for me to become head of this Navy."[64] Admiral McDonald was one of those military leaders, like Dwight Eisenhower, who did not savor war. "I saw no reason to send ships to the Mediterranean for six months, bring them back for three, and send them back for six again, in time of peace."

Repeatedly, he locked horns with McNamara. Before the *Liberty* incident, he told his right-hand man, Isaac Kidd, "I think I'll just turn in my suit. I just don't think I can do this any longer."[65] Kidd said of McNamara: "There was absolutely nothing that he wasn't privy to, as far as I was concerned."

McDonald articulated his frustration with Kidd's naval inquiry in a handwritten memo. "I think that much of this is extraneous and it leaves me with the feeling that we're trying our best to excuse the attackers," he wrote. He added a personal note: "Were I a parent of one of the deceased this release would burn me up. I myself do not subscribe to it." He challenged the statement that the court found no evidence that Israel's forces knew *Liberty* was an American ship. "Was there any which indicated that they didn't know?" he wrote.

He questioned the statement that there was no available indication that the attack was intended against an American ship. "Any that the attack wasn't intended?" he scribbled. "Hit by at least one air to surface rocket" became "attacked and hit." He added the word "classified" to conducted hearings.[66]

So Admiral McDonald scrutinized the text, which had been obviously designed to obfuscate. He cut the line "The attack was described by the Court as a 'major naval disaster of international significance.'" He bracketed the falsehood "in fulfillment of its obligation to protect its nationals and to evacuate those who desire evacuation. It was in fulfillment of such an obligation that USS *Liberty* was engaged." To this last line, he added two question marks.

He cut another of Kidd's lies outright: "Her flag, while flying, was not always fully extended due to a lack of wind and the ship's slow speed." He also cut "The court found that the calm conditions and slow ship speed may well have made the American flag difficult to identify." Admiral David Lamar McDonald did everything he could to obliterate the lie that Israel did not recognize that this was an American ship.

When Kidd speculated that "smoke from the burning whaleboat and other topside fires may have obscured her flag," Admiral McDonald cut this falsehood outright. Kidd also (shamefully) wrote of the torpedo boats, "I am sure that they felt they were under fire from USS *Liberty*." McDonald cut this. "How could anyone know what the Israeli torpedo boat captains 'felt'?" he asked. Admiral McDonald was not inclined to exonerate Israel, and so he cut the line "But the court found 'no available indications that the attack was intended against a U.S. ship.'"

"Not agreed," Admiral McDonald wrote in pencil. Nor could any navy admiral accept the absurdity that *Liberty*, with its four .50 caliber machine guns—nor *El Quseir*, with its two three-pounders—could have conducted a shore bombardment on El Arish. He soon discovered that the Pentagon "had little interest in making substantial changes to the draft."

On June 21, Admiral McDonald's chief assistant wrote him that "things seem to be moving rapidly in disturbing directions." Admiral McDonald was not pleased with the tone, the language, or the "import" of the summary. He had been left with "the feeling that we're trying our best to excuse the attackers."

Power ruled the day. McDonald was a full four-star admiral, and Kidd an insolent two-star admiral. But Kidd had John S. McCain behind him, and behind McCain were Cyrus Vance and Lyndon Johnson. McDonald, the navy's senior officer, faced superior power. So McDonald had asked Isaac Kidd, "Ike, was it intentional?"

"No," Isaac Kidd lied.[67]

All McDonald could do was dissociate himself from the cover-up and express his indignation in private. Later, ignoring the ignominy of the corrupted naval inquiry into the attack on the USS *Liberty*, his moral courage intact, McDonald regretted his acquiescence in the Vietnam War, which was entering its most virulent stage at the very moment of the attack on the USS *Liberty*:

> Maybe we military men were all weak. Maybe we should have stood up and pounded the table. . . . I was part of it and I'm sort of ashamed of myself too. At times I wonder, "Why did I go along with this stuff?"[68]

The betrayal of *Liberty* went too far, and he did not include it in this discussion. Admiral McDonald and his staff managed to make some minor adjustments to the naval inquiry. The final draft noted that the court determined the resemblance to *El Quseir* was "highly superficial" and that the attackers had "ample opportunity" to identify *Liberty* prior to the assault. It stated that the court had "sufficient information" to determine why the Israelis attacked (the author dissents).[69]

It noted that the court heard no evidence from Israel, language absent from the early draft. But the final draft included still that the flag may have been difficult for the attackers to see, even though that contradicted the testimony of every witness.

On June 18, the fact-finding team of the Joint Chiefs of Staff released its "Memo for the Chairman, JCS." Its focus was on the message(s) that supposedly failed to arrive in time and that supposedly would have moved the ship one hundred miles offshore. There were four such messages, it contended. Writing about the messages was a convenient means of avoiding the issue. Neither the court of inquiry nor the memorandum raised the issue of what or who put the ship in place, although, as noted above, Cyrus Vance and the 303 Committee are named as having sent *Liberty* to the Eastern Med. Kidd invoked General Burchinal and Admiral McCain as concurring in his conclusion that they should "scrupulously avoid getting into this matter on this issue at this time."

Kidd's strategy seems to have been to shut every door of inquiry, not least to the press; admit to nothing; and insist that everything was classified. He did not know that the Joint Fact-Finding team had inadvertently revealed the answer to this question. The Joint Chiefs staff had neglected to redact this one sentence: "It was the Deputy Secretary of Defense (Cyrus Vance) and the 303 Committee which 'initiated movement of the USS *Liberty* to the Eastern Mediterranean by way of Rota, Spain.'"[70]

On June 30, 1967, Cyrus Vance resigned as deputy secretary of defense. He pleaded ill health. Confusion would swirl around this incident for the next fifty years. Lyndon Johnson would call one of his speechwriters "a Zionist dupe" for suggesting that the president attend a pro-Israel rally.

"I have yet to understand why it was felt necessary to attack this ship or who ordered the attack," Richard Helms says in the documentary *USS Liberty: Dead in the Water*. Consenting to be interviewed as a favor to his old friend Dick Thompson, Helms says, "They [Israel] intended to attack this ship." Still, Helms was not generous with his office records for history.[71]

Hypocritically, Johnson, in apparently an effort to distance himself from what had been his own participation, encouraged what the Israelis called the "wicked insinuation" that Israel had intentionally attacked the ship. In an off-the-record briefing with *Newsweek*, Johnson used the term "deliberate attack." According to Israeli author Tom Segev, Ambassador Avraham Harman and the Israeli embassy spokesman, Dan Patir, "managed to tone down the *Newsweek* article."[72]

Arthur Goldberg, Johnson's UN ambassador—code-named Menashe in his efforts on behalf of Israel—revealed to Harman that the United States had intercepted communications of Israeli pilots identifying the ship as American.[73] Israel maintained the lie that they did not know the ship was American, while *Newsweek* added a question mark to its headline and dropped a sidebar commentary. Israel had other allies in the US publishing community. Martin Peretz in *Commentary* magazine wrote an article about the Six-Day War that was published in November 1967 without a single mention of the attack on the USS *Liberty*.[74]

The lobbyist for Israel, Abe Feinberg, learned that the United States had evidence of an Israeli pilot continuing to attack the ship even after verifying its identity.[75] Meanwhile, "Menashe" reported to the Israelis that the United States had recorded the Israeli pilots during the attack, again demonstrating that they knew the ship was American.

Israeli colonel Ram Ron's report blaming the victims was so blatantly dishonest that the Israelis ordered a second investigation presided over by Lieutenant Colonel and Judge Yeshayahu Yerushalmi. Yerushalmi promptly ruled that there was "insufficient evidence" warranting charges against any single individual. All Israeli military, from pilots to torpedo boat captains, had "acted reasonably under wartime circumstances."[76] With a flourish, Yerushalmi dismissed all charges.

On September 19, 1977, CIA director Admiral Stansfield Turner went on *Good Morning America* to deny that the Israeli government "knew about the USS *Liberty* before the attack" and to say that the attack was "not malicious" and had been "satisfactorily explained by Israel." On September 22, 1977, in the presence of Cyrus Vance, who was serving briefly as secretary of state, the United States fully embraced the idea that the attack was "a mistake by the Israeli air force."

In an advertisement in the *New York Times* taken out by Palestinian supporters, using documents from CIA, they declared that Moshe Dayan had ordered the attack. The headline was "Are We Welcoming the Murderer of Our Sons?"

The sailors of the USS *Liberty* had not forgotten this ruthless man. Five years earlier, in 1972, Lloyd Painter was working on a Secret Service detail to protect Abba Eban. Painter found himself in an elevator at the Waldorf Astoria Hotel in New York, standing beside Moshe Dayan. "I was armed and I wondered if old Moshe knew that I had survived the *Liberty* attack only five years earlier," Painter said. "I knew I could change the course of history, but would end up destroying my own life. I chose my own life."[77] Later, Painter told friends with his typical sardonic humor: "I had a gun and he didn't."

Honorable to a fault, Lloyd Painter emerged from this history with scant sympathy for Captain McGonagle, who lied to serve Isaac Kidd's corrupt naval inquiry to further his own career. "McGonagle betrayed his men," Painter told Bryce Lockwood.[78]

Admiral McDonald was relieved as Chief of Naval Operations three days after *Liberty* arrived at Little Creek Naval Station in Norfolk, Virginia. "He had been too openly critical of an operation that from his point of view made no sense," Peter Hounam writes.[79]

"Ward, they're not interested in the facts," Isaac Kidd confided to Boston. "It's a political matter and we cannot talk about it." Thirty years later, Ward Boston said that "LBJ had ordered us to put the lid on it. . . . I didn't speak up earlier because I was told not to," Boston admitted, invoking the code of obedience and acquiescence to authority that marks military service.[80] Boston had not been deficient in physical courage; he had flown photo reconnaissance missions over Tokyo and Iwo Jima in navy Hellcat fighters. Moral courage took longer.[81]

The transcript of Isaac Kidd's naval inquiry eventually released to the public was not the same text that Ward Boston had certified and sent to Washington. To cite one example, Lloyd Painter's testimony of witnessing the deliberate machine-gunning of the life rafts by the Israeli torpedo crews had been included in the original transcript and was now missing.

In 2004, Admiral Thomas Moorer termed the attack Israel committed, acts of murder against US servicemen, an act of war against the

United States. With the authority of having served as chairman of the Joint Chiefs of Staff (from 1970–1974), he demanded that Congress address Israel's motive "with full cooperation from the National Security Agency, the Central Intelligence Agency and the military intelligence services." Admiral Moorer searched for an explanation for an attack he deemed "absolutely deliberate." Any denial of that fact, he said, was a "damn lie." It would be the first time since the War of 1812 that the United States was attacked and Congress conducted no investigation.[82]

When he became Chief of Naval Operations, and later, as the chairman of the Joint Chiefs, Moorer tried to obtain information on why the rescue flights were recalled.[83] "There is simply no way that the Israeli pilots and torpedo boats could have concluded that it was anything other than a U.S. ship," Moorer remarked matter-of-factly. Despite his very high rank, Admiral Moorer could never obtain the information he sought about the rescue flights.

Few in Congress reacted at all, but the Congressional Record notes that John Rarick (D-La.) stood up on the floor of the House on September 19, 1967, to demand, "Who planned the attack on the *Liberty*, and why was it made?" Rarick noted the similarity between the blaming of Egypt and the 1898 blaming of Spain for the sinking of the *Maine* in Havana Harbor. He warned that another such incident "could be made to serve as a Pearl Harbor for World War III." Thomas G. Abernethy (D-Miss.) called the attack "incessant, heavy and hard."[84]

In 2004, Ward Boston swore out an affidavit calling the attack "a war crime" and the Israelis "murderous bastards." He revealed, finally, that Admiral Kidd had told him "that he had been ordered to sit down with two civilians from either the White House or the Defense Department, and rewrite portions of the court's findings."

Removed were transcriptions of intercepted instructions from Israeli commanders to their pilots, ordering them to "sink the American ship!" The final report did not include that the Israelis had jammed communications, proving foreknowledge that the ship was American, nor, of course, that the Israeli torpedo boats had machine-gunned the life rafts, despite there having been many witnesses. "They shot our life rafts out of the water," Moe Shafer says indignantly—fifty years later.[85]

Maurice Bennett talked to Senator J. William Fulbright and was told that the truth was hushed up on direct orders from President Johnson. Fulbright informed McGonagle and Admiral McDonald that the president knew the attack was deliberate and had ordered the information cover-up "for political reasons."[86]

When, shortly before his death, speaking at Arlington National Cemetery, McGonagle, who seems to have signed on to the cover-up in advance of the event, demanded the truth about the operation against the USS *Liberty* from the governments of the United States (now presided over by Bill Clinton) and Israel, he was ignored. He had long before rendered himself impeachable. He entrusted his papers to George Golden. "Those dirty bastards. They really did a number on us, George," McGonagle said.[87] Then he wept. Pitying his old friend, choosing to protect McGonagle's reputation, Golden destroyed the captain's papers.[88]

Shortly before McGonagle's death, Lloyd Painter wrote him a letter reflecting how he and others felt betrayed by what the captain had done. "We were sent there to die," Painter concluded. "We were expendable. Their worst nightmare was that we didn't sink."[89]

Another figure whom Isaac Kidd did not interview was Admiral William Inman Martin, whom he had known at the Naval Academy, and to whom he should logically have turned, since Martin was a principal in these events. Admiral Martin was interviewed by the team dispatched by the Joint Chiefs, but he did not tell them that *Liberty* had requested that he provide the ship with an escort.[90] In a myriad of ways, William Inman Martin revealed that he was part of the conspiracy. Soon after the attack, Admiral Martin, Jim Ennes writes, "came personally to the flagship's photo lab and confiscated all photographs and negatives depicting *Liberty*."[91]

Into the millennium, only a handful of sailors were ready to acknowledge the obvious: that the Israelis were acting with the acquiescence and collaboration of the Americans. One was Bob Scarborough, who perceived Isaac Kidd's lack of sincerity from the start. "He made us feel ashamed that we were there," he remembers.[92] Scarborough adds that Johnson and McNamara called back the rescue planes twice. Bill Knutson, a career navy aviator who flew one of the planes off the USS *America*, concluded that "there was a cover-up at the very top and pushed right down."[93]

Lloyd Painter testified to the machine-gunning of the life rafts, but this was omitted from the report, since it did not match the template that Israel had made an honest mistake by attacking a plainly marked US naval ship. This omission also skirted the nasty implication that the Israelis had committed war crimes. Chuck Rowley, the ship's photographer, took a photograph of the ship's flag flying in the breeze moments before the air attack began.[94] He showed it to the court of inquiry, where someone stamped it "TOP SECRET" and confiscated it; it was never to be seen again.

George Golden testified that during the General Quarters drill just prior to the attack, the captain had remarked that "anything could happen at any time." Wayne Smith testified that he had concluded they "were being attacked by the UAR." Anything else was unthinkable.

On June 15, 1967, Secretary of State Dean Rusk told the NATO ambassadors meeting in Luxembourg that Israel's attack was deliberate. Rusk had been one of those who met with Meir Amit in Washington, DC, during the last week of May. His remark was reported in European but not US papers. Years later, Rusk would grant an interview to Anthony Wells, the former agent of MI6 living in the United States. Wells would claim that his interview with Rusk was "classified" (by whom but himself?) and he could not release any of it.[95] So even those claiming to support the *Liberty* sailors would function as part of the cover-up.

This would remain the stance of officialdom. On July 14, the Senate Foreign Relations Committee, having received the transcript of the Naval Court of Inquiry, stated, "The information referred to is classified and in committee files." Hearings had been held on June 12, 14, and 26, 1967.

On July 18, the President's Foreign Intelligence Advisory Board declared that the Israeli high command had not made a "premeditated attack on a ship known to be American."[96] It justified Israel on the grounds that it was reasonable to conclude that El Arish was being shelled from the sea, an impossibility, and justified Israel's "error that *Liberty* was cruising at speeds over twenty knots." It accepted the Israeli lie that it had mistakenly identified *Liberty* as *El Quseir*. Mostly, the Foreign Intelligence Advisory Board concluded that the vessel was Egyptian, as in the original plan it had been required to do.

Israel stood steadfast in its ludicrous insistence that in this murderous attack, *Liberty* had been struck "by mistake."[97] Menachem Begin, in an effort to remove Israel entirely from culpability, said that "in Vietnam the Americans had mistakenly bombed their own ships a number of times," garbling what happened at the Gulf of Tonkin.

US politicians reinforced the cover-up put in place by a co-opted Admiral Kidd.

Israel did not fool everyone. On June 23, the Turkish military attaché in Tel Aviv arrived back in Turkey, where he briefed the Turkish general staff that the Israeli attack on *Liberty* was deliberate: "It was done because the *Liberty*'s electronic equipment was jamming Israeli military communications and intercepting Israeli intelligence."

One thing was clear. Israel's cover story was preposterous.

On July 26, Robert McNamara testified before the Senate Committee on Foreign Relations that it was "the conclusion of the investigatory body headed by an Admiral of the Navy in whom we have great confidence that the attack was not intentional." Many survivors believe that an early consequence of the cover-up was the firing on the USS *Pueblo*, a similar "spy ship" in international waters, on January 23, 1968. That month, the Department of Defense canceled the technical research ship program. In May, the Israeli government paid claims submitted for the thirty-four deaths "in accordance with domestic international damage laws."

On June 11, 1968, an undeserving Captain McGonagle was awarded a Medal of Honor—not at the White House by the president, but at the grubby Navy Yard southeast of Washington. The Faustian bargain of the *Liberty* story was now completed. William McGonagle was given a promotion, although he had been passed over twice, and a new command (in Hawaii) that would not likely have come his way otherwise. The United States awarded the medal to McGonagle only after assurances that Israel had no objections.[98] The Naval Security Group urged any *Liberty* sailors with whom they retained contact not to attend the Medal of Honor ceremony.[99]

The celebratory dinner was held at a grungy hotel, as if Lyndon Johnson felt only contempt for this man who had allowed himself to be bribed, who had betrayed his men. Jim Ennes told the author that "many of us feel (as I do and I think Joe Meadors and others do) that McG was traitorous to essentially go along with the official view of the attack. Certainly he was no heroic figure. . . . The whole affair reeks of hypocrisy. . . . He spoke of his guilt, but did not admit that he had taken a bribe."[100]

Four months before his death, McGonagle admitted, "After many years I finally believe that the attack was deliberate. I don't think there has been an adequate investigation of the incident."

McGonagle stated that it was "about time that the state of Israel and the US government provide the crew members of the *Liberty* and the rest of the American people the facts of what happened, and why it came out that the *Liberty* was attacked 30 years ago today." He demanded an explanation from both governments and was met, accordingly, with silence.

Only lies now accompany this story. In 1984, the Israelis claimed for the first time that they had made an inquiry at the American embassy on June 8, prior to the attack, as to whether American ships were in the area. Walworth Barbour stated emphatically and without reservation that the Israelis never made such an inquiry.[101]

CIA saw to it that Israel was shielded from blame, and when in July six *Liberty* crewmen were buried at Arlington National Cemetery, the monument read, "Died in the Eastern Mediterranean." This was replaced in 1982 with "Killed USS *Liberty*," not much improvement.

Over the years, beginning with Jim Ennes's book, *Assault on the*

Liberty: *The True Story of the Israeli Attack on an American Intelligence Ship*, which violated the ban against the sailors' discussing the incident, many have spoken out in defiance of the cover-up, ignoring the possible consequences and the threats. Ennes's book, while exemplary in many respects, makes little attempt to penetrate the motivations and purpose of the attack. Nor does it examine how the United States and Israel collaborated. Subsequent studies, like Peter Hounam's *Operation Cyanide*, written under the auspices of the BBC, do more to penetrate the purpose of the attack.

Several of the sailors have been far more politically astute. "Their worst nightmare was that we didn't sink," Lloyd Painter says. "That long voyage to Malta meant that the US government wanted us to sink." Kenneth Michael (Mike) Schaley says, "The more we found out, someone knew we were going to get attacked and sent us in anyway. We were on a suicide mission."[102] George Golden called the crew "guinea pigs," sacrificial lambs in the multiyear campaign to remove Nasser.

There is multifarious evidence that this was a joint operation of the two governments. Since Israel had conducted the attack, it fell to them to create a plausible tissue of lies. When a lie could no longer be maintained, another was set in its place. So arose the lie that the Israeli pilots had believed that the ship was *El Quseir*, an Egyptian freighter half the size of *Liberty*.

To reinforce this lie, the Israelis claimed they believed *Liberty* was moving at twenty-eight knots, rendering it a "legitimate target." *Liberty's* maximum speed was eighteen knots, and it was moving at five knots at the time of the attack. In another incarnation, Israel claimed the ship had been traveling at thirty-two knots. The goal was to create such confusion that critics would give up their attempts to penetrate what had actually happened. The Israelis claimed their pilots did not see the American flag waving in the light Mediterranean breeze; they claimed they did not notice the letters in the Roman alphabet emblazoned on the ship's hull: "GTR-5."

Yet the response of the Israeli government to the revelations of Operation Susannah, among other incidents, suggest that obfuscation was a feature of Israeli foreign policy as practiced by Ben-Gurion. They had kept Operation Susannah covered up for a year before admitting that the operation was a false flag Israeli scheme, with Egypt being blamed for terror attacks in Cairo and Alexandria that had been perpetrated by a spy network of Egyptian Jews under the auspices of Israeli intelligence.

Other lies by the Israeli government were blatant and easily dispelled. They insisted that prior to the attack, they had requested information from the American embassy in Tel Aviv about US ships operating off the Sinai. Yeshayeah Bareket, an Israeli air force intelligence officer, declared, "I personally called the American embassy."[103]

A State Department telegram stated, "No request for info on U.S. ships operating off Sinai was made until after *Liberty* incident. Had Israelis made such an inquiry it would have been forwarded immediately to the Chief of Naval Operations . . . and repeated to Dept."[104] That would have been Admiral David Lamar McDonald, who had already dissociated himself from this operation and was not likely to cooperate.

Scenting the danger of exposure, Lyndon Johnson himself denied that the Israelis had asked about ships being in the area prior to the attack. "We saw no need to inform Israel or any other party to the hostilities of the *Liberty*'s location since the ship was on a peaceful mission," he wrote to Congressman Joseph M. McDade (R-Penn.). "I have seen a report alleging that the Israeli Government had asked us about the presence of the ship prior to the attack, but that report is not true."[105]

Reportedly, in the hours after the attack, a "consensus report" was issued reflecting the view of all the American intelligence agencies that the attack was deliberate. This report was circulated, only to be abruptly withdrawn. All copies vanished. Higher US authority moved to cover for Israel. On June 8, the Department of Defense announced that Israel had apologized for the attack. But it was only on June 10 that the Israeli embassy in Washington, DC, sent an apology, one that labeled the attack "a tragic accident which occurred at the height of hostilities," which was false.

NSA scrambled to come up with reasons for sending *Liberty* to the Eastern Med. Searching in the files, "spook linguist" Marvin Nowicki discovered one reason: to provide VHF and UHF communication coverage. They had to rationalize, Nowicki says, "why the *Liberty* was there in the first place."

A week after the attack, James Angleton flew to Tel Aviv, where he conferred with Meir Amit. "With a special airplane," Amit recounted later, "we went from one place to another to show him what happened." Then, abruptly, Amit recovered himself and added, "But before there was no coordination."[106]

CHAPTER 10

AFTERMATH

*"Ward, they aren't interested in the facts or what hap-
pened. It's a political issue. They want to cover it up."*
— Admiral Isaac Kidd to his chief counsel,
Ward Boston, after delivering his
naval inquiry report in Washington, DC

By 11:17 a.m. EST on June 8, Lyndon Johnson was already covering up for Israel. *Liberty* had been torpedoed "by Israeli forces in error off Port Said," he wrote. "The carrier *Saratoga* had been instructed to dispatch aircraft to the scene to investigate." So, after the fact, lies were constructed to paper over the truth: that both carriers, *Saratoga* and *America*, had been involved; that one had sent planes to Cairo; and that afterward, there was first one launch toward the site of the attack, from *Saratoga*, followed nearly two hours later by two launches—another by *Saratoga* and the other by *America*. All these launches, one toward Cairo and three toward *Liberty*, had been aborted by Lyndon Johnson himself.[1]

At 12:10 p.m., on June 8, Kosygin replied that he had passed the message to President Nasser. At 5 p.m., Cyrus Vance, who had been for at least three months the most active member of the US government in implementing the operation against *Liberty*, and who would engineer the cover-up, telephoned John S. McCain, the commander in chief of US Naval Forces Europe, ordering that "all news releases on the *Liberty* affair would be made at the Washington level—no releases were to be made aboard ships."

This information was also relayed to Admiral William Inman Martin. Lyndon Johnson went on the air and said there had been a minor six-minute attack with ten sailors killed. The ship's log was rewritten with Captain McGonagle's cooperation to conceal the enormity of the attack.

Congress met on the afternoon of June 8, shortly after Israel had taken responsibility for the attack, making it clear that the attack had been well planned while insisting that it was an accident, a mistake, a fortuitous unfortunate error. Senator Robert F. Kennedy put himself forward, terming the attack "the tragic mistake of today." Illinois Democrat Roman Pucinski used the term "tragic mistake" twice, adding the phrase "when Israel mistakenly attacked an American ship." New York Republican Jacob Javits, a longtime supporter of Israel, called it a "tragic error." Soon to be orchestrated by Isaac Kidd in his naval inquiry, this was to be the party line ever after.

By 5 p.m., Johnson was meeting with his brain trust on the matter of the USS *Liberty*: McNamara; Secretary of State Dean Rusk; the chairman of the Foreign Intelligence Advisory Board, Clark Clifford; Under Secretary of State Nicholas Katzenbach; ambassador to Russia Llewellyn Thompson; special consultant McGeorge Bundy; and Special Advisor to the President on National Security W. W. Rostow. This was no small "accident," a blip on the screen of history to be swept into oblivion, an easily dismissed "mistake." Johnson dispatched Rostow to tell the chairman of the Joint Chiefs and the secretary of the navy to forget about *Liberty*.

Seven years earlier, being vetted by the State Department as a Kennedy appointee, Rostow had failed to pass State Department security because Otto Otepka, then handling security clearances for government employees, had deemed him a traitor, not fit to serve the government. David Halberstam, writing *The Best and the Brightest*, had called Rostow "like Rasputin to a tsar under siege." "I could never imagine any Israeli, no matter what his politics were, deliberately firing on the American flag," Rostow said sententiously in an effort to spread the idea that the attack was "a pure accident." Only newspapers free of the influence of the government, like the *Charleston (SC) News and Courier* and the *Shreveport*

Times dared challenge the government cover-up. The Shreveport paper called Israel's claim that the attack was a mistake "far-fetched."

On July 7, the *New York Times* published an Associated Press dispatch by an Israeli named Micha Limor, who wrote that the high masts and weird antennas showed that *Liberty* was a warship. He depicted the *Liberty* sailors as firing on the torpedo boats "with a heavy machine gun" ("they were shooting at us") and only then for the torpedo boats to have fired at *Liberty*. Limor, obviously working for the Israeli government, suggested that the Israelis hoped to "capture" *Liberty* rather than sink it. There is no evidence whatsoever that the Israelis had attempted to capture *Liberty*. Limor insists they could see no flag, which meant, he claimed, this was either "a ghost ship or an enemy ship."[2]

The profusion of lies issuing from many quarters is a measure of the desperation of both the United States and Israel that the truth not emerge. That the United States had conspired to murder its own men, that Israel had signed on to implement that policy, pointed to an America violating all it had stood for since the founding of the republic. *Liberty* had been sent to the East Med not to obtain intelligence, since, as Dave Lewis says, whatever they obtained had been obtained elsewhere.[3] As Admiral Lamar McDonald inferred, nothing obtained was of any consequence. They were placed there as "guinea pigs," George Golden believed: "We were the guinea pigs, to get shot up, to make it look like Egypt was doing this."[4] Golden, at Malta, where *Liberty* was sent to dry dock, ran into two naval officers whom he had known in the past.

"George, they really did it to you, old boy," one said.

"What are you talking about?" Golden said.

"You were a damned guinea pig," his friend said.

At a meeting on the Saturday afternoon after the attack, June 10, Defense Department officers searched for a rationale. Walter G. Deeley told the group, "Well, damn it, write down some reasons for sending that ship out there." Lieutenant Commander Birchard ("Bud") Fossett, in charge of scheduling of technical research ships, wrote, "*Liberty* was sent to the eastern Mediterranean in order to provide VHF and UHF communications coverage," which was so opaque that Deeley asked him to write down "*why* you needed that kind of coverage. Who needed it? What for? Write it all down."[5]

The task was impossible, yet, as Jim Ennes writes, a report more than two inches thick emerged from those weekend meetings. Ennes requested a copy of the report, only to be told it had been distributed on a "strict need-to-know basis." He filed a Freedom of Information Act case, only for the government to deny that such a report existed as CIA denied to the author the 303 Committee records, suddenly declaring that they did not exist, after first admitting that they did. Francis (Frank) A. Raven, a Pentagon civilian, had argued that the ship would be "defenseless out there. If war breaks out, she'll be alone and vulnerable." He was ignored. Raven wrote to Ennes in 1983 that he "blew up and started pushing panic buttons all over the place when he learned *Liberty* was moving toward the coast." His efforts were futile. The answer as to why the ship was "out there" seems plain: it was there to be sunk, to serve as the false flag pretext for the bombing of Cairo and the attendant fall of the demonized Gamal Abdel Nasser.

Treason resides in the interstices of political life. Thomas Lowe Hughes shared with me an example he discovered involving Joseph P. Kennedy. Serving as ambassador to the Court of St. James's, appointed by Franklin Roosevelt, Kennedy was caught copying Roosevelt's secret correspondence with Winston Churchill. It reveals how Roosevelt planned to enter World War II while at home declaring that he was not about to go to war.

Kennedy's plan for the two thousand cables and letters he accumulated, with a code clerk at the embassy named Tyler Kent who was involved in the same espionage, was to turn them over to the "America Firsters" and Colonel Charles Lindbergh, a Nazi sympathizer. Kennedy would then himself go on to support Wendell Wilkie for president against Roosevelt, who was about to seek his third term. Roosevelt outsmarted Kennedy and the cryptographer alike, which is another story.

Raven's boss, John E. Morrison Jr., an air force brigadier general, asked the Joint Chiefs of Staff to assume control of the ship. Something wasn't right. It seems clear, however, that the military, indeed the government, was not a monolith, and not everyone signed on or would have signed on to Angleton and Meir Amit's scheme to sink an unarmed surveillance ship and blame Egypt. Meanwhile, President Johnson's annoyance with Nasser was well-known to James Angleton, who used it to his advantage.

When Helms left the Agency, among the criticisms levied against him was that he had been "too trusting of Angleton." At the Angleton conference, David Martin said, "At some point, it's a director's responsibility to look at the costs and benefits, and Helms just never got around to that until way too late in the game."[6] CIA official historian David Robarge understates the issue in his introduction to the Richard Helms Collection: "Helms accorded the chief of the CI staff, James Angleton, much leeway in vetting assets, dealing with defectors and suspected double agents, and searching for 'moles' inside the Agency—despite the costs of disrupting legitimate operations and tarnishing officers' careers."[7]

NSA in its "fact-finding" report slyly exonerates Admiral William Inman Martin by suggesting that "judgment on the value of the intelligence to be gained could come only from DOD-level intelligence agencies—and in the case of *Liberty*, particularly from NSA." Uneasy, Marshall S. Carter went so far as to suggest that changes were needed "in the chain of command supervision and monitoring of just where the ship is, what is it doing and was it necessary," a view with which Admiral McDonald had agreed.[8] In a heavily redacted page of its report, NSA does speculate: "Speculation as to Israeli motivation varied. Some believed that as Israel expected that the complete destruction of the ship and killing of the personnel would leave the U.S. free to blame the U.A.R. for the incident and bring the U.S. into the war on the side of Israel. Ironically even though the *Liberty* had [*redacted*] others felt Israeli forces wanted the ship and men out of the way [*redacted*]."[9]

On July 22, Robert McNamara added further to the fabrications. Testifying before the Senate Foreign Relations Committee on foreign aid, he said: "I have examined the record of the investigation and I find no intent by the Israeli Government, and no intent by any representative of the Israeli Government to attack an individual vessel." Asked if it was an individual rather than a government decision, a relieved McNamara said, "Yes." At this moment, McNamara could not imagine that evidence would emerge of a "conscious Israeli intent to attack a U.S. vessel." He obviously believed at that moment that he was safe from history.[10]

From the intelligence component came extensive memoranda pinning the responsibility for the attack on Israel.[11] Thomas Lowe Hughes concluded that none of the information Israel had cooked up made sense, and the idea that they didn't know the ship was an American ship was ridiculous. "We assume," Hughes said, "that the Israelis thought that the thing would sink and blame it on the Egyptians. Otherwise it made no sense at all."

There was something amateurish about the plot. Among Jim Ennes's sources was an old salt named Raymond Linn, a chief petty officer who had been in the navy since before Pearl Harbor.[12] "I've never seen anything like this," Linn had told Ennes. "It's crazy to send an unprotected ship on an intelligence mission in a war zone. Spies just don't prance around like that in broad daylight near the front lines." Yet for these men, career military, where obedience to authority had to be second nature, questioning their highest superiors was not an option. It was inconceivable that their own commander in chief should sacrifice them, leave them behind to die. Yet this is what happened.

The blame would fall entirely on Israel, with Israel's acquiescence. Knowing where its military and financial interests lay, Israel would accept the full blame as the price to be paid for US military support. Israel would lie, absurdly, trumpeting forth easily disprovable lies about not knowing

Liberty was an American ship, even as its excuse—mistaking the USS *Liberty* for *El Quseir*—was not credible. Who would say otherwise?

Then, as now, America was not a society where the mainstream press in any meaningful manner challenged higher authority. Only a few dissident voices were raised. "The action was planned in advance," Drew Pearson and Jack Anderson wrote in the *Washington Post* of June 16, 1967. It was too well coordinated to be accidental. The *Washington Star* wrote on June 30 that Israel had to have known that *Liberty* was an American ship. The Associated Press stated that the purpose of *Liberty* was not the evacuation of Americans, as the United States claimed, but intelligence gathering. The *New York Times* was ready to justify the attack as among the mistakes that "invariably occur in war." Too clever by half, weighing in despite his obvious lack of access to the facts, star journalist Seymour Hersh writes that "The Israelis may have thought the *Liberty* was an Egyptian ship masquerading as a U.S. ship." As is customary with him, Hersh conceals his sources. Here he obviously used an Israeli source high in the chain of command.

Jim Ennes discovered that the deck log he himself had written had been falsified. The purpose was to minimize the attack, reducing its duration. This deck log, documenting the hours during the attack, was neatly written and listed the dead and wounded in alphabetical order, like Lyndon Johnson's voters who cast their votes from the cemetery and other places in the 1948 Texas senatorial election. McGonagle signed off on this log. It made no mention of the overflights during the morning. Admiral Kidd did not include the request by Captain McGonagle and Lieutenant Commander Lewis that Admiral Martin send a destroyer to accompany *Liberty* to its position in the Eastern Mediterranean.

In Tel Aviv, John Hadden and Ernest Castle were instructed to investigate the incident. They said that the bombing of *Liberty* was an error and that the presence of the American flag—which they acknowledged—"was taken by the Israeli pilots as a common military trick."[13] This indeed was a facet of the Israeli cover-up: "When they saw the U.S. flag, the Israelis thought it was probably the Egyptians pretending to be Americans and did not bother to check," Dan Raviv and Yossi Melman write in *Every Spy a Prince*.[14]

Castle attempted to rationalize the case with logic: If the thirty-knot ship could not have been *Liberty*, neither could it have been *El Quseir* with a maximum speed of fourteen knots, four less than *Liberty*. If the smoke that covered *Liberty* had made her difficult to identify was a result of the IDF attack, it could hardly be argued that the Israelis were trying to use it as an excuse that *Liberty* was throwing up a smoke screen to conceal her identity and was therefore an enemy ship."[15]

By 2:50 in the afternoon, Israeli lieutenant colonel Michael Bloch telephoned Ernest Castle and argued that because *Liberty* was not flying a flag (an outright lie), it had been mistaken for the Egyptian horse carrier *El Quseir*.

CHAPTER 11

COVER-UP CONTINUED: CIA AND *LIBERTY*

"This is pure murder."

—Anonymous Israeli general

Let us go back in time to see how the "spooks," as Captain Engen called them, responded to the attack on the USS *Liberty*. Although Richard Helms had dissociated himself and CIA from the order to bomb Cairo in the nick of time, thwarting the order sent to John Hadden in Tel Aviv, once the ship was bombed, CIA had no alternative but to participate in the cover-up. Less than a week after the attack, the Agency was ready with its own report. It was issued on June 10 and obviously designed to exonerate Israel of all blame. Maintaining the Israeli fiction that the attack had been an "accident," and issuing from the Directorate of Intelligence, the CIA report omits, exactly as Captain McGonagle had, the surveillance flights that began to fly over *Liberty* at dawn on June 8 and proceeded through the morning. It offers the lie that *Liberty* was "an electronics research ship which had been diverted to the crisis area to act as a radio relay station for U.S. embassies," that far-fetched fiction that CIA operative Bob Wilson mentioned at Malta.

The CIA report, reissued in 2016 in an unredacted form in response to the author's Freedom of Information request, asserts that the commander of the Sixth Fleet, declaring the attacking units "hostile," "sent attack aircraft" to protect the ship—omitting the devastating detail that the rescue planes had twice been recalled and that *Liberty* was left unaided until the morning of June 9. CIA's report does not, of course, acknowledge that planes had been on their way to Cairo from the USS *America* until they too were recalled.

CIA's point of view, its goal, in this document is to fortify Israeli's lying scenario. CIA writes that "the control tower at Hatzor [near Tel Aviv] through intercepted conversations with the helicopters leave little doubt that the Israelis failed to identify the *Liberty* as a US ship before or during the attack." No doubt the Agency counted on the sailors remaining silent and supine, because there are NSA intercepts that record Israeli pilots declaring "It's an American ship!" and their control tower handlers ordering them to attack it anyway.[1]

Unlike most CIA records, this unique document wanders into pure fiction. Israeli control tells a helicopter, "There is a warship there which we attacked. The men jumped into the water from it; you will try to rescue them!" In fact, no one jumped into the water from *Liberty*. The fabrication continues. US units "later searched the area [untrue] only to conclude that 'no survivors were recovered from the sea.'" So the ship would sink, leaving men in the water. Israelis and Americans alike would have been on the record as having searched the area only to discover no survivors. The ship would be identified as Egyptian, hostile, and a "warship," justifying the bombing of Cairo. Or the Israelis could sell the absurdity that *Liberty* had been mistaken for *El Quseir* "by an overzealous pilot." Intelligence services deal on a regular basis in scapegoats.

The CIA report spins its fable further: Hatzor instructs the helicopters: "If men were Egyptians to take them to El Arish; if they spoke English and were not Egyptians, to take them to Lydda." As the farce unfolds, CIA writes: "The Israelis suspected they may have hit an American or British and not an Egyptian ship." The jig, of course, was up, and the CIA report adjusts its perspective: there was no point in maintaining the scenario that the Egyptians had attacked *Liberty*. Events were moving swiftly, hence the contradictions. The Israeli offer of assistance [from Ernest Castle, the defense attaché], "Have you casualties?," is explained as a result of "the sensitive mission of the ship." Who knew otherwise? The ship in fact had no mission at all, except to serve as a scapegoat in a false flag operation.

CIA amplifies the farce, claiming that COMSIXTHFLEET then recalled the aircraft from the carriers *America* and *Saratoga* and sent two destroyers to assist *Liberty*. In fact, when help came in the early morning of June 9, it consisted of both destroyers and then the carriers. Admiral William Inman Martin had refused to send a destroyer to assist *Liberty* on June 8.

CIA issued several versions of this document. An early version admits that the hull number (GTR-5) "was prominently displayed and an American flag was flying." A variation on the theme has an intercept between an unidentified Israeli controller and helicopter 815: the pilot reports that GTR-5 is written on the ship's side, and the controller replies that this number "[has] no significance." In another wrinkle, the attack was called off not because a distress call had reached the Sixth Fleet, as was the case, but because the ship "seemed to be sinking." Israeli helicopters and the three torpedo boats searched the area until 6:04.

The CIA report mentions that "all of its [*Liberty's*] life rafts were lost" but excludes the fact that the torpedo boats machine-gunned the life rafts—and confiscated one as a souvenir, carrying it back to Tel Aviv, where it was later displayed in a museum. CIA includes a false casualty list of ten killed and ninety wounded, with twenty-two missing, "most of whom were probably trapped in the flooded compartments."

The "chronology of events" appended to this document picks up the Joint Chiefs' version of the cover-up, which was to concoct a byzantine thread of mishaps that led to the failure to arrive of messages ordering *Liberty* to move, alternately twenty or one hundred miles from shore, and so be out of harm's way. Dave Lewis suggests that Israel was known to pursue prey a hundred miles off, but should *Liberty* have moved that far out, as a consequence, Egypt could not have been blamed for the attack.[2] The whole lost message scenario was part of the cover-up.[3]

This was the Joint Chiefs' means of suggesting that the attack was an "accident" and "no one's fault." There is a reference to "a question raised by Chief of Naval Operations concerning the prudence of sending

USS *Liberty* to a position so close to the area of hostilities." But Admiral McDonald's concerns are buried deep within the report, and the Joint Chiefs quickly note that his concern was "not accompanied by a clarification of USS *Liberty*'s mission, without which no commander could have exercised military judgment." So CIA exonerates Admiral Martin.

(Within the National Security Agency, there was a dispute, with Frank Raven opposing the deployment of *Liberty* and General Morrison in favor. So confided Bud C. Fossett, who devotes much of his interview with NSA to Frank Raven's opposition to sending *Liberty* out alone into the Eastern Med. Most of Raven's remarks remain redacted even in the 2016 version of the document.)

In its ragged and inconsistent effort to make the story of the ship go away, CIA adds the myth that *Liberty* intentionally and effectively fired a machine gun at an Israeli torpedo boat at two thousand yards. As stated above, the sailor manning the machine gun had been killed, and the gun went off from the heat of the attacking rockets. A man had fired at the boats, only for Captain McGonagle immediately to have called for a cease-fire. CIA's adverb, "effectively," suggests the Agency overreaching in its effort to exonerate Israel and falsify its motivations.

The NSA, CIA, and the Joint Chiefs collaborated to inflate the preposterous message argument, weaving that well-worn, oft-repeated crooked trajectory from the Pentagon to San Francisco, Hawaii, the Philippines, and Eritrea. A human component invented to bring credibility to this disinformation is a sailor in Port Lyautey, Morocco, who had been chastised for getting his chief petty officer out of bed the previous watch and thus decided, fatally, to wait until morning to deliver this message, then forgot about it.

Uneasy with the *Liberty* cover-up from the start, CIA provided a newly unredacted copy of its June 13 description of the attack.[4] It fell to CIA to cover up for Israel and, in particular, to further the Israeli myth that it mistook *Liberty* for the Egyptian freighter *El Quseir*. "It could easily be mistaken for the latter vessel by an overzealous pilot," CIA offered. "Both ships have similar hulls and arrangements of masts and stacks." CIA does not mention that *El Quseir* was two hundred feet shorter or that *Liberty* hosted fourteen antennas and a moon dish prominently on deck.

In the unredacted version of this memo, newly released after the millennium, CIA does not seem quite so intractable. CIA records that it had requested from Israel the communications of the attacking aircraft and torpedo boats, only to be told that none of these communications were "available." CIA acknowledges that its custom had been to redact any information it obtained from a foreign government—an admission that CIA's assessment of the attack was built originally with consultation with the government of Israel.

CIA released yet another version of this document on June 10, 2016, adding these sentences:

> The intercepted conversations between the helicopter pilots and the control tower at Hatzor (near Tel Aviv) leave little doubt that the Israelis failed to identify the *Liberty* as a US ship before or during the attack. Control told (helicopter) 815 at 3:31 pm (8:30 a.m.) that there is a warship there which we attacked. The men jumped into the water from it. You will try to rescue them.

CIA then adds, penetrating Israeli disinformation:

> Although there were other references to a search for the men in the water and although US units later searched the area, no survivors were recovered from the sea, nor were there any indications that any of the 22 missing personnel from the *Liberty* had been lost overboard.[5]

A subsequent message from the control tower to the helicopter identified the ship as Egyptian and told the pilot to return home.

It seems clear that CIA had composed the original document from materials supplied by the state of Israel, embracing Israeli disinformation. The identification by the Israeli control tower of the ship as Egyptian exposed the original pretext. Another newly restored passage reads:

The weather was clear in the area of attack, the *Liberty*'s hull number (GTR-5) was prominently displayed, and an American flag was flying. The helicopter pilot was then urgently requested to identify the survivors as Egyptian or English-speaking (this being the first indication that the Israelis suspected they may have attacked a neutral ship). The helicopter pilot reported seeing an American flag on the *Liberty*. In another intercept between an unidentified Israeli controller and the helicopter number 815, the pilot reported that number GTR was written on the ship's side. The controller told the pilot the number "had no significance."

In this confusion, CIA refuses to accept the Israeli insistence that there was no American flag flying. But there is new information that the helicopter pilot was "urgently" requested to identify the survivors as Egyptian, a demonstration that CIA acknowledged the purpose of the attack and the pretext: the attack was to be blamed on Egypt as a pretext for the US bombing of Cairo, planes having been dispatched by Admiral Martin from the USS *America* at the time *Liberty* was attacked by two sets of jet planes.

The controller in Israel's version of the event attempts to persuade the pilot that the number GTR-5 "had no significance" despite the Roman letters indicating that it was an American ship, rather than Egyptian, in which case the letters would have been in Arabic.

Newly restored as well is this passage:

This was about 44 minutes after the last attack on the ship and the attack had apparently been called off, not because the ship had been identified, but because it seemed to be sinking. ... The US Defense Attaché in Tel Aviv reports that Israeli helicopters and the three torpedo boats searched the area until 6:04. ... The Israeli offer of assistance was declined because of the sensitive mission of the ship.

This was false. Ernest Castle's note, "Have you casualties?," was considered to be insulting—the bag containing his note landed next to a severed leg. His offer was declined not because of "the sensitive mission of the ship" but because his question, the answer to which was right before his eyes, was profoundly insulting and insensitive.

CIA adds: "According to US Navy reports, the ship was saved only through the efforts of her crew." This, of course, was true.

The CIA report goes on: "8 June 3:34 p.m. (8:34 a.m.) Israeli helicopter identified ship as 'definitely Egyptian.'" The helicopters were ordered back to base, as indeed, abruptly, the helicopters with their commandos aiming at sailors, and scurried off. Another Israeli falsehood continues in this version: "8 June 3:39 p.m. Hatzor control told helicopter to rescue men." CIA suddenly declares that Israel had known all day that *Liberty* was an American ship. These contradictory findings reflect, finally without ambiguity, the original plan: that Egypt would be blamed for attacking the ship.

The last, unredacted, version of CIA's report also provides proof of Israeli and CIA complicity. Within a week into the cover-up, CIA covers for Angleton's collaboration with Mossad. CIA concluded with the final pretext: that the ship "had been diverted to the crisis area to act as a radio relay station for US embassies."

"That's news to me," Dave Lewis says.[6] Cover stories for the media are designed at CIA's Office of Cover and Deception, as this one may well have been.

Following the convening of an intelligence working group to examine what led the NSA and Joint Chiefs to decide to move *Liberty* off Gaza after sending it there, CIA released an "Intelligence Information Cable" on November 5, 1967. A redacted name is said to have commented on the sinking of the US communications ship *Liberty*.

"They said that Dayan had personally ordered the attack on the ship and that one of his generals violently opposed this action and said 'This is pure murder.'"[7] This document refers to Dayan's "political ambitions" and to a nameless "Israeli Admiral," who disapproved of the action—and it was he who ordered it stopped, and not Dayan. Later, it would emerge that the person who instructed Dayan to order the attack was Meir Amit.

Throughout the autumn of 1967, the files continued to be papered with disinformation. A report by the legal advisor to the secretary of state, who was assigned to evaluate the Israeli excuse for the attack, was released on September 21, 1967. His name was Carol F. Salans, and his report's title was "The *Liberty*–Discrepancies between the Israeli Inquiry and U.S. Navy Inquiry," as if it were of importance to reconcile the contending stories.[8] Salans noted that the fighter aircraft carried out a run (one!) over the ship in an effort to identify a piece of disinformation that survived from the Israeli version of events.

As the following account will show, Anthony Wells is inaccurate in his contention that "the very top leadership [of Israel] was never informed until after the event what Moshe Dayan had ordered." Wells, a former MI6 operative and currently a CIA asset, would attempt to sell the idea that the responsibility for the attack rested entirely with the impetuous Dayan. Dayan might have been the most inflammatory of Ben-Gurion's disciples, but as has been established here, he did not come up with the idea of attacking the USS *Liberty*.

Lyndon Johnson requested Clark Clifford, chairman of his Foreign Intelligence Advisory Board, to offer his findings on the subject of the attack, and so Clifford produced his own report. Clifford wrote that the contention "that the *Liberty* could have been mistaken for the Egyptian supply ship *El Quseir* is unbelievable." After Johnson had made Clifford secretary of defense, Clifford telephoned LBJ and said, "Mr. President, I don't want to live in a world where the Israelis have nuclear weapons." Johnson hung up on him.[9]

The sane voice of George Ball may be heard summing up the damage Johnson's Middle East policy inflicted on America: "By assuring the Israelis that the United States would always provide them with a military edge over the Arabs, Johnson guaranteed the escalation of an arms race. ... By refusing to follow the advice of his aides that America make its delivery of nuclear-capable F-4 Phantoms conditional on Israel's signing the Nuclear Non-Proliferation Treaty, Johnson gave the Israeli's the impression that America had no fundamental objection to Israel's nuclear program."[10] Ball had attempted to persuade John F. Kennedy not to send sixteen thousand advisors to Vietnam, as he tried to convince Lyndon Johnson not to bomb North Vietnam. He remained a lone dissenter within the corridors of imperial power.

In the wake of the pressure to lie for Israel and for Johnson alike, officers and people in high positions contradicted themselves and lied shamefully. Ernest Castle, the US naval attaché, actually argued (on Thames Television) that "the attack could not possibly have been deliberate because Israel would never do anything contrary to American wishes."[11] In fact, of course, Israel had its green light and so was acting with full US knowledge and endorsement.

Admiral Kidd's corrupted naval inquiry did not mention that three sets of rescue planes had been recalled. There were non sequiturs studding the written record, including a statement by Admiral John S. McCain of his admiration for the effectiveness of the Israeli military, as if he approved of the attack and admired its execution. An admiral of the US Navy, it did not occur to him to sympathize with the sailors. He gave himself away.

Twenty years passed. Admiral McDonald was long gone from the navy. He had been succeeded by Admiral Thomas H. Moorer on August 1, 1967. Four-star admiral Moorer made the attack on *Liberty* his cause. At once he asserted that *Liberty* was "the most easily recognized ship in the US Navy," challenging Israel's fatuous argument that they didn't recognize *Liberty* when they attacked her. Moorer had twice served as chairman of the Joint Chiefs of Staff. In that capacity, he had attempted to uncover documents testifying to the planning of the attack. Despite his high position, he came up with nothing. The trail had been swept clean. No documents emerged.

It was twenty years after the attack when Dave Lewis, who thought of himself as a "lowly lieutenant commander," made Admiral Moorer's acquaintance. It was at the first reunion of the *Liberty* sailors. Learning the news that Lyndon Johnson personally had consigned the sailors to their deaths from Lewis, Admiral Moorer, a man of rare composure, expressed no emotion.

"I expected something like that had happened," Admiral Moorer said.[12] In their conversation, Moorer revealed to Lewis that Admiral Geis had died of hepatitis following a hip replacement. Only now was Lewis emboldened to reveal his knowledge, obtained from Admiral Geis, that Lyndon Johnson had personally canceled the rescue ships. "We all knew we had been betrayed, but we didn't know how badly," Admiral Moorer said, living up to his reputation as a sailors' admiral, using the first-person plural in solidarity with the sailors three times in one sentence.

"It was Israel's intent to sink the *Liberty* and leave as few survivors as possible," Admiral Moorer added. "Israel knew perfectly well that the ship was American."

Twenty-eight of the men who died on the USS *Liberty* had worked for Dave Lewis. Two had arrived at his office, retirement papers in hand, prior to the ship's departure from Norfolk. Both agreed to accept one last deployment—for him. Lewis would be forever tortured by the thought that they wouldn't have died had he not urged them to join *Liberty*'s final voyage. So it was important to Lewis to reveal what Admiral Geis had told him about Lyndon Johnson's malfeasance.

In the ensuing fifty years, the sailors and their advocates have defined the treason committed against them. By calling back the rescue flights, Lyndon

Johnson violated Article 99 of the Uniform Code of Military Justice: never to abandon a fellow wounded combatant in battle. Homicides at war were "unlawful killings," the consequences of "committing an act inherently dangerous to others" and exhibiting "a wanton disregard of human life."[13]

The accused must know that death or great bodily harm is a "probable consequence" of his conduct. This definition derives from Principle VI, adopted by all members of the United Nations and defined by the Nuremberg War Crimes Tribunal. Admiral Merlin Staring concluded that Johnson was guilty of a war crime.[14]

In keeping with the law, the USS *Liberty* Veterans Association filed a war crimes report with the secretary of the army, who served as the executive agent for the secretary of defense, at the Pentagon. Israel was named as a war criminal, but the veterans' petition does not mention Lyndon Johnson by name. When the author pointed this out to Ron Gotcher, who authored the war crimes report, he did not respond.

Perhaps taking advantage of this self-censorship, a form of participation in the cover-up, there was no response from the army to the sailors' petition. Nor would there be an honest government investigation over the ensuing fifty years to replace the corrupted, falsified record deposited by Isaac Kidd, not to mention the lying and embarrassing documents, and purported investigations, put forth by the state of Israel.

Twenty years passed before Isaac Kidd's threatening demand of silence would be violated by those who had experienced the attack, and a book be written by a sailor, Jim Ennes. Only in 1991 did Dwight Porter come forward, revealing that the CIA station chief in Beirut, where Porter was US ambassador, had showed him transcripts of intercepted Israeli messages. Now widely known, one had an Israel pilot commenting, "It's an American ship" and the pilot insisting that he could see the American flag, only for his control to demand, "Attack it!"

The cover-up seems to have been woven into history for eternity. In 2002, Peter Hounam and Christopher Mitchell made a documentary film called USS Liberty: *Dead in the Water*, sponsored by the BBC and financed by Dick Thompson. But Hounam told the author that the BBC had censored the final cut of the film, eliminating any suggestion of US-Israeli collaboration in the attack. *Dead in the Water* was aired in London late at night, far from prime time. In the United States, it was not broadcast at all, although it is available on the internet on YouTube and can be purchased from the USS *Liberty* Veterans Association. Censorship assumes many guises. You can discover the film on the internet under BBC: Dead In The Water.[15] It's on YouTube and can be purchased from the USS *Liberty* Veterans Association.

The Israelis considered it worth their effort to nourish the cover-up. In 2008, Brigadier General Iftach Spector, the lead pilot in the attack of the Mirage jets on the USS *Liberty*, published *Loud and Clear: The Memoir of an Israeli Fighter Pilot in Israel*. No US publisher could be found but for an obscure entity called Zenith Press, an imprint of MBI Publishing Company out of Minneapolis, which put out an English-language edition.[16]

Spector creates a scenario in which he had been patrolling the Suez Canal when he observed "a big ship" cruising off El Arish and was ordered to "go check the identity of this ship." He claims he made radio calls to the ship, which were not answered, and offers a description of the "forward superstructure, stack and mast" while not bothering to mention the most distinguishing components of *Liberty*'s appearance, the forty-five antennas and the giant moon dish on deck. He claims he was told, "If you are certain that this is a military vessel, you are cleared to attack." Spector would have us believe that because the letters GTR-5, which he supposedly read as CTR, were not in Hebrew, that it was not an Israeli ship, this alone justified his pulverizing the ship until his cannon were empty.

Spector claims he looked for a flag but could not find one, and that he was told the ship was "French." This allowed him to rest easy. Spector has nothing to say about the murdered innocent sailors, or that the deputy chief air controller at Air Control Central, overriding Kislev, the chief air controller at the IDF base, wanted to stop the napalm because "it's worth it just for the insurance." Spector's lack of affect is matched by Israeli author Avner Cohen, who called the attack on *Liberty* a "comedy of errors" in a brief telephone conversation with the author.[17]

And yet in 2003, now a brigadier general, Spector signed a letter in opposition to targeted killings carried out by Israel in the territories, air strikes on civilian population centers.[18]

There have also been seemingly independent efforts to confuse the issue. In 2005, a retired air force master sergeant named Mike Burke contacted Jim Nanjo. Burke had read Peter Hounam's book, *Operation Cyanide*, and now set out to discredit Nanjo's testimony that on the very early morning of June 8, he had been summoned by his Strategic Air Command superiors to ready his aircraft for action. So he had taxied onto the runway, his plane loaded with nuclear weapons, and waited for the order to take off.

Burke joined the USS *Liberty* Veterans Association, claiming he was "trying to help that bunch of old sailors get to the bottom of a 40-year-old controversy." Blindsiding Nanjo, he sent him excerpts of *Operation Cyanide*, which Nanjo had not yet seen. Seeing his words in print, his admission that he had readied his aircraft laden with nuclear weapons for action, Nanjo became agitated.

Burke then moved in for the kill, insisting that Nanjo must have had his timeline wrong and could not have been contacted by his superiors to ready his plane before the firing on *Liberty*, as he had said. Perplexed, unaware that the assault on the ship of course had to have been planned in advance since the cover-up had been so successful, Nanjo speculated that he must have been wrong about his having been contacted at between 2 and 4 a.m., since the ship had been attacked at 5 a.m. California time. "I am somewhat disturbed from you [*sic*] email, we reacted prior to the attack. I must have been mistaken in term [*sic*] of when the alert went on. . . . I cannot see any reason for us to be alerted before the incident occurred."

Having undermined Nanjo's testimony in a nine-email exchange, a leak in the cover-up having been patched up, this itinerant, lower-ranking air force officer disappeared. Burke did not as a member attend the fiftieth anniversary reunion of the Survivors of the Attack in Norfolk, hosted by the USS *Liberty* Veterans Association.

Beginning with Operation Susannah ten years earlier, in retrospect what we are witnessing was a new form of communication by nation states. False statements are made with no shame accruing to the obfuscators. Leaders could say anything they pleased, as Israel had erased the name of *Liberty* from its "combat information plot table" on the morning of the attack.

Israel could claim it had identified a decrepit Egyptian freighter.[19] Israel could brazen it out, laughing behind its hand. According to NSA, the US Department of State informed the Israeli government that "the later military attack by Israeli aircraft on the USS *Liberty* is quite literally incomprehensible."

NSA thought the attack should "at a minimum be condemned as an act of military recklessness reflecting wanton disregard of human life," which was all talk. The US Department of State asserted that "it expected the Government of Israel to take the disciplinary measures which international law requires in the event of wrongful conduct by the military personnel of a State." Meanwhile, the United States and Israel had buried the very notion of international law.

For the next fifty years, official and semiofficial inquiries would remain in the realm of farce. Official voices raised in opposition to the obfuscations were few. One who could not conceal his outrage was NSA deputy director Louis W. Tordella, who called the Israel Defense Forces Preliminary Inquiry "a nice whitewash for a group of ignorant, stupid, and inept xxx. If the attackers had not been Hebrew there would have been quite a commotion. Such crass stupidity—30 knots, warship, 2 guns, etc. does not even do credit to the Nigerian Navy."[20] Tordella obviously was not one of those in the loop. He was judging the incident on the evidence and so was appropriately outraged.[21]

In 1975, Dr. Kiepfer told documentary filmmaker Tito Howard that he was beginning to think that "The US government was at least cognizant, and it was done with their approval. . . . Both countries are involved and working together in a cover-up."[22] He concluded that the cover-up and conspiracy began even before the attack, that "the attack was planned in advance by both countries as a political stunt; like the Tonkin Gulf attack on the MTBs [motor torpedo boats], the loss of *Liberty* would give the US an excuse to attack Arab countries."

Three years later, author Richard Deacon, in a book about the Israeli secret services, pronounced the Six-Day War an event new to history. "Probably never before in history," he writes, "have Secret Services so completely dominated a war situation. It was in fact a joint plan between the American CIA and the Israeli Secret Service. . . . The war and the *Liberty* were a CIA-Mossad-Aman [the internal services, akin to FBI] plan."[23] Stranger still, the director of Central Intelligence, Richard Helms, despite CIA's official participation in the cover-up, far from being a proponent of these events, openly opposed them.

From their not-disinterested vantage, the Soviets saw things in exactly this way: they saw a war where the decisions were being made not by Congress or elected representatives but by intelligence operatives. Retired Soviet military intelligence (GRU) officer Oleg Korneevitch Sergeev stated matter-of-factly: "the attack on the USS *Liberty* was the joint action of two secret services, USA and Israel, which had one goal, combining forces for a war with Egypt."[24]

Looking back over the past fifty years, we discover precious few voices courageous enough to offer truth to power with respect to the USS *Liberty*. If you are surprised by Richard Helms speaking out, please return to that moment on Saturday, June 3, when his anger erupted upon discovering that John Hadden had been sent orders to bomb Cairo by Helms's underling Desmond Fitzgerald. At this very time, Helms was attempting to scuttle New Orleans district attorney Jim Garrison's investigation into the Kennedy assassination. On this matter, there are ample revelatory documents available. But when it came to the murder of unarmed American servicemen, Helms drew the line and went public.

None of CIA's official records of Helms's life and years of service to the Agency, not least those newly released in 2017, make reference to this honorable moment where he expressed outrage at the attack by the US government on its own sailors.

CHAPTER 12

"THE TRUTH, THE WHOLE TRUTH, AND NOTHING BUT THE TRUTH"

"I think Cristol's an Israeli agent."

—Admiral Isaac Kidd

Israel's most concerted publishing effort to defend its falsification of the events of June 8, 1967, is a 2013 book, *The* Liberty *Incident Revealed: The Definitive Account of the 1967 Israeli Attack on the U.S. Navy Spy Ship*. The author is an American, a retired Florida bankruptcy court judge named Aharon Jay Cristol.[1] Cristol's first book, it originated as a doctoral dissertation, and it is written entirely and shamelessly from the Israeli point of view. Praising his own service to the US Navy, Cristol neglects to say that he flew in two-seaters, in the back row, and that he was not a cryptologist.[2] How many trips he made to Israel in the service of this falsified history is difficult to enumerate. He admits to more than ten.

With arrogance to spare, Cristol claims that his book is "the truth, the whole truth, and nothing but the truth."[3] The dismaying preponderance of Israeli sources is the fruit of Cristol's having admittedly made those many trips to Israel for his "research." There are so many errors of fact and errors of omission as to render his book a curiosity of political propaganda. Perhaps the most interesting aspect of Cristol's book is that he and Israel felt the need at this late date to reiterate the old distortions.

Cristol claims that there have been five separate congressional investigations into the ambush of *Liberty* conducted since 1967, whereas the congressional library confirms that no government investigation has been conducted but for Admiral Kidd's narrowly conceived court of inquiry in the weeks after the attack. He insists that thirty-four of the sailors worked for the NSA. None did, except for the civilian translators. Everyone else served the US Navy and was subordinate to the Naval Security Group; NSA was required to apply to the Joint Chiefs of Staff to gain access to the intelligence collected by the USS *Liberty*, which was not an NSA ship, as Cristol claims, falsely.[4] It was a navy ship.

Cristol's most stunning omission is the machine-gunning of the life rafts by the Israeli torpedo boats. He remarks cynically that Admiral Kidd's report did not include Lloyd Painter's testimony as a witness to the torpedo boats machine-gunning the life rafts because "he must have been lying." Having seen the 2002 version of his book, Painter refused to be interviewed by Cristol. No matter; Cristol claims that Painter talked to him.

Among the dozens of flagrant errors riddling Cristol's book is his denial that *Liberty* ever requested an escort from Admiral Martin: William Inman Martin gives the lie to this view himself in the document released by the Joint Chiefs fact-finding investigation team. The Joint Chiefs team concluded that "an operational commander could not protect a ship like *Liberty* without providing escort and combat air patrol; he can only react to an attack once initiated or threatened which in this case was too late." As we have seen, Admiral Martin lied repeatedly in the aftermath of the attack.

Cristol's obsession with line of sight communications is specious and flawed. Dave Lewis says that Cristol should have known that line of sight is not rigid or inviolable, not absolute, especially in the highly ionized atmosphere of June 1967, a period of high sunspot activity.[5] This allowed aircraft in the area to hear the Israeli pilot who balked when he realized that he was being ordered to bomb an American ship.

Cristol assumes you can only intercept a signal within the horizon because it doesn't follow the curvature of the earth, but bounces around. Yet because of the sunspot cycle, at that moment you could at least partially follow that curvature. It was not inevitable that you could hear beyond line of sight, but it was at least possible on June 8, 1967.[6] (Tactical communications, local conversations in the field, are almost always line of sight, unlike strategic concerns.)

When Cristol argues that *Liberty*'s capacity for listening extended only to the horizon, twenty to twenty-five miles, he is referring to VHF/UHF (very high frequency/ultra high frequency), which is line of sight, ignoring 98 percent of the communications. They were at the peak of an eleven-year sunspot cycle, when the ionosphere was highly ionized, and so, using HF and not VHF, they could hear Tel Aviv talking to its troops. Seeing everything in black and white, Cristol fails to understand the variance involved. "Electrons and the sun's ionosphere don't always obey Cristol's edicts," Dave Lewis remarked to me with some irony. "He may be able to control the press, but he can't control communications."[7]

Cristol also infers that *Liberty*'s moon satellite could work only in the limited periods when the moon was visible to both the ship and the receiving antenna. This was not the case: for eighteen hours of the twenty-four hour day, the moon, the ship, and the shore station were in alignment. So Cristol stands behind a smokescreen of pseudoscience.

Cristol is particularly bent on undermining the transcripts of dialogue between Israeli air controllers and pilots because they establish that the Israelis knew *Liberty* was an American ship. He assumes American aircraft in the area couldn't hear Tel Aviv because it was more than twenty-five miles away, which is false. Along the way, he writes that Dave Lewis was assigned to the National Security Agency, which is also false. He was part of the Naval Security Group.

Nor did Cristol understand what CRITICOM communications were: these were "critical communications" set up by President Eisenhower so that the White House and Joint Chiefs would have a message within ten minutes. A CRITIC message could move from even a junior officer directly to the White House, bypassing FLASH emergency traffic and the Joint Chiefs of Staff, as we have seen in the case of US

Air Force Captain Richard Block. Those bypassed could even include COMSIXTH FLEET (Admiral William Inman Martin) and CINCUS-NAVEUR (commander in chief, US Naval Forces Europe—Admiral John S. McCain). They might receive a FLASH message, not a CRITIC. In his attempt to discredit Dave Lewis's testimony based on his conversation with Admiral Geis, Cristol insists that McNamara could not have called back because he could not use secure communication. Yet, in his panic, that is precisely what McNamara did. He used a plain, unsecure AUTODIN telephone on the Department of Defense telecommunications network.

Cristol goes to considerable lengths to validate Israel's lies. In his attempt to undermine the credibility of Lewis's testimony regarding Admiral Geis's statements that Lyndon Johnson personally had called back the rescue planes, Cristol libels Lewis, suggesting that he had been mentally impaired. (In his effort to rehabilitate Lyndon Johnson, Cristol is not alone. Another attempt to undermine Lewis's statements was James Scott's omission of Lyndon Johnson's personally calling back the rescue planes, despite the fact that Scott had talked to Lewis, as Lewis remembers, at least eight times.)[8]

Cristol opens his attack on Lewis, who reported on his conversation with Admiral Geis regarding the telephone calls of McNamara and Lyndon Johnson calling back the rescue aircraft, by challenging that Lewis ever requested an escort from the Sixth Fleet, which he assuredly did. That *Liberty* would not be able to defend itself in a firefight is why Lewis (and Captain McGonagle) requested a destroyer escort as soon as they were patched to the Sixth Fleet and heading for the turbulent zones of the Eastern Mediterranean.

It had been Lewis's idea, but he went through General Services Communication, which meant Captain McGonagle, although he was not obliged to consult the captain on this matter. Lewis was the officer in charge of USN-855, the designation of the cryptologic communications billeted on board *Liberty*. He had the authority to communicate with

Captain McGonagle's superiors, although he did not do so but, instead, consulted only the captain himself.

Cristol claims that he examined all messages and could not discover any that requested an escort of Admiral Martin. Yet the request had been teletyped. With limited knowledge of the protocols of a surveillance ship, Cristol, embarrassingly, demands to know how a puny lieutenant commander (Lewis) dared to ask a four-star admiral (Martin) for an escort. "Anyone who is familiar with US naval procedures," Cristol argues with braggadocio, "would find it very hard to believe that Lewis had authority to communicate with Admiral Martin." Yet it was so. Lewis communicated with the cryptologic unit on Admiral Martin's staff.

Moving beyond the pale of civilized discourse, Cristol writes that Lewis was so "badly burned" in the torpedo attack as to impair his judgment. Angry that the ship's chief intelligence officer declined to be interviewed for his book, Cristol concocts a scurrilous fantasy, arguing that Lewis' wounds "perhaps allowed imagination to fill in some of the gaps in his memory of the event and the immediate aftermath." Note the amateur's "perhaps."

His evidence in tatters, Cristol then accuses Lewis of "incredible audacity" for reporting Lyndon Johnson's statement, as conveyed to him by Admiral Geis, that he didn't want to "embarrass an ally," that line that revealed Johnson's prior knowledge of the identity of the attackers.

Cristol's book is replete with falsehoods. He terms *Liberty* "a warship by international law definition," when it was an unarmed noncombatant. On the issue of whether nuclear-armed planes took off from the USS *America*, he writes that "F-4B Phantom aircraft taking off from a US carrier" was "an impossibility in 1967." This is correct, but he neglects to inform the reader that the planes on the USS *America* that carried nuclear devices were A-4 Skyhawks and A-5 Vigilantes, which could be configured for nuclear weapons carries and releases. The F-4 Phantoms were loaded with Sidewinder and Sparrow missiles.

Cristol is helpful in one regard. It has been rumored that as soon as the SOS arrived, the Joint Chiefs had authorized the bombing of Haifa, the harbor from which the motorized torpedo boats had been launched. Cristol writes that it was Robert McNamara who canceled the Joint Chiefs' "use of force authorization," inadvertently confirming a fact that had been challenged and adding new information.

Cristol's final sentimental salvo is his blind assertion that had Israel really wanted to sink *Liberty*, it would have done so. He grants no credence to the competence of the sailors who accomplished the impossible. The images in Cristol's book purporting to be taken from gun camera film during the attack have been exposed as fake by military researcher Kenneth J. Halliwell.[9] Some of the photographs in Cristol's book were doctored. One supposed to be taken in the Med was actually a photograph of *Liberty* docked in Norfolk before it set sail.

There are many more factual inaccuracies. Cristol ignores the fact that the Israeli motorized torpedo boats machine-gunned *Liberty*'s life rafts and carried away one raft as a souvenir, a war crime. Cristol also omits that the Israeli planes shot deliberately at the stretcher bearers who had ventured out on deck in an attempt to rescue the wounded. And yet another of Cristol's lies of omission was that the United States did not experience a nuclear alert on June 8, 1967.

Cristol acknowledges the presence of only one reconnaissance flight on the morning of June 8, when there were at least eight, each recorded on a separate situation report. He never discovers that the ship was locked on "fire control," which meant that the attackers had to know that the ship was moving at five knots and could not have been involved in combat. He implies that *Liberty* and *El Quseir* were of equal size, and that the letters "GTR" on the hull could be mistaken for "CTR," denoting a Soviet ship. Why Israel would attack a Soviet ship at this moment is no more comprehensible than Israel's attacking an Egyptian horse freighter unrelentingly for close to two hours with weapons that included napalm, four days after Egypt had been defeated.

Cristol's sense of history and politics is also opaque. He argues that

McNamara and Johnson canceled the rescue planes because the US naval attaché, Ernest Castle, told them that Israel "had attacked the ship by mistake," which violates the timeline, certainly for McNamara's first cancellation call.

Cristol also claims that the ship was not able to send off a distress signal because someone "had accidentally moved the frequency one kilocycle and once this was discovered, *Liberty* was able to send off its SOS." In fact, one kilocycle was not very much, and the systematic destruction of the antennas and the jamming of the circuits were a conscious effort to prevent the ship from calling for help.

Cristol suggests that Israel may have been retaliating because *Liberty* had fired on the coastal town of El Arish. By 2013, the year his book was released, it was well-known that *Liberty* lacked the capability to fire on a city on shore. That would have required cannon; all they had were the four machine guns. It turned out that no one had fired on El Arish—the site, according to Israeli military historian Aryeh Yitzhaki, where Israeli troops killed at least one thousand Egyptian prisoners of war.

When the smoke cleared, Israel had forgotten its promise of "no territorial acquisition." The United States spoke of the "territorial integrity of the states Israel had invaded and occupied, while doing nothing to prevent Israel from altering its borders, then sending settlers in to occupy the freshly conquered lands."[10]

Two hours after his interview with Cristol, Isaac Kidd called Ward Boston. "I think Cristol's an Israeli agent," Admiral Kidd said. After thirty years of silence, on January 9, 2004, Ward Boston released an affidavit in which he declares that "Admiral Kidd was adamant that it was a deliberate, planned attack on an American ship." In 1990, Boston recalls, he had replied to a telephone call from Cristol about the court of inquiry, posing questions that Boston refused to answer. "At no time did I ever hear Admiral Kidd speak of Cristol other than in highly disparaging terms," Boston now said. "I find Cristol's claims of a 'close friendship' with Admiral Kidd to be utterly incredible."[11]

Boston saw himself as a victim of an effort at deception. He repudiated Cristol and his "misinformation" and wrote that "it is important for the American people to know that it is clear that Israel is responsible for deliberately attacking an American ship and murdering American sailors whose bereaved shipmates have lived with this egregious conclusion for many years."

Yet even Cristol uses the argument that it seemed "unlikely and without motive for Israel to attack the unarmed sailors of its sole and chief ally." He asks, rhetorically, "Is it reasonable that Israel would commit an act of war against the only nation in the world offering any support?" Boston (see affidavit, January 9, 2004) stated that "there is no question in my mind that those goddamned bastards tried to kill everyone on board." Yet why? And as this book has shown, Israel did not attack the "unarmed sailors of its sole and chief ally" as the sole perpetrator; the United States was a direct participant in the operation.

"Lyndon Johnson and Robert McNamara had directly ordered Admiral Kidd to conclude that the attack was a case of 'mistaken identity' despite overwhelming evidence to the contrary," Boston wrote.

"Ward, they're not interested in the facts," Isaac Kidd said. "It's a political matter and we cannot talk about it."

What inspired him to come forward after thirty years, Boston wrote, was Cristol's book, which "twists the facts and misrepresents the views of those of us who investigated the attack." His affidavit was a direct product of Cristol's lies: "It is Cristol's insidious attempt to whitewash the facts that has pushed me to speak out." Before Boston came forward, Cristol had termed him "a man of integrity." Now he was a "liar." Boston concluded that "Cristol must be an Israeli agent."[12] McNamara agreed to be interviewed by Cristol, only to claim that he never spoke on the telephone or radio to anyone in the Sixth Fleet that day.

Other efforts to argue for the Israeli position are no less flawed than Cristol's. In *The Secret History of the Jews*, John Loftus writes that *Liberty* was "intercepting Israeli communications and encrypting them, translating and altering their content and then sending them to Lebanon and Jordan in real time."[13] *Liberty* enjoyed no such capability. Loftus has produced a wild fantasy contrary to the facts.

Ernest Castle and Hadden signed on to what amounted to an endorsement of Cristol's falsified story. In an appendix to Cristol's book, they refer to "the failures of both U.S. intelligence and Israel intelligences services" which "might have prevented the tragedy." These "failures" are not enumerated; the idea itself is a well-worn evasion and means nothing. We do learn that Israel denied Castle's request to interview the pilots or torpedo boat commanders, a fact Castle kept to himself.

In Appendix II, "Hadden Recollections," John Hadden writes: "It was a foregone conclusion that Israel was going to start a preemptive war" once Egypt closed the Straits of Tiran and introduced troops into the Sinai.[14] Hadden writes that he hoped for "a period of at least three weeks to give the US President time to pose as a striver for peace . . . to exhaust all efforts to avoid war." The key word is "pose." Hadden knew that what became the "Six-Day War" was inevitable. Hadden writes "the Israelis kept President Johnson informed in detail during the crisis and during the War that followed. This effort exceeded anything I had experienced up to that time."

Without mentioning the attack on the USS *Liberty*, Hadden, in his typical circuitous manner, is suggesting that Johnson had foreknowledge of the attack on the USS *Liberty*. In the set of interviews he granted to his son, John L. Hadden, Hadden does not once refer to the attack on the USS *Liberty*. Cristol, however, blows Hadden's cover, writing that Hadden was "deeply involved in the collection and analysis of both overt and covert information and intelligence about the incident."

The enormity of the disinformation spread by Israel and its representatives, like Cristol, has discouraged the worldliest of observers. In his memoir, Clark Clifford states: "I do not know to this day at what level the attack on the *Liberty* was authorized and I think it is unlikely that the full truth will ever come out."

George Ball called the cover-up "an elaborate charade" with the United States complaining pro forma to Israel, which in turn "reacted by blaming the victims."[15] Later disinformation, even sloppier, included an anecdote about Captain McGonagle bringing *Liberty* to be repaired in Israel and McGonagle attending a July 4 celebration at the American embassy in Israel. The story, entirely false, appeared in *Ha'aretz* in 2007.

Lyndon Johnson had led the way in cloaking the cover-up in lies. In his 1971 memoir, *The Vantage Point*, when he had ample time to correct the figures, nonetheless he wrote that "ten of the *Liberty* crew were killed and a hundred were wounded." The actual figures were 34 and 174. "Carrier aircraft were on their way to the scene to investigate," Johnson lied, referring to the very planes he personally had called back and so prevented from flying to the site of the attack. By 1971, Israel was buying $600 million worth of American-made weapons a year. Two years later, the figure had climbed to more than $3 billion.

CHAPTER 13

TREASON

"Y ou call back a rescue, that's murder, isn't it?" I ask Dave Lewis.

"Yes, it is," he says. "It's called treason."[1]

Sailors like John Scott knew the truth. "I don't see how they make a mistake," he wrote to his parents at the time, managing to evade Admiral Kidd's edict that the sailors tell their families nothing. "It was too well-planned & coordinated. They [Israel] knew exactly where to hit us and they did." Scott's courage stands in stark contrast to the timidity of most of his shipmates. In the year 2015, Dave McFeggan remained wary of speaking out about his unorthodox role on the ship, even as he could not help but express his indignation at the complicity of Admiral Martin. McFeggan replied emphatically to the question of whether Admiral Martin had foreknowledge of the attack, as cited above: "Of course he knew." McFeggan spoke of his fear that the navy would cancel his pension should he talk.

To become Chief of Naval Operations, you had to be commander of a fleet, and Admiral Martin fully expected to be so promoted. Serving as an aviator was only one means of "punching your ticket" on the way to further promotions. He had held the Mediterranean Sea under his command and so had "punched another ticket." It was not to be.

Admiral John S. McCain Jr. had a similar ambition. He was Admiral William Inman Martin's immediate superior and believed he too was in line to be Chief of Naval Operations. He was an alcoholic and graduated 423rd out of his Naval Academy class of 441. Neither McCain nor his son did the navy proud. His son graduated from the Naval Academy 894th out of a class of 899. In the navy, John McCain III, later a US Senator, was notorious for a stunt he performed on the deck of the aircraft carrier USS *Forrestal* on July 29, 1967, a month after the attack on the USS *Liberty*. It was ten in the morning. He revved the engines on his plane, sending a blast of fire out the back of his aircraft. Normally such "hotrodding," as it was called, just scared the pilot behind him. But this time it caused the rockets on the plane behind him to explode, setting fire to the carrier *Forrestal* and killing 134 people. Had he not had an admiral for a father, he would have been court-martialed, Dave Lewis says. He was showing off for the hell of it, but the hell caught up with him. Shortly after, John McCain disobeyed the orders of his superior not to be flying so low, an action that led to his being captured by the North Vietnamese.

Years later, when Survivors of the USS *Liberty* requested a response to the naval inquiry and its insufficiencies, McCain brushed them off: "If my father did it, it must have been right."[2]

The public official most steadfast in refusing to sign on to the fabrications regarding the motivation behind Israel's vicious, pounding ambush of the unarmed USS *Liberty* was Richard Helms, who had been director of Central Intelligence at the time of the attack. "They intended to attack the ship," Helms repeated late in his life. "No excuse can be found that this was a mistake." It was rare for Helms to make public political pronouncements, let alone do so repeatedly, but he apparently had not forgotten Desmond Fitzgerald's unauthorized Saturday-morning cable to John Hadden ordering the bombing of Cairo. That CIA had authored a document covering up for Israel in the days following the attack did not prevent Helms from repudiating the Israeli point of view in his later years.

Helms wanted to be heard. "It was no accident," Helms said more than once.[3] The attack was "no mistake." He was plainly urging that people not accept the official explanations, even all these many years later. As a life-long intelligence operative, he could do no more. There were others who told the truth, like Walter Deeley, an official at NSA, who wrote: "There is no way that they [Israel] didn't know that the *Liberty* was American."[4]

After the attack on the USS *Liberty*, John Hadden remained in Tel Aviv. On occasion, he drove his automobile as close to the nuclear reactor at Dimona as he dared and collected soil samples for radioactive analysis. It was 1967, and 1968, and he was concerned that Israel, despite its denials, was engaged in the manufacture of nuclear weapons. Invariably, he was trailed by the Shin Bet. He was a man to whom physical courage came easily.

Once, in 1968, an Israeli helicopter landed near his automobile. When security personnel demanded to examine his identification, Hadden flashed his US diplomatic passport. A year after the events of this story, John Hadden would go on to become a whistle-blower, exposing that Israel had stolen a considerable amount of weapons-grade uranium from a depot of NUMEC, a US Navy contracting company situated in Apollo, Pennsylvania, that was handling nuclear waste for the US Atomic Energy Commission. Hadden came to believe that NUMEC was an Israeli front, the uranium having been destined for Israel from the start. When he first heard it, Hadden said he hated the term "whistle-blower," but that is what he became.

By now, Hadden was despised by Mossad, who spoke of him as "*Ha mamseah gadol*," the big bastard. He returned to CIA headquarters, where Hadden served at both the Israel and Middle East desks. He fell under the sway of James Angleton and participated in the CIA cover-up of the attack on the USS *Liberty*. He found that Angleton's attitude and treatment of his peers "was so awful that the minute one became DCZ, he was gone. Their hatred of him was at such a level that because I was on his staff most refused to talk or deal with me."[5]

At the Israel desk, where they played cat and mouse for years, Angleton prevented Hadden from receiving communiqués from people in Israel. Hadden walked a delicate line, managing to remain friends with his old contacts in Israel, despite Angleton's interference. Hadden attempted to persuade the Israelis to go easy; flexing their muscles would do them in.

Running America was not in their interests. The Israelis did not see things John Hadden's way.

Hadden spent much of the last third of his career assembling a report on the development of the Israeli bomb, documenting how Israel had funneled one hundred kilograms of weapons-grade uranium from the NUMEC plant. An irony was that his own father, Gavin Hadden, had worked on the Manhattan Project and written its official history. John Hadden found that there had been "deep collusion by American corporate and federal entities that were working with the Israelis."[6] No copy of this report would survive.

One day at Langley, Angleton ambushed John Hadden. "When did they pitch you?" Angleton said, as if Hadden were the "fifth man" in a group of traitors that ultimately included Kim Philby, Guy Burgess, Donald MacLaine, Anthony Blunt, and John Cairncross, the "Cambridge Five." By "they," Angleton was referring to the KGB, implying that the Soviets had approached Hadden as a person of interest with a view toward recruiting him as a source, asset, contract agent, or agent in place. It was a profound insult, slanderous and false.

Angleton was revealing that beneath his suave façade, he was rude and barbaric and was, like Bill Harvey, something of a thug, whatever his effete appearance. Always he played dirty. John Hadden was to spend eight years at the Israel desk under James Angleton, even as he clung to the idea of himself as an honorable person.

Years later, Hadden admitted in an interview with Peter Hounam that there was "a difference in tone between Angleton and Helms. Anybody who was anti-Soviet was Angleton's friend," Hadden said.[7] But then he suggested that Hounam was "ascribing too much power to Angleton." By the close of their conversation, Hadden had persuaded Hounam that he "admired" Angleton. As for Helms, he never cut the umbilical cord that tied him to Angleton, and as ambassador to Iran, where he was exiled after leaving the Agency, on the rare occasions that he returned to the United States, he asked that meetings be arranged for him with Angleton.[8]

Hadden maintained a correspondence with Meir Amit and Efraim

Halevy late in his life. See, for example, his March 17, 1980, letter to "Nachick."

"You may not believe it," Hadden writes, "but a recent poll showed 50% of all Americans do not realize that we import any oil at all!"[9] Hadden suggests that only "until something like Pearl Harbor happens— something really close to the bone like a direct Soviet attack on Western Europe . . . will US policy toward the Middle East improve."

In his characteristic convoluted manner, Hadden added a fact to his rambling about the Six-Day War: "Washington had actively wanted the Israelis to go all the way and unseat Nasser, but to America's chagrin, Dayan and the Israeli government had refused."

Nasser, indeed, had been a useful enemy to Israel. Hadden opposed what he called "the politicization of our espionage apparatus" and presidential meddling.[10] Those who thought otherwise became Richard Helms's enemies, like General Vernon A. Walters, who told Helms, in the context of Nixon having nastily engineered Helms's fall from grace, "Well, Dick, we all have to retire sometime." Helms had received a note from the White House "ordering him to claim that any investigation in Mexico concerning the Watergate people would interfere with Agency operations there." Like John Hadden's, Helms's life was crisscrossed with demands that he lie and obfuscate.

The attack on the USS *Liberty* bedeviled John Hadden all his life, and the part he played in it had embittered his soul. On July 30, 2001, in search of solutions to the Arab-Israeli conflict, he invoked a question raised by nineteenth-century Russian philosopher Nikolay Chernyshevsky, and famously embraced by Vladimir Ilyich Lenin in 1902: "What is to be done?" Hadden noted: "No wonder there are those who would like to shift all responsibility for the ME Middle East) to the USG."[11] So he told Peter Hounam that he had "spent two months investigating the attack on the USS *Liberty* and reached the conclusion it was a mistake."

Liberty, he said, "in my view is a very unimportant event." When Hounam mentioned a document claiming that Moshe Dayan had ordered the attack (as the reader may recall, it was Meir Amit who is entitled to that honor), Hadden's forthrightness burst through. "That's absolutely out of the question," Hadden said. "I don't know who told you that. Anything like that that you're describing I would have seen it, if not written it." John Hadden lived out his life knowing the true story of the USS *Liberty* and, as an expression of his loyalty to his government, kept silent.

What Hadden came to believe, according to his son, John Hadden Jr., was that "there was a progression of corruption in every aspect of American life, and of course it was as much within the Agency as it was within the Pentagon, as it was within the Congress, as it was within the presidency—it was everywhere."

Knowing well the Israeli proclivity to interfere in American publishing, thwarting the publication of books distasteful to them, Hadden decided to put what he knew about the Israeli atomic bomb production into a novel he called "BOMB."[12] The main character of "BOMB," Ezra, a Kibbutznik, "skeptical, cynical and ironic," bears a strong resemblance to the author. Unlike John Hadden, however, he is short and stout, with thinning hair, and is "a modern buccaneer." His son, Amos, a Sabra, born in Israel, would perish during the Six-Day War "scaling the Golan Heights" in Syria.

"BOMB" chronicles the birth of the Israeli nuclear arms program in the early 1960s, aided by Israel's "own Dr. Strangelove." Israel's nuclear program would be "in the name of our survival." Ezra is blackmailed by Mapai, the Ben-Gurion party. He complies, knowing he "couldn't refuse."

It is Ezra's older brother, Shmuel, who carries the author's views. "I fear what may happen to a people wholly caught up in the mechanics and ways of war," he says. "Of what use is our existence to the world if all we can come up with is the Uzi sub-machine gun?" Shmuel adds: "Will history see us as latter-day Spartans or even, God forbid, Prussians?"

"BOMB" chronicles the logic by which Israel decided that they must be the first in the Middle East to build an atomic arsenal, and under conditions of "absolute secrecy." Mistrusting the durability of French assistance ("Who knows what the *Goyim* will do to us next?"), they moved forward, even as they mistrusted Mossad to maintain secrecy. There is a scene in "BOMB" at the "gold dome of the Bahai temple," the very building that the Soviets had targeted for annihilation should Cairo have been bombed. The war will end with the first Arab victory, one character states. There was no going back.

"BOMB" concludes with ever more lethal nuclear weaponry being produced in Israel. In writing this story, John Hadden was attempting to keep the issue of Israeli nuclear war power open, all the while tantalizing the reader with his acute knowledge of the intrigue between Israel, the United States, and the Soviet Union. His son recounts that Hadden "couldn't satisfy the publisher's requests to make it more Ian Flemingish, so it fizzled."[13]

Among John Hadden's favorite quotations was one by Sir Arthur Conan Doyle from *Rules of Sherlock Holmes*: "There is nothing more deceptive than an obvious fact." Another was a version of Winston Churchill's "Truth deserves a bodyguard of lies," which he is said to have addressed to Josef Stalin. Hadden preferred: "Lies are so precious they need a bodyguard of Truth." He was a man most comfortable with subtlety.

"Dear Menachem," Hadden wrote to a friend on 19 November 2001, "I believe that history, the rights and wrongs, who struck first, who is at fault, where might justice lie, what would fairness dictate, is, as the Germans say, (back to Munich) Wurst!"[14] With respect to the USS *Liberty*, there is every indication that he was tougher on the United States for its complicity than he was on Israel, as was proper.

James Angleton was fired by William Colby on December 20, 1974, in the wake of the exposé of his organizing a spying program on US dissenters and antiwar protesters. Helms had retired in 1973, and it was only once Helms was gone that Angleton could be rooted out of his nest at CIA.

Appalled by the Church Committee revelations, as well as his own stifling knowledge of Angleton's malfeasances, for the last three months of Angleton's tenure at CIA, the new director of Central Intelligence,

William Colby, consigned him to an eight-by-eight-foot cubicle.[15] Angleton was not provided with a telephone number or office. "This is where you will be eight hours a day," Colby said. Angleton stuck it out for three months. This information derives from Dick Thompson.

Two weeks later, Colby drowned in a canoeing accident. On the day of his disappearance, his wife noted later, he had violated his usual routine, one he followed religiously. He had left his breakfast dishes unwashed. He had gone out without a life vest.

Dick Thompson spent more than $700,000 of his own money on his documentary, *USS* Liberty: *Dead in the Water*. When he took an interest in the *Liberty* story, a colonel in the air force told him, "Given your oath to the country, you're not allowed to do what you're doing."[16] People were tailing him, and he knew it. "If you find out one thing," Thompson remarked to a friend, "you find out something else." He was an American patriot who loved his country so much that when he came upon the story of the USS *Liberty*, he devoted a good portion of his time to efforts to uncover the truth of what had taken place.

He remained a man who didn't want anyone to notice him. He didn't want anyone to know his name, and you will not find it among the credits for *Dead in the Water*. He appreciated honest people and traveled to the North Country to visit Dave Lewis, promising that one day he would take Lewis to the best Russian restaurant in Montreal, just over the Canadian border. (Thompson's deep contacts with the Soviets derived from his intelligence background.) They should go there, Thompson said. He was fun loving and enjoyed life. They never made it.

Dick Thompson died when his old Cadillac hit a tree in South Carolina. He was on his way home from a reunion of the *Liberty* veterans. His final act had been to turn over the rights to *Dead in the Water* to the USS *Liberty* Veterans Association to help fund their efforts to make their story better known.

After he left the Agency, James Angleton visited William F. Buckley Jr. at the offices of the *National Review* in New York. CIA had long funded the magazine, and in 1977 and 1978, Angleton saw Buckley frequently.

After James Angleton's death, tribute was paid to him in Israel's Hall of Honor for Mossad agents. There were two monuments, bronze plaques, erected in his honor. One is on a hillside a few miles from Jerusalem, the other in a park near the King David Hotel, site of an infamous *Irgun* attack. The first was dedicated as a "Memorial Corner" to Angleton by Jerusalem mayor Teddy Kollek, long an intelligence colleague of Angleton, and defense minister Yitzhak Rabin.

The dedication of one of the plaques was attended by Israeli intelligence chiefs past and present. Later, on an assignment in Israel, a television reporter sought out one of the Angleton memorials. After some difficulty he was able to locate it, but something seemed odd. On closer inspection, Angleton's plaque turned out to be made not of bronze but of cardboard. The trees and the plaque were at the end of a garbage dump. The plaque read: "In Memory of a Good Friend." This message is duplicated on a wall overlooking the Old City of Jerusalem.

"This guy sold out his country for the bloody Israelis, and this is the way they pay him back!" the cameraman remarked.[17]

John Hadden had grown weary of America's obsession with empire, its imperial aspirations, which, as an avid historian, he connected to Rome. Hadden retired in 1973. In his later years, he pursued his hobbies: woodworking, making dioramas chronicling local history (he had settled in Brunswick, Maine) and toys for his grandchildren. He found himself crying at "sugary" sentimental movies. He gave a talk on the sex life of the lobster.

Hadden remembered an America that had enjoyed the sympathy of the rest of the world "and just threw it away. Destroyed it." His final advice to his son, John, was "Don't trust anyone!" He is to be remembered for refusing to be the person who gave the Israelis a green light to pursue the Six-Day War, "flickering" or otherwise. They had to go to Washington to get it. John Hadden would not grant it to them in Tel Aviv.

In 1980, he was in correspondence with Meir Amit. "It seems that we think along the same lines, and share the same views," Amit wrote Hadden, a far cry from their meeting in May 1967, when Amit was rushing around in search of an American endorsement of Israel's pursuit of what came to be known as the "Six-Day War" and Hadden sought to delay it.[18]

"Your letters from Israel are of immense help and interest to me," Hadden wrote.

In 2006, the State Department held a conference on the Six-Day War, where the Survivors of the attack on the USS *Liberty* were denied the opportunity to speak; their dignity was redeemed by author James Bamford, who read out Ward Boston's repudiation of Jay Cristol's book and pronounced John S. McCain's so-called naval inquiry an utter fraud. Observing the spectacle, John Hadden called the conference organizers "stupid," then went off to lunch with Ernest Castle. None of the scholars or pundits or former spooks mentioned that Angleton had collected dirt on Richard Helms and other DCIs.

When his son asked him yet again about the USS *Liberty*, Hadden retreated into a final silence on this subject.[19] Yet, as Hadden junior put it, "he served a mythological America that he himself considered more and more fraudulent." Prescient, John Hadden noted that "the best example of such dangers is our creation of the Muslim extremist threat, which, without our arms and money, would never have assumed the danger they have." He was a skilled, effective operator, yet at heart an idealist. "For intelligence to be useful," he believed, "it must serve only one master and that is Truth, even if that truth is contrary to the ideology and beliefs of our political leadership."

Hadden himself said that he "wasn't very good at spying." At the age of eighty, he summed up his CIA career as an "ongoing circus" and a "puerile occupation," not a serious line of work at all. In the year of his death, Hadden said, simply, "I never felt that working for CIA was a good choice."[20]

John Hadden died on May 27, 2013, at the age of eighty-nine in his home in Brunswick, Maine. When Hadden died, CIA violated its customary procedure and took no formal notice of his passing. It was more than a year before the Association of Former Intelligence Officers noted Hadden's death in its June 25, 2014, *Weekly Intelligence Notes* e-newsletter. One retiree, an admirer of John Hadden named Grant Smith, was dumbfounded that the passing of so senior a CIA officer should be ignored by the Agency he had served so well.

John Hadden, living in Maine after he retired from CIA. (Photo courtesy of John L. Hadden.)

Gamal Abdel Nasser died of a heart attack in 1970. He was fifty-two years old. Five million people in emotional anguish gathered for his funeral.

Liberty's wounded were offered paltry, woefully inadequate compensation. Dave Lewis met with State Department officers on three occasions to hammer out how much he would be awarded.

The amount of reparation was figured according to your base pay and the percentage of your disability as determined by the Veterans Administration, reduced by the amount you would earn if you put your money in a savings account. The calculations for Dave Lewis assumed due course promotions through captain (a promotion that he was unjustly denied), reduced by 4 percent, which would be what you would earn if you put in a savings account, with a 20 percent disability.

When Lewis closed in on retirement, and attempted to negotiate with them, the State Department denied they had ever met with him.[21] They claimed they had no record of their meetings. From the VA, Lewis received $81,000 in reparations, with which he bought a house and two hundred acres of land, a pond, and an apple orchard. He had done "penance," as his superior and advocate Admiral Ralph Cook put it, by creating a box for electronics that could fit into a helicopter hanger and would replace surveillance ships like *Liberty*. This was in 1970 or 1971.

"It's disheartening when your own government turns its back on you," Dave Lewis says. His last post was as executive officer, number two in command of the Naval Communications Master Station, Western Pacific, in Guam. One day, his brother Harold asked for a favor: a ship was pulling in. Could Dave host a fiesta for the sailors, complete with food, strippers and other favors for the sailors, six hundred in all? When the ship's leave was canceled, Dave was stuck with all the food and the booze. He took it all with good humor. He could never be accused of taking life too seriously.

On July 31, 1979, Dave Lewis retired after twenty-six years in the navy. Only then did his wife, Dolores, learn that he had been a "professional cryptologist." He moved to his hometown, Colebrook, New Hampshire, where he clerked for thirteen years in the local hardware store. He could not vote for Hillary Clinton for president, he says, because she was passing TOP SECRET CODE WORD information in the clear.

Many sailors faced a lifetime of surgeries. By 1980, Moe Shafer had ribs removed to release pressure on his neck, two neck fusions, and six lower back fusions, all related to the attack. His ears were still ringing. His medical records had gone astray, and he was denied veterans benefits. The Israelis offered him $500 in reparations.[22] Larry Weaver endured a lifetime of pain; he emerged with a stainless steel left shoulder, two knee replacements, nerve damage to the right side of his body. Old age would be accompanied by the use of only his right thumb and index finger, with a square foot of mesh holding his abdomen together, and sixty pieces of shrapnel in his body. He had survived thirty-one major surgeries. Yet on his DD-214 discharge form, the navy made no mention of the USS *Liberty*. It took him twenty-nine years to obtain benefits from the Veterans Administration.

For second- and third-degree burns from the blast of the torpedo, Bryce Lockwood was awarded $26,000 in reparations.[23] Ron Kukal received $24,000 "in full and final settlement."

To negotiate these ungenerous payments, Israel had hired a high-powered Washington lawyer named David Ginsburg, who was aided by Nicholas Katzenbach and Yitzhak Rabin. It was a farce; Israel wrote a check for $3,323,500, although the money would come out of American pockets, American aid to Israel.

Israel also balked at paying for repairs to the ship they had blasted into futility. Why should they pay, since the United States had failed to order *Liberty* further from shore? they argued. The United States presented a claim for the damage to the ship to the Israeli government for $7,644,146. Israel rejected the claim. The final settlement, for $6 million, was devised by Mossad agent Rafi Eitan, leader of the task force that had captured Adolf Eichmann and smuggled him to Israel. Eitan had also secured the uranium from NUMEC in Apollo, Pennsylvania.

The "six million," of course, was an invocation of the Holocaust, a reminder to the world that no matter what evils Israel perpetrated, they could not approach the horrors of World War II. It was as if the Holocaust immunized Israel for any future actions. Dean Rusk's response was that Congress merely increased the annual Israeli aid by that amount.

It was now December 1980. Johnson and McNamara were gone. It had already cost $20 million to refit the ship and would have cost an additional ten. It didn't seem worth it. Meanwhile, there were new methods of surveillance, including the one initiated by Dave Lewis himself.

Settlements in what had been Palestinian territory began on June 10, 1967. By the millennium, three hundred thousand settlers had moved to land that had not been part of Israel before June 1967. In 1968, aid to Israel from the United States increased at least fourfold. James Angleton's imperial schemes, in which Israel had been enlisted, carried the day.

In claiming that the attack was an "accident" and a "mistake," it was Israel that was protecting its ally, the United States, which was equally responsible for murdering and maiming those sailors. No ally of Israel has believed that Israel would commit so heinous an act of war, one studded with war crimes, against the United States. So Rafi Eitan admitted that he knew the facts behind the attack but was committed to silence out of "signature" (a quaint term) and "loyalty to my country." Eitan acknowledged that he was familiar with the term "Operation Cyanide."

That the United States and Israel collaborated on an operation to sink an unarmed American intelligence ship and send everyone on it to the bottom of the sea remains among the darkest secrets of the twentieth century. In whose interest was the removal of Gamal Abdel Nasser is for history to speculate. Even intelligence asset Anthony Wells confirms that planes took off for Cairo, even as Wells ignored the false flag aspect of the intended attack.

History often supplies someone who chooses not to remain silent. In this story we have the diaries of Moshe Sharett, who elucidates the strategies during these years of the Mapai party of David Ben-Gurion, Pinhas Lavon, Shimon Peres, Moshe Dayan, and Binyamin Gibli, all bent on the demonization of Nasser. Mapai leader David Hacohen declared himself convinced that the Israelis should behave in the Middle East as if they were crazy in order to terrorize the Arabs and blackmail the West.[24] Encouraged by CIA, in particular James Angleton, but Allen Dulles as well, innocent American servicemen, many under twenty years old, became the collateral damage, the scapegoats, caught in the web of David Ben-Gurion's obsession to "topple" Nasser. At the same time, their brothers in Vietnam were suffering 58,220 casualties in an equally futile endeavor.

Israel steadfastly maintained its silence about what happened in what looks now like a form of political blackmail. A former CIA officer with the clandestine services, Victor Marchetti, put it this way: "The CIA and Israel's intelligence agency, the Mossad, have become so entwined over the years that the Mossad is now in a position to blackmail the CIA—and therefore the U.S. government."[25]

The United States would be munificent in its aid to Israel. Israel would not reveal, indeed not so much as hint, that the attack on the USS *Liberty* was a collaboration between the United States and Israel, the United States having sacrificed its own unarmed sailors to serve one more attempt to remove Nasser from power. That Lyndon Johnson sacrificed American men to serve his own political ends, committing murder, would not be exposed, and every US president and every congressperson since has honored the Faustian bargain made with Israel. Lyndon Johnson's mainstream biographers have chosen not to notice his role in the affair of the USS *Liberty*.

Not surprisingly, much time was devoted during the proceedings of Admiral Kidd's naval inquiry to the preposterous argument that the failure of those specious messages was to blame for the ship being attacked. Kidd's report adds that the Asmara station "was handling an abnormally large amount of high precedence message traffic on 8 June 67."[26] It was as if the trumped-up human comedy of errors was not sufficient, providing the United States with cover the likes of which history has rarely encountered.

An NSA cryptologist who had been stationed at Bremerhaven in 1964, intercepting Russian naval communications in the Baltic and North Sea, pronounced "Operation Cyanide" "a clandestine CIA and Mossad plan." His name was J. P. Feldmann, and he had been trained as a Russian Morse code intercept operator, a cryptologic technician third class in the US Navy, one among the few who uncovered the truth and was willing to speak out.[27]

The plot was not invisible. The first director of Mossad, Isser Harel, recognized "the US is interested in toppling Nasser's regime. . . . On the matter of Nasser it prefers its work to be done by Israel."

That their own government should have killed and maimed them and their shipmates was so horrifying a thought for these lifetime military men that when the Survivors filed their war crimes charges against Israel in 2004, they did not name Lyndon Johnson in the petition, although he had abandoned American sailors to die in violation of the military code, a crime against humanity. So horrific was Johnson's conduct that no president since has been willing to examine the motives behind the Israeli attack. Representative Craig Hosmer (D-Calif.) posed a rhetorical question, referring to Lyndon Johnson: "How can you court martial a President?"

Ernie Gallo says that Johnson could have been impeached for violating the code of military justice and leaving wounded people behind on a field of battle. Gallo went on to serve for twenty-three years with CIA. One day, an Agency officer of his acquaintance presented him with two photographs taken through the periscope of a submarine watching the attack. Taken from the surface level, as from a boat, the photographs show the ship before and after the attack. These photographs had resided in CIA files until he gave them to Ernie. Gallo did not make them public because he did not want the fellow who gave him the pictures to get into trouble.

Photographs of the USS *Liberty* taken from the periscope camera of either the USS *Amberjack* or the *Andrew Jackson*, one before the attack, the other after. June 8, 1967. (Photos courtesy of Ernie Gallo.)

Over the years, determined to expose the truth, on behalf of the sailors, efforts were made to interview Secretary of Defense McNamara. Colonel William Barrett Taylor III, a personal friend of McNamara's, wrote him a request, suggesting that they discuss what happened. They scheduled a luncheon at the Senate Dining Room, and Taylor mailed McNamara a copy of James Ennes Jr.'s book, *Assault on the* Liberty, as well as a copy of the documentary *Dead in the Water*.

Taylor requested that he and Admiral Tom Moorer meet with McNamara. There was no written reply to this invitation, only a few lines on the second page of the letter. "I don't recall," McNamara writes. "I would like to help, but . . ." McNamara claimed that he could locate no written comments he had made, "no memos." His handwriting was a hopeless scribble.

Meanwhile, writers would periodically become available to serve disinformation to the public, like Stewart Steven, who wrote that the "torpedo boats and jet aircraft" had "orders to disable the vessel rather than sink it," and blamed *Liberty* for sailing "knowingly into a war zone."[28]

Steven praises Meir Amit for the "extraordinary mission" he undertook on his own personal initiative on June 1 when he flew to the United States and supposedly called Richard Helms, then head of CIA, from the airport, demanding an immediate audience. Steven does not mention that the first person Amit saw was not Helms but James Angleton. Steven does not mention Angleton at all.

He praises Amit for doubling the size of Mossad.[29] Amit would be remembered not for his efforts on behalf of the Six-Day War but for the Lavon affair and the assassination of Mehdi Ben Barka, the opposition leader in Morocco who was kidnapped in 1965 outside the Brasserie Lipp in Saint-Germain-des-Prés in Paris. Behind this Moroccan-Israeli deal stood King Hassan, who saw his fate mirrored in that of King Farouk of Egypt, whom Nasser and his fellow officers deposed. Amit retired in 1969. Amit's successor would be someone who had no background in intelligence.

Had Lyndon Johnson's order that the rescue planes be called back to base achieved its intended result, the sinking of *Liberty* with no surviving witnesses; had Egypt (with or without Soviet assistance) been framed for the attack as intended; had the United States then retaliated by bombing Cairo, armed with those nuclear devices at the ready on the USS *America*; had the Soviets then responded with a nuclear retaliation of their own against Israel, as Captain Shashkov of the Soviet submarine K-172 has testified that they had been ordered to do and were prepared to do; and had the Strategic Air Command then further retaliated with its hydrogen bombs, as they were prepared to do as well, raising the ante, Lyndon Johnson's legacy would have been World War III. He came close.

In the years that followed, it became in some circles shameful to have served on the USS *Liberty*. Glenn Oliphant had joined the American Legion. At the Legion convention in Minneapolis in 2012, he addressed five hundred veterans. The *Liberty* Survivors in attendance handed out a thousand pieces of literature and five hundred buttons and sold many items. Oliphant believed the Legion supported them.

When he was invited to the American Legion convention in Indianapolis in 2012, Glenn accepted and traveled to the venue in the company of shipmate Ernie Gallo.[30] Arriving, they discovered that their registration had not been recorded. They had requested a booth, having brought everything needed, only to be told by the organizers that there was no room for them. Then the vendor booth organizer, having been sent by Legion Headquarters, told them they would be removed by force if necessary. Her name was Andrea Watson, and she had brought with her several security guards.

Oliphant inquired if their application had arrived, only to be told that if it had, it would have been sent back. When they offered to pay for another booth on the spot, she refused. When the security guards weighed in, Oliphant and Gallo decided to leave. Oliphant was a gentle soul and led the Bread Oven Ministry at his church, United Methodist in White Bear Lake, Minnesota. He was so disappointed that he decided, after twenty-two years, that he no longer wanted to be a member of the American Legion.

He removed his membership card from his wallet and turned to hand it to Watson. She had a radio in one hand and a clipboard in the other. Without thinking, he placed the card into the top of her blouse. He did not touch her. Oliphant and Gallo went out to the loading dock, only for the security guard to prevent them from leaving. The head of the convention appeared with Oliphant's membership card in his hand.

He said he was charging Oliphant with assault. Watson claimed he had touched her. Before the police arrived, Oliphant apologized to Watson. He asked her to accept his apology, and she said she did. It seemed she was not happy about lying. But the head of the convention somehow got her to change her story and tell the police Oliphant had touched her.

Attempting to mediate was veterans' advocate Ted Arens, who had served in Vietnam, and who talked to the judge advocate of the Legion, Phil Onderdonk. Onderdonk insisted that Oliphant had "grabbed Watson's chest." And they were pressing assault charges.

"The ship should never have been there," Onderdonk said. "It was a spy ship!" As if these sailors were responsible for the actions of the 303 Committee and Cyrus Vance on behalf of Lyndon Johnson and James Angleton, who had thrust them in harm's way in the Eastern Mediterranean.

Oliphant was arrested and tossed into jail. There he languished until 1 a.m., when he was led in front of a judge. He was charged with a misdemeanor, and $150 bail was set. At 2:30 a.m., this Orwellian scenario concluded, and he was released.

Onderdonk went on to call the Survivors "anti-Semites" because they had criticized Israel for its part in the attack. That most Survivors remained content to blame Israel alone for the entire operation, inaccurately, fed fuel to the fires. It was, indeed, something of an act of anti-Semitism to place all the responsibility for the injuries and the murders on Israel alone.

Ted Arens serving in Vietnam. Ted Arens appealed to the American Legion's national leadership to support "our comrades of the USS *Liberty*." (Photo courtesy of Ted Arens.)

Not all veterans' organizations took the stance of the American Legion. Over the years, the Veterans of Foreign Wars (VFW) passed ten resolutions supporting the crew of the USS *Liberty*. Invoking "our freedom of speech that we all [as veterans] fought for," Ted Arens appealed to the American Legion's national leadership to support "our comrades of the USS *Liberty*."[31]

Commemorative monument to the USS *Liberty* organized by Ted Arens with quotation from William Inman Martin (see text).

Then, finally, embracing the position of the VFW, at the American Legion's 2017 annual convention in Reno, the organization approved "Resolution 40" calling for the first full US government investigation of Israel's 1967 attack on the USS *Liberty*. Rejecting Onderdonk's position, the Legion called for the "115th United States Congress to publicly, impartially, and thoroughly investigate the attack on the USS *Liberty* and its aftermath and to commence its investigation before the end of 2017, the fiftieth anniversary year of the attack." The American Legion, at last, had embraced the reality that the attack on the USS *Liberty* had been nothing less than an attack on the United States of America.[32]

Glenn Oliphant says that "there is finally justice and truth for the *Liberty* Veterans in their efforts against the American Legion. The Israeli apologists that thought they controlled the membership have found out that the truth cannot be defeated."[33] James Joyce wrote in *Ulysses* that if history repeats itself, it's "with a difference," so it is best at this moment not to invoke the credibility of the Warren Commission, the 9/11 Commission, and other government investigations. Yet in 2018, the *Liberty* veterans were again refused a place at the annual meeting of the American Legion.

In 2018, the *Liberty* group applied once more for a booth at the American Legion's annual event, only to be told that they were "banned for life."[34]

Dave Lewis places the responsibility for the attack at 60–40, with 60 percent of the blame going to Israel and 40 to the United States. At the turn of the New Year 2017, he wrote checks in support of the Free Palestine Movement and Jewish Voice for Peace. He speculates: "If it was premeditated, we were set up. Had the ship been sunk, had the helicopters picked off all the survivors, and had the debris washed ashore and been discovered by the Israelis, who would they blame? They would blame Egypt." As for Lyndon Johnson, "he was treasonable."[35]

"If your organization wishes an additional investigation of the USS *Liberty*, you should make your wishes known to your congressional representatives and senators," Onderdonk had told Arens. Over the years, the Survivors have approached their members of Congress, only to meet with stone walls.

Dave Lewis approached his own senator, one known to be willing to talk to everyone. Bernie Sanders came on the line, only to tell Lewis that it would be "inappropriate" for him to support the sailors. When Lewis suggested to Sanders that he reply through a local rabbi who looked favorably on the cause of the sailors, the reply was the same. This too was "inappropriate."[36] His other senator, Patrick Leahy, wrote "Mr. and Mrs. Lewis" that "on December 17, 1987, the issue was officially closed by the two governments."

Adlai Stevenson III, both as a US Senator and later, became a supporter of the idea that the truth of what happened to *Liberty* should be investigated. When he ran for governor of Illinois in 1982, a strong effort by the American/Israel Public Affairs Committee (AIPAC) resulted in his narrow defeat. He lost by one-seventh of one percent. A recount was denied by one vote. A judge named Seymour had admitted to a mutual friend, Bernard Peskin, that he voted as he did "because of Israel." All it took for AIPAC to mobilize was Stevenson's avowed intention to investigate the attack on *Liberty* as chairman of the Senate Subcommittee on Collection and Production.

Stevenson concluded: "The Lobby represents neither Israel nor the liberal, progressive opinions of most American Jews. It is The Lobby by default with a well-developed network of individuals and organizations trained to react against critics of Israeli policies and reward its political minions with money. It preempts and intimidates mainstream Jews."[37]

Asked why they had opposed Stevenson, AIPAC officials replied that he was "anti-Semitic" and if he were not stopped in Illinois, "he might run for President," an idea, Stevenson admits, that "had in fact crossed my mind."

The son of Adlai Stevenson Jr., who represented progressive views throughout the 1950s and was a great admirer of Mrs. Eleanor Roosevelt, could hardly be termed an anti-Semite.[38] But lies had become the cornerstone of discourse of the *Liberty* story from the moment Israel claimed that its ferocious attack on the ship was an "accident." Another of those who reject the Israeli cover story that this was an "accident," who is certain the Israelis knew that *Liberty* was an American ship, is Admiral Bobby Inman.[39]

John Hadden, clear-eyed as ever at the turn of the millennium, wrote to Peter Sichel at Christmas: "I doubt if today any American President can withstand AIPAC's control of Congress."[40]

The cover-up of the attack on the USS *Liberty* did not come to a halt after a mere fifty years. At the fiftieth-anniversary commemoration at Arlington National Cemetery, the navy sent only a color guard and a bugler, no officer. The respect of their government remained elusive for these Survivors.

By 1973, Israel was "purchasing three million dollars' worth of armaments and aircraft a year from the U.S." Israel has zealously guarded the secret it holds of the joint US and Israeli collaboration in the attack on the USS *Liberty*. Keeping the Middle East open to American investment had been behind the attempt to remove the socialistic Nasser, and it remained a goal facilitated by Israel, now an American political and economic outpost.

Here is a list of some of those whom available evidence suggests bear responsibility for the murderous attack on the USS *Liberty*:

Meir Amit
James Angleton
Lyndon Johnson
Cyrus Vance
Robert McNamara
Moshe Dayan
Levi Eshkol
John S. McCain
Donald D. Engen
William Inman Martin

The list of those who knew about the operation, yet remained silent, even as they were appalled by the sacrifice of unarmed American sailors, includes Richard Helms and John Hadden. You cannot emerge from serving a government engaged in immoral actions with clean hands.

Group of Survivors, reunion in 2014 in Manatee, Michigan.
(Photo courtesy of Ted Arens.)

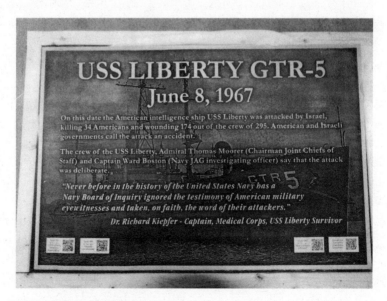

Commemorative plaque.

There were also those who were clearly not implicated in this false flag Israeli-American operation: the Chief of Naval Operations, Admiral David Lamar McDonald; Frank Raven, a senior official at NSA, chief of the G group in charge of eavesdropping on the noncommunist world; Deputy Director Louis Tordella and Director Marshall Carter at NSA; and, among other sailors, lonely Captain Joseph Tully of the USS *Saratoga*, whose dedication to duty and commitment to protecting the navy's finest in a time of conflict may remind the reader of the open-hearted, if taciturn, sea captains of novelist Joseph Conrad.

The Six-Day War was an early example of what would later become customary in American wars. Rather than by elected officials, decisions were made more often than not by a shadow government, here the 303 Committee with its component of CIA involvement, leaving the commander in chief safe in his plausible deniability. Intelligence services have been at the forefront of our wars since Vietnam. Private contractors have hovered.

Surely, had Nicholas Katzenbach remained alive, he might have changed his mind regarding whether it was in the interest of the United States that some hard truths be allowed to surface, the better to change direction, the better to restore our integrity and remind us of the principles for which we stand.

NOTES

PREFACE

1. For the role of CIA in the murder of Patrice Lumumba and of his followers, see the report of the Belgian government. The Church committee took up the subject but contributed little factual intelligence (1978). The parliamentary inquiry of the Belgian government was released in 2001.

2. See "Gamal Abdel Nasser Interviewed in English," Gamal Abdel Nasser, interview by Clifton Daniel, *New York Times*, April 19, 1969, YouTube video, 58:40, https://www.youtube .com/watch?v=cU_4PYR50ek (accessed June 28, 2018).

3. Walter J. Jacobsen, "A Juridical Examination of the Israeli Attack on the USS *Liberty*," *Naval Law Review* 36 (1986): 110. Federal law requires the following: Art. 3: "A MILITARY AIRCRAFT SHALL BEAR AN EXTERNAL MARK INDICATING ITS NATIONALIST AND MILITARY CHARACTER"; Art. 7: "The external marks required by the above articles shall be so affixed that they cannot be altered in flight. They shall be as large as practicable and shall be visible from below and from each side"; Art 19: The use of false external marks is forbidden."

4. According to international law, "the great ocean expanses [are] left as free as possible from national jurisdiction claims over them" except in cases of "legitimate self-defense." 1958 Geneva Convention on the High Seas (2 U.S.T. 2312, TI.A.S. No. 5200, 450 U.N.TS. 82), to which both Israel and the United States were parties. See Myres S. McDougal, "Authority to Use Force on the High Seas," *Naval War College, International Law Studies, 1947–1977*, ed. E. Lillich and J. Moore (Naval War College Press, 1980), p. 95. The "high seas" refers to "all parts of the sea, except internal waters and territorial sea of a coast state."

Jacobsen writes: "Absent hostilities, intelligence gathering on the high seas is lawful." See Walter J. Jacobsen, "A Juridical Examination of the Israeli Attack on the USS *Liberty*," *Naval Law Review* 36 (1986). Israel had no claim of self-defense, since *Liberty* was not armed. Jacobsen notes that by June 8, Israel had reopened the Straits of Tiran and had conquered Jordanian territory. There was no issue of self-defense. Jacobsen was not aware that *Liberty* was not conducting intelligence gathering on Israel.

5. *Liberty* was not gathering intelligence on Israel at all. David Edwin Lewis, in discussion with the author, June 21, 2014. Jacobsen, "Juridical Examination," p. 93.

6. There are other examples of division within CIA on crucial matters, and far more than agency apologists like Tennent Bagley suggest: "For a few years after the Agency in 1968 made

its official finding in Nosenko's favor," Bagley writes, "CIA did not speak with a single voice. The leadership of its Counterintelligence Staff under James Angleton judged [Yuri] Nosenko to be a KGB plant, and its operations chief Newton S. ('Scotty') Miler continued to probe into what lay behind the KGB's operation." Tennent H. Bagley, *Spy Wars: Moles, Mysteries, and Deadly Games* (New Haven & London: Yale University Press, 2007), p. 212.

7. Wilbur Crane Eveland, *Ropes of Sand: America's Failure in the Middle East* (London and New York: W. W. Norton, 1980), p. 309.

8. For insight into the methods and thinking of Mossad, see the works by Victor Ostrovsky, a former Mossad agent: Victor Ostrovsky and Claire Hoy, *By Way of Deception* (New York: St. Martin's, 1991) and Victor Ostrovsky, *The Other Side of Deception: A Rogue Agent Exposes the Mossad's Secret Agenda* (New York: HarperCollins, 1994). Ostrovsky explained in an interview with Australian magazine *New Dawn*, no. 33 (November–December 1995) that he "wanted to stop the Mossad's use and abuses of the Israeli and outside Jewish communities." In response to questions from the Knesset, Mossad admitted they wanted to buy time to stop the publication of *By Way of Deception* so that they could kidnap him, as they had kidnapped Mordechai Vanunu and put him in jail to stop him from telling his story about the Israeli nuclear program.

9. Eveland, *Ropes of Sand*, p. 326.

10. Quoted in Laura Dawn Lewis, "Remembering Our Fallen Heroes," *Spotlight* (magazine).

11. Isabella Ginor and Gideon Remez, *Foxbats over Dimona: The Soviets' Nuclear Gamble in the Six-Day War* (New Haven, CT: Yale University Press, 2007), pp. 111–12ff. A Foxbat is a type of Soviet aircraft.

12. Ibid., p. 31.

13. John L. Hadden, in discussion with the author, March 1, 2017. Halevy had written to Hadden on October 3, 1979, of "true friendship and brotherhood." Halevy had gone on to be director of Mossad from 1998–2002.

14. Stewart Steven, *The Spymasters of Israel* (New York: Ballantine, 1980), p. 122.

15. Deputy Attorney General Nicholas Katzenbach's comments on how the Kennedy assassination should be handled are analogous to how he responded to the facts involving the Israeli attack on the USS *Liberty*. See "Memorandum for Mr. Moyers," November 25, 1963. Katzenbach wants to release only information that would "satisfy people that all the facts have been told" and that the evidence was such that Oswald would have been convicted at trial. Katzenbach's memorandum to Johnson aide Bill Moyers is available online, for instance at Mary Ferrell Foundation, https://www.maryferrell.org/showDoc.html?docId=62268#relPageId=29 (accessed September 9, 2018).

16. Thomas Lowe Hughes, in discussion with the author, August 2, 2016.

17. See Frank Bruni, "Where's Jared Kushner?" *New York Times* (op-ed), February 1, 2017, p. A27. See also Michelle Goldberg, "Why Is This Hate Different from All Other Hate?" *New York Times*, April 2, 2017, p. 3.

18. Joseph Daichman, *History of the Mossad* [in Russian] (Smolensk, Russia: Rusich, 2001). The book has not been translated into English. Summaries courtesy of the papers of Richard Thompson.

19. Eveland, *Ropes of Sand*, p. 325. Eveland uncovers the origins of the US-Israel operation to invade Egypt and remove Gamal Abdel Nasser, the operation to which the USS *Liberty* was collateral damage.

Eveland was working undercover as an engineer in the Middle East at the time of the attack on the ship.

CHAPTER 1. JOHN HADDEN CONFERS WITH MEIR AMIT

1. For a description of the American embassy in Tel Aviv, see Seymour M. Hersh, *The Samson Option: Israel's Nuclear Arsenal and American Foreign Policy* (New York: Random House, 1991), pp. 159–61.

2. Dick Tracy was among the first police procedurals; the comic strip appeared in newspapers from 1931 to 1977.

3. Descriptions of John Hadden at home come from conversations and emails with his son, theater director and playwright John L. Hadden.

4. John Hadden, *Conversations with a Masked Man: My Father, the CIA, and Me* (New York: Arcade, 2016), p. 35.

5. This biographical summary comes from an essay by John Hadden, "What INTELLIGENCE Can and Cannot Do for You," papers of John Hadden, courtesy of John L. Hadden.

6. Hadden, *Conversations with a Masked Man.*

7. Ibid., p. 5.

8. John Hadden to Peter Sichel, April 1, 2013. Papers of John Hadden.

9. See Joan Mellen, *The Great Game in Cuba: CIA and the Cuban Revolution* (New York: Skyhorse, 2016), p. 163.

10. Hersh, *Samson Option*, pp. 161, 159–71.

11. John L. Hadden, email to the author, August 3, 2015.

12. Hadden, *Conversations with a Masked Man*, p. 79.

13. Ibid., p. 4.

14. Wilbur Crane Eveland, *Ropes of Sand: America's Failure in the Middle East* (London and New York: W. W. Norton, 1980), p. 323.

15. Andrew Cockburn and Leslie Cockburn, *Dangerous Liaison: The Inside Story of the U.S.-Israeli Covert Relationship* (New York: HarperCollins, 1991), p. 69.

16. Richard Curtiss, *A Changing Image: American Perceptions of the Arab-Israeli Dispute* (Washington, DC: American Educational Trust, 1982).

17. For more information about Kennedy's relationship to the Middle East, see Avner Cohen, "Kennedy and the Israeli Project," chap. 6 in *Israel and the Bomb* (New York: Columbia University Press, 1998).

18. Alfred M. Lilienthal, *The Zionist Connection: What Price Peace?* (New York: Dodd, Mead, 1978), p. 544ff.

19. Ibid., p. 855.

20. Hersh, *Samson Option*, p. 147.

21. John Hadden to Peter Sichel, May 31, 2003. Papers of John Hadden.

22. John Hadden, "Hadden Recollections," appendix to "The USS *Liberty* and the Role of Intelligence," by A. Jay Cristol, http://www.thelibertyincident.com/docs/liberty-intelligence.pdf.

23. Tom Segev, *1967: Israel, the War, and the Year That Transformed the Middle East*, trans. Jessica Cohen (New York: Metropolitan, Henry Holt, 2007), p. 252.

24. Ibid., p. 329.

25. Hadden quoted in Andre Gerolymatos, *Castles Made of Sand: A Century of Anglo-American Espionage and Intervention in the Middle East* (New York: Thomas Dunne Books, 2010), p. 169.

26. Livia Rokach, *Israel's Sacred Terrorism*, 3rd ed. (1985). Available online at https://archive.org/details/IsraelsSacredTerrorism (accessed June 28, 2018). With appendices and substantial quotations from the unpublished diaries of Moshe Sharett. See also Livia Rokach, *Israel's Sacred Terrorism: A Study Based on Moshe Sharett's Personal Diary and Other Documents* (Belmont, MA: Association of Arab-American University Graduates, 1986), p. 52.

27. Hadden, *Conversations with a Masked Man*, p. 33.

28. Ibid., p. 1.

CHAPTER 2. FIRE AT A SHIP!

1. Arutz Sheva Staff, "Minister Katz Warns Ex-Mossad Chiefs to Keep Quiet," Arutz Sheva, April 2, 2016.

2. Efraim Halevy, interview by Mehdir Hasan, *Israel National News*, November 22, 2016, http://www.israelnationalnews/com/News/News.aspz/210193 (article unavailable as of August 2018).

3. See Michael Holzman, *James Jesus Angleton: The CIA and the Craft of Counter-intelligence* (Amherst, MA: University of Massachusetts Press, 2008), p. 224.

4. For Meir Amit's career, see Steven Stewart, *The Spymasters of Israel* (New York: Ballantine, 1980), pp. 156–57.

5. Note found in the papers of John Hadden.

6. Report of a meeting with John Hadden, May 25, 1967, top secret: for the addressee only (Levi Eshkol). Provided by Meir Amit, August 2002 to Isabella Ginor and Gideon Remez, authors

of *Foxbats over Dimona: The Soviets' Nuclear Gamble in the Six-Day War* (New Haven, CT: Yale University Press, 2007). Among the chosen journalists was also Ronen Bergman, who cites Amit's memo in his article, "Will Israel Attack Iran?" *New York Times* (magazine), January 25, 2012.

Although this conversation has not been cited in any explanation of how the attack on the USS *Liberty* originated, it illuminates the incident more fully than the eyewitness accounts of the incident.

7. Wilbur Crane Eveland, *Ropes of Sand: America's Failure in the Middle East* (London and New York: W. W. Norton, 1980), p. 324.

8. Ginor and Remez, *Foxbats over Dimona*, p. 111.

9. Thomas Lowe Hughes, in discussion with the author, August 2, 2016; Dan Raviv and Yossi Melman, *Every Spy a Prince: The Complete History of Israel's Intelligence Community* (Boston: Houghton Mifflin, 1990), p. 195.

10. Shabtai Teveth, *Ben-Gurion and the Palestinian Arabs: From Peace to War* (New York: Oxford University Press, 1985), p. 189.

11. Ariel Sharon as reported by *Agence France Press*, November 15, 1998.

12. Hughes, in discussion with the author.

13. Eveland, *Ropes of Sand*, p. 324.

14. Hughes, in discussion with the author. Hughes had been offered the job that went to Eugene Rostow, and at lunch one day, Eppy Evron, deputy minister at the Israeli embassy, told Hughes, "You should have taken the job last August. There wouldn't have been a war." Hughes was not a man to be bamboozled. "You've got to be kidding," he said.

15. Report of a meeting with John Hadden.

16. Michael Collins Piper, *Final Judgment: The Missing Link in the JFK Assassination Conspiracy* (Wolfe Press, 1995), p. 52.

17. Andrew Cockburn and Leslie Cockburn, *Dangerous Liaison: The Inside Story of the U.S.-Israeli Covert Relationship* (New York: HarperCollins, 1991), p. 91.

18. Piper, *Final Judgment*, p. 52.

19. NUMEC was a privately owned nuclear enriching plant located in Apollo, Pennsylvania, owned by Zalman Mordecai Shapiro, a Jew with close ties to Israel. See Seymour M. Hersh, *The Samson Option: Israel's Nuclear Arsenal and American Foreign Policy* (New York: Random House, 1991), chap. 14.

20. Shimon Peres's conversation with President Kennedy has been well documented. See Israeli minutes of the unscheduled meeting between Shimon Peres (then Israel's deputy minister of defense) and President John Kennedy, held at the White House April 2, 1963, document 1, Miscellaneous Hebrew Documents, National Security Archive/Israel State Archive. See also Rebecca Shimoni Stoil, "Mr. Peres Goes to Washington," *Times of Israel*, October 1, 2016. "I came through the rear door accompanied by Ambassador Avraham Harman. Kennedy started to question me like a machine gun. It was the day our chief of intelligence resigned. All of a sudden Kennedy said, 'DO you have a nuclear bomb?' I said Israel will not be the first to introduce a nuclear bomb in the Middle East."

21. Tom Segev, "Shimon Peres: A Man of Peace?" *New York Times*, October 2, 2016.

22. In 1978, John Hadden told the BBC that the uranium processing facility in Apollo, Pennsylvania, had been "an Israeli operation from the beginning." Hadden remarked sardonically, "They are pretty good at removing things." NUMEC, the company in question, had hosted longtime Israeli operative Rafael (Rafi) Eitan. The uranium shipments from NUMEC to Israel began in 1965 when employees reported they saw people loading boxes about the size of highly enriched uranium-235 canisters onto a ship bound for Israel. NUMEC was handling nuclear waste for the US Atomic Energy Commission.

In 2011, CIA declassified wiretap transcripts of conversations between NUMEC founder Zalman Shapiro and venture capitalist David Lowenthal, revealing illegal storage practices and a dangerous nuclear spill. CIA blocked the release of 225 pages. The FBI and CIA investigated Shapiro and Lowenthal in the 1960s under suspicion of diverting highly enriched uranium (HEU) from NUMEC into the clandestine Israeli nuclear weapons program.

For decades, CIA has blocked the release of its files and equity content in other government agency reports about NUMEC. Certainly by 1968 CIA knew that "NUMEC material had been diverted by the Israelis and used in fabricating weapons." Israel lobbyist Abraham Feinberg was a promoter of Israel's nuclear weapons program, and also a supporter of Lyndon Johnson. When Johnson's chief aide Walter Jenkins was arrested in a public toilet on October 14, 1964, at least $250,000 that Feinberg had raised for Johnson was found in Jenkins's office safe. In 1968, when Secretary of Defense Clark Clifford telephoned LBJ and said, "Mr. President, I don't want to live in a world where the Israelis have nuclear weapons," Johnson hung up on him.

23. John Hadden voiced these views only forty years later. Hadden, "John Hadden Recollections," appendix to "The USS *Liberty* and the Role of Intelligence," by A. Jay Cristol, http://www.thelibertyincident.com/docs/liberty-intelligence.pdf.

24. See chapter 4, "Toppling Nasser."

25. Department of Defense, *Plan for US Military Intervention in Cuba Codenamed Northwoods* (Washington, DC: National Archives at College Park, July 23, 1962).

26. Ginor and Remez, *Foxbats over Dimona*, p. 113.

27. Peter Hounam, *Operation Cyanide: Why the Bombing of the USS* Liberty *Nearly Caused World War III* (London: Vision, 2003), pp. 266–67.

CHAPTER 3. JAMES JESUS ANGLETON: TREASON AT THE TOP

1. Arnold M. Silver, "My Wars, Hot and Cold: Autobiographical Notes of Arnold M. Silver" (unpublished manuscript, undated). Contributed for this book by a retired CIA officer who prefers to remain anonymous.

2. John Hadden to Peter Sichel, April 1, 2013. Papers of John Hadden.

3. See Paul L. Williams, *Operation Gladio: The Unholy Alliance between the Vatican, the CIA, and the Mafia* (Amherst, NY: Prometheus Books, 2015), pp. 41, 44.

4. Williams, *Operation Gladio*, p. 41.

5. Quoted in Tennent H. Bagley, *Spy Wars: Moles, Mysteries, and Deadly Games* (New Haven, CT: Yale University Press: New Haven & London, 2007), p. 214.

6. William Colby said this frequently. See David Wise, "The Spookiest of the CIA's Spooks," *Los Angeles Times*, December 24, 2006. Interviewed by Wise, who asked why he had to fire James Angleton, Colby said, "I honestly couldn't figure out what the devil they were doing." See also John Prados, *William Colby and the CIA: The Secret Wars of a Controversial Spymaster* (Lawrence: University Press of Kansas: Lawrence, 2009), p. 257.

Colby took counterterrorist functions away from Angleton's staff. Prados writes: "He also took away Angleton's responsibility for liaison with the Federal Bureau of Investigation and much of his previous gadfly role in vetting almost every DOD activity. Some other portfolios Angleton held had to be decided at a higher pay grade, but Colby recommended that these too be taken away from the Counterintelligence Staff. One was CIA liaison with Israeli intelligence, which Jim had handled since the inception of the state of Israel."

7. Tom Mangold, *Cold Warrior: James Jesus Angleton: The CIA's Master Spy Hunter* (New York: Simon & Schuster, 1991).

8. Bagley, *Spy Wars*, p. 23.

9. Ibid., p. 219.

10. Joseph C. Goulden, "Soviet Deception, Recruiting an Enemy," *Washington Times*, February 29, 2004.

11. Mangold, *Cold Warrior*, p. 50.

12. For an example of Angleton's double-talk, peruse his garbled testimony before the Church Committee in 1975. Here he is offering his reply to a question about CIA's mail-opening program (HT/LINGUAL): "Here, I mean in terms of the perspective of our assets, the mail program loomed as an extremely important object, I mean in terms of ex-sight [*sic*] and insight into Soviets who were traveling here, Soviet students, and we had an active program of recruitment, attempted recruitments of Soviet students, our knowledge that partially every Soviet student is at the sufferance of KGB, where it is worked in necessarily into the mechanism. It is also the grounds for preparing young people in American realities who come back and go into the service and more active roles." He persuaded CIA to open all mail to and from the Soviet Union, and Helms went along with it. No useful intelligence was ever obtained, as CIA's Inspector General concluded when the operation was reviewed. See David C. Martin, *Wilderness of Mirrors: Intrigue, Deception, and the Secrets That Destroyed Two of the Cold War's Most Important Agents* (Guilford, CT: Lyons Press, 1980), p. 70. For Angleton's testimony before the Church Committee, see "Testimony of James Angleton, 17 Sep 1975," SSCIA record number 157-10014-10007, agency file number 01-H007, hosted at the Mary Ferrell Foundation, https://www.maryferrell.org/showDoc.html?docId=1435.

Asked about the FBI mail-opening efforts, Angleton replied with more of his best double-talk: "My understanding only is that it was based specifically on a piece of information regarding some operational matter of the opposition."

To some questions, Angleton lied outright. Asked, "Are you aware of any mail intercept projects where the Bureau cooperated with the Agency or any other Agency actually provided mail to the CIA?" Angleton, who was among the FBI's most highly placed informants, said, "No." In fact, he had masterminded the opening of George de Mohrenschildt's mail in Haiti. In a rare twenty-four-page memorandum that Angleton himself signed, he outlines exactly whose mail he was intercepting and forwarding to the FBI so that the writer could be investigated—at Angleton's pleasure.

On Angleton as a Bureau informant, see W. A. Branigan to A. H. Belmont, "James Angleton, CIA," April 30, 1954, FBI; V. P. Keay to A. H. Belmont, "James Angleton, Central Intelligence Agency," March 17, 1965, FBI; D. J. Brennan Jr. to W. C. Sullivan, "Bureau Informant 100," April 9 and 20, 1970, FBI. All letters from SP Letter Series, record number 124-10326-10105, agency file number 62-99724-81.

Another of his fabrications was that "the Agency, unlike the Soviets, does not have an assassination department": "Testimony of James Angleton, 19 Jun 1975," SSCIA record number 157-10014-10005, agency file number 01-h05, hosted at the Mary Ferrell Foundation, https://www.maryferrell.org/showDoc.html?docId=1447. CIA's "Executive Action" component was already in place. Angleton also lied about Lee Harvey Oswald's having been debriefed by CIA's Soviet Russian division in June 1962 upon his return from the Soviet Union. Angleton later accused David Murphy, who headed this division, of being a Soviet mole, a KGB agent, on Soviet defector Anatoliiy Golitsyn's say-so. Murphy in turn, denied Golitsyn access to his files. Retaliating, Angleton had Murphy assigned to Paris as station chief, at the same time warning the head of French intelligence that Murphy was a Soviet agent. See Martin, *Wilderness of Mirrors*, pp. 198–99.

None of this was ever established. Among others whom Golitsyn accused of being a Soviet spy, with Angleton's approval, was W. Averell Harriman, who had been US ambassador to Moscow during World War II. Harriman would also go on to be governor of New York (1955–1958). Another of Golitsyn's targets was British Labour prime minister Harold Wilson.

Angleton also devoted no small amount of time to attacking *Ramparts* magazine for pursuing themes "used consistently in the Soviet and block propaganda campaign against the United States" and stressing "militancy in the 'Standard Communistic' sense of an outright advocacy of violence." There were many Jews on the *Ramparts* staff, he noted, concluding that their position was to protect Nasser. See: Director, FBI to SAC SF, November 6, 1967, FBI, record number 124-10274-10319, agency file number CR 100-445393-88; "RAMPARTS Issues of June, July and September 1967," memorandum for Director, Federal Bureau of Investigation, Attention: Mr. S. J. Papich, September 20, 1967, CIA, 239226.

In its coverage of the Middle East during the summer of 1967, *Ramparts* does not mention the attack on the USS *Liberty*. Angleton took a direct interest in *Ramparts*, and the counterintelligence documents on the subject, unusually, were signed by him.

In his June 15, 1978, interview with the House Select Committee on Assassinations (record number 100-10110-10089, agency file number 096-JFK), Angleton does not mention either Israel or Mossad.

In 1975, Angleton, out of the Agency, exercised his skill at double-talk before the Church Committee: "Going back to OSS days," he said, brushing aside that CIA was violating its charter forbidding it to operate domestically, "we've had operations where [we] were domestic, in the war, all the way through."

In his interviews with government agencies, Angleton did not mention Israel or Mossad: House Select Committee on Assassinations, record number 200-20220-10089, agency file number 096-JFK, National Archives and Records Administration, College Park, MD.

13. Bagley, *Spy Wars*, p. 23.

14. Silver, "My Wars."

15. "Soviet Deception, Recruiting an Enemy," *Washington Times*, February 29, 2004.

16. Martin, *Wilderness of Mirrors*, p. 56.

17. Ronald Kessler, in Bruce Hoffman and Christian Ostermann, eds., *Moles, Defectors, and Deceptions: James Angleton and His Influence on US Counterintelligence* (Washington, DC: Woodrow Wilson International Center for Scholars, 2014), p. 37, https://www.wilsoncenter .org/sites/default/files/moles_defectors_and_deceptions_james_angleton_conference _report.pdf (accessed September 9, 2018). Kessler was speaking at the conference exploring Angleton's legacy, "Moles, Defectors, and Deceptions: James Angleton and His Influence on US Counterintelligence," which was sponsored by the Woodrow Wilson International Center for Scholars and Georgetown University's Center for Security Studies and held at the Wilson Center in Washington, DC, March 29, 2012.

18. Malcolm Blunt, UK researcher who worked closely with Tennent Bagley and assisted in his research, in discussion with the author.

19. Martin, *Wilderness of Mirrors*, p. 57.

20. David Robarge, official CIA historian, speaking at the Angleton conference, in Hoffman and Ostermann, *Moles, Defectors, and Deceptions*, p. 100.

21. Yossi Melman and Dan Raviv, "Spies Like Us: Spy vs. Spy Intrigue between CIA and Israel Centered around US Embassy in Tel Aviv," *Tablet*, April 8, 2010, https://www.tabletmag .com/jewish-news-and-politics/30106/spies-like-us. San Francisco lawyer Bartley Crum served as one of six Americans on President Truman's Anglo-American Committee of Inquiry into Palestine. Before his service ended, Crum had persuaded Truman to recognize the state of Israel. Truman was very early in this matter, and he reaped some honor for his courage. After Crum's death, his daughter, the writer Patricia Bosworth, was told, "As a result of his devotion to Israel—to Zionism—and his incessant speechifying, often for no pay, streets were named in his honor throughout the Holy Land, and money was being raised for forests to be planted in the deserts—forests that would be named 'Bartley Cavanaugh Crum.'" Later Bosworth, writing about her father, asked Israelis from Tel Aviv and Haifa if they knew of streets in their cities named "Crum." They didn't. Nor were there forests named for her father. She asked the library in Jerusalem to please check. Back came a fax that read, "There is no record of any street or any forest in the state of Israel named Bartley Cavanaugh Crum." See Patricia Bosworth, *Anything Your Little Heart Desires: An American Family Story* (New York: Simon & Schuster, 1997), p.

366. Apparently gratitude was in short supply in the state of Israel. Both Crum and Angleton served Israel long and faithfully.

22. Michael Holzman, *James Jesus Angleton: The CIA and the Craft of Counterintelligence* (Amherst, MA: University of Massachusetts Press, 2008), p. 151.

23. Andrew Cockburn and Leslie Cockburn, *Dangerous Liaison: The Inside Story of the U.S.-Israeli Covert Relationship* (New York: HarperCollins, 1991), p. 41.

24. Andre Gerolymatos, *Castles Made of Sand: A Century of Anglo-American Espionage and Intervention in the Middle East* (New York: Thomas Dunne Books, 2010), p. 168. See also Thomas Powers, *The Man Who Kept the Secrets: Richard Helms and the CIA* (New York: Alfred A. Knopf, 1979), p. 322.

25. Tom Segev, *1967: Israel, the War, and the Year That Transformed the Middle East*, trans. Jessica Cohen (2005; New York: Metropolitan, Henry Holt, 2007). This book is particularly useful for its translations from the Hebrew of passages from Meir Amit's memoir, *Head to Head: A Personal Look at Great Events and Secret Affairs* (Tel Aviv: Hed-Arzi, 1999).

26. Thomas Lowe Hughes, in discussion with the author, August 2, 2016.

27. Steven Stewart, *The Spymasters of Israel* (New York: Ballantine, 1980), p. 119.

28. Robarge, in Hoffman and Ostermann, *Moles, Defectors, and Deceptions*, p. 37.

Among the Angleton conference participants was Ronald Kessler, who writes on *Newsmax*, March 28, 2012, "As the author of three books on the CIA, I was honored to be asked to participate as a speaker. But my first thought on hearing about the conference was: Why waste time on Angleton?

"Today, no one in the CIA or FBI considers Angleton, who died in 1987, to have been anything other than a paranoid conspiracy theorist who paralyzed CIA intelligence operations against the Soviet Union and never caught a spy. Upon further reflection, however, I recognized how important the conference is. That's because defenders of Angleton continue to confuse the public about Angleton's legacy and his approach." Kessler adds: "Angleton was chief of counterintelligence for more than 20 years. Fear was the secret to his longevity. Angleton kept huge files with names of CIA officers who had come under suspicion based on his amateurish theories. Anyone who called his bluff could become a target. Angleton would continue to poison the air until William E. Colby, as director of Central Intelligence, finally fired him in 1974."

Christopher Andrew, a professor at Cambridge, gave the keynote address. Carl Colby, William Colby's son, was a panelist. He had directed a documentary film about his father, *The Man Nobody Knew: In Search of My Father, CIA Spymaster William Colby*. Ronald Kessler had written nineteen books about the intelligence community and had been a reporter for the *Wall Street Journal* and the *Washington Post*.

Speaking over the internet from Belgium, retired CIA officer Tennent Bagley said, "Until we learn much more about that world of moles and deceptions in the Cold War, we'll have to recognize that any truly fair assessment of Jim Angleton's work in it will have to wait." Bagley came in praise, arguing that "having been so long in that central position, Angleton became a symbol, practically the personification of American counterintelligence." Bagley protected

Angleton, insisting, "We all should know by now, paranoia or no paranoia, there *were* moles inside CIA in Angleton's time."

In his talk before the conference, Kessler was emphatic: "I can assure you, the FBI and the CIA today consider James Angleton to be a menace, someone who actually never caught a spy, who really was a nut case, paranoid, constantly weaving conspiracy theories, and, ultimately paralyzing intelligence gathering against the Soviet bloc when intelligence was most needed."

Barry Royden served with CIA for forty years and another ten "on contract." Angleton was not a KGB mole, Royden said. "He had merely become victim to having been too-long buried in the wilderness of mirrors that is counterintelligence." Charles Battaglia noted the "disorganization of the [CI] files." Bagley was persistent in his efforts to rehabilitate Angleton as an intelligence officer: "Jim Angleton had an enormous well of common sense," he added. "He would not have believed for a moment that Bill Colby was someone else's agent."

Christopher Andrew had written the first history of MI5 as well as *The Sword and the Shield: The Mitrokhin Archive and the Secret History of the KGB*. He spoke about Angleton's engagement with British intelligence. Andrew wisely noted that "the monster KGB conspiracy theories of the 1960s were . . . fueled by historical ignorance." As a historian, Andrew was able to set the record straight on a number of issues.

A high point came when Loch Johnson, who had interviewed Angleton for the Church Committee, quoted Angleton saying, "It is inconceivable that a secret intelligence arm of the government has to comply with all the orders of the government." Johnson recalled how at the public hearing, Angleton "lamented that the nature of the threat posed by the Soviet Union was insufficiently appreciated. He shot back at [Frank] Church: 'When I look at the map today and the weakness of power of this country, that is what shocks me.'" Included as well was a retired KGB major general, Oleg Kalugin. Kalugin was Angleton's Soviet counterpart. Kalugin concluded that Angleton and Soviet figure Vladimir Kryuchkov were equally dangerous: "In both cases, their distrustful mentalities eroded intelligence and could really have led the world to the brink of danger."

Associated Press reporter David Martin summed it up sensibly. Angleton, he said, "served at a time when almost everyone believed that the US and Soviet Union were involved in a life-and-death struggle." He noted that a "CIA director doesn't have time to hunt for moles. He has to trust someone else to do it, and Helms trusted Angleton, which meant he pretty much just let him have his way. At some point, it's a director's responsibility to look at the costs and benefits, and Helms just never got around to that until way too late in the game." Robert Hathaway, who worked at the Center, added about Helms: "Helms simply was not prepared" to supervise Angleton "even though he was being urged by others to do so." Hathaway was one of two coauthors of the history of Helms as DCI.

In the final panel, David Robarge attempted to create a balance by referring to Angleton as a "through-and-through counterintelligence officer," a rarity. Robarge attempted to offer a biographical approach to Angleton's life and career. Robarge also tried to challenge Seymour Hersh's approach to Angleton. The final speaker was author David Wise, who concluded that Angleton "did more harm than good."

29. See Robert Littell, *Young Philby* (New York: Thomas Dunne Books, 2012), p. 264.

30. Mangold, *Cold Warrior.*

31. Silver, "My Wars."

32. Holzman, *James Jesus Angleton*, p. 154.

33. John Hadden, quoted in Cockburn and Cockburn, *Dangerous Liaison*, p. 80.

34. Martin, *Wilderness of Mirrors*, p. 57.

35. Silver, "My Wars."

36. Quoted in Gerolymatos, *Castles Made of Sand*, p. 165.

37. Ibid.

38. Cockburn and Cockburn, *Dangerous Liaison*, pp. 132–33.

39. Stewart, *Spymasters of Israel*, p. 119.

40. Dan Raviv and Yossi Melman, *Every Spy a Prince: The Complete History of Israel's Intelligence Community* (Boston, MA: Houghton Mifflin, 1990), p. 153.

41. Isabella Ginor and Gideon Remez, *Foxbats over Dimona: The Soviets' Nuclear Gamble in the Six-Day War* (New Haven, CT: Yale University Press, 2007), p. 112.

42. See Thomas Powers, *The Man Who Kept the Secrets: Richard Helms and the CIA* (New York: Alfred A. Knopf, 1979), p. 322.

43. Holzman, *James Jesus Angleton*, p. 169.

44. Ibid., p. 169.

45. "Testimony of James Angleton."

46. Silver, "My Wars."

47. Raviv and Melman, "Spies Like Us."

48. Richard Curtiss, *A Changing Image: American Perceptions of the Arab-Israeli Dispute* (Washington, DC: American Educational Trust, 1982).

49. Powers, *Man Who Kept the Secrets*, p. 67. Powers's description of Angleton is embarrassing: "His long mouth is so sensitive to inner mood that he can express two emotions at the same time, registering a dourness close to despair at one end, while turning up in sardonic comment at the other" (p. 168).

50. Ibid.

51. Angleton thought these people would help Israel, since they were Jewish, but he needed to be sure of their loyalty to Israel. MHCHAOS was a CIA operation designed to uncover foreign influence on race and antiwar protests—an influence that was nonexistent. MHCHAOS turned out to be no more than an expression of Angleton's rabid anticommunism.

52. Seymour M. Hersh, *The Samson Option: Israel's Nuclear Arsenal and American Foreign Policy* (New York: Random House, 1991), p. 145. These Angleton files were never brought to the attention of the House or Senate intelligence committees. Government cover-ups were the rule rather than the exception, and not the particular province of the attack on the USS *Liberty*.

53. See Holzman, *James Jesus Angleton*, p. 154.

54. Charles Battaglia speaking at the Angleton conference. In Hoffman and Ostermann, *Moles, Defectors, and Deceptions*, p. 34.

55. Thomas Lowe Hughes, in discussion with the author, August 2, 2016.

56. Mangold, *Cold Warrior*, p. 114.

57. Christopher Andrew speaking at the Angleton conference. In Hoffman and Ostermann, *Moles, Defectors, and Deceptions*, pp. 46–48. Ronald Kessler noted that Angleton suspected everyone except Kim Philby (the British agent and Angleton's long acquaintance who was in fact a Soviet spy): Kessler speaking at the Angleton conference, in Hoffman and Ostermann, *Moles, Defectors, and Deceptions*, p. 37. Angleton also accused David Murphy, chief of the Soviet Russia Division, of being a KGB agent on the strength of a charge by Soviet defector Anatoliiy Golitsyn: Barry Royden speaking at the Angleton conference, in Hoffman and Ostermann, *Moles, Defectors, and Deceptions*, p. 34. See also Martin, *Wilderness of Mirrors*, pp. 198–99.

In 1967, Angleton was distracted by heightened mole hunting following his contention that the KGB had penetrated CIA. In 1966, in the company of his favorite Soviet defector, Anatoliiy Golitsyn, he traveled to London on a twenty-four-hour jaunt where Angleton announced to a group of British intelligence operatives that included the head of MI5 and "C," the head of the British SIS, that the Sino-Soviet split was a "deception," that there was no enmity between Communist Russia and Communist China. By now, in his mad effort to discredit KGB defector Yuri Nosenko, Angleton was allowing Golitsyn access to his secret files. It may have been that both Golitsyn and Nosenko were moles. Certainly both seemed to be self-serving opportunists.

Some noted the absurdity of Golitsyn's insisting the United States was penetrated and Angleton's conclusion that there was nothing that happened in the US government (Martin, *Wilderness of Mirrors*, p. 191) that Moscow did not know in twenty-four hours. After 1,277 days of confinement and 292 days of interrogation, Bruce Solie, the powerful head of CIA's Office of Security, had concluded that Nosenko had not yet been debriefed. All the while, Angleton had never actually met Nosenko. Helms awarded Solie a medal for his work in rehabilitating Nosenko, so that some began to accuse Angleton himself of being the Soviet mole. One might interject that Angleton certainly does not appear to have been loyal to the United States in the part he played in organizing the attack on the USS *Liberty*.

William Harvey was among those who accused Angleton of being a Soviet agent. Finally, William Colby fired Angleton in 1974.

Another of Angleton's errors in judgment would be that the Soviet Union was behind Gamal Abdel Nasser, when in fact their alliance was tenuous.

58. See Stewart, *Spymasters of Israel*, p. 119.

59. Deputy Director for Operations (DDO), the clandestine services. This was the original name for the Deputy Director for Plans (chief of the clandestine services). In 1973, the name was changed back to Deputy Director for Operations.

60. See Alfred M. Lilienthal, *The Zionist Connection: What Price Peace?* (New York: Dodd, Mead, 1978), pp. 567–68.

61. See Wilbur Crane Eveland, *Ropes of Sand: America's Failure in the Middle East* (London and New York: W. W. Norton, 1980), p. 323.

62. Ibid., p. 307.

63. See Richard B. Parker, *The Six-Day War: A Retrospective* (Gainesville, FL: University Press of Florida, 1996).

CHAPTER 4. TOPPLING NASSER

1. Howard M. Sachar, *A History of Israel: From the Rise of Zionism to Our Time* (New York: Alfred A. Knopf, 2007), p. 472.

2. Livia Rokach, *Israel's Sacred Terrorism: A Study Based on Moshe Sharett's Personal Diary and Other Documents* (Belmont, MA: Association of Arab-American University Graduates, 1986), p. 43.

3. G. B. Erskine, memorandum, 1956, quoted in Stephen Green, *Taking Sides: America's Secret Relations with a Militant Israel* (Brattleboro, VT: Amana Books, 1988), pp. 332–34.

4. Rokach, *Israel's Sacred Terrorism*, p. 56.

5. Ibid., p. 71.

6. Alfred M. Lilienthal, *The Zionist Connection: What Price Peace?* (New York: Dodd, Mead, 1978), p. 364.

7. Avri el-Ad, *Decline of Honor* (Chicago: Henry Regnery Company, 1976), p. 105.

8. Ibid., pp. 116–17. El-Ad/Seidenwerg/Frank's superior told him: "Do you realize what will happen if the British pull out? They'll abandon to Nasser the mightiest military bases in the Middle East: thirty-seven military installations, including two fully equipped airfields, docks, dumps, hospitals, radar stations, ordnance depots.... With those forward bases, Nasser's air force will stare right into our eyes ... he'll have complete control of the canal ... Israel's shipping will be shut off forever." The solution was to terrorize the United Kingdom into not pulling out. "We can furnish them with the excuse to retract. To stay ... If we poison the atmosphere around him then what little trust the West has in place in him will end abruptly. Then we have accomplished what must be done for Israel." Ibid., pp. 118–19.

9. Richard Thompson, email message, July 23, 2003. Email provided to the author by Dave Lewis.

As a CIA asset, Thompson would have access to such information connecting to "Cyanide" and Operation Frontlet 615. Thompson believed that "because operation 'Cyanide' was called off by the USA, Israel refused to accept the fact and began Operation Frontlet 615 early. They demanded the *Liberty* be moved. She was to have been attacked by an unmarked aircraft."

The facts of Operation Cyanide: thanks to Philby's relationship with Angleton, Israel had a detailed battle plan prepared and rehearsed for the Golan Heights. Another provocative note by Thompson is that the plan for Israeli goals of the Golan right wing of the Israel government moved the attack date from the fifteenth to the fifth. ("Frontlet 615" had been in play for many months prior to June 1967.) US communication, both defensive and blocking, were in place, and the *Liberty*'s signals were actuarially blocked at first by US systems provided, resulting in knowledge of all used channels. Thompson also suggests that "the reason that opening the facts today is very difficult [is it] would show the grip that Israel has on the US government." Lurking behind these events as well was Israel's suspicion that the US would support Egypt's call for a cease-fire and equal suspicion that USS signals transmitted to the US were being intercepted by the Soviets.

10. See El-Ad, *Decline of Honor*, pp. 29, 65.

11. Ibid., p. 291.

12. Andrew Cockburn and Leslie Cockburn, *Dangerous Liaison: The Inside Story of the U.S.-Israeli Covert Relationship* (New York: HarperCollins, 1991), p. 55.

13. Ben-Zvi quoted in Rokach, *Israel's Sacred Terrorism*, p. 76.

14. Cheryl A. Rubenberg, *Israeli and the American National Interest: A Critical Examination* (Urbana and Chicago: University of Illinois Press, 1986), p. 59–60.

15. Steven Stewart, *The Spymasters of Israel: The Definitive Inside Look at the World's Best Intelligence Service* (New York: Ballantine, 1980), p. 73.

16. Shabtai Teveth, *Ben-Gurion's Spy: The Story of the Political Scandal That Shaped Modern Israel* (New York: Columbia University Press, 1996), p. 81.

17. Rokach, *Israel's Sacred Terrorism*, p. 91.

18. Lilienthal, *Zionist Connection*, p. 365.

19. Aviezer Golan, *Operation Susannah* (New York: Harper & Row, 1978), p. 65.

20. Rokach, *Israel's Sacred Terrorism*, p. 92.

21. Ibid., p. 90.

22. Ibid., p. 127.

23. Sharett quoted in Rokach, *Israel's Sacred Terrorism*, p. 92.

24. Marcelle Ninio, Victor Levy, Robert Dassa, and Philip Natanson quoted in Golan, *Operation Susannah*.

25. Ibid., p. 141.

26. Ibid., p. 375. For a memoir of the travails of "Paul Frank," also known as Avri Seidenwerg, see El-Ad, *Decline of Honor*.

27. Quoted in Lilienthal, *Zionist Connection II: What Price Peace?* (New Brunswick, NJ: North American, 1982), p. 323. Israeli papers sympathized with the conspirators and accused the Egyptians of anti-Semitism.

28. Stewart, *Spymasters of Israel*, p. 121.

29. El-Ad, *Decline of Honor*, p. 192. The reasoning was that were the truth told, the public would lose faith in the army, tantamount to losing faith in the country. By the middle of Paul Frank's trial, Motke Ben-Nasur had admitted that everything Frank said was true (p. 195). Mossad had not been involved in the planning of Operation Susannah, but stood ready to make Aman (army intelligence) subservient to its increasing power. Avri El-Ad was persuaded that "loyalty to his country" demanded that he lie about the real dates of the sabotage because any action before July 22 would have exonerated Lavon. El-Ad was told that if he had not lied in the

Lavon framing, he would have been accused of the sabotage having been his own idea without orders or the knowledge of the government (p. 236). He rewrote his field reports to coincide with Gibli's fraudulent case against Lavon, who resigned on February 17, 1955. By November, Ben-Gurion would again be both prime minister and defense minister.

30. Quoted in Rokach, *Israel's Sacred Terrorism*.

31. Ibid., p. 680. In conflict, horror-stricken and lost, completely helpless, Sharett wrote in his diary of January 10, 1954, "What should I do? What should I do?"

32. El-Ad, *Decline of Honor*, p. 189.

33. Ibid., p. 184.

34. Allen Dulles tried to get Nasser to commute the death sentences. Cockburn and Cockburn, *Dangerous Liaison*, p. 57.

35. Golan, *Operation Susannah*, p. 90.

36. Moshe Sharett, "Diary," January 25, 1955, in Rokach, *Israel's Sacred Terrorism*, p. 680.

37. Cockburn and Cockburn, *Dangerous Liaison*, p. 57.

38. Golan, *Operation Susannah*, p. 142.

39. Sharett, "Diary," January 10, 1954, in Rokach, *Israel's Sacred Terrorism*, p. 639.

40. Sharett, "Diary," January 14, 1955, in ibid., p. 654.

41. Sharett, "Diary," January 25, 1955, in ibid., p. 685.

42. So Dayan explained his sudden visit to the United States: "In the latter half of July, 1954, while I was on a three and a half years' visit to the Army bases in the USA, the [Special Services] Unit initiated an operation which thereafter was always referred to as 'the security mishap.' A detachment carried out a few small-scale sabotage actions in Cairo and Alexandria. The result was the arrest and trial of eleven of its members. Some were sentenced to long terms of imprisonment. The tragic climax was the suicide of one member and the execution of two others on January 1, 1955." Richard Deacon, *The Israeli Secret Service* (New York: Taplinger, 1978), p. 67.

43. Rokach, *Israel's Sacred Terrorism*, p. 96.

44. Sharett, "Diary," May 26, 1955, in ibid., p. 1021.

45. Golan, *Operation Susannah*, p. 3.

46. Ibid., p. 352.

47. El-Ad, *Decline of Honor*, p. 183.

48. Ibid., pp. 121–26.

49. Sharett, "Diary," January 26, 1955, in Rokach, *Israel's Sacred Terrorism*, p. 685.

50. Ibid., p. 789.

51. Moshe Sharett recorded in his diary the day of his departure from the government at a cabinet meeting: "None of my colleagues raised his head to look at me. None got up to shake my hand, despite everything. It was as if all their mental capacities were paralyzed, as if the freedom of movement was banned from their bodies, the freedom of expression was taken from their hearts and the freedom of independent action from their conscience. They sat heavy and staring in their silence. I crossed the whole length of the meeting room and left." "Diary," June 18, 1956 in Rokach, *Israel's Sacred Terrorism*.

52. Sharett, "Diary," pp. 874–75, in ibid., p. 99.

53. Rokach, *Israel's Sacred Terrorism*, p. 100. See also: Sharett, "Diary," March 30, 1955 and April 24, 1955, in ibid., p. 100.

54. Golan, *Operation Susannah*, p. 73.

55. Deacon, *Israeli Secret Service*, pp. 169–70.

56. Ibid., p. 170.

57. Ibid., p. 178.

58. Anthony Pearson, *Conspiracy of Silence: The Attack on the USS* Liberty (London: Quartet, 1978), p. 13.

59. Seymour M. Hersh, *The Samson Option: Israel's Nuclear Arsenal and American Foreign Policy* (New York: Random House, 1991), p. 35.

60. Stewart, *Spymasters of Israel*, pp. 128–29.

61. Lilienthal, *Zionist Connection*, p. 568.

62. Deacon, *Israeli Secret Service*, p. 170.

63. Isabella Ginor and Gideon Remez, *Foxbats over Dimona: The Soviets' Nuclear Gamble in the Six-Day War* (New Haven, CT: Yale University Press, 2007), p. 51.

64. Rokach, *Israel's Sacred Terrorism*, p. 377.

65. Dayan outlines his provocations: "'We would send a tractor to plow an area where it wasn't possible to do anything. . . . It was in the demilitarized zone, and we would know in advance that the Syrians would start to shoot. And then we would use artillery and later the air force.' He thought the Golan would have to be given back to Syria if there were ever to be peace in the region and that keeping it would result in the loss of many Israeli soldiers," explains James Akins. Dayan continues: "I can tell you with absolute confidence that [they] were not thinking about [security]; they were thinking about the Heights' land. . . . I saw them; I spoke with them. They didn't even try to hide their greed for that land." See James Akins, "The Attack on the USS *Liberty* and Its Cover-Up" (annual distinguished lecture; Washington, DC: Center for Policy Analysis on Palestine, September 1999), pp. 7–8.

66. Sharett, "Diary," January 31, 1954, in Rokach, *Israel's Sacred Terrorism*, p. 23.

67. Hersh, *Samson Option*, p. 22.

68. Rokach, *Israel's Sacred Terrorism*, p. 44.

69. Pearson, *Conspiracy of Silence*, p. 17. Pearson, a British reporter with contacts deep in British intelligence, learned that the British had penetrated the KGB network in Yemen, and so knew from the Russians that they were aware that an American-Israeli plan existed. Pearson is less reliable on the details of the attack on the USS *Liberty*. His book suffers a loss in credibility because there are no source notes, nor does Pearson feel free to name his sources.

70. Mohamed Hassanein Heikal, *The Cairo Documents: The Inside Story of Nasser and His Relationship with World Leaders, Rebels, and Statesmen* (Garden City, NY: Doubleday, 1973), p. 233.

71. Pearson, *Conspiracy of Silence*, pp. 18–21.

72. Ted Gup, *The Secret Lives and Deaths of CIA Operatives* (New York: Anchor, 2001), p. 222.

73. John Hadden, *Conversations with a Masked Man: My Father, the CIA, and Me* (New York: Arcade, 2016), pp. 150–51.

74. Quoted in Ginor and Remez, *Foxbats over Dimona*, p. 76.

75. Wilbur Crane Eveland, *Ropes of Sand: America's Failure in the Middle East* (London and New York: W. W. Norton, 1980), p. 323. Wilbur Crane Eveland was a CIA officer stationed in the Middle East. After the Six-Day War he requested—in a private meeting with Allen Dulles—that he be transferred from the Middle East to Africa. Eveland went to Africa under one of the deep-cover positions with private industry organized by Thomas Karamessines. Having observed James Angleton's manipulations with Israeli intelligence, with Eppy Evron on the ground in Washington and with Meir Amit at a distance, he wanted no connection to the Middle East. He titled one particularly trenchant chapter in his honest book, *Ropes of Sand*, "On the Outside Looking In." So he had observed how Angleton and Allen Dulles stood together as Cold War fanatics, and now Angleton, with Dulles in his camp and with Helms standing by, was free to operate.

76. Cockburn and Cockburn, *Dangerous Liaison*, pp. 146–47.

77. Here is the statute establishing the 303 Committee by law: "A Special Group is established under the National Security Council to approve and review covert operations, acting on the basis of unanimity. The Special Group shall consist of the Secretaries of State and Defense, or representatives designed by them; a representative of the President designated by him; and the Director of the Central Intelligence Agency."

78. Powers, *Man Who Kept the Secrets*, pp. 321–22.

79. Special Committee of the NSC "*Liberty*," national security file, 1967, box 10, Lyndon B. Johnson Library, Austin, TX.

80. I am indebted to Thomas Lowe Hughes for his interviews with me: August 2, 2016, in Chevy Chase, Maryland, and by telephone, August 9, 2016.

81. Victor Marchetti and John D. Marks, *The CIA and the Cult of Intelligence* (New York: Alfred A. Knopf, 1974), p. 326.

82. Ibid., p. 327.

83. John Prados, *Safe for Democracy: The Secret Wars of the CIA* (Chicago: Ivan R. Dee, 2009), p. 380.

84. In regard to the extant document of the 303 Committee: Special Committee of the NSC "*Liberty*," national security file, 1967, box 10, Lyndon B. Johnson Library, Austin, TX. This document refers to a US submarine in UAR (Egypt and formerly Syria) waters. There is a reference to "615," suggesting that events would commence on June 15. All that remains of the intriguing idea of the submarine was that it would shadow the USS *Liberty*, beginning on June 7. It would then be submerged, never to be seen again, but for its periscope, which would surface with sufficient time to photograph the attack. One photograph would fall into the hands of a *Liberty* survivor who went on to work for CIA named Ernie Gallo.

The camera was used by the periscope to take the photographs. The periscope itself was developed to take photographs of Soviet ships. The entire installation was known as an

AN-BRD-7 and was developed by Sanders Associates in Nashua, New Hampshire. It cost $495 million. It served all the functions of an intelligence ship, yet was small enough to put in a helicopter hangar.

Two subs were there on black ops: the *Andrew Jackson* and the *Amberjack*. One was on Operation Cyanide tapping the Mediterranean cables from all countries.

85. Eveland, *Ropes of Sand*, pp. 324–25.

86. Ronald Kukal, email to the author, November 16, 2015. See also Ed Offley, "Former Crewman Thinks a Sub Saw It All," *Navy Times*, June 30, 1997. Offley quotes Doug Gaston, son of an *Amberjack* officer who told Offley that "his father had told him on several occasions the *Amberjack* stumbled into the *Liberty* attack as it was patrolling near the Egyptian coastline. . . . his sub was on a mission over there and he and other officers watched the attack through the periscope . . . for over an hour." The skipper of the *Amberjack*, August Hubal, said, "his crew mistakenly believed the combat incident they witnessed was the *Liberty*, but what else could it have been?" These events remain shrouded in obfuscation and mystery.

87. Information about Foy Kohler courtesy of Thomas Lowe Hughes.

88. Hughes, in discussion with the author, August 2, 2016.

89. Richard Sturman, in discussion with the author, December 28, 2016.

90. Ernie Gallo, in discussion with the author, June 8, 2014.

91. Richard L. Block, in discussion with the author, December 6, 2014.

CHAPTER 5. MEIR AMIT ON THE MOVE

1. The phrase is biblical. I found it among the personal papers of John Hadden.

2. When Karamessines, now deputy director for plans, went through the CIA staff vaults and safes, he found chaos. Karamessines and his staff worked for months on archival operational files and even chased down leads provided by agents and defectors that had never been acted upon by Angleton. His approach was entirely subjective.

3. Christopher Andrew speaking at the Angleton conference. In Bruce Hoffman and Christian Ostermann, eds., *Moles, Defectors, and Deceptions: James Angleton and His Influence on US Counterintelligence* (Washington, DC: Woodrow Wilson International Center for Scholars, 2014), p. 48, https://www.wilsoncenter.org/sites/default/files/moles_defectors_and _deceptions_james_angleton_conference_report.pdf (accessed September 9, 2018).

4. Richard Helms, "Views of General Meir Amit. Head of the Israel Intelligence Service, on the Crisis in the Middle East," Central Intelligence Agency memorandum, June 2, 1967, National Archives and Records Administration, College Park, MD. Copies of this memo went to Dean Rusk, Robert S. McNamara, and Walt W. Rostow. Its attachment was classified as SECRET.

5. R. Jack Smith, "In His Own Words," interview with Richard Helms, June 3,

1982. Attachment to David Robarge, *A Life in Intelligence: The Richard Helms Collection* (Washington, DC: CIA Center for the Study of Intelligence, 2008), p. 29, https://www.cia .gov/library/readingroom/collection/life-intelligence-richard-helms-collection.

6. Robert Hathaway speaking at the Angleton conference. In Hoffman and Ostermann, *Moles, Defectors, and Deceptions*, p. 78.

7. For a detailed discussion of the week leading up to the Six-Day War, see Tom Segev, "Three Days to War: The Decision," chap. 11 in *1967: Israel, the War, and the Year That Transformed the Middle East*, trans. Jessica Cohen (New York: Metropolitan, Henry Holt, 2007).

8. Helms, "Views of General Meir Amit."

9. Tom Segev, *1967: Israel, the War, and the Year That Transformed the Middle East*, trans. Jessica Cohen (New York: Metropolitan, Henry Holt, 2007), p. 326.

10. Dave Lewis, in discussion with the author, December 16, 2014.

11. Segev, *1967*, p. 331.

12. Wilbur Crane Eveland, *Ropes of Sand: America's Failure in the Middle East* (London and New York: W. W. Norton, 1980), p. 527.

13. Amit speaking in Christopher Mitchell's documentary about the attack on the USS *Liberty*, *Dead in the Water* (London: BBC, 2002).

14. Segev, *1967*, p. 331.

15. Hamodia staff, "Was There an American Spy in the Israeli Government?" *Israeli News*, June 23, 2004.

16. Andrew Cockburn and Leslie Cockburn, *Dangerous Liaison: The Inside Story of the U.S.-Israeli Covert Relationship* (New York: HarperCollins, 1991), pp. 146–47.

17. Segev, *1967*, pp. 332–33.

18. In his memoir, *As I Saw It* (New York: W. W. Norton, 1990), Dean Rusk does not mention his meeting with Meir Amit during Amit's fateful visit to the United States during the last week of May and the first days of June 1967 on the cusp of the Six-Day War. Still, even for an intransigent cold warrior like Rusk, as it would be for lifelong CIA officer Richard Helms, the Israeli attack on unarmed American sailors was going too far. "Through diplomatic channels, we refused to accept their [Israel's] explanations," Rusk writes in his 1990 memoir, revealing that he operated, indeed, from the premise that neither the victims nor the public, who paid his salary, were entitled to transparency. "I didn't believe them then, and I don't believe them to this day," Rusk says. "The attack was outrageous" (p. 388). Yet Rusk writes, disingenuously, as if the attack were entirely an Israeli operation. Even as he ostensibly does not believe that the attack was "an accident" or "a mistake," he maintains the cover-up.

19. Quoted in Segev, *1967*, p. 332.

20. Meit Amit, "Will Israel Attack Iran?" interview with Ronen Bergman, *New York Times*, January 25, 2012.

21. John Lloyd Hadden Jr., in discussion with the author, July 9, 2014.

22. John Hadden to Peter Sichel, April 1, 2013. Papers of John Hadden.

23. Ernie Gallo, in discussion with the author, June 8, 2014.

24. Segev, *1967*, p. 333.
25. See Cockburn and Cockburn, *Dangerous Liaison*, p. 145ff.
26. Ibid., pp. 145–46.
27. Segev, *1967*, p. 334.
28. Cockburn and Cockburn, *Dangerous Liaison*, p. 154.
29. Segev, *1967*, p. 330.

CHAPTER 6. "HEROES IN THE SEAWEED"

1. Dave Lewis, in discussion with the author, August 23, 2016.
2. Joint Chiefs of Staff Fact-Finding Team, "Report of the JCS Fact-Finding Team, USS *Liberty* Incident 8 June 1967—Declassified at 12 Year Intervals," p. 6, National Archives and Records Administration, College Park, MD. Whenever there is a mention of "the ship's mission" in this Joint Chiefs memorandum from their fact-finding team, sentences are redacted (see p. 7). The many redactions following the statement that it was 303 and Vance that sent *Liberty* into harm's way suggest that this crucial detail was inadvertently left unredacted.
3. Thomas Lowe Hughes, in discussion with the author, August 9, 2016.
4. Joint Chiefs of Staff Fact-Finding Team, "Joint Chiefs Fact Finding Report. Done between 12 June and 18 June, Visiting Stuttgart; Athens; and the Sixth Fleet (USS *America* and USS *Little Rock*); Athens, Malta, London, Washington, DC." There is one name redacted from the roster of persons visited.
5. Robert "Bob" Wilson, in discussion with the author, June 8, 2017, fiftieth anniversary of the *Liberty* attack, Norfolk, Virginia.
6. Ibid.
7. Dave Lewis, in discussion with the author, May 2, 2017.
8. Dave Lewis, in discussion with the author, August 24, 2017.
9. Clyde W. Way, "Oral History Interview," interview by Henry Schorreck et al., National Security Agency, June 8, 1980, https://www.nsa.gov/news-features/declassified-documents/uss-liberty/assets/files/interviews/interview_c_way.pdf (accessed July 9, 2018). Way worked in long-distance communications on the ship and was supervisor of Section 3 of the NSDB, thirty megs and above.
10. Dave Lewis, email to the author, July 21, 2014. "After the attacking aircrafts were identified as Israeli," Lewis says, "my watch supervisors gave orders to find out what they were saying between planes and to Tel Aviv in plain language." Dave Lewis, in discussion with the author, May 10, 2017.
11. "Affidavit of Fact dated August 3, 1999. David E. Lewis, CDR USN Ret." State of Vermont, County of Essex. Vermont General Affidavit from David E. Lewis, April 22, 2012. Courtesy of David Edwin Lewis.

12. Dave Lewis, email to the author, October 28, 2016.

13. Dave Lewis, in discussion with the author, January 18, 2017.

14. Bryce Lockwood, in discussion with the author, June 8, 2014.

15. Dave Lewis, in discussion with the author, March 12, 2014, and May 19, 2015. Lewis says the crew came to believe that Johnson's "girlfriend," Mathilde Krim, was an agent of Mossad. They were primarily interested in the Soviets and their connection with the United Arab Republic.

16. Dusty (Paddy) Rhodes, "Oral History Interview," interview by Henry Millington and Bob Farley, National Security Agency, June 13, 1980, https://www.nsa.gov/news-features/declassified-documents/uss-liberty/assets/files/interviews/interview_p_rhodes.pdf (accessed July 9, 2018).

17. "Bud" C. Fossett, "Oral History Interview," interview by Robert D. Farley, National Security Agency, May 15, 1980, https://www.nsa.gov/news-features/declassified-documents/uss-liberty/assets/files/interviews/interview_b_fossett.pdf (accessed July 9, 2018).

18. James G. O'Connor, "Oral History Interview," interview by Bill Gerhard et al., National Security Agency, May 22, 1980, https://www.nsa.gov/news-features/declassified-documents/uss-liberty/assets/files/interviews/interview_j_oconner.pdf (accessed July 9, 2018).

19. Anthony Wells: "Was it possible that *Liberty* was listening to the Soviets listening to the Israelis?" This question appears in Wells's October 2013 review of A. J. Cristol's *The Liberty Incident Revealed: The Definitive Account of the 1967 Israeli Attack on the US Navy Spy Ship* (Annapolis, MD: Naval Institute Press, 2013). See also Dave Lewis, in discussion with the author, July 23, 2016.

20. Dave Lewis, in discussion with the author, June 30, 2014.

21. John E. Borne, *The USS* Liberty: *Dissenting History vs. Official History* (PhD diss., New York University, September 1993), p. 22.

22. David S. Collins, "Ed Lewis and the Attack on the USS *Liberty*," *Northern New Hampshire Magazine* (March 1998): 8–9.

23. The discussion of Dave Lewis's childhood is based on interviews in New Hampshire and Vermont, June 21, 2014 (among other dates).

24. For the US involvement in the Six-Day War involving aerial reconnaissance of the Egyptian air bases, see Stephen Green, *Taking Sides: America's Secret Relations with a Militant Israel* (Brattleboro, VT: Amana Books, 1988), pp. 205–11.

25. During the course of Green's effort to verify this information about a secret aerial effort by the United States, "Air Force intelligence contacted several former members of the Tactical Reconnaissance Squadron," which accomplished the mission of "reminding them of their obligation to maintain silence on any previous intelligence missions in which they have been involved." Ibid., pp. 209–10.

26. Lockwood, in discussion with the author, April 2, 2014.

27. Peter Hounam, *Operation Cyanide: Why the Bombing of the USS* Liberty *Nearly Caused World War III* (London: Vision, 2003), p. 219.

28. The date was May 23, 1967. Green, *Taking Sides*, p. 201.

29. Ibid., p. 187.

30. See Joseph Daichman, *History of the Mossad* [in Russian] (Smolensk, Russia: Rusich, 2001). A Soviet writer, Daichman thought that the attack on *Liberty* was designed to deprive American intelligence of its "eyes and ears" at the moment when the Israelis were moving on from the Egyptian to the Syrian front.

As the deputy chief of Aman (Israeli military intelligence) told author Peter Hounam, *Operation Cyanide*, p. 227, "the decision to attack Syria was made by the Minister of Defense on Day Five in the middle of the night, without any need for any preparations, and there was nothing they could monitor on the subject. Let's say that this boat would not have been attacked. Do you think that we would have not attacked Syria anyway?" Whether the United States had aided Israel in its efforts prior to the outbreak of the Six-Day War, Shlomo Gazi suggested, "The man to confirm or to disprove it, of course is General Amit." This, of course, is true. The dynamics of these events lay at the door of the head of Mossad. When the *Liberty* survived, another plan that was aborted was Israel's annexation of Damascus.

31. See Ed Offley, "Former Crewman Thinks a Sub Saw It All," *Navy Times,* June 30, 1997. Doug Gaston's father, a junior officer on the *Amberjack*, told him on several occasions that the *Amberjack* stumbled into the *Liberty* as it was patrolling near the Egyptian coastline, and so watched the attack for an hour. Torpedoman Second Class Rex Blumeyer said, "We took a hell of a down angle and went deep to evade the attackers." Captain Augustine Hubal said his men were "confused in their memories." They encountered "a different combat incident that his crew mistakenly believed was the *Liberty* under attack," which seems far-fetched. Soviet witnesses also came forward. The Polaris missile submarine *Casimir Pulaski*, armed with sixteen nuclear-tipped ballistic missiles, was on patrol close to the *Liberty*: a former crewman said that, on one particular day, "We were on station moving at a very low rate of speed. We heard explosions, loud noises, through the hull and immediately they aborted their track."

Beginning on June 11, the Soviet fleet activity in the Eastern Mediterranean was gradually decreased.

32. *Christian Science Monitor*, August 5, 1982.

33. Nikolai Shashkov, interview by Nikolai Cherkashin, *Rodina* magazine. From the papers of Dick Thompson.

34. Joint Chiefs of Staff Fact-Finding Team, "Addendum. ECJC/JRC, USNAVEUR for N-31 and 32. Subj: USS *Liberty*(U)/ 08686," National Archives and Records Administration, College Park, MD.

35. *The Link* 30, no. 3 (July–August 1997).

36. Fossett, "Oral History Interview."

37. Isabella Ginor and Gideon Remez, *Foxbats over Dimona: The Soviets' Nuclear Gamble in the Six-Day War* (New Haven, CT: Yale University Press, 2007), p. 76.

38. Richard Block (flight commander on Crete), email to the author, August 13, 2016. Charles Tiffany, quoted in "Selected Documents about the June 8, 1967 Attack on the USS *Liberty*." Classified Top Secret.

39. Dave Lewis, email to the author, August 7, 2017.

40. William D. Gerhard and Henry W. Millington, *United States Cryptologic History: Attack on a Sigint Collector, the U.S.S.* Liberty *(S-CCO)*, Special Series Crisis Collection, vol. 1 (Washington, DC: National Security Agency/Central Security Service, 1981). Originally classified TOP SECRET UMBRA; classified by NSA/CSSM 123-2. Papers of Richard Thompson.

41. Robert J. Cressman, "*Liberty* III (AGTR-5). 1964–1970," Naval History and Heritage Command, September 16, 2017, p. 11, https://www.history.navy.mil/research/histories/ship-histories/danfs/l/liberty-agtr-5-iii.html (accessed July 9, 2018). Note that Cressman does not mention that the *Liberty* would have come under the command automatically on June 2, passing through the Straits of Gibraltar. The ship would send a message to the new command (Sixth Fleet) that "we are here." Lewis assumed that passing through Gibraltar, they would have come under the command of the Sixth Fleet. It was tradition in the navy that as soon as you enter the waters of another command, you transfer to the authority of that command.

42. See *Remember the Liberty* (Washington, DC: US Congressional Committee on Armed Services, May 1971). The failure of these supposed messages is termed, p. 19: "one of the most incredible failures of communications in the history of the Department of Defense." An "immediate precedent" category was assigned, but not the highest priority, which was "FLASH." The entire chronicle of the lost messages seems specious.

43. Ibid.

44. Joe Lentini, in interview with the author, May 4, 2014, Nashville, Tennessee. Lentini contends there were no such messages "lost"—messages ordering the ship to be moved first twenty, then one hundred miles from shore. "Think about it," Lentini adds. "Why would anyone send a ship of the 6th fleet a message and route it to a shore station? To see the problem, you first need to understand how the Navy sends messages to its ships." Joe Lentini, email to the author, May 15, 2017. See also Joe Lentini, emails to the author, August 1, 2017, and August 2, 2017.

45. This note was sent for action to Op-92, copy to 09, with instructions to Op-92 to provide a reply to reach McDonald on his return to the Pentagon from Annapolis not later than 1430 (2:30 p.m.), June 7.

46. Personal files of David Edwin Lewis. Subject: RE USS *Liberty* CIA documents labeled "Operation Cyanide." Courtesy of Commander Lewis.

47. David K. E. Bruce, "The National Intelligence Authority," *Virginia Quarterly Review* (Summer 1946): 360.

48. The story made the front page of the *New York Times*, Youssef M. Ibrahim, "Egypt Says Israelis Killed P.O.W.'s in '67 War," September 21, 1995.

49. Dave Lewis, email to the author, May 2, 2014.

50. National Security Agency, "Secret Savin" document regarding the USS *Liberty*, p. 4. Declassified and approved for release by NSA on January 16, 2007. "Chronology of Events." That a cover-up was already in place is suggested by the NSA document including this: "Since Ambassador Goldberg had stated at the UN that no US Navy ships were within 350–400 nautical miles of the UAR/Israel area."

51. Richard Harvey, interview by W. M. Gerhard, H. Millington, and R. D. Farley, National Security Agency, July 16, 1980. Harvey insists that "we had provided them at the stop in Rota with a package of tech material on targets that they would be tasked against as well as some people that went aboard. So we have equipped them reasonably well at Rota." Dave Lewis denied that he had received any such package. The people who went aboard were Arabic and Russian translators.

52. Ibid.

53. James M. Ennes Jr., *Assault on the* Liberty: *The True Story of the Israeli Attack on an American Intelligence Ship* (1979; Reintree Press, 2013), p. 38.

54. David McFeggan, officially a *Liberty* communications technician, in discussion with the author, June 18, 2014.

55. Dave Lewis, in discussion with the author, July 11, 2016.

56. Dave Lewis, email to the author, October 11, 2016. For the date of the request being June 2 or 3: Dave Lewis, in discussion with the author, May 2, 2017.

57. Anthony Wells would run the *Liberty* Document Center in Middleburg, Virginia. Wells, who professed close CIA associations, contended in our interview in Middleburg that the mission of the *Liberty* was "secret." Anthony Wells, in discussion with the author, May 7, 2014.

58. Dave Lewis, in discussion with the author, May 10, 2014, and July 11, 2016. Disputing Wells's contention, Lewis notes that the movements of the escort would also be classified. Joint Chiefs, "Report of the JCS Fact-Finding Team," p. 13.

59. James Bamford, *Body of Secrets: Anatomy of the Ultra-Secret National Security Agency: From the Cold War through the Dawn of a New Century* (New York: Doubleday, 2001), p. 197.

60. Ibid., pp. 197–98.

61. Joint Chiefs, "Report of the JCS Fact-Finding Team," p. 48. The argument by CIA asset Tony Wells that the presence of a destroyer by its side would have exposed the *Liberty*, whose existence was secret, is specious. Dave Lewis points out that where they were going and who they were was common knowledge in Rota. And thus the report avoids chastising Admiral William Inman Martin.

62. Ibid., p. 17.

63. David McFeggan, in discussion with the author, June 18, 2015.

64. See Bamford, *Body of Secrets*, pp. 180–81. For the trajectory of the *Valdez*, see pp. 185–87.

65. Terry McFarland, interview by William Gerhard, Henry Schorreck, and R. D. Farley, National Security Agency, August 23, 1980.

66. Bamford, *Body of Secrets*, p. 202. Later, one of the surviving prisoners talked. Four hundred were executed at El Arish alone.

67. Joint Chiefs, "Report of the JCS Fact-Finding Team," p. 12.

68. McFeggan revealed this detail to author Hounam; see *Operation Cyanide*, p. 192.

69. Carol Moore, in discussion with the author, December 10, 2014. Moore was a protégé of Dick Thompson on business projects.

70. Facts compiled from interview with Tim Thompson, June 22, 2014; Dave Lewis, in discussion with the author, December 9, 2014; Moore, in discussion with the author.

71. Dave Lewis, in discussion with the author, December 9, 2014, who had several meetings with Thompson; Thompson's son, Tim, in discussion with the author.

72. The 303 Committee would rule the world: Unknown Israeli Writer [pseud.], "Chapter Ten—A Day to Remember" (unpublished manuscript, included among the papers of Richard Thompson). Courtesy of Ernie Gallo and Tim Thompson.

73. Dave Lewis, in discussion with the author, June 8, 2017, Norfolk, Virginia.

74. Interview with Brown & Root pilot Jack Robbins by Christopher J. Castaneda for the biography *Builders: Herman and George R. Brown* (College Station, TX: Texas University Press, 1999). Castaneda and his coauthor deposited the papers of their research for their biography of Herman and George Brown at Rice. George Rufus Brown referred to the government as a "partner of business": George Rufus Brown, "Oral History Interview," National Archives and Records Administration, Lyndon Baines Johnson Library, April 6, 1968.

75. In 2009, the United States amended the Freedom of Information Act to protect CIA interests in oil. B-1, an exclusion, allows CIA to keep secret any information "in the interest of national defense or foreign policy." Section B-9 protects one particular client, the oil industry, allowing CIA to keep secret "geological and geophysical information and data, including maps, [and] concerning wells."

76. CI/R&A, "Garrison and the Kennedy Assassination," CIA memorandum no. 8, January 11, 1968, National Archives and Records Administration, College Park, MD.

See also Sarah K. Hall to "Chief: LEOB/SRS," "Memo: December 1967 Ramparts Article Entitled 'The CIA's Brown and Root Dimensions,'" memorandum, December 20, 1967, CIA record number 104-10117-10203, National Archives and Records Administration, College Park, MD. See also: "Garrison Investigation of the Kennedy Assassination," memorandum to George Musulin, January 4, 1968, CIA, National Archives and Records Administration, College Park, MD.

For the George Brown reference, see the chief of the DCS office in Houston's memorandum, "James Garrison/George Brown—Possible Attempt to Embarrass Agency," December 17, 1967, CIA, HOU-251-67, National Archives and Records Administration, College Park, MD. See also the Houston office chief's memorandum to Director, Domestic Contact Service and Musulin, "Case 49364—Possible Involvement of George Brown in Garrison Matter. REF: Haynes/Musulin Telecon 5 Jan 68," January 11, 1968, CIA, National Archives and Records Administration, College Park, MD.

77. Livia Rokach, *Israel's Sacred Terrorism: A Study Based on Moshe Sharett's Personal Diary and Other Documents* (Belmont, MA: Association of Arab-American University Graduates, 1986).

78. Anthony Wells, "Moshe Dayan and the Attack on the United States Ship *Liberty*, June 8, 1967," September 2013. A copy of this essay was provided to the author by Dave Lewis. In our interview in Middleburg, Virginia, on May 7, 2014, Wells emphasized that Moshe Dayan was behind the attack. I was to accept this view, and during our luncheon he offered to write an introduction to my book.

Not subscribing to the "great man" view of history, I continued my research, only to discover that Meir Amit, head of Mossad, gave the order to Dayan to initiate the attack on the USS *Liberty*.

When I asked Wells for the texts of his interviews with Dean Rusk and Richard Helms, he pleaded "clear security reasons relating to sources and methods inside Israel and other parts of the Middle East plus collateral HUMINT intelligence from the British." The invocation of "sources and methods" had long been the standard CIA excuse for not revealing information otherwise accessible to the public. "Sources and methods" has long been an empty euphemism.

79. Cyrus Vance, *Hard Choices: Critical Years in America's Foreign Policy* (New York: Simon & Schuster, 1983), p. 197.

80. Ibid., p. 41.

81. "The radio shack was topside. They dial a knob and set up the frequencies and patch the circuit to the crypto center. When they go through the key card, it scrambles and then de-scrambles it. You type your message on your typewriter. It goes into the cryptographic machine and comes out scrambled. The output message is sent to the radio shack which has set up the circuit for whomever the recipient was and sends it to the recipient." Richard Sturman, in discussion with the author, December 28, 2016.

82. Tim Thompson, in discussion with the author, June 22, 2014.

83. Terence Halbardier to John Gidusko, January 25, 2014. Dave Lewis, email to the author.

84. Dave Lewis, in discussion with the author, June 24, 2016.

CHAPTER 7. CONSPICUOUS GALLANTRY

1. This term was used by the US Navy in awarding a Silver Star to a deceased USS *Liberty* sailor.

2. Robert L. Wilson, "Oral History Interview," interview by Robert D. Farley, Henry F. Schorreck, and Henry Millington, National Security Agency, May 6, 1980, https://www.nsa.gov/news-features/declassified-documents/uss-liberty/assets/files/interviews/interview_r_wilson.pdf (accessed July 12, 2018).

3. Bob Scarborough, in discussion with the author, August 24, 2014; Ron Grantski, in discussion with the author, August 23, 2014. There was no possibility that the attack was an "accident," invalidating the book by Judge Aharon J. Cristol, stem to stern. See A. J. Cristol, *The Liberty Incident Revealed: The Definitive Account of the 1967 Israeli Attack on the US Navy Spy Ship* (Annapolis, MD: Naval Institute Press, 2013). See also Jeff Jardine, "50 Years Later, Truth Still Matters to USS *Liberty* Crewman Who Survived Attack by Israelis," *Modesto Bee*, May 27, 2017.

4. Ron Grantski, in discussion with the author, August 23, 2014. I could not corroborate

this. Both Dave Lewis and Bob Scarborough pointed out that the order was *not* to intercept messages emanating from Israeli sources. Both were dubious about how this CT obtained the information. Lewis and Scarborough noted as well that there were no Hebrew linguists aboard and no Hebrew dictionaries.

5. Ron Grantski's information about how the Israelis locked "fire control" onto the USS *Liberty* was confirmed to me by Bob Scarborough, August 24, 2014: "When they came to attack, all they had to do was push a button because fire control was locked on us. We knew this from Morse code intercepts. [Ron McFarland acknowledges that they sent STRUMS or Morse Strums to NSA, manual Morse mainly.] We sent out a critic about 'attacking an American base.' They didn't put the two together; the CRITIC did not mention fire control. The Israelis themselves said they were going to attack an American base. We broke their encryption. There was no reply to the CRITIC."

6. Joseph L. Meadors, vice president, USS *Liberty* Veterans Association, to the Honorable John S. McCain, May 16, 2000.

7. Stephen Green, *Taking Sides: America's Secret Relations with a Militant Israel* (Brattleboro, VT: Amana Books, 1988), p. 320.

8. Bud C. Fossett, "Oral History Interview," interview by Robert D. Farley, National Security Agency, May 15, 1980, https://www.nsa.gov/news-features/declassified-documents/uss-liberty/assets/files/interviews/interview_b_fossett.pdf (accessed July 9, 2018): "USN-855 [Dave Lewis] in their mission in very large measure was controlled and directed by NSA. The CO of the USS *Liberty* was in no way controlled by NSA. . . . He was the bus driver and he worked for the Sixth Fleet."

9. Jim Kavanagh, in discussion with the author, August 14, 2014; Moe Shafer, in discussion with the author, August 14, 2014.

10. Seth Mintz, in discussion with Paul McCloskey, October 16, [1986?]. Included in the Paul McCloskey file.

11. Rowland Evans and Robert Novak, "Twenty-Five Years of Cover-Up," *Washington Post*, June 1992, at USSLiberty.org, http://www.ussliberty.org/mintz.txt.

12. Rowland Evans and Robert Novak, "Remembering the *Liberty*," *Washington Post*, November 6, 1991.

13. Ibid. See also Seth Mintz, "Attack on the *Liberty*: A Tragic Mistake," letter to the editor, *Washington Post*, November 9, 1991. This letter is a retraction. "As I told Mr. Evans and Mr. Novak," Mintz writes, "I believe the real villain in this tragedy not to be Israel, but whoever in the American chain of command denied the presence of an American ship in the area. I am certain that had the American Embassy told the Israelis that the ship was American, it never would have been attacked."

14. Evans and Novak, "Remembering the *Liberty*."

15. Rich Carlson, email to the author, July 2, 2017.

16. Seth Mintz addressed a reunion where he told the sailors that the Israeli navy had the USS *Liberty* AGTR-5 on their plotting board, having identified it from *Jane's Fighting Ships*.

Dave Lewis attended this event. The Israelis had claimed that they destroyed all documents not by the day but by the watch.

17. Pinchasy's identification of *Liberty* has been much quoted. See James Bamford, *Body of Secrets: Anatomy of the Ultra-Secret National Security Agency: From the Cold War through the Dawn of a New Century* (New York: Doubleday, 2001), p. 204. It is important, given Israel's subsequent denial, that they knew that they were bombing an unarmed American intelligence ship.

18. Phillip F. Tourney, *Erasing the* Liberty: *My Battle to Keep Alive the Memory of Israel's Attack on the USS* Liberty (Crestview, FL: Money Tree, 2016), p. 26.

19. See Wilson, "Oral History Interview."

20. The description of the Israeli aircraft is from Tourney, *Erasing the* Liberty, p. 48.

21. Terry L. McFarland, "Oral History Interview," interview by William Gerhard, Henry Schorreck, and R. D. Farley, National Security Agency, June 23, 1980, https://www.nsa.gov/news-features/declassified-documents/uss-liberty/assets/files/interviews/interview_t_mcfarland.pdf (accessed July 12, 2018). In this interview, McFarland confirms that the collection effort, the SIGINT group, was not tasked with intercepting Israeli communications.

22. Joseph L. Meadors, email to the author, July 2, 2017.

23. For descriptions of the aerial attacks, I am indebted to Engineer Third Class Kenneth M. Schaley, with whom I spoke on March 25, 2015, and Jack Beattie, with whom I spoke in June 2014. Beattie had been seventeen when he joined the navy, and so his mother signed for him.

24. *El Quseir* was 275 feet shorter and 8,040 tons lighter than *Liberty*. A dilapidated horse freighter, it was harbored in Alexandria with inoperable boilers and destined for the scrap heap at the time of the attack.

25. Ed Lewis, emails to Thomas Schaaf, June 14, 2012; Thomas Schaaf, email to Ed Lewis, June 14, 2012; Ed Lewis, in discussion with the author, May 17, 2017. Dave Lewis attempted to reach Hubal himself through one of Hubal's roommates at the Naval Academy, Jack Hyatt. The third Naval Academy roommate was Phillip Armstrong, who was killed in the attack.

26. Dave Lewis, email to the author, May 18, 2015. Hubal was in Dave Lewis's class at the US Naval Academy. Dave's naval brother confirmed that Hubal and the *Amberjack* were on a black op. Hubal told his classmate Thomas Schaaf that he was between fifty and one hundred miles away when the *Liberty* was attacked, "but I never believed him" (Thomas Schaaf, email to the author, May 21, 2015). Dave also notes that a submarine in the area would rescue survivors from the water if the ship was going down. "If a US sub was told to help us they could easily have torpedoed the three Israeli torpedo boats." Dave Lewis, email to the author, May 19, 2015.

27. Lloyd Painter, email to the author, June 30, 2014.

28. Dave Lewis, in discussion with the author, June 30, 2016.

29. Dave Lewis, in discussion with the author, December 4, 2017.

30. John E. Borne, *The USS* Liberty: *Dissenting History vs. Official History* (PhD diss., New York University, September 1993), p. 30.

31. Larry Weaver, in discussion with the author, March 21, 2014. See also Larry Weaver on "Down the Rabbit Hole with Popeye," radio broadcast, June 6, 2014.

32. George H. Golden LCDR to the Honorable Senator John McCain, May 25, 2000. Papers of Richard Thompson.

33. William R. Chandler to James M. Ennes, October 3, 1987. Included in the Paul McCloskey file.

34. Anthony Pearson, *Conspiracy of Silence: The Attack on the USS* Liberty (London: Quartet Books, 1978), p. 125. Pearson's book, originally serialized in *Penthouse* magazine, is marred by the absence of source notes and by the use of nameless sources in the text.

35. Richard L. Block, in discussion with the author, June 22, 2014, Miami, Florida.

36. Charles B. Tiffany, memorandum, "The *Liberty* Cover Up and Me." Courtesy of Ernie Gallo, from the papers of Richard Thompson.

37. See Marvin E. Nowicki to James Bamforth [*sic*], March 3, 2000.

38. Marvin E. Nowicki, "Assault on the *Liberty*: The Untold Story from SIGINT," from the papers of Richard Thompson. Nowicki recounts morning flights on June 7 and June 9, monitoring the Israelis using UHF receivers. See also, "Letter to the Editor" of the *Wall Street Journal*, "Tragic 'Gross Error' in a 1967 Attack," May 16, 2001. Many years later, Nowicki earned a PhD in political science, but at the time he was able to offer no historical or political perspective on the history of Israel or of Israeli relations with Egypt.

39. Nowicki ultimately came to the conclusion that the attack was "mistaken." His reference to "young sabras" protecting their country betrays his sentimental attachment to Israel and predisposition to protect them. He has no idea who put the ship "in harm's way" despite his PhD and blames the NSA, Pentagon, US Navy, and Theater Commanders, including LANTFLT, NAVEUR, and SIXTHFLT. Nowicki went on to argue that the attack "was carried out by the Israelis in the heat of battle," although there was no battle in the area by Thursday; the Egyptians had been thoroughly routed. He never learned (or would admit) that the motor torpedo boats continued machine-gunning the *Liberty* forty minutes after the torpedo hit. That the planes were "probably engaged in more pressing activity to protect their country" is plainly false. Later, Oliver Kirby was sent to NSA to investigate and saw the transcript of Nowicki's Navy EC-121.

40. For the Dwight Porter evidence, see also the column of Evans and Novak, November 6, 1991. See also, James Akins, Distinguished Lecture Series, no. 2 (Washington, DC: Center for Policy Analysis on Palestine, March 2000). Akins had been US ambassador to Saudi Arabia. The lecture took place on September 21, 1999.

41. Jim Ennes to Trevor Armbrister, July 10, 2003. A *Reader's Digest* editor, Armbrister was at work on a book about the attack on the USS *Liberty*. He died before the work could be completed.

42. See W. Patrick Lang, USSLiberty.org, August 10, 2007, http://ussliberty.org/patricklang.htm (accessed July 12, 2018).

43. Clyde Way, "Oral History Interview," interview by Henry Schorreck et al., June 8, 1980, https://www.nsa.gov/news-features/declassified-documents/uss-liberty/assets/files/interviews/interview_c_way.pdf (accessed July 12, 2018).

44. Eileen Fleming, "Remember the USS Liberty's MD in honor of National Dr. Day," *Arab Daily News*, March 23, 2014, https://thearabdailynews.com/2014/03/23/remembering-uss-libertys-md-honor-national-dr-day/ (accessed September 9, 2018).

45. Ibid.

46. Dave Lewis, in discussion with the author, May 9, 2017.

47. Brian Wright, "A Dark Place in the Past: Veterans of Attack on USS *Liberty* Work to Make Sure It Isn't Forgotten," June 16, 2015 (article unavailable as of August 2018).

48. Fleming, "Remember the MD."

49. Terry McFarland, "Oral History Interview," interview by William Gerhard, Henry Schorreck, and R. D. Farley, National Security Agency, August 23, 1980, https://www.nsa.gov/news-features/declassified-documents/uss-liberty/assets/files/interviews/interview_t_mcfarland.pdf (accessed July 12, 2018).

50. Richard Sturman, in discussion with the author, December 28, 2016.

51. Terence Halbardier to John Gidusko, January 25, 2014.

52. Ibid.

53. Jim Ennes, in discussion with the author, June 2, 2014. Ennes told me that Bennett was unpopular on the *Liberty* and later at the Naval Security Group Headquarters where Ennes and Bennett encountered each other again. Dave Lewis had intended to write a "less than perfect" fitness report for Bennett. But after the attack, it was difficult to write that anyone was unsatisfactory. When Lloyd Painter was nominated for a Silver Star, Bennett, experiencing no such hesitation, told Golden that Painter was cowardly during the attack. Ennes concluded that those who deserved medals didn't receive them, and people who barely deserved medals did.

54. Quoted in Alan Hart, *Zionism: The Real Enemy of the Jews*, vol. 3, *Conflict Without End?* (Atlanta GA: Clarity Press, 2010), p. 91.

55. Law Offices of Paul N. McCloskey Jr. to file, memorandum, October 16, 1991. Included in the McCloskey file. This memorandum describes McCloskey's contacts with Tavni over a period of four years, 1983–1986. McCloskey had lost to Pete Wilson in the California Republican Senate primary in June 1982, having served fifteen years in the House. The key issue was Wilson's announced support of Israel's right to annex the territories occupied in the 1967 war, as opposed to McCloskey's "contention that the Jewish lobby had become too powerful in its control of Congress on Mideast issues." As a lawyer, McCloskey had on a pro bono basis incorporated the USS *Liberty* Veterans Association as a nonprofit, tax-exempt entity. It was Ennes who was contacted by Tavni. At the time, living in the US, Even Tov was awaiting trial for bank forgery.

56. Paul McCloskey to file, "Re: James Ennes/Even Tov," memorandum, January 3, 1986. At Leavenworth, Tov became a champion chess player; in Israel he had published a magazine called *Guys and Dolls*.

57. Paul McCloskey to file, "Jim Ennes," memorandum, August 3, 1983. Included in the Paul McCloskey file.

58. Paul McCloskey to Joseph Adragna, Esq., August 16, 1983. Included in the Paul McCloskey file. Tov pleaded guilty to larceny by trick or fraud.

59. The quotations from Amnon Tavni come from the Paul McCloskey file.

60. Paul N. McCloskey, memorandum, October 28, 1991. Included in the Paul McCloskey file. See also Paul "Pete" McCloskey to file, "RE: Victor Ostrovsky," memorandum, October 20, 1991. Included in the Paul McCloskey file. Written on October 19, 1991, following a three-hour meeting with Ostrovsky.

61. Borne, USS Liberty, p. 20.

62. Phil G. Goulding, Confirm or Deny (New York: Harper & Row, 1970), pp. 133–34. Goulding was McNamara's press secretary.

63. Ibid., p. 134.

64. Memorandum, June 8, 1967. From the files of Admiral David Lamar McDonald.

65. Joint Chiefs of Staff Fact-Finding Team, "Report of the JCS Fact-Finding Team, USS Liberty Incident 8 June 1967—Declassified at 12 Year Intervals," p. 19, National Archives and Records Administration, College Park, MD.

66. Forslund preferred to share his testimony with military people, the survivors of the USS Liberty, even as he was too honest and forthright a person to maintain silence. Still, he was uncomfortable with sharing his experience with a civilian author (female) of an unknown political persuasion. Steve Forslund, email to the author, December 16, 2014. Forslund wrote: "I could only witness to a single document that I recall reading." Forslund's statement to the Liberty veterans was made in 2003.

67. Evidence from Jim Nanjo comes courtesy of Peter Hounam.

68. Bryce Lockwood says the entire US nuclear force was on alert starting the morning of June 8: Bryce Lockwood, in discussion with the author, June 8, 2014. Washington, DC.

69. Charles B. Tiffany, memorandum, "The Liberty Cover Up and Me." Courtesy of Ernie Gallo, from the papers of Richard Thompson.

70. It was only after the torpedo struck that the fuel oil tanks were ruptured and oil poured out. Richard Sturman says that "the only way those Israeli pilots could have seen oil coming from the USS Liberty would have been after the torpedo attack ruptured our fuel oil tanks." "You hit her, you hit her good!" an Israeli pilot had said. "There's oil coming out of her!" That the Israeli pilots were well aware of the identity of their target comes from another pilot, who reported: "Oil is spilling out into the water. Great! Wonderful! She's burning! She's burning," and the air controller echoes, "She's burning! The warship is burning!" disinformation buried in his enthusiasm. There was no evidence whatsoever that Liberty was a warship.

71. Admiral Thomas H. Moorer; General Raymond G. Davis, United States Marine Corps; Rear Admiral Merlin Staring, United States Navy (ret.); former Judge Advocate General of the navy, Ambassador James Akins (ret.), former United States ambassador to Saudi Arabia, Findings of the Independent Commission of Inquiry into the Israeli Attack on USS Liberty: The Recall of Military Rescue Support Aircraft while the Ship was under Attack, and the Subsequent Cover-Up by the United States Government (Independent Commission of Inquiry, October 22, 2003). The panel highlighted Ward Boston's affidavit revealing "that the court was ordered by the White House to cover up the incident" and finding that Israel's attack was "a case of mistaken

identity." See Admiral Thomas Moorer, "Israeli Attack on US Navy Ship Led to Cover-Up," *Washington Report on Middle East Affairs*, January 11, 2004.

72. Dave Lewis, in discussion with the author, May 12, 2017.

73. Dave Lewis, in discussion with the author, March 21, 2014.

CHAPTER 8. WITH THE SIXTH FLEET

1. Phillip F. Tourney, *Erasing the* Liberty: *My Battle to Keep Alive the Memory of Israel's Attack on the USS* Liberty (Crestview, FL: Money Tree, 2016), p. 60. See also James Scott, *The Attack on the* Liberty: *The Untold Story of Israel's Deadly Assault on a US Spy Ship* (New York: Simon & Schuster, 2009), pp. 215–16.

2. Phil Tourney's radio show: *USS* Liberty *Massacre Hour*, radio broadcast, Rense Radio, October 6, 2017.

3. Robert L. Wilson, "Oral History Interview," interview by Robert D. Farley, Henry F. Schorreck, and Henry Millington, National Security Agency, May 6, 1980, https://www.nsa .gov/news-features/declassified-documents/uss-liberty/assets/files/interviews/interview_r _wilson.pdf (accessed July 12, 2018).

4. Harold Six ran into David McFeggan on the USS *America*. Harold Six, in discussion with the author, June 10, 2017, Norfolk, Virginia.

5. Bryce Lockwood, email to the author quoting chief engineer George Golden, June 14, 2017.

6. See Andrew Weir, "The Spy Ship Israel Torpedoed," in *Middle East*, October 1983, p. 34: "When the Joint Chiefs of Staff in Washington heard of the attack, they furiously ordered an air strike by the USS aircraft carrier in the Mediterranean against the Israeli naval base at Haifa, but the order was countermanded by President Johnson." The source was a former CIA officer, likely Patrick McGarvey.

7. Patrick J. McGarvey, *CIA: The Myth and the Madness* (Baltimore, MD: Penguin, 1973), p. 17.

8. See Richard Deacon, *The Israeli Secret Service* (New York: Taplinger, 1978), p. 182. See also McGarvey, *CIA*, p. 17. McGarvey served with CIA at the time.

9. Brad Knickerbocker, "A Former Navy Pilot Recalls the *Liberty* Incident," *Christian Science Monitor*, June 4, 1982.

10. Jim Ennes, email to the author, September 5, 2017.

11. James M. Ennes Jr., "About Vice Admiral Donald Engen's Letter," April 16, 1999. Courtesy of Dave Lewis.

12. John E. Borne, *The USS* Liberty: *Dissenting History vs. Official History* (PhD diss., New York University, September 1993), p. 37. Borne's research seems meticulous.

13. Dave Lewis, in discussion with the author, August 8, 2016.

14. Dave Lewis, in discussion with the author, March 14, 2014.

15. Ennes, "About Vice Admiral Donald Engen's Letter." Ennes's conclusion is beside the point: "Admiral Martin was fully aware of our presence in the area and had promised immediate air support if needed. If he made that promise without passing it along to the carrier commanders [Tully and Engen] then that was a failure of Admiral Martin and his staff. If Admiral Engen allowed his aircraft to be so involved in a drill that he could not have reacted to an emergency, then that is also something that should have been investigated at the time."

16. Bill Knutson, in discussion with the author, June 9, 2015. These tests were done every three months. It was Alert 5 condition, and so it was easy to dispatch one or more planes to Cairo with nuclear capabilities. It was not a "nuclear weapons loading exercise," however, but the actual operation.

17. Dave Lewis, in discussion with the author, June 30, 2016.

18. George E. Sokol, quoted in Tourney, *Erasing the* Liberty, p. 152ff. Sokol, in a telephone call to the author on June 22, 2017, expressed his doubt that nuclear-armed planes went to Cairo, but against his opinion is the testimony of Captain Engen himself as well as others, and the circumstantial evidence that those planes were directed to return to Crete since nuclear-armed planes could not return to an aircraft carrier.

19. Rich Young, email to Jim Ennes and Joe Meadors, November 25, 2002. The day after the attack, Young helped carry "your dead and wounded aboard our ship."

20. Chuck Rowley to Jim Ennes, May 25, 1980. Courtesy of Jim Ennes.

21. Richard L. Block, in discussion with the author, June 22, 2014, recounting Captain Block's sources on the USS *America*. Strictly speaking, this is hearsay, confirmed not by documents but by the reality that Captain Engen and Admiral Martin covered for each other.

22. Captain Engen to a fellow officer on the USS *America*. It was repeated to air force intelligence officer Richard L. Block.

23. Moe Shafer, in discussion with the author, June 10, 2017. On the USS *Little Rock*, his flagship, Martin, upset by his participation in the operation, in a rare moment confided to five sailors in the hospital on *America*, including Shafer, who was interviewed by the author.

24. Joseph Tully, radio interview by Don Brooks, WOJB, Wisconsin, February 12, 1990.

25. Bill Knutson, email to the author, July 21, 2016. Ken Halliwell, email to the author, July 21, 2016. Halliwell, an engineer who did these calculations as well, concluded that the A-4 lacked air-to-surface missiles and cannon. Based on a message from *Saratoga* to COMSIXTHFLT, "the estimated time of arrival for A-1H propeller fighter aircraft launched from the USS *Saratoga* was three hours." The F-4 was capable of higher speeds, but did not contain a rapid-fire cannon, only air-to-air missiles to defend aircraft carriers and A-4s from possible air attack. Auxiliary fuel tanks and munitions under the wings slowed these planes down.

26. W. D. Knutson, in discussion with the author, November 10, 2014.

27. Bill Knutson, emails to the author, August 8, 2017, and August 10, 2017. I asked Knutson to explain what a "barrel roll" is: "A barrel roll starts from level flight. The aircraft nose is elevated slightly and the pilot puts in full right or left aileron, which causes the aircraft to roll

around the line of flight. The aircraft makes a full revolution back to horizontal flight. It is called a barrel roll because the aircraft really rolls in an arc and not a point. The arc is similar to a round barrel—thus the 'barrel' roll."

28. Some pilots launched from *Saratoga* heard voices from *Liberty* requesting help while they were being recalled. One wrote a magazine article about it for *Counterattack* (July 1967). When John E. Borne came to write his dissertation, he discovered that all copies of this magazine had disappeared from New York libraries. See Borne, *USS* Liberty, p. 38.

29. Ibid., p. 38.

30. Donald D. Engen USN (ret.) to Captain J. M. Tully, USN (ret.), October 15, 1992. Courtesy of Dave Lewis and Jim Ennes. See also Ennes, "About Vice Admiral Donald Engen's Letter." Courtesy of Dave Lewis.

31. Alan Hart, *Zionism: The Real Enemy of the Jews*, vol. 3, *Conflict Without End?* (Atlanta: Clarity Press, 2010), pp. 90–91.

32. Dave Lewis, email to the author, May 20, 2014; Jim Ennes, *Assault on the* Liberty*: The True Story of the Israeli Attack on an American Intelligence Ship* (1979; Reintree Press, 2013), p. 86.

33. Dave Lewis, in discussion with the author, May 28, 2015.

34. Dave Lewis, in discussion with the author, March 12, 2014. The *Liberty* was attacked at 6:58 a.m. EST. By 7:50 a.m., LBJ should have been called by Walt Rostow, McGeorge Bundy, or Robert McNamara, who would have received the FLASH message that the ship was being attacked. No phone call to Johnson was recorded by anybody. At 8:08 a.m., LBJ called Mike Mansfield, and at 8:13 a.m., he called Mansfield again. At 9:48 a.m. and at 9:49 a.m., Kosygin called LBJ.

35. "Declaration of David E. Lewis, Commander USN Ret." Courtesy of Dave Lewis.

36. Richard Sturman, in discussion with the author, December 28, 2016.

37. Engen to Tully, but see also Ennes, "About Engen's Letter."

38. Engen to Tully. In the October 15, 1992, letter, the captain of the USS *America* and now Vice Admiral Donald D. Engen refers to the "screw-up [that] was part and parcel to the spooks keeping so quiet about what they were doing and eventually this was rectified in the early 1970s." He was being optimistic. Captain Tully sent a copy of his letter to Jim Ennes, who shared it with Dave Lewis, which is how it came to be available to the reader.

39. "Memorandum for the Record" is document 219 in Harriet Dashiell Schwar, ed., *Foreign Relations of the United States, 1964–1968*, vol. 19, *Arab-Israeli Crisis and War, 1967* (Washington, DC: Government Printing Office, 2004).

40. *The Link* 30, no. 3 (July–August 1997).

41. Moe Shafer, in discussion with the author, June 20, 2017, Norfolk, Virginia.

42. COMSIXTHFLT to a List of Recipients, Naval Message, with a Corrected Copy Later, June 9, 1967.

43. Peter Flynn, in discussion with the author, March 22, 2014.

44. Moe Shafer, emails to the author, May 13, 2015, and August 14, 2014; Shafer, in discussion with the author, June 10, 2017.

45. Terence Halbardier to John Gidusko, January 25, 2014.

46. Ibid.

47. Moe Shafer, emails to the author, August 12 and 14, 2014; May 13 and 14, 2015; June 24, 2016; and August 6, 2016; Shafer, in discussion with the author, June 10, 2017.

48. Anthony Pearson, *Conspiracy of Silence: The Attack on the USS* Liberty (London: Quartet Books, 1978), pp. 56–57. See also Patrick J. McGarvey, *CIA: The Myth and the Madness* (Baltimore, MD: Penguin, 1973), p. 17.

49. Moe Shafer, in discussion with the author, June 10, 2017.

50. Dave Lewis on *The People Speak*, radio broadcast, produced by Mike Kim, hosted by Edward Jones, Marilyn Meadors, and Mike Kim, BBS Radio, July 15, 2008.

51. Ennes, *Assault on the* Liberty, p. 138.

52. Borne, *USS* Liberty, p. 54.

53. George F. Bogardus, "Letter to the Editor," *Washington Post*, April 1999. Former consult Bogardus is asking in 1999: "Why were two [*sic*] fighters launched by the Sixth Fleet to rescue the *Liberty* recalled almost at once to their carrier? Who gave superior orders to the Sixth Fleet? Why was the *Liberty* wittingly abandoned to bloody attack?" Bogardus also asks: "At one point Air Force General David Burchinal asked the Joint Chiefs of Staff, 'Who, repeat who, are the enemy?'" meaning Soviets or Israelis. The Joint Chiefs did not reply for two days.

54. David G. Nes, in interview with Ted Gittinger for the Association for Diplomatic Studies and Training, Foreign Affairs Oral History Project, November 10, 1982. Available at the Lyndon Baines Johnson Library.

CHAPTER 9. COVER-UP

1. The cable: 1967 June 8: FM: AMEMBASSY TEL AVIV. TO: RUEHC/SECSTATE WASHDC IMMEDIATE 165. NAR 8. REF: CONF. 0825. Barbour writes that the Israelis "do not intend give any publicity about vessel." Nor did they "intend give any publicity to incident. Urge strongly that we too avoid publicity. If it is US flag vessel its proximity to scene conflict could feed Arab suspicions of US-Israel collusion. . . ."

2. Article in the *Norfolk Virginian Pilot*, June 11, 1967.

3. Seymour M. Hersh, *The Samson Option: Israel's Nuclear Arsenal and American Foreign Policy* (New York: Random House, 1991), p. 161.

4. Ibid., p. 12.

5. Barbour's June 8, 1967, cable following the attack is housed at the Lyndon Baines Johnson Library. This cable has been declassified. EHB635, FN ANENBASST TEK AVUV'TI RYEGC.SECSTATE WASGDC IMMEDIATE 165. 1967 JUNE 8 17 53. Lyndon B. Johnson Library, Austin, TX.

6. Richard Nolte, telegram to Lyndon B. Johnson, "AMEMBASSY CAIRO TO SECSTATE WASHDC," June 8, 1967, Lyndon B. Johnson Library, Austin, TX.

7. Phillip F. Tourney, *Erasing the* Liberty: *My Battle to Keep Alive the Memory of Israel's Attack on the USS* Liberty (Crestview, FL: Money Tree, 2016), pp. 170 and 198.

8. Jim Ennes, in discussion with the author, June 2, 2014.

9. Dave Lewis, in discussion with the author, February 24, 2015.

10. James M. Ennes Jr., *Assault on the* Liberty: *The True Story of the Israeli Attack on an American Intelligence Ship* (1979; Reintree Press, 2013), pp. 113–14. To many, and to this day, McGonagle remained the captain, their leader, even in the face of evidence of his malfeasance.

11. James O'Connor, "Oral History Interview," interview by Bill Gerhard et al., National Security Agency, May 22, 1980, https://www.nsa.gov/news-features/declassified-documents/uss-liberty/assets/files/interviews/interview_j_oconner.pdf (accessed July 19, 2018).

12. Joseph Conrad, "Author's Note" to *The Shadow-Line* in *Typhoon and Other Stories* (London: Heinemann, 1903; New York: Everyman's Library, 1991), p. 248.

13. Lloyd Painter, email to the author, July 10, 2014.

14. Louis W. Tordella, Deputy Director, National Security Agency, for the record, "SECRET SAVIN," memorandum, June 8, 1967, document ID: 3847449. Released under FOIA case #62845.

15. James Scott, *The Attack on the* Liberty: *The Untold Story of Israel's Deadly Assault on a US Spy Ship* (New York: Simon & Schuster, 2009), p. 145.

16. Ibid., pp. 146–47.

17. Admiral William Inman Martin to Jim Ennes, March 1, 1984. Courtesy of Jim Ennes.

18. Reply to a letter from Richard G. Schmucker to His Excellency Yuli M. Vorontsov, Embassy of the Russian Federation, Washington, DC, October 8, 1997. Papers of Richard Thompson.

19. John Hrankowski, "The Israeli Attack on the USS *Liberty*, Mistake or Stab in the Back?" interview in *Pravda*, July 4, 2002, http://www.pravdareport.com/news/russia/04-07-2002/45729-0/ (accessed July 19, 2018). See also "War Without End: Another Pravda Article on USS *Liberty* Attack by Israel," *Pravda* (article unavailable as of September 2018).

20. Larry Broyles, email to Commodore Dave Lewis, May 15, 2014; Larry Broyles, "To Whom It May Concern, Concerning Larry Broyles," interview by Glenn Oliphant, April 4, 2013; Larry Broyles, in discussion with the author, August 20, 2016.

21. Bud C. Fossett, "Oral History Interview," interview by Robert D. Farley, National Security Agency, May 15, 1980, https://www.nsa.gov/news-features/declassified-documents/uss-liberty/assets/files/interviews/interview_b_fossett.pdf (accessed July 9, 2018). Classified "Top Secret Codeword Sensitive" at Fossett's request.

22. Robert L. Wilson, "Oral History Interview," interview by Robert D. Farley, Henry F. Schorreck, and Henry Millington, National Security Agency, May 6, 1980, https://www.nsa.gov/news-features/declassified-documents/uss-liberty/assets/files/interviews/interview_r_wilson.pdf (accessed July 12, 2018).

23. Ron Kukal, telephone conversation with the author.

24. John E. Borne, *The USS* Liberty: *Dissenting History vs. Official History* (PhD diss., New York University, September 1993), p. 73.

25. Ennes, *Assault on the* Liberty, p. 136.

26. Bryce Lockwood, in discussion with the author, April 2, 2014.

27. Quoted in Tourney, *Erasing the* Liberty, p. 17t.

28. Ron Grantski, in interview with the author, August 23, 2014.

29. Don Pageler, "The USS *Liberty*'s Impact on My Life" (unpublished statement, undated). Provided to the author by Don Pageler.

30. There were twenty Bronze Stars, nine Navy Commendations, a Presidential Unit Citation, the Medal of Honor, two Navy Crosses, and thirteen Silver Stars.

31. Lloyd Painter, email to the author, August 5, 2014.

32. Broyles, "To Whom It May Concern."

33. Ron Kukal, in discussion with the author, May 28, 2014.

34. William D. Gerhard and Henry W. Millington, *United States Cryptologic History: Attack on a Sigint Collector, the U.S.S. Liberty (S-CCO)*, Special Series Crisis Collection, vol. 1 (Washington, DC: National Security Agency/Central Security Service, 1981), p. 44. Originally classified TOP SECRET UMBRA; classified by NSA/CSSM 123-2. Papers of Richard Thompson.

35. Marshall S. Carter, "Oral History Interview," interview by Robert D. Farley, National Security Agency, October 3, 1988, Colorado Springs, Colorado.

36. Thomas Lowe Hughes, in discussion with the author, August 9, 2016.

37. Carter, "Oral History Interview."

38. Dave Lewis, in interviews with the author, including June 8, 2017. In Norfolk, Gary Brummett, who served under Golden in the engineering department of the ship, insisted that Golden was not Jewish, so I reinterviewed Dave Lewis on the subject. Dave was close to Golden and remained in contact with George Golden's wife, Bessie, after Golden's death.

39. Bryce Lockwood, email to the author, June 14, 2017.

40. George Koromah, in discussion with the author, June 8, 2017.

41. Bob Wilson in Malta seems not to have been treated with any special trust or consideration, despite his being seconded by CIA. Wilson did not discuss his intelligence work on *Liberty* with the author. The details of his brief stay in Malta are from his interview with the NSA.

42. James M. Makris, quoted in Tourney, *Erasing the* Liberty, pp. 165–67.

43. Glenn Oliphant, email to the author, November 23, 2014.

44. Lloyd Painter, email to the author, November 30, 2014. Painter noted that A. J. Cristol had access to a lot of inside information. Painter had been nominated for a Silver Star, but it was rejected at some level of the chain of command. "I never spoke to anyone about that, but Cristol somehow learned of it."

45. Lloyd Painter, email to the author, June 30, 2014.

46. Lloyd Painter to Richard Schmucker, May 8, 2000. Papers of Richard Thompson.

47. Sandy McGonagle said this to survivor Gary Brummett in 2005 at the Army-Navy Club banquet reunion. Gary Brummett, in interview with the author, January 12, 2015.

48. Dave Lewis, in interviews with the author, June 21 and June 22, 2015.

49. Ward Boston, affidavit, January 9, 2004. Available online, for instance at If America Knew, https://ifamericaknew.org/us_ints/ul-boston.html (accessed September 10, 2018).

50. Borne, *USS* Liberty, p. 77.

51. Ibid., p. 78.

52. The Israelis denied that they saw an American flag on the ship. In fact, the flag, shattered by gunfire, had to be replaced twice. Joe Meadors, email to the author, July 2, 2017.

53. Merlin H. Staring to David Walsh, July 17, 1984. Files of Paul McCloskey.

54. Ibid.

55. Merlin H. Staring to Senator John Warner, September 2, 2005.

56. Dave Lewis, in discussion with the author, June 30, 2016.

57. Merlin H. Staring to Senator John Warner. "The survivors," Staring wrote, "have been denied the honor that should have been theirs of recognition as prime exemplars of the Navy's historic tradition: 'DON'T GIVE UP THE SHIP.'"

58. See Scott, *Attack on the* Liberty, pp. 230ff.

59. Isaac Kidd Jr., "LIBERTY Inquiry Findings Relative to Communications (U)," memorandum, June 21, 1967, Op-OO Memo 00345-67, SECRET SENSITIVE (DECLASSIFIED), US Navy Archives. See also: Op-002, Op-00 Memo 00317-67 of June 9, 1967, "Movements of USS LIBERTY (U)."

60. Scott, *Attack on the* Liberty, p. 231.

61. "David L. McDonald's Comments/Recommended Changes on *Liberty* Press Release—1300," June 23, 1967, box 112. *Liberty* Press Releases immediate office files of the CZNO, Operational Archives Branch.

62. For biographical details of the life of Admiral David Lamar McDonald, see David Lamar McDonald, *The Reminiscences of Admiral David Lamar McDonald, US Navy (Retired)* (Annapolis, MD: US Naval Institute, November 1976).

63. Ibid., p. 201.

64. Ibid., p. 344.

65. Ibid., p. 420. See also p. 388. McDonald's interviewer, John T. Mason Jr., told him, "Admiral, that's an interesting aspect of your character, your ability to speak out and say the truth, as you felt the truth to be, without fear of consequences."

66. Scott, *Attack on the* Liberty, p. 232.

67. Bryant Jordan, "Israel Attack on USS *Liberty* 'No Accident,' Says Helms," *Navy Times*, July 7, 2002.

68. McDonald, *Reminiscences*.

69. "The court determined that the *Liberty* sailed in international waters, flew the American flag, and sported clean and freshly painted hull markings." Scott, *Attack on the* Liberty, p. 227.

70. Joint Chiefs of Staff Fact-Finding Team, "Report of the JCS Fact-Finding Team, USS *Liberty* Incident 8 June 1967—Declassified at 12 Year Intervals," p. 6, National Archives and Records Administration, College Park, MD.

71. See George A. Manfredi, Rockefeller Commission, *Memorandum for the Record: Subject: Examination of a Portion of the Records of Richard Helms* (Washington, DC: Commission on CIA Activities within the United States, March 19, 1975). National Archives and Records Administration. Documents destroyed included Helms's correspondence files and his desk calendars, 1965 through March 1973.

72. Tom Segev, *1967: Israel, the War, and the Year That Transformed the Middle East*, trans. Jessica Cohen (New York: Metropolitan, Henry Holt, 2007), p. 568.

73. Scott, *Attack on the* Liberty, p. 196–97.

74. Martin Peretz, "The American Left & Israel," *Commentary* 44, no. 5 (November 1, 1967): 27–34.

75. Segev, *1967*, p. 569.

76. Quoted in Scott, *Attack on the* Liberty, p. 264.

77. Lloyd Painter, email to the author, June 20, 2016.

78. Bryce Lockwood, in discussion with the author, April 2, 2014.

79. Peter Hounam, *Operation Cyanide: Why the Bombing of the USS* Liberty *Nearly Caused World War III* (London: Vision, 2003), p. 265.

80. See James W. Crawley, "Ex-Officer Alleges Cover-Up in Probe of Spy Ship Attack," *Union-Tribune*, February 17, 2004.

81. Boston quoted in Crawley, "Ex-Officer Alleges Cover-Up."

82. Thomas Moorer, "Israeli Attack on US Navy Ship Led to Cover-Up," *Washington Report on Middle East Affairs*, January 11, 2004.

83. Admiral Moorer never could obtain any information about why the rescue flights were recalled. Borne, *USS* Liberty, p. 213.

84. Congressional Record: House. September 19, 1967. H 12170. "Attack on U.S.S. 'Liberty': Another Pearl Harbor?" Mr. Rarick (at the request of Mr. Hechler of West Virginia) was granted permission to extend his remarks at this point in the record and to include extraneous matter.

Rarick, now deceased, was a close friend of mine. As a judge, he was a rabid segregationist, yet that doesn't tell the whole story, as witness his kindness to Leonard Caesar when he was incarcerated in the East Feliciana State Hospital at Jackson, a notorious insane asylum. This story is told in my book *Jim Garrison: His Life and Times* (Southlake, TX: JFK Lancer Productions & Publications, 2008). I interviewed John several times, yet never once did he mention the USS *Liberty*. He was modest in a style rarely seen today.

85. Moe Shafer, email to the author, August 14, 2014. The most egregious war crimes were the shooting of the stretcher bearers; the shooting at the firefighters; and the shooting up of the life rafts, according to Ernie Gallo, in interview with the author, June 8, 2014. Gallo believes Johnson's leaving wounded people behind on a field of battle warranted impeachment.

86. Maurice Bennett quotes Senator William Fulbright, January 21, 1974. Files of documentary filmmaker Tito Howard.

87. Gary Brummett, in discussion with the author, January 2014.

88. Dave Lewis, in discussion with the author, June 2017, at the fiftieth-anniversary reunion of the survivors of the attack.

89. Lloyd Painter, in discussion with the author, June 30, 2014.

90. Joseph R. Russ, Major General, USA Chief, JCCRG, to the Chairman, Joint Chiefs of Staff, "Fact-Finding Team," memorandum, Joint Command and Control Requirements Group, June 18, 1967. The cause of the messages not arriving is listed as "(1) human error, (2) high volume of communications traffic, and (3) lack of appreciation of sense of urgency regarding the movement of LIBERTY." The reasons for delays "on the Flagship of COMSIXTHFLT [the USS *Little Rock*] were internal staffing, a delay in transmitting due to other traffic of the same and higher precedence, and the commander and his staff were deeply involved in high priority press activity directed by DOD and plans for evacuation of dependents"—this latter most obviously strictly cover and of no validity. There were no plans for the evacuation of dependents. The Joint Chiefs' participation in disseminating this disinformation reveals their complicity in the cover-up. The Joint Chiefs' memo closes on the note that they gleaned their information from "facts previously collected by the Court of Inquiry."

91. Ennes, *Assault on the* Liberty, p. 319.

92. Bob Scarborough, in discussion with the author, August 24, 2014.

93. Bill Knutson, in discussion with the author, June 9, 2015.

94. Chuck Rowley, in interview with Jim Ennes, June 12, 2000.

95. Since Wells will not release the transcript, I don't know whether Rusk requested that the interview be "classified" and hence not made available to historians. Wells just told me it was "classified."

96. The President's Foreign Intelligence Advisory Board and the 303 Committee were two distinct and separate entities. The PFIAB was a small group of notables from industry, academia, and the legal profession; intelligence retirees; and those with past political experience in providing advice to the president. The 303 Committee was comprised of more hardcore intelligence participants, but the relationship between the two groups was symbiotic. They were aware of each other's product, and the president saw both. "Advisory" meant advising the president. 303 was involved in intelligence analysis, end product, and recommendations.

97. Segev, *1967*, p. 386.

98. Paul Findley, "Even As USS *Liberty*'s Heroic Captain Receives New Honor, Cover-Up of Israeli Attack on His Ship Continues," *Washington Report on Middle East Affairs*, March 1998, p. 26. Findley was a former Illinois congressman and the author of *They Dare to Speak Out: People and Institutions Confront Israel's Lobby* (Chicago: Lawrence Hill Books, 2003) and *Deliberate Deceptions: Facing the Facts about the US-Israeli Relationship* (Washington, DC: American Educational Trust, 1995).

99. O'Connor, "Oral History Interview," p. 54.

100. Jim Ennes, email to the author, April 20, 2014.

101. Walworth Barbour's telegram to the State Department was released on September 22, 1982: FM AMEMBARRY TELAVIV TO SECSTATE WASHDC IMMEDIATE. CONFIDENTIAL TEL AVIV 4178 REF: STATE211695. "NO REQUEST FOR INFO ON U.S. SHIPS OFF SINAI WAS MADE UNTIL AFTER LIBERTY INCIDENT. HAD ISRAELIS MADE SUCH AN INQUIRY IT WOULD HAVE BEEN FORWARDED

IMMEDIATELY TO THE CHIEF OF NAVAL OPERATIONS AND OTHER HIGH NAVAL COMMANDS AND REPEATED TO DEPT. BARBOUR." In his 1970 memoirs, Yitzhak Rabin, the army chief of staff, wrote that Israel had requested "the United States either withdraw all its vessels from our shores, or inform us of the exact location of all vessels close to our shores." He claimed that he had made this request to Ernest Castle, the US military *charge d'affaires*. Rabin was lying. Shortly after the attack, Castle denied that any such request for information ever took place. Castle noted that had such a request been made, it would have been forwarded to Admiral McDonald. American Embassy Tel Aviv to US Secretary of State, message 4178, June 1967.

102. Mike Schaley, in discussion with the author, March 25, 2015.

103. Sailor Richard (Rocky) Sturman, "Statement," USSLiberty.org, http://www.ussliberty.org/rocky.htm (accessed September 5, 2018).

104. Borne, *USS* Liberty, p. 283.

105. This evidence courtesy of Sturman, "Statement."

106. Interview with Meir Amit in Hounam, *Operation Cyanide*, p. 230.

CHAPTER 10. AFTERMATH

1. An after-the-fact effort: The Joint Chiefs would have preferred that "faulty U.S. communications practices" be blamed. See "Foreword" to William D. Gerhard and Henry W. Millington, *United States Cryptologic History: Attack on a Sigint Collector, the U.S.S. Liberty (S-CCO)*, Special Series Crisis Collection, vol. 1 (Washington, DC: National Security Agency/Central Security Service, 1981). Originally classified TOP SECRET UMBRA; classified by NSA/CSSM 123-2. Papers of Richard Thompson. This document is heavily redacted. Even the names of translators and editors are missing. A Central Intelligence Agency representative told the Defense Department that the frantic efforts to move *Liberty* messages sent by NSA and the Joint Chiefs were prompted by an intelligence report from the Office of the US Defense Attaché in Tel Aviv indicating that the IDF planned to attack *Liberty* if she continued to operate in Israeli coastal water, more obfuscation. It has taken fifty years to wade through the disinformation. See Stephen Green, *Taking Sides: America's Secret Relations with a Militant Israel* (Brattleboro, VT: Amana Books, 1988), p. 239.

2. Micha Limor, "Israeli Navy Man Describes the Attack on USS *Liberty*," *New York Times*, July 7, 1967, at USSLiberty.org, http://www.ussliberty.org/limor.htm (accessed September 6, 2018).

3. Dave Lewis, in discussion with the author, November 14, 2016.

4. Golden is quoted in Peter Hounam, *Operation Cyanide: Why the Bombing of the USS Liberty Nearly Caused World War III* (London: Vision, 2003), pp. 240–41.

5. Jim Ennes, *Assault on the* Liberty: *The True Story of the Israeli Attack on an American Intelligence Ship* (1979; Reintree Press, 2013), p. 132.

6. Here is David Martin, author of *Wilderness of Mirrors: Intrigue, Deception, and the Secrets That Destroyed Two of the Cold War's Most Important Agents* (New York: HarperCollins, 1980; Lyons Press, 2003). Martin is speaking at the Angleton conference. In Bruce Hoffman and Christian Ostermann, eds., *Moles, Defectors, and Deceptions: James Angleton and His Influence on US Counterintelligence* (Washington, DC: Woodrow Wilson International Center for Scholars, 2014), p. 72, https://www.wilsoncenter.org/sites/default/files/moles_defectors_and _deceptions_james_angleton_conference_report.pdf (accessed September 9, 2018).

7. David Robarge understates the case of Helms affording James Angleton "much leeway": See Robarge, "Overview," introduction to *A Life in Intelligence: The Richard Helms Collection* (Washington, DC: CIA Center for the Study of Intelligence, 2008), p. 17, https:// www.cia.gov/library/readingroom/collection/life-intelligence-richard-helms-collection.

8. Gerhard and Millington, *Attack on a Sigint Collector*, p. 62.

9. Ibid., p. 64.

10. McNamara's testimony is quoted in James Scott, *The Attack on the* Liberty: *The Untold Story of Israel's Deadly Assault on a US Spy Ship* (New York: Simon & Schuster, 2009), p. 255.

11. Thomas Lowe Hughes, in discussion with the author, August 2, 2016.

12. Ennes, *Assault on the* Liberty, p. 18.

13. Joseph Daichman, *History of the Mossad* [in Russian] (Smolensk, Russia: Rusich, 2001), cited in the papers of Richard Thompson. The book has not been translated into English.

14. Dan Raviv and Yossi Melman, *Every Spy a Prince: The Complete History of Israel's Intelligence Community* (Boston, MA: Houghton Mifflin, 1990), p. 162.

15. See Anthony Pearson, *Conspiracy of Silence: The Attack on the U.S.S.* Liberty (London: Quartet, 1978), p. 69.

CHAPTER 11. COVER-UP CONTINUED: CIA AND LIBERTY

1. Issuing from the Directorate of Intelligence, the CIA report "The Israeli Attack on the USS *Liberty*" is dated June 13, 1967. Responding to FOIA requests, CIA finally released a mostly unredacted version of this document.

2. Dave Lewis, email to the author, March 30, 2016. Dave reminded me that it was the captain who had made the original decision to leave their position where it was, and his major consideration was that line of sight communications would have been affected.

3. The Joint Chiefs' fact-finding report (see chap. 6, note 2) obfuscates regarding the reason of why *Liberty* did not receive the message to move one hundred miles before the attack: "because it was missent to the Pacific by the Department of the Army Communications Center" (p. 35). The JCS report offers an unconvincing reason: "Since a majority of the US Navy Mobile Fleet messages are destined for the Pacific, local procedures in the Department of the Army Communications Center allow direct transmission to the communications center

serving the taskforce, by-passing the normal path through the relay at Cheltenham, Maryland" referring to "a series of personnel errors resulting in misrouting the message to the Pacific area. Four years later, the House Armed Services Committee wrote, "the circumstances surrounding the misrouting, loss and delays of those messages constitute one of the most incredible failures of communications in the history of the Department of Defense." (See Stephen Green, *Taking Sides: America's Secret Relations with a Militant Israel* [Brattleboro, VT: Amana Books, 1988], p. 217.) No one in authority made the connection between these "incredible" errors and the motivation for the attack on the USS *Liberty*.

4. "The Israeli Attack on the USS Liberty," memorandum, CIA Directorate of Intelligence, June 13, 1967. Access on Crest computer at National Archives and Records Administration, College Park, MD. Per #058375. August 31, 1977.

5. Ibid. p. 3.

6. David Edwin Lewis, in discussion with the author, March 23, 2016.

7. Information Report. November 9, 1967 Central Intelligence Agency. Unevaluated Information. Country: Israel. Subject: Prospects for Political Ambitions of Moshe Dayan/ Attack on USS Liberty Ordered by Dayan. Report No: B-321/33403-67.

8. State Department documents, i.e., To: U-The Under Secretary Through: S/S from: L- Carl F. Salans. SUBJECT: "THE Liberty"—Discrepancies Between Israeli Information Memorandum. September 21, 1967. "The Navy Court Finding of facts, plus testimony of various members of the crew indicates reconnaissance overflights of the *Liberty* at 0515, 0850, 1030, 1056, 1126, 1145, 1220, and 1245." Situation reports were filed for each of these overflights. Suffice it to say that Israel had ample opportunity to identify the USS *Liberty* that morning. The naval inquiry reports no such identification run, and Commander McGonagle's testimony "that he observed one air-reconnaissance flight approximately five to six miles from the ship at an altitude of 7,000." McGonagle was used profusely by the government to falsify the description of what took place during the attack.

9. Clark Clifford, *Counsel to the President* (New York: Random House, 1991).

10. George W. Ball and Douglas B. Ball, *The Passionate Attachment: America's Involvement with Israel, 1947 to the Present* (New York: W. W. Norton, 1992), p. 66.

11. John E. Borne, *The USS Liberty: Dissenting History vs. Official History* (PhD diss., New York University, September 1993), p. 152.

12. Dave Lewis, in discussion with the author, May 26, 2014.

13. "Misbehavior before the Enemy," Uniform Code of Military Justice, article 99. Available online, for instance at http://www.au.af.mil/au/awc/awcgate/ucmj2.htm#899.%20ART.%20 99.%20MISBEHAVIOR%20BEFORE%20THE%20ENEMY (accessed September 10, 2018).

14. Steve Forslund and Ron Gotcher were enlisted in the US Air Force and worked as intelligence analysts for the Joint Chiefs of Staff when the attack occurred. Gotcher was stationed in Vietnam and Forslund at Offutt Air Force Base outside Omaha. Both saw transcripts of Israeli air-to-air and air-to-ground communications during or after the attack. Both said Israel knew the ship was American and was determined to sink it.

15. *Dead in the Water* censored by the BBC: Peter Hounam, in discussion with the author, July 31 to August 3, 2015, Scotland.

16. Iftach Spector, *Loud and Clear: The Memoir of an Israeli Fighter Pilot* (Minneapolis: Zenith Press, 2009), pp. 131–38.

17. Avner Cohen, in telephone conversation with the author, July 17, 2016.

18. Arieh O'Sullivan, "27 Pilots Refuse to Carry Out Targeted Killings," *Jerusalem Post*, September 25, 2003. Spector was the highest-ranking signatory.

19. William D. Gerhard and Henry W. Millington, *United States Cryptologic History: Attack on a Sigint Collector, the U.S.S. Liberty (S-CCO)*, Special Series Crisis Collection, vol. 1 (Washington, DC: National Security Agency/Central Security Service, 1981), p. 41. Originally classified TOP SECRET UMBRA; classified by NSA/CSSM 123-2. Papers of Richard Thompson.

20. Tordella wrote this as a penned, longhand comment attached to a copy of the Israeli Defense Forces Preliminary Inquiry. Ibid.

21. *The USS* Liberty, Public Affairs Series 34 (New York: Americans for Middle East Understanding, December 2002), http://www.ameu.org/Resources-(1)/USS-Liberty-(1).aspx (accessed September 10, 2018).

22. Dr. Kiepfer is quoted from a film, *Justice for the* Liberty (Break of Dawn Productions, 2015). See also Notes of Tito Howard, July 29, 1975. Papers of Richard Thompson.

23. Richard Deacon, *The Israeli Secret Service* (New York: Taplinger, 1978), p. 178.

24. Reply to a letter from Richard G. Schmucker to His Excellency Yuli M. Vorontsov, Embassy of the Russian Federation, Washington, DC, October 8, 1997. Papers of Richard Thompson.

CHAPTER 12. "THE TRUTH, THE WHOLE TRUTH, AND NOTHING BUT THE TRUTH"

1. A. J. Cristol, *The* Liberty *Incident Revealed: The Definitive Account of the 1967 Israeli Attack on the U.S. Navy Spy Ship* (Annapolis, MD: Naval Institute Press, 2013).

2. Tom Schaaf, in discussion with the author, October 26, 2014.

3. Cristol, Liberty *Incident Revealed*, p. xii. Cristol writes that Admiral Martin told a press conference that he did not get any instructions from Washington at any time and that he, not Tully and not Geis, ordered the *Liberty*-defense aircraft launched and recovered (p. 104). Note that he does not mention Donald D. Engen, captain of the USS *America*. Other of Cristol's obfuscations are on page 208, when he denies that Moshe Dayan "personally ordered the attack" and challenges Dave Lewis's statement that Lyndon Johnson said he did not want to embarrass our ally, Israel. On page 106, Cristol states: "Lewis was badly burned in the torpedo attack on the Liberty. His perception of events that day and during his period of recuperation

has perhaps allowed imagination to fill in some of the gaps in his memory of the event and the immediate aftermath."

4. Dave Lewis, in interview with the author, June 21–24, 2014, New Hampshire.

5. On ionization, Lewis added that given the sunspot cycle, it was very likely signals would be heard beyond the horizon. They were at the peak between high and low ionization. Cristol was basing his calculations on the US Department of Transportation *Instrument Flying Handbook*, which was not reliable. During heavy ionization, transmitted distances are in excess of normal. It was about propagation, how a radio wave is transmitted through the ether (atmosphere) in HF communications. When a light wave hits the ionosphere, it changes direction. In HF communications, the electromagnetic wave is bent, like light as it goes through a glass of water.

When they hit the ionosphere, both VHF and UHF waves are diverted straight up into the air. Extremely low frequencies propagate through the earth. High frequencies from three to thirty megacycles bounce back and forth between the earth and the ionosphere. Unless there is extremely heavy ionization in the sunspot cycle, the sound waves are bent back rather than refracted and are reflected back to the ground so you have more than the line of sight. The opposite extreme is ELF, extremely low frequency, below thirty kilocycles. That travels between earth and the ionosphere around the earth. The wave is so long it will go all the way around the world. A two-hundred-million-watt transmitter will go around the world twice. Instead of its being a short wave reflected by the ionosphere, the ionosphere and the earth are the two boundaries.

In June 1967, they were at the peak of an eleven-year sunspot cycle, and the ionosphere was heavily ionized. That meant that the VHF signals would curve rather than follow the line of sight. In 1956, in Bremerhaven, they were copying five-watt transmitters out of Chicago taxicabs.

The extremely low frequencies that a submarine uses go through the water and the earth and don't go into the air at all. In the event of a nuclear bomb detonating and destroying the ionosphere, communications are not affected. The electromagnetic pulse of a nuclear warhead in the atmosphere complexly destabilizes the ionosphere, so no communications are possible.

This is why you need submarines around. The problem with submarine communications is the wavelength is so long you can only send five words a minute. You can send code, "War's broken out," but you can't send a five-hundred-word message saying, "This is what I think happened." Cristol points out that the Department of Transportation publication advises pilots of the VHF distances that they can be heard reliably. They can't wait to find out what the sunspot cycle is doing. So everything is VHF, which was highly improbable at the time. He doesn't have any proof because most strategic communications were HF, they weren't VHF. Cristol doesn't make the distinction. The Israeli intelligence network must have heard *Saratoga* launch aircraft toward *Liberty* in the first launch by Captain Tully. They knew they had to cover themselves. That was when the helicopter suddenly said, "Do you need help?"

6. Dave Lewis, in interview with the author, March 14, 2014.

7. Dave Lewis, in discussion with the author, June 2, 2015.

8. See James Scott, *The Attack on the* Liberty*: The Untold Story of Israel's Deadly Assault on a US Spy Ship* (New York: Simon & Schuster, 2009).

9. Kenneth J. Halliwell, email to the author, April 24 and 30, 2016. See also Halliwell, "An Evidentiary Study of the USS *Liberty* Attack," USS Liberty Inquiry, July 15, 2014, https://sites.google.com/site/usslibertyinquiry/home (accessed September 9, 2018); Halliwell, email to the author, August 3, 2014.

10. John E. Borne, *The USS* Liberty*: Dissenting History vs. Official History* (PhD diss., New York University, September 1993), p. 17.

11. Ward Boston, affidavit, January 9, 2004. Available online, for instance, at If America Knew, https://ifamericaknew.org/us_ints/ul-boston.html (accessed September 10, 2018).

12. Ward Boston, interview, *Washington Report on Middle East Affairs*, 1998.

13. John Loftus and Mark Aarons, "The Liberty Incident," chap. 12 in *The Secret War against the Jews; How Western Espionage Betrayed the Jewish People* (New York: St. Martin's Griffin, 1994).

14. A. Jay Cristol, Ernest Castle, and John Hadden, "The USS *Liberty* and the Role of Intelligence."

15. George W. Ball and Douglas B. Ball, *The Passionate Attachment: America's Involvement with Israel, 1947 to the Present* (New York: W. W. Norton, 1992), p. 58.

CHAPTER 13. TREASON

1. Dave Lewis, in discussion with the author, July 11, 2016.

2. Dave Lewis, telephone call with the author, September 1, 2018.

3. Helms made this statement on May 29, 2002. Bryant Jordan, "Conflicting Comments Rekindle LIBERTY Dispute, Key Investigators Express Belief That Israel Deliberately Attacked US Ship," *Navy Times*, June 26, 2002.

4. James Bamford, *Body of Secrets: Anatomy of the Ultra-Secret National Security Agency: From the Cold War through the Dawn of a New Century* (New York: Doubleday, 2001), p. 232.

5. John Hadden to Peter Sichel, April 1, 2013. Papers of John Hadden.

6. John Hadden, *Conversations with a Masked Man: My Father, the CIA, and Me* (New York: Arcade, 2016), p. 21.

7. Peter Hounam, *Operation Cyanide: Why the Bombing of the USS* Liberty *Nearly Caused World War III* (London: Vision, 2003), p. 233.

8. See, for example, Ambassador Helms, "Priority," eyes only for Charles Naas. Attached to David Robarge, "Overview," introduction to *A Life in Intelligence: The Richard Helms Collection* (Washington, DC: CIA Center for the Study of Intelligence, 2008), p. 17, https://www.cia.gov/library/readingroom/collection/life-intelligence-richard-helms-collection.

9. These statistics derive from the papers of John L. Hadden.

10. John Hadden to "Dear Bill," August 18, 2007. Papers of John Hadden.

11. John Hadden to Efraim Halevy, July 30, 2001. By this time, Halevy had completed his service to Mossad.

12. Quotations from John Hadden's unpublished novel come from: "BOMB: Section and Outline." Papers of John Hadden. The name of the author on the title page is "Anonymous."

13. John Hadden Jr., email to the author, April 3, 2017.

14. John Hadden, to "Dear Menachem," November 19, 2001. Papers of John Hadden.

15. Gary Brummett, in interview with the author, January 12, 2015, and June 7, 2017, Norfolk, Virginia.

16. Gary Brummett, in discussion with the author, based on recollections of Dick Thompson, January 12, 2015. See also Gary Brummett on *The People Speak*, BBS Radio Network, July 15, 2008.

17. Quoted in Victor Marchetti, "Secret of Nuclear Capability Discovered by U.S. Spy Ship," *Spotlight*, June 9, 1997. Duplicated on a wall: Andrew Cockburn and Leslie Cockburn, *Dangerous Liaison: The Inside Story of the U.S.-Israeli Covert Relationship* (New York: HarperCollins, 1991), p. 16. It had been a long time since a Mossad chief (Isser Harel) could call the founders of Israel "a bunch of Russians, socialist Russians."

18. "Think along the same lines": Meir Amit to John Hadden, January 4, 1980; "of immense help and interest to me": John Hadden to Meir Amit, March 17, 1980. Papers of John Hadden. In a letter to Hadden of December 17, 2000, Amit writes, "We have to recognize the Palestinian state," a far cry from his 1967 reflections about attacking a ship.

19. John L. Hadden, in discussion with the author, July 8, 2014.

20. John Hadden to Peter Sichel. Papers of John Hadden.

21. Dave Lewis, in discussion with the author, July 11, 2016.

22. Moe Shafer, email to the author, July 12, 2016. See also Ted Arens, in conversation with Larry Weaver, at the fiftieth anniversary reunion in Norfolk, Virginia, June 2017. Courtesy of Ted Arens. Email from Ted Arens, January 5, 2018.

23. Bryce Lockwood, email to the author, July 12, 2016.

24. Livia Rokach, *Israel's Sacred Terrorism*, 3rd ed. (1985). Available online at https://archive.org/details/IsraelsSacredTerrorism (accessed June 28, 2018). With appendices and substantial quotations from the unpublished diaries of Moshe Sharett. See also Livia Rokach, *Israel's Sacred Terrorism: A Study Based on Moshe Sharett's Personal Diary and Other Documents* (Belmont, MA: Association of Arab-American University Graduates, 1986), p. 102.

25. Marchetti, "Secret of Nuclear Capability Discovered by U.S. Spy Ship." The title of this article is not accurate. The United States had long known, of course, about Israel's nuclear capability.

26. Attachment to Court of Inquiry Draft. Hundreds of pages of irrelevant messages and details about why the messages were not delivered were attached to the naval inquiry. They are larded with officialese and are an embarrassment. They are designed to support the "accident" thesis. The exoneration of Israel was the first order of business.

27. J. P. Feldmann concurs: Operation Cyanide was "a clandestine CIA and Mossad plan." NSA memo, August 11, 2005.

28. Steven Stewart, *The Spymasters of Israel* (New York: Ballantine, 1980), p. 235.

29. Ibid., p. 302.

30. Glenn Oliphant, email to the author, September 26, 2016.

31. Ted Arens to the American Legion (Commander Helm, Adjutant Wheeler, Judge Advocate Onderdonk, Treasurer Buskirk, Historian Mason, Chaplain Cash, Sergeant-at-arms Hagan), March 23, 2015. Onderdonk replied to Arens's letter sanctimoniously: "If your organization wishes an additional investigation of the USS *Liberty*, you should make your wishes known to your congressional representatives and senators." P. B. Onderdonk Jr., National Judge Advocate, to Ted Arens, April 7, 2015. Onderdonk persisted in slandering Oliphant ("One of your members committed assault and battery on one of our female staff and was convicted of his crimes.").

32. Moe Shafer, email to the author, August 24, 2017.

33. Glenn Oliphant, email to the author, August 26, 2017.

34. Ernie Gallo, email to the author, August 22, 2018.

35. Dave Lewis, email to the author, October 26, 2016.

36. Dave Lewis, in discussion with the author, July 20, 2017.

37. Adlai Stevenson III, email to the author, January 9, 2017. "Represents neither Israel nor the liberal, progressive opinions of most American Jews": Adlai Stevenson III, *The Black Book: Restoring American Values to American Politics* (Self-published, 2009), p. 203. (Reissued in Chinese in 2017.)

38. Adlai Stevenson III, email to the author, July 21, 2017.

39. Admiral Bobby Inman, in discussion with the author, July 13, 2016. "Bobby Inman was on the inside of all that," Dave Lewis says. "He was part of the intelligence community all his life."

40. John Hadden to Peter Sichel, December 25, 2001. Courtesy of John L. Hadden.

BIBLIOGRAPHY

Aid, Matthew M. *The Secret Sentry: The Untold History of the National Security Agency*. New York: Bloomsbury Press, 2009.

Allen, Robert J. *Beyond Treason: Reflections on the Cover-Up of the June 1967 Israeli Attack on the USS* Liberty, *an American Spy Ship*. Self-published, CreateSpace, 2012.

Bagley, Tennent H. *Spy Wars: Moles, Mysteries, and Deadly Games*. New Haven, CT, and London: Yale University Press, 2007.

Bagley, Tennent H. *Spymaster: Startling Cold War Revelations of a Soviet KGB Chief.* New York: Skyhorse, 2013.

Baker, Bobby, with Larry L. King. *Wheeling and Dealing: Confessions of a Capitol Hill Operator*. New York: W. W. Norton, 1978.

Ball, George W., and Douglas B. Ball. *The Passionate Attachment: America's Involvement with Israel, 1947 to the Present*. New York: W. W. Norton, 1992.

Bamford, James. *Body of Secrets: Anatomy of the Ultra-Secret National Security Agency, from the Cold War through the Dawn of a New Century*. New York: Doubleday, 2001.

Beschloss, Michael. *Reaching for Glory: Lyndon Johnson's Secret White House Tapes, 1964–1965*. New York: Touchstone, 2001.

Black, Ian & Benny Morris. *Israel's Secret Wars: A History Of Israel's Intelligence Services*. New York: Grove Press, 1991.

Bregman, Ahron. *Israel's Wars: A History Since 1947*. London and New York: Routledge, 2003.

Brown, Madeleine Duncan. *Texas in the Morning: The Love Story of Madeleine Brown and President Lyndon Baines Johnson*. Baltimore, MD: Conservatory Press, 1997.

Bryce, Robert. *Cronies: How Texas Business Became American Policy—And Brought Bush to Power*. New York: Public Affairs, 2002.

Byrd, David Harold "Dry Hole." *I'm an Endangered Species: The Autobiography of a Free Enterpriser*. Houston: Pacesetter, 1978.

Carle, Glenn L. *The Interrogator: An Education*. New York: Nation Books, 2011.

Carlson, Elliot. *Joe Rochefort's War: The Odyssey of the Codebreaker Who Outwitted Yamamoto at Midway*. Annapolis, MD: Naval Institute Press, 2011.

Caro, Robert A. *The Years of Lyndon Johnson: Master of the Senate*. New York: Vintage Books, 2003.

Caro, Robert A. *The Years of Lyndon Johnson: Means of Ascent*. New York: Alfred A. Knopf, 1990.

Caro, Robert A. *The Years of Lyndon Johnson: The Passage of Power*. New York: Alfred A. Knopf, 2012.

Caro, Robert A. *The Years of Lyndon Johnson: The Path to Power*. New York: Vintage Books, 1982.

Charitan, Wallace O., Charlie Eckhardt, and Kevin R. Young. *Unsolved Texas Mysteries*. Plano, TX: Wordware, 1991.

Christiansen, Rupert. *I Know You're Going to Be Happy: A Story of Love and Betrayal*. London: Short Books, 2013.

Clarence, John, and Tom Whittle. *The Gold House: The True Story of the Victorio Peak Treasure, Book 2: The Lies, The Thefts*. Las Cruces, NM: Soledad, 2012.

Cockburn, Andrew, and Leslie Cockburn. *Dangerous Liaison: The Inside Story of the U.S.-Israeli Covert Relationship*. New York: HarperCollins, 1991.

Cohen, Avner. *Israel and the Bomb*. New York: Columbia University Press, 1998.

Cohen, Warren I., and Nancy Bernkopf Tucker, eds. *Lyndon Johnson Confronts the World, American Foreign Policy 1963–1968*. Cambridge: Cambridge University Press, 1994.

Collins, Max Allan. *Ask Not*. New York: Forge, 2013.

Conrad, Joseph. *Typhoon and Other Stories*. London: Heinemann, 1903; New York: Everyman's Library, 1991.

Cottrell, Richard. *Gladio: NATO's Dagger at the Heart of Europe*. Rev. ed. San Diego, CA: Progressive, 2015.

Cowger, Thomas W., and Sherwin J. Markman. *Lyndon Johnson Remembered: An Intimate Portrait of a Presidency*. Lanham, MD: Rowman & Littlefield, 2003.

Cristol, A. J. *The Liberty Incident Revealed: The Definitive Account of the 1967 Israeli Attack on the U.S. Navy Spy Ship*. Annapolis, MD: Naval Institute Press, 2013.

Dallek, Robert. *Camelot's Court: Inside the Kennedy White House*. New York: Harper, 2013.

Dallek, Robert. *Flawed Giant: Lyndon Johnson and His Times 1961–1973*. New York: Oxford University Press, 1998.

Dallek, Robert. *Lone Star Rising: Lyndon Johnson and His Times 1908–1960*. New York: Oxford University Press, 1991.

Dallek, Robert. *Lyndon B. Johnson: Portrait of a President*. New York: Oxford University Press, 2004.

Deacon, Richard. *The Israeli Secret Service*. New York: Taplinger, 1978.

Dismukes, Bradford, and James M. McConnell, eds. *Soviet Naval Diplomacy*. New York: Pergamon Press, 1979.

Dugger, Ronnie. *Our Invaded Universities: Form, Reform, and New Starts: A Nonfiction Play for Five Stages.* New York: W. W. Norton, 1974.

Dugger, Ronnie. *The Politician: The Life and Times of Lyndon Johnson.* Old Saybrook, CT: Konecky & Konecky, 1982.

Durham, Robert B. *False Flags, Covert Operations, and Propaganda.* Self-published, Lulu, 2014.

El-Ad, Avri. *Decline of Honor.* Chicago: Henry Regnery, 1976. This is the memoir of "Paul Frank," also known as Avraham or Avri Seidenwerg or Seidenberg.

Engen, Donald D. *Wings and Warriors: My Life as a Naval Aviator.* Washington, DC, and London: Smithsonian Institution Press, 1997.

Ennes, James M., Jr. *Assault on the* Liberty*: The True Story of the Israeli Attack on an American Intelligence Ship.* New York: Random House, 1979; Gaithersburg, MD: Reintree Press, 2013.

Epstein, Edward Jay. *The Assassination Chronicles: Inquest, Counterplot, and Legend.* New York: Carroll & Graf, 1992.

Epstein, Edward Jay. *James Jesus Angleton: Was He Right?* New York: FastTrack Press, 2014.

Estes, Billie Sol. *Billie Sol Estes: A Texas Legend.* Granbury, TX: BS Productions, 2005.

Estes, Pam. *Billie Sol: King of Texas Wheeler-Dealers.* Granbury, TX: Pemelaco Productions, 2004.

Eveland, Wilbur Crane. *Ropes of Sand: America's Failure in the Middle East.* London and New York: W. W. Norton, 1980. As a former CIA operative, Eveland uncovers the origins of the US-Israel operation to invade Egypt and remove Gamal Abdel Nasser, the operation to which the USS *Liberty* was collateral damage.

Gallo, Ernest A. *Liberty Injustices: A Survivor's Account of American Bigotry.* Palm Coast, FL: ClearView Press, 2013.

Ganser, Daniele. *NATO's Secret Armies: Operation Gladio and Terrorism in Western Europe.* London and New York: Frank Cass, 2005.

Gates, Jeff. *Guilt by Association: How Deception and Self-Deceit Took America to War.* Santa Barbara, CA: State Street, 2008.

Gentry, Curt. *J. Edgar Hoover: The Man and the Secrets.* New York: W. W. Norton, 1991.

Gerolymatos, Andre. *Castles Made of Sand: A Century of Anglo-American Espionage and Intervention in the Middle East.* New York: Thomas Dunne Books, 2010.

Gibson, James N. *Nuclear Weapons of the United States: An Illustrated History.* Atglen, PA: Schiffer, 1996.

Gilboa, Amos, and Ephraim Lapid. *Israel's Silent Defender. An Inside Look at Sixty Years of Israeli Intelligence.* Jerusalem: Israel Intelligence Heritage and Commemoration Center, 2012.

Ginor, Isabella, and Gideon Remez. *Foxbats over Dimona: The Soviets' Nuclear Gamble in the Six-Day War.* New Haven, CT: Yale University Press, 2007.

Golan, Aviezer, as told to by Marcelle Ninio, Victor Levy, Robert Dassa, and Philip Natanson. *Operation Susannah.* New York: Harper & Row, 1978.

Golan, Galia. *Soviet Policies in the Middle East from World War Two to Gorbachev.* Cambridge, MA: Cambridge University Press, 1990.

Goldstein, Gordon M. *Lessons in Disaster: McGeorge Bundy and the Path to War in Vietnam.* New York: Henry Holt, 2008.

Goodwin, Doris Kearns. *Lyndon Johnson and the American Dream.* New York: St. Martin's Press, 1991.

Goulding, Phil G. *Confirm or Deny: Informing the People on National Security.* New York: Harper & Row, 1970.

Green, Stephen. *Taking Sides: America's Secret Relations with a Militant Israel.* Brattleboro, VT: Amana Books, 1988.

Gulley, Bill, and Mary Ellen Reese. *Breaking Cover.* New York: Simon & Schuster, 1980.

Gup, Ted. *The Book of Honor: The Secret Lives and Deaths of CIA Operatives.* New York: Anchor Books, 2001.

Hadden, John. *Conversations with a Masked Man: My Father, the CIA, and Me.* New York: Arcade, 2016.

Hadden, John. "Travels with a Masked Man." *American Letters & Commentary* 17 (2005): 182–91.

Haley, J. Evetts. *A Texan Looks at Lyndon: A Study in Illegitimate Power.* Canyon, TX: Palo Duro Press, 1964.

Hart, Alan. *Zionism: The Real Enemy of the Jews.* 3 vols. Atlanta: Clarity Press, 2009–2010.

Hart, John Limond. *The CIA's Russians.* Annapolis, MD: Naval Institute Press, 2005.

Hatonn, Gyeorgos Ceres. *Winging It.* Las Vegas, NV: Phoenix Source, 1994.

Heikal, Mohamed Hassanein. *The Cairo Documents: The Inside Story of Nasser and His Relationship with World Leaders, Rebels, and Statesmen.* Garden City, NY: Doubleday, 1973.

Heikal, Mohamed. *The Sphinx and the Commissar: The Rise and Fall of Soviet Influence in the Middle East.* New York: Harper & Row, 1978.

Helms, Richard, with William Hood. *A Look over My Shoulder: A Life in the Central Intelligence Agency.* New York: Random House, 2003.

Hersh, Burton. *Bobby and J. Edgar: The Historic Face-Off Between the Kennedys and J. Edgar Hoover That Transformed America*. New York: Basic Books, 2007.

Hersh, Seymour M. *The Samson Option: Israel's Nuclear Arsenal and American Foreign Policy*. New York: Random House, 1991.

Hershman, D. Jablow. *Power beyond Reason: The Mental Collapse of Lyndon Johnson*. Fort Lee, NJ: Barricade, 2002.

Herzog, Chaim. *The Arab-Israeli Wars: War and Peace in the Middle East*. New York: Vintage Books, 2010.

Holzman, Michael. *James Jesus Angleton: The CIA, and the Craft of Counterintelligence*. Amherst: University of Massachusetts Press, 2008.

Hounam, Peter. *Operation Cyanide: Why the Bombing of the USS* Liberty *Nearly Caused World War III*. London: Vision, 2003. According to Commander David Edwin Lewis, this title is a misnomer. Lewis discovered that "Operation Cyanide" referred not to the attack on the USS *Liberty* but to the transference of communications to a submarine should there be a nuclear attack, when high-frequency signals would not be able to penetrate the radiated atmosphere. A submarine utilizes extremely low frequencies. In the event of a nuclear bomb, electromagnetic pulse stabilizes the ionosphere so no communication is possible. You must rely on a submarine, although the wavelength is so long that you can only send five words a minute.

Hughes, Thomas L. *Anecdotage (Some Authentic Retrievals)*. Self-published, 2013.

Jacobsen, Walter J. "A Juridical Examination of the Israeli Attack on the USS *Liberty*." *Naval Law Review* 36 (1986).

Johnson, Lyndon Baines. *The Vantage Point: Perspectives of the Presidency 1963–1969*. New York: Holt, Rinehart and Winston, 1971.

Karnow, Stanley. *Vietnam: A History*. New York: Penguin Books, 1984.

Klieman, Aaron S. *Soviet Russia and the Middle East*. Studies In International Affairs 14. Baltimore, MD, and London: Johns Hopkins Press, 1970.

Knickerbocker, Brad. "A Former Navy Pilot Recalls the *Liberty* Incident." *Christian Science Monitor*, June 1982.

Lasky, Victor. *It Didn't Start with Watergate*. New York: Dial Press, 1977.

Lilienthal, Alfred M. *The Zionist Connection: What Price Peace?* New York: Dodd, Mead, 1978.

Littell, Robert. *Young Philby*. New York: Thomas Dunne Books, 2012.

Loftus, John, and Mark Aarons. *The Secret War against the Jews: How Western Espionage Betrayed the Jewish People*. New York: St. Martin's Griffin, 1994.

Macintyre, Ben. *A Spy among Friends: Kim Philby and the Great Betrayal*. New York: Crown, 2014.

Mangold, Tom. *Cold Warrior: James Jesus Angleton: The CIA's Master Spy Hunter.* New York: Simon & Schuster, 1991.

Marchetti, Victor, and John D. Marks. *The CIA and the Cult of Intelligence.* New York: Alfred A. Knopf, 1974.

Martin, David C. *Wilderness of Mirrors: Intrigue, Deception, and the Secrets That Destroyed Two of the Cold War's Most Important Agents.* Guilford, CT: Lyons Press, 1980.

Marvin, Daniel. *Expendable Elite: One Soldier's Journey into Covert Warfare.* Walterville, OR: Trine Day, 2006.

Mattson, Roger J. *Stealing the Atom Bomb: How Denial and Deception Armed Israel.* Self-published, 2016.

McClellan, Barr. *Blood, Money, & Power: How L.B.J. Killed J.F.K.* New York: Hannover House, 2003.

McDonald, David Lamar. *The Reminiscences of Admiral David Lamar McDonald, U.S. Navy.* Annapolis, MD: US Naval Institute, 1976.

McDougal, Myres S. "Authority to Use Force on the High Seas." In U.S. Naval War College International Law Studies: Readings in International Law from the Naval War College Review 1947–1977, edited by E. Lillich and J. Moore. Annapolis, MD: Naval War College Press, 1980.

McGarvey, Patrick J. *C.I.A.: The Myth and the Madness.* Baltimore, MD: Penguin Books, 1973.

McMaster, H. R. *Dereliction of Duty: Lyndon Johnson, Robert McNamara, the Joint Chiefs of Staff, and the Lies That Led to Vietnam.* New York: Harper Perennial, 1997.

McNamara, Robert S. *In Retrospect: The Tragedy and Lessons of Vietnam.* New York: Vintage Books, 1995.

Mellen, Joan. *The Great Game in Cuba: CIA and the Cuban Revolution.* New York: Skyhorse, 2013.

Melman, Yossi, and Dan Raviv. *Friends in Deed: Inside the U.S.-Israel Alliance.* New York: Hyperion, 1994.

Neff, Donald. *Warriors for Jerusalem: The Six Days That Changed the Middle East.* New York: Linden Press, 1984.

North, Mark. *Act of Treason: The Role of J. Edgar Hoover in the Assassination of President Kennedy.* New York: Skyhorse, 2011.

Oglesby, Carl. *The Yankee and Cowboy War: Conspiracies from Dallas to Watergate and Beyond.* New York: Berkley Medallion, 1977.

Oren, Michael B. *Six Days of War: June 1967 and the Making of the Modern Middle East.* New York: Ballantine Books, 2003.

Ostrovsky, Victor, and Claire Hoy. *By Way of Deception*. New York: St. Martin's Paperbacks, 1991.

Ostrovsky, Victor. *The Other Side of Deception: A Rogue Agent Exposes the Mossad's Secret Agenda*. New York: HarperCollins, 1994.

Pacalo, Patrick J. *The Liberty Cipher*. Cold Warfare IV. Self-published, PublishAmerica, 2011.

Parker, Richard B., ed. *The Six-Day War: A Retrospective*. Gainesville: University Press of Florida, 1996.

Pearson, Anthony. *Conspiracy of Silence: The Attack on the U.S.S. Liberty*. London: Quartet Books, 1978.

Phillips, David Atlee. *The Night Watch: 25 Years of Peculiar Service*. New York: Atheneum, 1977.

Piper, Michael Collins. *Final Judgment: The Missing Link in the JFK Assassination Conspiracy*. Washington, DC: Wolfe Press, 1995. Piper's summary of James Angleton's long relationship with Mossad and the state of Israel is outstanding.

Powers, Thomas. *The Man Who Kept the Secrets: Richard Helms and the CIA*. New York: Alfred A. Knopf, 1979.

Pratt, Joseph A., and Christopher J. Castaneda. *Builders: Herman and George R. Brown*. College Station: Texas A & M University Press, 1999.

Rabin, Leah. *Rabin: Our Life, His Legacy*. New York: G. P. Putnam's Sons, 1997.

Raviv, Dan, and Yossi Melman. *Every Spy a Prince: The Complete History of Israel's Intelligence Community*. Boston: Houghton Mifflin, 1990.

Reedy, George. *Lyndon B. Johnson: A Memoir*. New York: Andrews and McMeel, 1982.

Ro'i, Yaacov. *From Encroachment to Involvement: A Documentary Study of Soviet Policy in the Middle East*. New York: John Wiley & Sons, 1974.

Rokach, Livia. *Israel's Sacred Terrorism: A Study Based on Moshe Sharett's Personal Diary and Other Documents*. 3rd ed. With appendices and substantial quotations from the unpublished diaries of Moshe Sharett. Belmont, MA: Association of Arab-American University Graduates, 1986; Archive.org. https://archive.org/details/IsraelsSacredTerrorism.

Rusk, Dean. *As I Saw It*. New York: W. W. Norton, 1990.

Sachar, Howard M. *A History of Israel: From the Rise of Zionism to Our Time*. New York: Alfred A. Knopf, 2007.

Safran, Nadav. *Israel: The Embattled Ally*. Cambridge, MA: Belknap Press of Harvard University Press, 1981.

Sandler, Martin W., ed. *The Letters of John F. Kennedy*. New York: Bloomsbury Press,

2013. See especially President Kennedy's strong stand on international inspection of the Israeli nuclear facilities at Dimona.

Saunders, Frances Stonor. *Who Paid the Piper? The CIA and the Cultural Cold War.* London: Granta Books, 1999.

Schoenman, Ralph. *The Hidden History of Zionism.* Santa Barbara, CA: Veritas Press, 1988.

Schwar, Harriet Dashiell, ed. *Foreign Relations of the United States, 1964–1968.* Vol. XIX, *Arab-Israeli Crisis and War, 1967.* Washington, DC: United States Government Printing Office, 2004.

Scott, James. *The Attack on the* Liberty: *The Untold Story of Israel's Deadly Assault on a U.S. Spy Ship.* New York: Simon & Schuster, 2009.

Segev, Tom. *1967: Israel, the War, and the Year That Transformed the Middle East.* Translated by Jessica Cohen. New York: Metropolitan Books, 2007. Originally published in Jerusalem in 2005. This book is useful for its translations from the Hebrew of Meir Amit's memoir, *Head to Head: A Personal Look at Great Events and Secret Affairs.* Tel Aviv: Hed-Arzi, 1999.

Shultz, Richard H., Jr. *The Secret War against Hanoi: The Untold Story of Spies, Saboteurs, and Covert Warriors in North Vietnam.* New York: Perennial, 1999.

Silver, Arnold M. "My Wars, Hot and Cold: Autobiographical Notes of Arnold M. Silver." Unpublished notes dictated into a tape recorder from early 1990 into 1993. Contributed for this book by a retired CIA officer who prefers to remain anonymous. See also "Questions, Questions, Questions: Memories of Oberursel," *Intelligence and National Security* 8, no. 2 (April 1993). Silver was with CIA from its inception until he was fired by Stansfield Turner in the wake of the Church Committee hearings in 1978. Silver is frank in his assessment of Agency operations. At one point, he accuses William Harvey of "singing the old song of our people who don't want to face realities." Of the Bay of Pigs operation, he points out that "the entire project was riddled with penetrations by Raul Castro's intelligence people working under the direction of the KGB."

Smiley, Tavis. *Death of a King: The Real Story of Dr. Martin Luther King's Final Year.* New York: Little, Brown, 2014.

Smith, Grant F. *Divert! NUMEC, Zalman Shapiro, and the Diversion of US Weapons Grade Uranium into the Israeli Nuclear Weapons Program.* Washington, DC: Institute for Research, Middle Eastern Policy, 2012.

Spector, Iftach. *Loud and Clear: The Memoir of an Israeli Fighter Pilot.* Minneapolis: Zenith Press, 2009.

Stevenson, Adlai, III. *The Black Book: Restoring American Values to American Politics.* Self-published, 2009.

Stewart, Steven. *The Spymasters of Israel.* New York: Ballantine Books, 1980.

Stinnett, Robert B. *Day of Deceit: The Truth about FDR and Pearl Harbor.* New York: Touchstone, 2001.

Teveth, Shabtai. *Ben-Gurion and the Palestinian Arabs from Peace to War.* New York: Oxford University Press, 1985.

Thomas, Gordon. *Gideon's Spies: The Secret History of the Mossad.* New York: Thomas Dunne Books, 2012.

Tolley, Kemp. *Cruise of the Lanikai: Incitement to War.* Annapolis, MD: Naval Institute Press, 1973. The author was a rear admiral in the US Navy.

Tourney, Phillip F., and Mark Glenn. *What I Saw That Day: Israel's June 8th, 1967, Holocaust of US Servicemen aboard the USS* Liberty *and its Aftermath.* Self-published, *Liberty* Publications, n.d.

Tourney, Phillip F. *Erasing the Liberty: My Battle to Keep Alive the Memory of Israel's Attack on the USS* Liberty. Crestwood, FL: Money Tree, 2016.

Twain, Mark. *Eruption: Hitherto Unpublished Pages about Men and Events.* Rev. ed. with an introduction by Bernard Devoto. New York: Harper and Brothers, 1940.

Valentine, Douglas. *The CIA as Organized Crime.* Atlanta: Clarity Press, 2017.

Vance, Cyrus. *Hard Choices: Critical Years in America's Foreign Policy.* New York: Simon & Schuster, 1983.

Weiner, Tim. *Legacy of Ashes: The History of the CIA.* New York: Doubleday, 2007.

Weir, Alison. *Against Our Better Judgment: The Hidden History of How the US Was Used to Create Israel.* Self-published, CreateSpace, 2014.

Wells, Anthony R. *A Tale of Two Navies: Geopolitics, Technology, and Strategy in the United States Navy and the Royal Navy, 1960–2015.* Annapolis, MD: Naval Institute Press, 2017.

Wilford, Hugh. *The Mighty Wurlitzer: How the CIA Played America.* Cambridge, MA: Harvard University Press, 2008.

Williams, Paul L. *Operation Gladio: The Unholy Alliance between the Vatican, the CIA, and the Mafia.* Amherst, NY: Prometheus Books, 2015.

Zelizer, Julian E. *The Fierce Urgency of Now: Lyndon Johnson, Congress, and the Battle for the Great Society.* New York: Penguin Books, 2015.

INDEX

Pages in *italics* indicate photographs. Names of those aboard USS *Liberty* are followed by an asterisk (*).

on Egypt and Nasser, 28, 29
  on CIA plan to launch a coup
    against Nasser, 84
  and Eppy Evron, 82, 163
  firing of, 49, 329–30
    reasons why not fired, 357n6
  on importance of oil, 158
  and John Hadden, 46, 55, 87, 103,
    325–26
  legacy of, 359n17, 360n28
  on Nasser and Egypt, 64, 84
  and Operation Gladio, 49
  and Richard Helms, 87, 293, 393n7
  and the Six-Day War, 100, 107
  use of double-talk, 51, 357n12
  and the Vatican, 54–55
  and William F. Buckley Jr., 331
Anglo-American Committee of Inquiry
  into Palestine (US), 359n21
anti-Semitism, 51, 99, 198, 235, 346
  Egypt accused of, 73, 80, 365n27
  Survivors of the USS *Liberty* accused
    of, 342
Apollo, PA. *See* NUMEC
Aqaba, Gulf of, Nasser's closing of, 30,
  41, 48, 55–56
  Israel goading Egypt to attack, 106
Aqaba, Straits of. *See* Gulf of Aqaba,
  Nasser's closing of
Arab League, 82
Arab Liberation Movement, 29
Arafat, Yasser, 51, 60, 84
Arens, Ted, 342, *343*, 344, 399n31
Arlington National Cemetery, fiftieth
  anniversary commemoration of the
  attack, 347
Armbrister, Trevor, 380n41

Armstrong, Phillip*, 116, *116, 173*, 182,
  183, 187, 196, 379n25
Assault on the Liberty: *The True Story of
  the Israeli Attack on an American Intel-
  ligence Ship* (Ennes), 286, 340
Associated Press, 291, 295, 360n28
Aswan Dam, 68, 83
Atomic Energy Commission (US), 325,
  356n22
Azar, Shmuel, 70, 74

Baghdad Pact, 68
Bagley, Tennent, 50, 52, 351n6, 360n28
Baldwin, Roger, 74
Ball, George, 38, 305, 322
Bamford, James, 144, 332
Bandung Conference, 83
Barbour, Walworth, 27, 241–42, 285,
  386n1, 391n101
Bareket, Yeshayeah, 287
"barrel-roll" (aircraft maneuver), 224,
  384n27
Bat Gallim (Israeli ship), 66–67
  as a false flag operation, 68
Battaglia, Charles, 360n28
Bay of Pigs operation, 27
BBC documentary, 207
Beattie, Jack*, 168, 256
Begin, Menachem, 37, 284
"below the salt," 140
Ben Barka, Mehdi, 340
Ben-Gurion, David, 29, 38, 40, 53, 54,
  56, 67, 287, 304, 337
  desire for war with Egypt, 76–77
  as minister of defense, 74
  and Moshe Sharett, 81
  on Nasser and Egypt, 81, 86

Makris, James M., 264
Mangold, Tom, 50, 54
Manhattan Project, 326
Man Nobody Knew, The: In Search of My
Father, CIA Spymaster William Colby
(documentary film), 360n28
Manor, Amos, 53, 56
Mansfield, Mike, 233
Mapai party (Israel), 75, 78, 80, 83, 337
Marchetti, Victor, 88, 337
Marines (US), 31
Marks, John, 88
Martin, David, 293, 360n28
Martin, William Inman, 30, 110, *133*, 140,
 223, 247, 274, 316, 374n61, 384n20
  and the attack on USS *Liberty*, 289,
   347
    believing that USS *Liberty* had
     been sunk, 217
    CIA exonerating, 300, 375n61
    claiming that attack was made
     by Egypt, 238
    foreknowledge of, 147, 214,
     247, 269, 323
    NSA exonerating Martin, 293
    on provision of an escort, 111,
     141–42, 144, 247, 282, 295,
     299, 314, 317
  claiming clearly marked US ships
   safe in international waters,
   142–43
  Cristol's errors about, 395n3
  delaying message to USS *Liberty*, 138
  getting orders from 303 Committee,
   155
  hoping for promotion to chief of
   naval operations, 323

making an inspection of USS *Liberty*
 on June 9, 234
meeting with some of USS *Liberty*
 crew trying to convince them they
 hadn't been abandoned, 234–35,
 254, 384n23
nickname "Fast Charger," 142, 217,
 223
not interviewed by Kidd for Naval
 Court of Inquiry, 282
part of the cover-up, 135, 196, 216,
 244, 289, 323, 384n21
  claiming that USS *Liberty* not
   part of his command, 142,
   144, 233
  claiming that Sixth Fleet planes
   were at scene of attack, 200
  claim of conducting a SIOP
   drill on USS *America*, 24,
   218–19
  confiscating materials that had
   been aboard the ship, 282
  confusion on when USS *Liberty*
   came under his command,
   133, 134, 141
  contradicting self, 231
  denying that USS *Liberty* was a
   spy ship, 241, 247
  sending a message to Pentagon that USS *Liberty* was
   attacked by Egypt, 238
  sending USS *Liberty* on overly
   lengthy trip to be repaired, 254
  and William McGonagle,
   111–12, 142, 144
promising air support for USS
 Liberty, 218, 384n15